Equity
Markets
in Action

Founded in 1807, John Wiley & Sons is the oldest independent publishing company in the United States. With offices in North America, Europe, Australia, and Asia, Wiley is globally committed to developing and marketing print and electronic products and services for our customers' professional and personal knowledge and understanding.

The Wiley Trading series features books by traders who have survived the market's ever changing temperament and have prospered—some by reinventing systems, others by getting back to basics. Whether a novice trader, professional, or somewhere in-between, these books will provide the advice and strategies needed to prosper today and well into the future.

For a list of available titles, visit our Web site at www.WileyFinance.com.

Equity Markets in Action

The Fundamentals of Liquidity, Market Structure & Trading

ROBERT A. SCHWARTZ
RETO FRANCIONI

WILEY

John Wiley & Sons, Inc.

Published by John Wiley & Sons, Inc., Hoboken, New Jersey.
Published simultaneously in Canada.

For general information on our other products and services, or technical support, please contact our Customer Care Department within the United States at 800-762-2974, outside the United States at 317-572-3993 or fax 317-572-4002.

Wiley also publishes its books in a variety of electronic formats. Some content that appears in print may not be available in electronic books.

For more information about Wiley products, visit our web site at www.wiley.com.

Library of Congress Cataloging-in-Publication Data:

ISBN 0-471-46922-X

Printed in the United States of America.

10 9 8 7 6 5 4 3 2 1

For our wives, Jody and Karin,
and our children, Emily, Ivo, and Alessandro

The prices of stocks—and commodities and bonds as well—are affected by literally anything and everything that happens in our world, from new inventions and the changing value of the dollar to vagaries of the weather and the threat of war or the prospect of peace. But these happenings do not make themselves felt in Wall Street in an impersonal way, like so many jigglings on a seismograph. What registers in the stock market's fluctuations are not the events themselves but the human reactions to these events, how millions of individual men and women feel these happenings may affect the future.

Bernard M. Baruch
My Own Story
Henry Holt and Company, New York, 1957, page 84

Contents

Preface

This book is about liquidity, market structure, and trading. It is about the powerful combination of technological, competitive, and regulatory forces that have transformed equity markets on both sides of the Atlantic. It is about issues that have been debated for years and never been resolved, including market transparency, the consolidation of order flow, the nature of intermarket linkages and the vibrancy of intermarket competition.

The book contains a computer simulation model that is purposed to give you a taste of what it is like to actually trade in an equity market. When you put the enclosed CD in your computer, you will be able to enter your orders to buy or to sell in an electronic order book market that also receives machine-generated order flow. If you trade too fast, you will push prices away from you. If you trade too slowly, you might miss the market. This is part of the real world of trading.

Our book is addressed to practitioners, academicians, and other students of the market. Market structure is intricate; we seek to give the reader the big picture concerning the interplay between liquidity, market structure, and trading. Trading is intricate, and one does not become a professional trader overnight; we seek to highlight the major considerations that are faced by those who facilitate the implementation of portfolio decisions and turn orders into trades. The material in this book is also relevant for portfolio theory and capital markets courses in MBA programs. Risk and return get the lion's share of attention in standard MBA finance courses, while liquidity, the third attribute of a stock or portfolio, is typically ignored. We wish to rectify the imbalance.

We have both been involved in the equity markets for many years, but in somewhat different ways. Robert Schwartz is a U.S.-based academician whose major research focus has been equity market structure and trading. Reto Francioni is a European-based practitioner who has had major responsibility as a market architect in both Zurich and Frankfurt. We have interacted over the years, have found ourselves to be on the same wavelength, and have joined forces to produce this book.

We have done so at a particularly exciting time for the industry. During the last quarter of the twentieth century, equity markets emerged as one of the most dynamic sectors in national economies on both sides of the Atlantic Ocean. Mutual funds and pension funds, in their infancy three decades ago, are today dominant in the market. In the United States, Nasdaq, which grew to become a powerful market center since its inception in 1971, has reengineered itself from a competitive dealer market into a modern hybrid market, as has the London Stock Exchange on the other side of the Atlantic.

Today, in exchanges throughout Europe, Canada, and the Far East, an electronic trading platform is the major trading vehicle, and alternative electronic trading systems are making substantial inroads in the United States. Along with changing the technicalities of trading, modern hardware and software technology are opening new avenues for compiling information and creating orders on the basis of systematic information processing. As a by-product of computer technology, electronic transaction records are now available that include all quotes, trades, and volumes for individual stocks with time stamped in fractions of a second. The data have shown the extent to which portfolio performance can be eroded by execution costs. Increasingly, investors are seeking to control these costs. They can do so by their selection of a broker, by smart order handling, and by avoiding illiquid stocks and illiquid marketplaces. Ultimately, however, the only way to reduce costs across the board for all issuers and for all investors is to build a better stock market.

Despite all the recent market structure developments, much more is expected for the future. It is a big task to amass liquidity, contain short-period volatility, discover appropriate share prices, and enable trades—particularly the big institutional trades—to be made at reasonable cost. Much remains to be learned about how to accomplish this task, and the equity markets remain a work in process. From our perspective, this makes our subject relevant and exciting. We hope to share the excitement with you.

OVERVIEW OF THE BOOK

The book is structured as follows. In Chapter 1, we consider the defining characteristics of a market center and its value chain. In so doing, we identify an exchange's mission, focus on its customers and their objectives, and discuss the impact of technology on a market center's operations. In Chapter 2, "From Information to Prices," we make the transition from the perfect, frictionless world that characterizes modern finance theory to the actual world that is replete with transaction costs, imperfections, and imperfect information. Chapter 3 focuses on liquidity and its converse, illiquidity, the attribute of securities and portfolios that makes our subject important.

Against this background, in Chapter 4, "What We Want from Our Markets," we focus specifically on the meaning of market quality and further identify what a market center's function should be. Then, in Chapter 5, "Institutional Order Flow," we zero in on the special needs of large traders and on the impact their orders have on the market.

The next four chapters turn to market architecture. We consider the economic forces at play in an order-driven market (Chapter 6) and in an intermediated market (Chapter 7). Chapter 8 describes the evolving scene in the United States, and Chapter 9 focuses on the evolving scene in Europe.

In Chapter 10, we turn to the final element in the value chain—clearing and settlement. Chapter 11 deals with one of the most critical forces impacting the markets: regulation. Chapter 12 then describes the simulation model that is included with this book. The simulation is our attempt to deliver something promised in the book's title—to see an equity market in action.

More technical discussion is contained in four appendixes at the end of the book: "Prices and Returns," "From Portfolio Decisions to Trading in a Frictionless Environment," "Dimensions of Informational Efficiency," and "The Concept of Self-Regulation."

PRIOR PUBLICATIONS

Some of the material in this book was originally covered in Robert A. Schwartz, *Reshaping the Equity Markets: A Guide For the 1990s* (Harper Business, 1991, reissued by Business One Irwin, 1993). Additional material originated in the following books from Kluwer Academic Publishers: *Coping with Institutional Order Flow* (2004), *A Trading Desk's View of Market Quality* (2004), *Call Auction Trading: New Answers to Old Questions* (2003), *Regulation of U.S. Equity Markets* (2001), and *The Electronic Call Auction: Market Mechanism and Trading* (2001). Other previous publications by the authors are cited where relevant in the text.

ACKNOWLEDGMENTS

A number of people have contributed substantially to the production of this book. We thank Richard Meier in particular for his major and selfless inputs, one being that he participated as a coauthor of Chapter 9, "The

Evolving Scene in Europe." Thanks also to Michael Jaeggi, who coauthored Chapter 10, "Clearing and Settlement," and to Bruce Weber who co-authored Chapter 12, "Simulated Trading." We extend a very special thanks to Antoinette Colaninno, Dror Parnes, and Nelly Baccaro for their assistance in gathering and assembling information and for helping keep us organized. Leigh Woods produced some of the more complicated graphs and figures, and we are grateful. We are indebted to Bill Abrams and Bruce Weber, who were codevelopers of the trading simulation software that is part of this book, and to Oliver Rockwell, who produced the simulation software. Some of our colleagues at Baruch College and SWX have read drafts of the manuscript and have given us valuable feedback. In particular, we thank Lin Peng, John Merrick, David Christie, Scott McCleskey, and, especially, Avner Wolf for his encouragement and support during the production process. We are also grateful to Bill Abrams, Paul Davis, Puneet Handa, Holly Stark, Benn Steil, Bruce Weber, Bob Wood, and Steve Wunsch for the comments, assistance, and support that they have given us over the years. Important conceptual foundations were developed with Kalman Cohen, Puneet Handa, Thomas Ho, Steven Maier, Ashish Tiwari, and David Whitcomb, and we are grateful to them. Finally, we express our gratitude to Pamela van Giessen and Lara Murphy at Wiley and Christine Furry at North Market Street Graphics for their most valuable guidance and assistance in the production of this book.

ROBERT A. SCHWARTZ
RETO FRANCIONI

New York, New York
Zurich, Switzerland
June 2004

CHAPTER 1

The Role of an Equity Market

A securities exchange is an organized and supervised marketplace where trades are made based on an approved set of rules and regulations.[1] A securities exchange is a *secondary market*. A *primary market* is where newly issued shares are publicly offered (commonly in an *initial public offering*, or IPO). Stock exchange members trade as brokers (agents) and/or as dealers (principals). The securities traded include stocks, bonds, and warrants. Orders can be executed at prices set in an order book, via periodic call auction principles, and/or with the use of market-making facilities.

The settlement of trades executed on a securities exchange takes place in a settlement organization such as Euroclear, Clearstream, and Sega Inter Settle (SIS) in Europe, and Depository Trust & Clearing Corporation (DTCC) in the United States. These settlement organizations maintain technical interfaces with the stock exchanges and their members, and they organize the exchange of cash and securities on a delivery-versus-payment basis. Additionally, in many equity markets, a *central counterparty* (CCP) is contractually interposed between the trading parties. A CCP provides posttrade anonymity, netting, and counterparty risk management services. We discuss this in further detail in Chapter 10, "Clearing and Settlement."

THE VALUE CHAIN OF A SECURITIES EXCHANGE

Shares of a stock are issued by a listed company. Orders to trade those shares originate with investors and are brought to an exchange by intermediaries. The confirmation of each trade by the stock exchange goes both to members and to settlement organizations and CCPs. The settlement organizations subsequently confirm settlement of the trades to the stock exchange members, who in turn send confirmation to the end buyers and end sellers (the investors). This is all part of the *value chain* of a securities exchange.

Elements of the Value Chain

In this subsection, we look more closely at the elements in the complete value chain.

Issuers: The Listed Companies   As noted, the term *primary market* refers to the initial issuance in the case of shares.[2] The products traded (the securities) are "delivered" by issuers (the companies who are obtaining equity financing through new share issuance). Interestingly, an exchange may itself be an issuer. This is the case if an exchange's governance structure is that of a for-profit organization that is equity based, as distinct from a mutual organization owned by its members. The New York Stock Exchange, for example, is a membership organization—membership is obtained through the purchase of a seat. The Stockholm Stock Exchange, the first exchange to *demutualize* (it incorporated in January 1993), is equity-based. Subsequently, the Swedish company, OM, absorbed the exchange, and shares of OM are traded (where else?) on the Stockholm Stock Exchange.

By listing on an exchange through an *initial public offering* (IPO), a company that has previously been in private hands goes public. An IPO involves fixing the issuing price and placing the shares, usually via a consortium, with investors. The issuing price is an indication of the initial price determined at the stock exchange. However, the initial price set by trading after an IPO can, and commonly does, differ from the IPO price, depending on the accuracy with which the IPO price was set and owing to the varying pressures of supply and demand in the secondary market.

Exchange   An exchange is a *secondary market*. A stock exchange neither holds securities on its own account nor owns the securities. The main responsibility of an exchange is fair and orderly price discovery for already issued securities (which are not consumed, but merely exchanged).

Official exchange prices are set, following approved rules and regulations, under the surveillance of special regulators. In the United States, for example, the Securities and Exchange Commission (SEC) supervises the equity markets. Market centers also have a *self-regulatory organization* (SRO) obligation.

Exchanges are interactive, information-driven, and volume-driven marketplaces. The overall objective of an exchange is to attract liquidity, to execute orders with reasonable speed and at minimal cost, and to find appropriate prices for customers (members and investors). In accomplishing this, an attractive portfolio of listed stocks is a major asset for an exchange.

Investors   The investors include retail and institutional customers who want to buy or to sell securities and who, for this purpose, hold cash and securities accounts with an intermediary. We consider the trading needs of one major class of investors in particular in Chapter 5, "Institutional Order Flow."

Intermediaries   The intermediaries are exchange members who are either brokers acting on behalf of investors as agent or dealers acting on their own accounts as principal. A broker facilitates trading, whereas a dealer participates in trading (as a principal). Intermediaries are supervised banks and financial entities that generally have specific regulatory requirements. In many markets, a custodian (a separate intermediary with whom the broker-dealer also interacts to effect settlement) maintains investors' cash and securities accounts.[3]

Settlement Organizations   Settlement organizations ensure delivery versus payment of the traded securities and payment of the money within a predefined period of working days. In both the United States and Europe, settlement is usually two or three working days after a trade (T + 2 or T + 3). A physical exchange of cash and products rarely takes place anymore, as the securities exchanged are all standardized and dematerialized. That is, book entries in an accounting system have, often by law, replaced paper certificates as evidence of ownership. Settlement organizations accept the risk of nondelivery of shares or cash from their members, and the members accept this risk vis-à-vis their customers (the investors). In this sense, the intermediaries are "risk buffers" for a stock exchange.

Central Counterparty (CCP)   In many equity markets, a CCP is contractually interposed between the trading parties. As we have noted, the CCP provides posttrade anonymity, netting, and counterparty risk management services. We discuss this further in Chapter 10, "Clearing and Settlement."

Functional Overview

Exhibit 1.1 shows a trade schematically. Assume an investor B (a buyer) wants to buy a specific number of shares of a stock at a specific price. His or her order arrives at the exchange via an intermediary (a member of the stock exchange who can be either a bank or a broker). At the exchange, the order is matched against a contra-side order, that of investor S (a seller). The matching is done in terms of price, size, and time. As a result of the matching, a trade occurs.

On an electronic trading platform (e.g., London's SETS, Deutsche Börse's Xetra, or Switzerland's SWX), the exchange maintains an open, central order book and matches orders according to predetermined rules. Another way to bring orders together is to route them to the book of a *specialist* (who is a market maker at the New York Stock Exchange).[4] Orders may also be brought together in periodic call auctions or crossing facilities. We discuss these alternatives in Chapter 6, "Order-Driven Markets" and Chapter 7, "Intermediated Markets."

On electronic trading platforms, the matching algorithms (the prede-

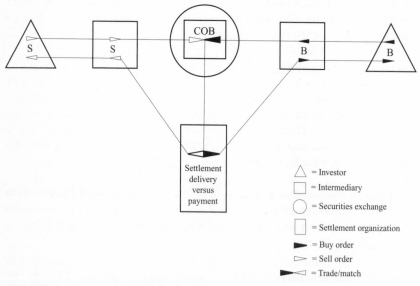

EXHIBIT 1.1   The value chain: Overview.

termined rules) generally include price-time priority. Namely, the most aggressively priced orders are matched first, and if multiple orders have been placed at the most aggressive price, those that were placed first are matched first. In the opening and closing procedures of the electronic trading platforms, the algorithm also aims to execute the highest possible number of shares. We discuss these procedures in Chapter 6.

To settle completed trades, instructions are transmitted (usually electronically) to the corresponding settlement organization. The information conveyed includes:

Security identification number of the stock (typically ISIN in Europe, and CUSIP in the United States.

Price, size, and time of the trade and, commonly, the calculated settlement amount, including currency details.

Identification of the two *participating intermediaries* (for example, SWIFT's BIC, or bank identifier code),[5] and, often, information about their clearing and settlement accounts.

Identification of the original *buy and sell orders*, and unique exchange reference to the trade.

The relevant settlement organizations (e.g., Euroclear, Clearstream, and SIS in Europe, and DTCC in the United States) settle the trades within a predefined period of time (usually T + 3), and deliver the securities to the buyer versus payment of the cash amount to the seller. Where a central counterparty is involved, the CCP becomes a party to the trade. Effectively, two back-to-back identical settlement transactions are instructed. The natural seller delivers shares to the CCP as buyer, and the CCP, as seller, in turn delivers shares to the natural buyer (the delivery of funds goes in the opposite direction).

This all takes place between the CCP, the settlement organization, and the intermediaries. Their corresponding intermediaries inform investors B and S, who are holding their cash accounts and shares with their intermediaries. Here is what happens:

Buyer's intermediary. Debits investor B's cash account by the calculated settlement amount (number of shares times price) plus transactions fees and credits investor B's securities account by the shares bought.

Seller's Intermediary. Debits S's securities account by the shares sold and credits S's cash account by the calculated settlement amount (number of shares times price) minus transaction fees.

Trust is one of a securities market's biggest assets. It is therefore of utmost importance that all buy and sell orders be executed in a timely, fair, and orderly fashion. This means that exchange members as one group and investors as another group must be treated equally. This involves:

Transparency. Having the same chance to get information about the central order book and the listed companies.

Accessibility. Having the same chance to access the matching facility where the trades take place, be it an electronic central order book or the order book of a market maker.

Speed of order handling and trade execution. Speed enables a security position to be converted rapidly into cash (or cash into a security position) as an investor enters or leaves a market. Speed represents an important asset for a market, but it is not one that comes for free, especially for less liquid securities. As we discuss in a number of places in this book, fast trading generally results in the investor incurring higher costs.
- Speed becomes more important as the volatility of a security increases (i.e., the greater the rate at which a stock's price can change). Ideally, there should be minimal risk of a price changing between the time an order has been entered and the time it is executed.
- Fast order handling is also important for trading a basket of securities, especially if the basket is being hedged in the derivatives markets. Because of the time differences involved and the order imbalances that can occur, an inability to execute quickly in both the cash and the derivative markets results in substantial monetary risks.

The rules and regulations of a securities exchange are applied and enforced on two levels: (1) by a national or federal agency—such as the Securities and Exchange Commission (SEC) in the United States, the Financial Services Authority (FSA) in London, the Bundesanstalt für Finanzdienstleistungen (Bafin) in Germany, the Commission des operations de bourse (COB) in France, or the Swiss Federal Banking Commission (SFBC) in Switzerland; (2) by the market surveillance and enforcement organizations run by the securities exchanges themselves for their own self interests and also in light of their SRO obligations. Stringent rules of enforcement enable customers to place their trust in an exchange. A market-oriented, effective surveillance organization is a major asset for a regulated capital market.

Technical Overview of an Electronic Trading Platform

Today's stock exchanges are high-tech organizations. Having looked at the functional value chain of a securities market, let us next see what is behind the scene in terms of technology. The main parts of an electronic trading platform are shown in Exhibit 1.2. They are:

- The user *front end*, consisting of a trading system (optional) and trading interface (API, FIX, etc.).
- The *network*, consisting of access points to a wide area backbone network and interfaces that are provided to members (typically via a gateway).
- The *back end*, which handles the major functions of trading and trade management, market supervision and control, information dissemination, supporting functions (e.g., billing and statistics), and provides central interfaces to settlement organizations, information vendors, market data vendors, and the like.

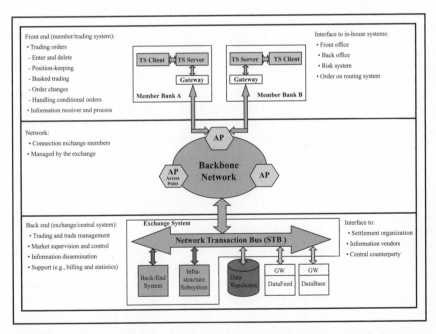

EXHIBIT 1.2 Technical view of an electronic trading platform. Modified example based on the *SWX Platform and Associated Systems*, SWX Swiss Exchange, November 2002, page 4.

The back end is the heart of a trading platform. It performs a number of functions as the central system for exchange applications. To handle the requisite volume of transactions, a highly sophisticated computer system must be secure, modular, performant, robust, scalable, flexible, have an open architecture,[6] and contain adequate backup and redundancy features. The main elements of the back end are:

Trading. Building up and maintaining the central order book is the main task. The trading module provides various market models, such as the order book and its related matching algorithms. This includes all of the functions relating to the capture, processing, and execution of orders. All securities listed at the stock exchange must be covered. The trading module also provides facilities for off-order book, bilateral trading (e.g., indications of interest and addressed offers), and trade and transaction reporting.

Trade management. This module covers all of the posttrade facilities provided by an exchange. All trades (both those matched[7] and reported[8]) are handled. This module allows enquiry; the entry, limited modification, and deletion of trades; trade publication; and the management of trade reversals and other posttrade correction facilities. This module also passes trades on to CCPs and settlement organizations for clearing and settlement.

Information dissemination and management. This module immediately disseminates, from the exchange, all information that results from trading activity (recalculated indices, news, etc.) to the marketplace (members, surveillance personnel, data vendors, etc.). Most stock exchanges provide their own value-added information services that complement raw market data.

Market supervision and control. This module includes monitoring and controlling the market on a day-to-day basis. It also provides features for handling exceptional situations. The main focus is on the order book and trading activity.

Data and Statistics. This module maintains data and ensures statistical completeness, accuracy, and consistency for all data concerning members, issuers, and products. It also enables the production of a wide range of reports and statistics.

With an electronic exchange, all of the preceding modules are programmed into its software. This software has to be run, maintained, and enhanced through new software releases.[9] This represents a major, never-ending task. The advantages of an electronic platform running an open order book with continuous matching include:

The *concentration of liquidity* in one single order book per security, which enables customers to get the best price.

A *transparent order book* with full information, which enables customers to see what they get.

Decentralized market access, which enables participants to trade from anywhere and to get what they see.

Relatively efficient, lower-cost *centralized surveillance.*

The electronic exchange has important interfaces with the following external organizations (see Exhibit 1.3):

Members. The technology enables seamless access to trading and reporting facilities provided by the exchange. Pretrade anonymity is provided by the exchange.

CCPs and settlement organizations. The technology manages payments, delivery, collateral, and settlement on the due date. This requires a specialized interface that contains many details specific to the counterparties. Posttrade anonymity is provided by the CCPs.

Regulatory and surveillance organizations. The electronic technology supports investigations into an array of rules breaches and is used to support various legal reporting requirements.

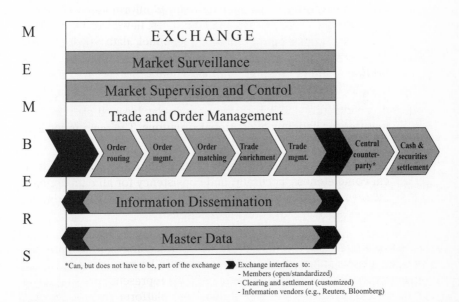

EXHIBIT 1.3 Overview of an exchange.

Market Models:
The Heart of Price Determination

Of the various elements that define an exchange, the most fundamental is its market model (including the matching algorithm). A market model, in essence, is the combination of an exchange's trading phases and trading forms. As such, a market model defines the procedures used for price discovery. The overall objective of a trading platform is fair and orderly price discovery. Also of importance are the interaction of participants with the stock exchange, the exchange's product range, the segments traded, and the hours of operation.[10] In addition, the following must be specified:

Who the market participants are, along with their trading capacities, user types, and so forth.

What the market segments are. Instruments may be grouped in a variety of ways—for example, by industry sector, geographical area, market liquidity, capitalization, and inclusion in indices.

What the actual market model itself is (i.e., the type of matching mechanism).

The trading phases of a market include preopening, the opening itself, continuous trading, trading interruptions and restarts, and the closing.

The trading forms include periodic call auctions, continuous trading, and market making with single or multiple market makers.

We depict the modular market model in Exhibit 1.4. The trading form applicable to highly liquid stocks (a pure high-volume business) is the order-driven, open order book market model that we discuss in Chapter 6, "Order-Driven Markets." In less liquid and illiquid markets, market making is the more appropriate trading form. We discuss this market model in Chapter 7, "Intermediated Markets." A periodic call auction can be used to open and to close almost any type of market. We discuss this market model in Chapter 6.

How should the parts of an exchange's market model be combined? This question must be answered in light of customer requirements and the particular needs of the different products traded. There are no dogmas with regard to market architecture. The choice is not only between call auctions and continuous trading. The question is also how best to combine call auctions with continuous trading. All possibilities must be taken into account to establish the optimal microstructure. Consequently, most trading platforms have modular models that can combine different price

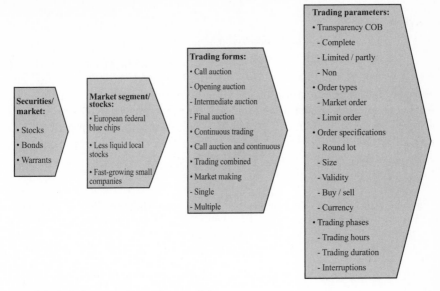

EXHIBIT 1.4 Modular market model.

discovery components into tailor-made market architecture. Most of the functionality is highly configurable in terms of the time for which an order is valid, the sizes in which the stocks can be bought or sold, the minimum price variation allowed,[11] the order types accepted, and so forth.

There are two generic market models for trading: *order-driven* (the orders of some public participants establish the prices at which other public participants can trade) and *quote-driven* (dealer or market-maker quotes establish the prices at which all public participants trade).[12] The order-driven model can be enriched by liquidity-enhancing market-making functions such as the sponsors in Xetra and the specialists on the New York Stock Exchange. Hybrid combinations of the two generic models are common and effective.

The modularity of functions, an ability to customize important features (e.g., trading hours, lot size, and currency) and the power to offer effective flexibility for customers enables customized, tailor-made micro-structure solutions to be achieved. Flexibility also enables faster adjustment of market structure and functionality to changing trading circumstances. It is of utmost importance for the matching algorithm that principles of equal treatment, price-time priority, and executing the highest possible volume be generally adhered to. In addition to simplicity, one of the key criteria for the matching algorithm is consistency as perceived by market participants.

To ensure consistent, transparent price determination, an exchange's algorithm can accept only two order types: limit orders and market orders.[13] If, for instance, two buy limit orders are at the best market bid of 52, with one of them being a simple order to buy 400 shares at 52 and the other being an all-or-nothing order to buy 700 shares at 52, a total of 1,100 shares to buy at 52 could not be shown on the book. If it were, other participants would have no way of knowing that a market order to sell 600 shares could not be executed fully against the 1,100-share aggregated bid at 52.[14]

Therefore, the central limit order books of the European stock exchanges all accept only limit and market orders. Other orders (the conditional orders) must be handled outside of the matching model, typically in the front ends of members.[15] To be entered into the matching procedure of an electronic order book, all conditional orders must be converted into either market or limit orders. However, specialists on a trading floor offer a special service to deal with conditional orders by taking them on their own books. One special order type can be placed in the book, however. It is an *iceberg order*, where only part of the order's size is disclosed to the market, along with a disclosure that the order does in fact contain a hidden size. Iceberg orders are sometimes referred to as *hidden orders*. Order types in the central limit order book are shown in Exhibit 1.5.

	Attribute order type	Size	Buy or sell	Price	Condition
Unconditional orders*	Market	X	X	—	—
	Limit	X	X	X	—
Conditional orders†	Conditional:				
	▪ Fill or kill	X	X	(X)	X
	▪ All or none	X	X	(X)	X
	▪ Stoploss	X	X	(X)	X
	▪ Immediate or canceled etc.	X	X	(X)	X

*Shaded areas = good for direct matching.
†For definitions of conditional orders, see, for example, New York Stock Exchange, Constitution and Rules, Rule 13.

EXHIBIT 1.5   Order types and COB.

We next focus on price determination and the use of order types in the context of an open order book in an order-driven, continuous electronic market. The rules of price determination are highest executable volume (leaving the lowest surplus)[16] and price-time priority.[17] Further, as noted previously, only market and limit orders are accepted by the matching procedure as a necessary condition to ensure transparency, consistency, and equal treatment.

For a central limit order book system, the following instructions are necessary and sufficient for matching:

Unconditional orders are always acceptable for a direct match. These orders indicate "at market," or a limit price (the maximum to be paid for a purchase or the minimum to be received for a sale), and the period for which an order is valid (e.g., "good for the day," "good till canceled"). Iceberg orders need additional parameters. Order types with special conditions are not entered in the order book but can nevertheless result in matches.

Conditional orders must be transformed either into a market order or into a limit order for matching purposes. This is possible as long as the corresponding situation applies in the central order book. Therefore, a permanent cross-check between a stored conditional order and the status of the central order book is required.

A market model is part of the rules and regulations of a stock exchange. It is also the basis for monitoring and supervising a market. The market model can be provided by a software package on the back end of a trading platform, or it can be operated by a specialist on a trading floor. Market models can also be operated by electronic communication networks (ECNs) or by alternative trading systems (ATSs). We discuss these further in Chapter 8, "The Evolving Scene in the United States."

After a trade is completed, the delivery of shares (by the seller) and the payment of cash (by the buyer) must take place as reliably, as quickly, and as cheaply as possible. Trade settlement has no impact on price discovery, but it has a big impact on the overall fee structure of a trade. It is therefore a key element in the value chain of the secondary market.

In European markets, a strong pressure exists to bring trading and settlement activities under one roof (examples are Deutsche Börse AG, Euronext, and the Borsa Italiana). Combining trading, clearing, and settlement organizationally is termed *vertical integration*. The United States has a hybrid structure of multiple exchanges but just one clearing and settlement venue.[18]

Cross-border transactions are usually settled through a complex chain of brokers, settlement systems, and, mostly at the national level, payment systems. In Europe, with all of its separate national systems, relatively high settlement costs are a significant impetus for the consolidation of cross-border settlement. Consolidation along these lines would have a major positive impact on the European cash markets. We discuss this further in Chapter 9, "The Evolving Scene in Europe," and Chapter 10, "Clearing and Settlement."

MARKET PARTICIPANTS

We now turn to the three types of participants who interact with each other in a securities market: investors, brokers and dealers, and issuers.

Investors

Investors are the basic source of order flow and the primary customers of an exchange. They include two broad groups: individuals (retail customers) and institutions (including mutual funds, pension funds, and insurance companies). Exchange members acting on their own account can also be considered investors.[19] The investors buy (invest in) and sell (divest) securities at an official price on their own account. When their orders execute at an exchange, customers get an *official price.*

The orders of institutional customers are typically far larger than those of retail customers, but other than this there is no longer a clear difference between retail and institutional participants. Good tools and good information are publicly available for all investors. However, large institutional orders are far more difficult to cope with because of their size. Consequently, we devote a chapter to institutional trading (Chapter 5, "Institutional Order Flow").

When holding stocks, investors put their money at risk to get a return. To monitor their risk, they need quality information that is timely and appropriate about the companies they have invested in. The know-how and skills of investors have improved dramatically in recent years. So, too, have the quality of data and information. The sophisticated trading tools now available to retail customers meet professional standards. Sophisticated investors, both large and small, these days have easy and reliable access to major exchanges at any time, from almost anywhere, via the Internet or through their brokers. Their decision-making speed is high and their ability to act and react is extremely good. For the retail customers, immediacy has become almost a commodity. Derivatives on stocks and/or stock indices and other tools are also available for knowledgeable retail and institutional investors to handle equity risk effectively.

Brokers and Dealers

A broker is an exchange member who acts as an intermediary between an investor and an exchange. Brokers do not take orders on their own books, but merely route them to a market. A broker acts as an agent, in his or her own name, on the client's account. Brokers are responsible for knowing their customers and for delivering either cash or shares if a customer fails to do so. In other words, these intermediaries must stand behind their customers.

For their services, brokers receive a brokerage fee (commission). To fulfill his or her role, a broker operates a cash and securities account in the name of the investor. A major asset for a broker is his or her receipt of order flow, and thus his or her portfolio of customers.

Intermediaries also supply marketability services to public investors by trading in their own names on their own accounts. When an intermediary does so, he or she is termed a *market maker* or *dealer*. The distinction between a market maker and a dealer is that the former is contractually committed to provide liquidity to a marketplace by putting up quotes on both sides of the market (one to buy and one to sell). The market maker is also required to maintain a fair and orderly market. A dealer has no such obligation.

Whether a stock exchange member acts as a broker or as a dealer is termed his or her *trading capacity*. Acting as both a broker and a market maker (NYSE specialists, for instance, perform both functions) is termed *dual capacity*. Within a given broker-dealer firm, however, these two roles must be strictly separated, and so, too, must be their accounting. The reason is that customer risk and the firm's own risk must be duly separated to prevent a broker-dealer firm from shifting risk, either by intent or inadvertently, to its customers. A device commonly referred to as a *Chinese Wall* separates the two roles.

Through their activities, brokers and dealers are an important element in the risk structure of a marketplace. Brokers bear the risks involved in order routing (although it almost never happens with an electronic infrastructure, an IT glitch could result in an order being lost or misdirected) and posttrade clearance and settlement (brokers must stand behind their customers). The unique risk borne by dealers is the exposure to price changes that they face when carrying unbalanced inventory positions that are acquired in the process of trading with their customers.

Issuers

The shares that are traded at an exchange (the product) have been delivered by public companies that, in the exchange context, are referred to as *issuers*. An issuer is a legal entity that issues and distributes its securities to investors in public markets that are ruled by law. A corporation's objective when listing at a stock exchange through an initial public offering (IPO) is (1) to raise equity capital at a better price, (2) subsequently to be able to obtain additional capital required to finance growth, and/or (3) to optimize its capital structure.

To issue stocks, both the requirements of law and the rules and regulations of the exchange must be fulfilled. To be issued and listed, shares must be standardized and fungible. These days, shares are typically not traded *physically* (as paper certificates) at a securities exchange, but by book entry in the accounting systems of settlement organizations and custodians.

An important task for a listed company is to keep investors informed about its business so that they can analyze and manage their investments on the basis of sound information. To this end, after it has completed its IPO, a listed company must continue to fulfill a number of ongoing requirements, including the publication of news,[20] the issuance of periodic (usually quarterly or semiannual) balance sheet statements, profit and loss statements, and special reports. These statements and reports must follow the international accounting standards promulgated by the International Accounting Standards Committee (IASC), U.S. generally accepted accounting principles (GAAP), and other corporate governance guidelines.

MISSION

The mission of a market center involves macroeconomic and microstructure objectives and various legal, operational, and social objectives.

Macroeconomic Objective: Capital Allocation

A well-functioning capital market is a necessary condition for the economic growth and development of a free market economy. Companies need capital to invest in profitable projects and skills. Investors are looking to acquire portfolios with attractive risk and return characteristics. Both parties meet (indirectly) at the stock exchange. In this context, a stock exchange's specific role is to enable a company's shareholders to achieve cost-effective trading in an efficient secondary market. Only if this is delivered will investors buy newly issued shares in the primary market. The key prerequisites include an efficient organization, open and flexible rules and regulations, and effective surveillance.

A stock exchange, through the intermediation structure created by a broad set of rules and regulations pertaining to membership organizations and settlement organization, is interposed between issuers and investors in the primary market, and between the investors (buyers and sellers) in the secondary market. A clear separation exists between (1) financing and risk taking in the primary market and (2) the clearly defined mechanics of exchanging securities for cash in the secondary market. A secondary market has a risk profile that may change dramatically with, for example, disintermediation or the introduction of a central counterparty. Appropriate risk handling, as a component of investor protection, is one of the major legal goals of an exchange. The information needed by market participants must be sufficient, reliable, and timely. For this to be the case, transparency is absolutely critical.

Microstructure Objective: Price Discovery

Various participants in a market can have radically different time perspectives and motives for placing an order. A fund manager may be prepared to wait several days to work a large order, whereas a day trader will want an extremely fast turnaround. Some participants seek to trade because of their own receipt and analysis of information; others do so for their own liquidity purposes; and some trade on the basis of technical analysis. Seen from the point of view of the marketplace, all these flows are broken down into atomic transactions that meet (more or less) in real time on the exchange.[21] As they meet, prices are discovered.

Price discovery is at the heart of exchange operations. Fair and orderly price discovery is key to a market's trustworthiness. The specific way in which the price discovery function is carried out defines the microstructure of an exchange. Bookbuilding and the matching algorithm of an order book must fulfill at least the following criteria:

Equal treatment concerning transparency, technical and functional access, and information availability.

Timely information concerning news about the listed companies.

Transparency in terms of at least part of the order book. Members of the stock exchange usually have, by the rules and regulations, more information than investors.

A predefined, consistent matching algorithm and, therefore, prices that are foreseeable, given the order flow. Executing the highest possible volume with the lowest buy-sell imbalance and price-time priority (the most aggressive orders, first in price and then in time, are served first) are common principles.[22]

Fast and easy access. Immediacy matters both in terms of how it is perceived by market participants, and in terms of the technical connections required.

Accurate posttrade information about trade executions.

A particularly thorny problem concerning price discovery is how best to integrate large orders (consisting of hundreds of thousands of shares or more) and smaller orders (100 or so shares). Markets commonly identify *round-lot orders* as the smallest number of shares that can be traded on an exchange's main trading platform. Historically at the NYSE, a round lot has been 100 shares, and in the past the NYSE has used special procedures to economize on the cost of handling *odd-lot orders* (orders that are smaller than one round lot).[23] Increasingly, electronic technology has made special procedures unnecessary and has enabled one round lot to be one share of stock (this is called *round-lot one*).

This was not always the case. In Germany in the 1980s, for example, round-lot size was enormous in the blue-chip segment (sometimes thousands of shares). Therefore, only institutional investors (no retail investors at all) and members dealing on their own account traded within this segment at the exchange. With round-lot one, the German market is now available for retail investors. With major stock exchanges having round-lot one, a real task of an exchange is to integrate both small and large orders.

Legal Objective: Protection

Investor protection, as provided by law and the rules and regulations of an exchange, is of critical importance. It is important not solely for the individual investor, but also for the entire secondary market as a system. Market protection means:

- Fair and orderly price discovery.
- Transparency of price discovery and news about listed companies.
- Efficient settlement.
- Reliable and performant trading platforms and settlement systems.
- Lowest possible transaction costs.

Today, every federal capital market has a law regulating its exchanges. The rules and regulations of an exchange must be specified based on these laws. Typically, a federal securities commission (e.g., the SEC in the United States and the Swiss Federal Banking Commission in Switzerland) applies and enforces the law and the rules and regulations. In addition, there is an enforcement organization at each exchange. Unfortunately, in today's dynamic environment, the laws, rules, and regulations are, almost by definition, always lagging behind market developments. Therefore it is sensible to delegate a degree of self-regulation to each exchange (which can act more appropriately because of its nearness to the market). Market protection should be formulated in an appropriate, market-oriented way. Overly detailed specifications can unduly limit the freedom of exchanges and intermediaries to act. Both must be allowed sufficient freedom to react to fast-changing market conditions.

Operational Objective: Reliability

Operational reliability means performant, secure, user-friendly systems and easy access.[24] It also means having failure-tolerant systems, backup systems, and efficient implementation of system upgrades (releases). Guaranteed, fault-tolerant message delivery is also required, and immediate access to a market must be technically possible so that a public customer can obtain immediacy if he or she is willing to pay immediacy's price.

A set of system requirements must be specified to guarantee reliability. The technical requirements are stated in the *service-level requirements* of an exchange. These generally include:

Integrity. Security is needed to maintain data integrity. Huge projects and investments are made in this area so that an exchange can offer the highest degree of security.

Fault tolerance. A system's tolerance against failure has to be continually checked (e.g., process fail-over, recovery procedures).

Disaster recovery. Facilities must be put in place and exchange teams must be trained to react quickly and flexibly. They must therefore periodically exercise recovery procedures.

Recoverability. This means data integrity (storability) for system data and messages.

Availability. This measures the total time that a system is operationally available for trading. Typically, the electronic exchanges in Europe must be, and have been, available for well over 99.998 percent of normal working hours per year. That is, they have been down for less than 0.002 percent of the time, which translates into only a few minutes per year. Even better, the world's largest derivatives market, Eurex, has achieved 100 percent availability since it began operating in May 1998.

Volume capacity. This is given in terms of the maximum number (x percent plus contingency) per day for trades, orders, quotes, and trade reports, along with the maximum number of traded instruments (both liquid and illiquid). Capacity requirements must reflect both average and peak load numbers for orders per unit of time, both in the aggregate and per instrument traded.

Scalability. Of critical importance is the scalability of the aforementioned features within a reasonably short period of time. Scalability is essential to support further volume growth.

Response time. This is the order request response time and message sequencing in seconds for average and peak broadcast times.

Execution speed. This is the time necessary for auction execution.

General requirements. General requirements concerning the system include portability (using standards where possible), maintainability (easy and at low cost with reduced complexity), and auditability (ability to meet the demands of regulatory authorities and other auditors).

Additionally, there are overriding criteria including equal treatment, transparency, immediacy, and low costs. These criteria are interdependent. Each is a necessary but not a sufficient condition for market integrity. The different weightings given to these factors in an ever-changing market environment are decisive for the success of an exchange that is striving to attract, to maintain, and to enhance liquidity at reasonable cost.

Social Objective: Equal Treatment

Justice requires fairness,[25] and fairness requires equal treatment. Fairness is a two-way relationship: Two people must both be fair to each other. In our context, fairness applies to investors and to intermediaries. Fairness is a noble objective, but what does it mean? Philosophical discussion about this topic goes back at least several hundred years.[26] The following example suggests one difficulty in applying the fairness principle.

Consider a group of four people—a heavy construction worker, a professional marathon runner, a grandfather, and a baby. Assume that they have four loaves of bread to share and nothing else to eat. How should the bread be distributed? Here are two alternatives:

1. Each person gets one loaf (equal distribution).
2. The bread is distributed on the basis of need or other criteria such as an individual's age, weight, or contribution to social welfare (proportional distribution).

Construction worker	1¾ loaves
Marathon runner	1½ loaves
Grandfather	½ loaf
Baby	¼ loaf

Which do you think is fairer, scenario 1 or 2? This is a slippery philosophical issue. However, when raised in the context of a concrete situation, the term *equal treatment* can gain content and become relevant.

Equal treatment for exchange members means:

No one is disadvantaged in terms of access to the open interface.

Within the interface, participants have equal treatment for routing, storing, and executing orders.

Accurate and equal information exists about price discovery.

The timing of information release and dissemination does not favor any one member over any other.

Members are treated fairly in terms of performance, volume, recovery procedures, and backup.

The same fee and pricing structure applies for the same service provided.

Equal treatment for investors means:

Public information is available at the same moment in time for every party who may have an interest in getting it. If there is any disequilibrium in the public release of exchange information caused by the exchange itself, trading must be halted.

Individual investors should receive equal treatment with respect to their access to the marketplace. This falls under the responsibility of the members.

TRENDS AND TRIGGERS

Three major forces are impacting exchange development: technology, competition, and regulation. In this section, we give particular emphasis to the first two, technology and competition. We turn to a more extended dis-cussion of the third in Chapter 11, "Regulation."

Information Technology as a Catalyst

The computerization of operations has made exchanges far more efficient in handling heavy volume in a timely fashion and at reasonable cost. Fur-ther, information technology (IT) enables geographically dispersed mar-ketplaces to be more effectively consolidated. The strategic advantage of an electronic trading platform can be summarized as follows. It is a neces-sary condition for:

- A full and efficient integration of trading and settlement (vertical inte-gration).
- A national and an international strategy (horizontal integration).
- Decentralized market access for market participants.
- Extended trading hours.
- Better support for members.
- Better functionality for members.
- Effective centralized market surveillance.

A market center strives to offer fast and reliable access, from any-where at any time, to a fully integrated *straight-through process* (STP). STP means that, once an order has entered the order routing channel, it is in a seamless, fully integrated online procedure, from its entrance on the order book, to matching, and on through to clearance and settlement. STP, at minimum, requires the vertical integration of a capital market on a tech-nical level.

In Europe, almost every national capital market is de facto vertically integrated in this way, and some are legally vertically integrated. Switzer-land, where vertical integration was achieved 15 years ago, has always been on the leading edge in this regard. Interestingly, the international nature of the Swiss market has led to a combination of vertical and hori-zontal approaches to service provision. These developments have resulted in a strong interrelationship between the integrated marketplace and its members. It is of utmost importance that functional change be coordinated across all of the service providers in a given market. This in turn drives markets toward consolidation and standardization.

Rationalizing the processing chain and efficiently handling an ever-increasing transaction volume with a well-performing system is a never-ending task. Exhibit 1.6 shows how Eurex, the German/Swiss options and

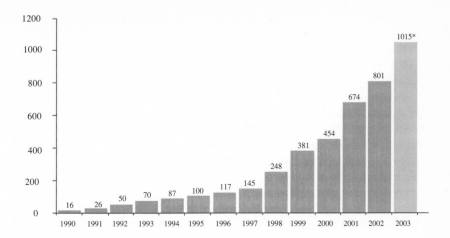

*Figures for 2003 extrapolated, based on YTD August 2003.

EXHIBIT 1.6 Eurex futures and options total trading volume, in million contracts.

futures market, has developed over the years despite the heavy demands the expansion has placed on its IT infrastructure. Highly effective IT management was clearly required. System complexity and costs were reduced dramatically through (1) modular functionality, (2) configuration and modularity in technical areas, and (3) open interfaces to members and to clearing and settlement organizations. The reliability and availability of these trading platforms is significantly more than 99.995 percent of trading hours. This is a compelling reason to trust these platforms.

Because of the open interface between the exchange and its members, a new industry has developed in the front-end area. Sophisticated, user-friendly trading front ends at a professional level are now publicly available. An open architecture enables a consolidation of marketplaces to take place in the front end (see Exhibit 1.2). This consolidation makes virtual accessibility to parallel markets immediately possible at the same time from anywhere. Further consolidation or compilation of several markets in the same front end is now technically feasible. For example, one can trade all European blue chips and their corresponding derivative products from the same front end. This means that basket trading and hedging are possible with the same tool and, at the same time, both locally and cross-border.

Consolidation in the front end also facilitates the use of tailor-made trading clusters. By *trading cluster*, we mean trading the same security in different marketplaces at the same time and thereby achieving a virtual consolidation of multiple marketplaces. Note, the consolidation is in the front end of the members and investors, not in a merged exchange.

The trading networks have also become more efficient and more reliable on the back end.[27] Customized nets between exchanges and their members, and also the Internet, are increasingly being used between exchange members and investors. In the future, the Internet will no doubt also be used as a low-cost solution for connecting an exchange, its members, and its customers.

All told, an exchange's IT has a direct impact on its efficiency and competitive strategy. IT has been and will be a core competence in the know-how and skills of an exchange.[28] Given its pervasive impact on an exchange's service level and profit and loss statement, IT will continue to be a decisive catalyst for future change and development.

Competition

We next consider the following aspects of competition: (1) the battle for order flow between market centers and their members (the broker-dealer firms); (2) the drive toward integration (both vertical and horizontal) that could result in the elimination of competitive pressures; (3) a product that one would like competition to produce—the development of market structure for all investors (both institutional and retail); (4) market segmentation, which defines the broader context within which the interplay of competitive forces takes place.

The Battle for Order Flow   Let us look again at the value chain in light of two related industry practices, internalization and netting. We do so with the aid of Exhibit 1.7. Internalization means that an exchange member firm that has received orders from its clients is pooling customer orders for a period of time and then, in a procedure called *netting*, is matching the corresponding buy and sell orders for a security. The matching takes place at the same price as the exchange price prevailing at the time when the netting takes place.[29] Only the net (the excess of sells over buys or of buys over sells) is then routed to the exchange. In this way, the member takes advantage of the information inherently available in the flow of orders across his or her book and displays the net only to the marketplace. Nevertheless, because the individual trades included in the internalized net do not go through the exchange and are reported only to the regulatory authorities, the central marketplace cannot as fully realize economies of scale.

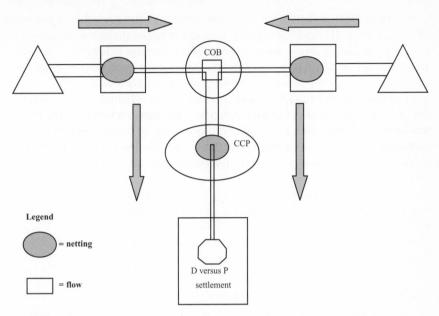

EXHIBIT 1.7 Netting of order flows: Internalization and central counterparty.

Trades can also be netted in the posttrade settlement process. This normally is economically efficient only in markets that include central counterparty services. Posttrade netting requires relatively complex processing on the member side to reconcile the settlement net with each of the individual customer orders.

We note the following about netting. First, the volume of order flow to an exchange can be diminished appreciably by netting. Second, only big players generally have enough volume to make internalization worthwhile. Third, there is an inherent trade-off involved—many customers seek immediate execution, whereas, for the members, a longer netting period enables more orders to be traded in-house. Fourth, netting implies competition between an exchange and its members for order flow. When, how, and where this competition will heat up in the future is an open issue. In any event, the bigger and stronger are its member firms, the greater is the threat to an exchange and the more intense is the pressure put on the market center to innovate and to improve the efficiency of its systems.

Integration Integration has two dimensions: vertical and horizontal. *Vertical integration* refers to the integration of five elements of the value chain—the exchange, investors, intermediaries, settlement organizations, and a central counterparty (where a CCP exists). The ultimate objective of vertical integration is to achieve fully unified straight-through processing of security transactions. *Horizontal integration* refers to the merging of (and also cooperation between) trading organizations (exchanges), of settlement organizations, and of other secondary market service providers. Both vertical and horizontal integration raise serious competitive issues between the various service providers involved. That is, along with the efficiencies that integration may bring, inefficiencies will also appear if a fully integrated system becomes complacent in the absence of vibrant competition.

The effects of vertical integration are:

Costs. Fixed costs are lower, as are order handling costs, transaction costs, and surveillance costs. However, there is also a temptation to cross-subsidize within the vertically integrated structure. Cross-subsidization raises the risk of closing out lower price providers who are not part of the vertical silo.

Reliability. Service can be made more reliable in terms of immediacy, performance, security, and safety, since the systems are more readily integrated when their operators are aligned.

The effects of horizontal integration are:

Competitive advantage. For an exchange, lowering a spectrum of costs creates a more attractive product portfolio, offers the potential for synergy between the members, enhances liquidity, strengthens investor protection, and reinforces market integrity.

Customer needs. In Europe in particular, customers would benefit from having one market for the blue chips with one set of rules and regulations, one point of access to trading, pooled liquidity, one technology, and more efficient portfolio risk management. This would result in enhanced liquidity, better transparency, less system complexity, and reduced market fragmentation.

Issuers. In Europe in particular, issuers would benefit from having one market for raising capital, one marketplace to fulfill all information requirements, the elimination of double listings, and one arena for marketing.

No clear trade-off exists between vertical and horizontal integration. The two can coexist simultaneously. In the trading area, there is a clear need for a European blue-chip market. On the other hand, the national capital markets need local exchanges for listing and trading local securities. This is because security markets develop from the bottom up, never from the top down.[30] In Europe, trading can be carried out at both a European level and a local level using the same technology and trading platform. This applies to the settlement business, too, and in the future will also be seen in the clearing business. Achieving a global marketplace requires a further step, primarily because of the different time zones involved. The global level will remain fragmented for considerably longer. Nevertheless, the first signs of consolidation are already being seen on the global level.[31]

As we have seen, there is considerable pressure to consolidate and standardize to reduce overall costs. This process (which is driven as well by mergers among market players looking for increased market share) will inevitably result in the need for component organizations in the value chain to come together. They can do so via alliances and even mergers. Over time, this will reduce the number of technological platforms and, inevitably, will require market players to switch from their particular market structure to a new, consolidated one. Ironically, if the component organizations become too large or unwieldy, they may then even fragment again. However, whatever comes to pass, the stronger the technical and organizational interdependencies between exchanges and their members becomes, the more important it will be to have solid investor protection.

Investor Revolution   Fifteen years ago in Europe, floor-based trading was the name of the game. Investors had neither fast access to the markets nor timely, accurate information about the order books and recent trade executions. Big round lots resulted in big order sizes. The floor broker who took a client's order was responsible for executing it on a best-effort basis. Even under the most favorable circumstances, an order, by today's standards, would take a long time to execute. In the meantime, the investor did not have accurate information about what was in the book at the exchange. The investor's broker and the broker's representative on the floor also did not commonly know what was on the book. Better clients could call up their brokers, but most retail customers had to wait hours and sometimes days to get confirmation of their trade executions, and the confirmations were typically delivered by letter (snail mail).

The situation has changed dramatically in Europe. Today, retail investors can obtain high-quality, up-to-the-minute, generally independent information about the state of the market. Every retail investor can, via the Internet, with a time delay measured in just seconds, discover a security's bid-ask spread in the central limit order book, along with (typically) the five best cumulated quotes on each side of the market. Investors can also *route* their orders—now usually at round lot one—via the Internet to their brokers, who in turn seamlessly route the orders on, within seconds, to the exchange's central limit order book. These changes have gone a long way

	Market	Liquidity/ Market Capitalization/ Free Float	Indices	Derivatives and Exchange-Traded Funds	Market model	Most Common Order Types	Sectoral Approach	Examples
Blue chips	Europa, (partly global)	High/ high/ significant	Yes	Yes	Order-driven (central limit order book)	Market and limit orders	Yes	Euro-Stoxx 50 / DAX 30-Stocks
Local/ regional stocks	Local	Low to medium/ low/low	Partly Mostly Not	No (exception: maybe based on an index)	Market making (single or multiple)	Limit and conditional orders	Mostly not	"Over-the-counter" markets "New markets" in Germany, France, Italy, United Kingdom, and others

EXHIBIT 1.8 Market segmentation: Liquidity view (Europe).

to blurring the boundaries between professional traders and sophisticated retail customers.

Market Segmentation   Market segmentation is a necessity because:

- Markets grow from the bottom up, not from the top down (which also means from small to big, from local to global).
- The market architecture for special market segments is driven by investor needs.
- Due to technical flexibility (modular and configurable systems) and the range of competing suppliers available, competition can lead to fragmentation.
- On a European level, the benefits of harmonization that can be achieved by building a European blue-chip segment are widely accepted, but the approach is also widely contested.[32]

Different customized market models are required depending on (1) the needs of investors and intermediaries and (2) other product-based criteria (liquidity, sector, etc.). Institutional customers might require a large round-lot size, while round-lot one is best for a retail investor. Much depends on a stock's liquidity as determined by its market cap and free float. For instance:

- The more liquid the market for a stock, the more suitable continuous trading is for fair and qualitatively good price discovery.
- The less liquid a market for a stock, the more call auctions (discussed in Chapter 6) and market marking (discussed in Chapter 7) are needed for good price discovery.
- Based on the liquidity view, we display more detail about the corresponding segmentation and its consequences in Exhibit 1.8.

SUMMING UP

A securities market is a complex institution. Because customer needs are continually changing, an exchange is under never-ending pressure to adapt, to modify, and to enhance its operations. But the quality of a market is neither easily defined nor readily measured. The ISO-norm 9000 describes quality ". . . as an integration of features and characteristics that determine the extent to which output satisfies customer needs." We suggest that more of an explanation is needed. In the ensuing chapters of the book, we delve deeper into the issue.

NOTES

1. We use the term *securities exchange* broadly. Much of what we say applies to dealer networks as well as to traditional exchanges. An exchange itself is not easily defined. The institution is commonly taken to be a market where intermediaries meet to deliver and execute public orders. In the United States, an exchange is an organization with this function that has registered with the U.S. Securities and Exchange Commission as an exchange.

2. In the case of warrants, the issuer is *not* the listed company, but the actual writer of the option.

3. Another major custodial service is securities lending. For investors, the custodian is usually the exchange member (broker-dealer firm). For the exchange member, custodian services are delivered by the clearing and settlement organizations.

4. We discuss the specialist operations in further detail in Chapter 8, "The Evolving Scene in the United States."

5. SWIFT is the industry-owned cooperative supplying secure, standardized messaging services and interface software to 7,500 financial institutions in 200 countries. The Bank Identifier Code (BIC) is a unique address, which, in telecommunication messages, identifies precisely the financial institutions involved in financial transactions.

6. *Performant* means that the system meets all speed, capacity, and throughput requirements needed to support the market activity. *Scalable* means that the throughput per time unit of a system can be enlarged significantly without making a major investment in hardware/software and/or incurring higher operating costs. *Open architecture* involves providing access to functions in a publicly defined way, wherever possible, following widely used standards.

7. These are trades executed "on" the exchanges, that is, the parties to the trade met on the exchange, typically in a central limit order book.

8. These are trades that took place "off" the exchange and are subsequently reported to the exchange in order to comply with rules and regulations (generally, this should ensure that sufficient market transparency is achieved).

9. A *release* is the implementation and activation of a bundle of functional changes. It makes the process of rolling out changes to the members more manageable.

10. Not only are the operating hours of the systems relevant, but also the specific trading periods for various security segments during the day.

11. For instance, the United States recently moved from sixteenths to decimal-based price steps.

12. As noted, we discuss the order-driven model in Chapter 5 and the quote-driven model in Chapter 6.

13. A *limit order* specifies the highest price a participant would be willing to pay to acquire shares or the lowest price that he or she would be willing to receive

to sell shares. A *market order* is an unpriced order to buy or to sell at market (the best price established by limit orders and/or dealer quotes).

14. An all-or-nothing (AON) order is an instruction to buy or to sell the entire number of shares stated on the order or, if this is not possible, to buy or sell nothing at all. Other special order types that cannot be included in a transparent electronic limit order book include fill-or-kill orders (if the order cannot be executed immediately, cancel it), stop-loss orders, and cross-price-conditioned orders (e.g., buy 300 shares of xyz.com at 49 if the price of abc.com is 28 or higher).

15. Definitions of the various conditional orders are given in the *New York Stock Exchange Rule Book* (see Rule 13).

16. We discuss additional criteria for setting prices at the auctions in Chapter 6, "Order-Driven Markets."

17. Price is the primary priority rule of order execution. Other secondary priority rules include time priority, size priority, random selection, and pro rata selection.

18. This is true only for the cash markets in the United States, which all use DTCC for clearing and settlement. This is also true for the London Market place with the London Stock Exchange, CREST, as a settlement organization and the London Clearing House. The derivatives markets are organized differently.

19. For an exchange itself, an order is nothing but an order. Neither how long it lasts nor its size is relevant to the exchange.

20. The publication of information that can affect the price of a given security must be timely, and all investor classes should in principle have equal access to the information so that "insider trading" cannot occur.

21. For brevity's sake, this analysis assumes that all orders are interacting in a single market. In reality, shares often trade simultaneously on multiple markets. This raises the question of how best to integrate trading in these markets so that price discovery can remain efficient and not suffer from the effects of fragmentation. An important means for achieving an integrated order flow is the use of an effective best-execution policy that takes into consideration the best prices available on all the markets trading the shares in question.

    Put simply, *best execution* is the regulatory requirement to execute a client's order under the best available terms (e.g., the best price available on any exchange, net of trading costs). By requiring orders (at least for retail customers) to be routed across markets to execute at the best price, best-execution regulation helps to ensure integration through cross-border order interaction. In many cases, such as in the United States and Germany, firms have made a business of offering best execution for their retail customers. Similarly, exchanges such as virt-x in Europe have sought to provide a platform on which shares listed elsewhere may trade at superior prices.

    For a more detailed discussion of the relationship between best execution, order interaction, and market integration, see S. McCleskey, *Achieving Market Integration: Best Execution, Fragmentation and the Free Flow of Capital*, Oxford: Butterworth-Heinemann, 2004.

22. Additional or alternative criteria to lowest surplus could be: market pressure, taking into consideration a reference price (e.g., last paid price or an average price). See also Chapter 6, "Order-Driven Markets."

23. For instance, an order to buy 50 shares of General Motors (GM) is an odd lot. If the order is for 250 shares of GM, there are two round lots and an *odd-lot portion* of 50 shares.

24. For a discussion of how to manage operational risk, see, for example, Christopher L. Culp, *The Risk Management Process*, John Wiley & Sons (finance series), 2001, p. 432 ff.

25. See J. Rawls, *A Theory of Justice*, The Belknap Press of Harvard University Press, 1975.

26. For example, two famous philosophers who have grappled intensively with this issue are Aristotle (284–322) and Immanuel Kant (1724–1804).

27. And storage capabilities and capacities as well as processing power and speed are still growing on a two-digit percentage rate per year.

28. With regard to the outsourcing debate, we note the following. There are no industry standards for IT. All solutions are tailor made and customized. Therefore, once outsourced, the corresponding exchange basically has no alternatives, because a change in IT (realizing that valuable alternatives exist) is, in light of switching cost and time to market, very expensive, slow, and almost never feasible from a member's point of view.

29. This is clearly different from a best-execution procedure. *Best execution* means executing an incoming order immediately at least at the price (bid-ask or better) of a reference exchange such as virt-x for Swiss blue chips, Xetra for German blue chips, and SETS for British blue chips.

30. A glance at the life cycle of a security makes this clearer. The smaller a company is in terms of its balance sheet, market capitalization, P&L and so forth, the more locally it is traded. It is said, for example, that investors in the majority of small to medium-sized companies are generally based no more than 100 miles (160 km) from the headquarters of the company concerned! Only truly regional companies are traded regionally, and only truly global companies are traded globally. At the time of its IPO (i.e., the birth of a security from the point of view of the capital markets), a company is typically local. As it then develops, it first becomes interesting regionally. Only a relatively few securities (such as IBM, which is listed in a significant number of world markets) ever make it into the global league.

31. An example is the Global Equity Market (GEM) initiative of a number of the larger world stock exchanges.

32. See for example Deutsche Börse AG, IPO Analyst Presentation: *Deutsche Börse Goes Euroboard*, March 31, 2000, p. 25. The benefits of harmonization include:
    • A common market for liquid segments (blue chips, growth market) with harmonized trading rules.
    • A single point of access for all products of the common market.
    • Reduced spreads due to a single point of liquidity.
    • Cost reduction due to network standardization, and increased quality due to competition between exchanges.

CHAPTER 2

From Information to Prices

Information is the input that drives investment decisions and therefore also trading. Security prices are a result (output) of the process. In efficient markets, information should be reflected in prices with an accuracy that leaves no investor an incentive to search for additional information or to trade. If information is perfectly reflected in prices and if trading is a frictionless (seamless and costless) process, then security prices will follow a random walk (i.e., a stock's price will change randomly over time). However, when the realities of actual markets are taken into account, it is clear that trading is not frictionless and that share prices do not follow random walks. Understanding this is crucial to appreciating the importance of instituting efficient market architecture.

In most of this chapter, we consider the relationship between information and prices in a perfect world. Our discussion encompasses concepts of information, expectations, and random walks. In the last section of this chapter, "Information and Prices," we leave the frictionless environment behind and head toward real-world markets. More technical background pertinent to this chapter is contained in three appendixes located at the end of the book. Appendix A, "Prices and Returns," depicts the relationship between these two variables. Appendix B, "From Portfolio Decisions to Trading in a Frictionless Environment," discusses price determination in a perfect, frictionless world. Appendix C, "Dimensions of Informational Efficiency," presents five dimensions of informational efficiency that are noted in the fourth section of this chapter ("Informational Efficiency, Prices, and Random Walks").

CAPM—A PERFECT, FRICTIONLESS WORLD

In the opening paragraph of his classic 1952 *Journal of Finance* paper, Harry Markowitz set forth two stages of portfolio selection:[1] "The first stage starts with observation and experience and ends with beliefs about the future performances of available securities. The second stage starts with the relevant beliefs about future performances and ends with the choice of portfolio." Markowitz's paper focused on the second step and, in so doing, rigorously established risk as a major consideration for portfolio selection along with expected return. This analysis has provided the basis for the capital asset pricing model. Thirty-eight years later, in 1990, Markowitz was awarded the Nobel Prize in Economics.

Given the enormous complexity of real-world markets, it is standard economic methodology to construct models based on simplifying assumptions that, of necessity, are unrealistic. The capital asset pricing model (CAPM), a major pillar of modern portfolio theory, follows this methodology. Three economists, working separately, developed the CAPM: William F. Sharpe, who also received a Nobel Prize in Economics in 1990, John Lintner, and Jan Mossin.[2] Key CAPM assumptions include:

- There are no taxes, no transaction costs, and no short-selling restrictions.
- Investors are fully informed and, being fully informed, have the same (homogeneous) expectations about what prices will be in the future.
- Unlimited amounts can be borrowed or lent at a constant, risk-free rate.
- Markets are perfectly liquid.

Viewed comprehensively, these assumptions roll into one: The world is a frictionless environment.

In the frictionless environment, the information presented to all investors is in the form of the ultimate bottom line. Namely, in the perfect world, all investors know the distributions of future returns for all stocks and for all portfolios. Further, investors all know that the actual returns are drawn randomly over time, but are correlated across stocks for any slice in time, and the covariance terms are known. Finally, investors know that the distributions are normal,[3] and that normal distributions are characterized by two parameters: mean and variance. Consequently, all information in the perfect world is summarized by (1) the means and variances of returns distributions for individual stocks and portfolios and (2) the covariance of returns across stocks and portfolios.

The frictionless world is elegant in its simplicity. An analysis of it provides important insights into (1) the definition and measurement of risk, (2) the risk reduction that can be achieved through portfolio diversification, (3) the nature of risk and return relationships, and (4) the pricing relationships between a market portfolio (a basket of all stocks), the set of risky stocks that comprise that portfolio, and the risk-free asset.

To understand the equilibrium that is achieved in the frictionless environment, we consider in Appendix B both individual investor demand and aggregate market demand to hold (1) shares of the market portfolio, (2) the risk-free asset, and (3) shares of the individual stocks. Under CAPM, on both the individual investor and the market level, the demand to hold shares of the market portfolio is downward sloping, while the demand to hold shares of each individual stock in the basket is horizontal (infinitely elastic) at the stock's equilibrium price. Horizontal demand means that a stock has an *intrinsic value:* At any price above the equilibrium value, no shares at all will be held, and at any price below the equilibrium value, an unlimited number of shares will be held.

An individual stock has an intrinsic value in the perfect world because its price depends only on how its return covaries with the return on the market portfolio. That the covariance is the only factor that matters can be explained as follows. First, each stock's expected return (and hence its current price) is uniquely related to its covariance with the market portfolio.[4] Second, a stock's covariance with the market can, at zero cost, be replicated by appropriately combining two or more other stocks. Third, all participants are in perfect agreement about the covariance parameters for all stocks. Fourth, the first three conditions imply that perfect substitutes for each and every stock exist. With the availability of perfect substitutes, each stock has an intrinsic value (the price that locates the stock's infinitely elastic, horizontal demand curve).

INFORMATION

Let us now look at what lies beneath the information depicted by returns distributions. In actual markets, the raw information available pertains to market conditions and to the fundamental determinants of share value. To be useful, the raw information has to be collected, processed, and analyzed. In light of the enormity of the available information set, individual participants cannot be expected to know it all or to process what they do know in identical ways.

Taking an aerial view, we classify information into two broad categories: market (trading) information and fundamental information relative to the investment decision (the basic determinants of share value).

Market information includes knowledge of the current quotes, last-transaction prices, and transaction volume. In addition, some traders take account of recent high-low prices, the daily opening price, and the previous day's close. Furthermore, it would be of value to have information on orders that have not yet executed, including knowledge of the limit order book, knowledge of orders held by traders in the crowd[5] (which are partially revealed), and statements of buying or selling interest by block, institutional, and other large traders (which are partially available on systems such as AutEx).

Fundamental information relating to the investment decision pertains to the determinants of future share value. The most useful form for information to take would be a direct statement of the means, variances, and covariances of security returns. However, one can at best form expectations on means, variances, and covariances, given the information set that is available:

Recent share price history. Knowledge of the historic values of the means, variances, and covariances of returns, and so on.

Current financial information. Information concerning current capital structure, earnings forecasts, and so on.

Current strategy of management. Knowledge about the current strategic business and outlook.

Current economic information. Information concerning the firm's product market, the firm's competitors, national and international economic conditions, and so on.

Structural change. Knowledge of recent acquisitions, divestitures, discoveries, regulatory change, and so on.

Organizational efficiency. Knowledge of corporate structure, managerial ability, and so on.

The six categories of information pertain to the environment and to the firm whose security is being evaluated. One might view information even more broadly, however. The relevant set encompasses attributes of the decision maker—the technical knowledge and experience that allow a good assessment of relevant facts. This information ranges from the decision maker's experience and skill at assessing intangibles (e.g., managerial ability) to formal knowledge of portfolio theory and the capital asset pricing model. Information of this type may be nothing more than enlightened intuition; nevertheless, it is a key input into decision making.

Security analysis involves the assessment of share value. But, as we have noted, security analysts do not undertake a treasure hunt to find a golden number that one might call an *intrinsic value.*[6] Rather, share prices are set the way they are for most resources. They are set in the marketplace—in relation to the forces of demand and supply. There are, however, a few exceptions to this rule. Some prices are used for trading or valuation purposes outside the market in which they are established. When so used, the price can be viewed as an intrinsic value. This is commonly referred to as *derivative pricing* or as *price basing.* Derivative pricing applies when one market (e.g., a regional exchange) operates within a context provided by another market (e.g., the NYSE). Price basing is used when a price determined in the derivative market is used to set price in the related cash market, or vice versa.

Information can be classified in another way—it can be characterized as public information, as inside information, or as private information:

- *Public information.* Widely disseminated information that is readily available to the public. Being readily available does not necessarily mean, however, that the information is provided free. For instance, real-time data on market quotes and transaction prices, and many historic databases, must be paid for.
- *Inside information.* Information possessed by only a select set of people who have a special position with regard to the information. Corporate officers and others with business ties to a company (e.g., an investment banker, a lawyer, or a proofreader) are commonly in possession of inside information.
- *Private information.* Information that participants may individually possess because of their own investigations and analyses.

  Comprehensively viewed, the set of available information is, in a word, enormous. Consequently, individuals see only parts of it, and each participant typically assesses information in a way that, to some extent, is unique to his or her own vantage point. For this reason, private information plays a major role in the formulation of individual expectations.

Tapping effectively into even a relatively specific information set can require considerable skill and expense, but an analyst who can do this successfully may earn handsome returns. An article in the *Wall Street Journal* on October 6, 2003, is illustrative.[7]

The *Journal* reported that, between June and August of 2003, certain large institutional investors using two detailed pharmaceutical databases that cost subscribers between $25,000 and $50,000 a year were able to determine that the drug company, Schering-Plough, was losing market share for its hepatitis C medicine to a competitor, Roche Holding AG.[8] The investing public got hints of the development in July, but full information was not available until August 22. During this period, Schering peaked at $20.47 on June 18, then drifted down, dipping below $17 as July turned into August. On August 21, the stock closed at $16.48. Strikingly, on August 22, the day when Schering confirmed the declining sales trend for its product, shares opened down $2.18, at $14.30. The *Journal*'s comment? "While nobody did anything wrong in this case—the investors weren't acting on inside information and the company violated no disclosure rules—it highlights an information chasm in the drug business that essentially punishes smaller investors." The underlying reality is that the large investors were acting on *private information*, and they were richly rewarded for their efforts. Undoubtedly, this story can be told many times over for many different industries.

EXPECTATIONS

Individuals form expectations about a company's future returns, given the current information set. Expectations link current information to the market value of shares.

Homogeneous Expectations

Much formal analysis in financial economics assumes that different investors have the same expectations concerning security returns. Even though the assumption of homogeneous expectations is known to be unrealistic, models based on it (e.g., the standard capital asset pricing model) give much insight into how the market determines prices for various assets according to their risk and return characteristics. In the context of the capital asset pricing model, the assumption of homogeneous expectations is equivalent to the assumption that decision makers have perfect information concerning the means and variances of returns for the full set of stocks.

Rational decision making may seem to imply the homogeneity of expectations. This is because such decision making considers what a rational person would conclude, given the facts. Presumably, what one rational person would conclude, all rational people should conclude. However, having considered the elements that comprise the information set, we may better understand why the assumption of homogeneous expectations is unrealistic. It is plausible for a group of investors to have homogeneous expectations only if they share the same information set, process it in an identical way, and do not have private information.

Divergent Expectations

The term *divergent expectations* is used to characterize an environment where investor beliefs are not homogeneous. Individuals are commonly observed to differ in their assessments of information, and this is not difficult to explain. Information sets are vast, complex, and challenging to understand. Different individuals possess only part of the information that is publicly available, and some investors have private information. As we discuss next, stock selection is, to an extent, a beauty contest, where everyone is guessing what everyone else is expecting (and guessing).

Furthermore, individuals may also reassess their individual valuations based on what they come to know that others are thinking. We can refer to these reassessments as either *adaptive valuations* or as *interdependent valuations*. To illustrate, assume that the Fed announces in a depressed market environment that interest rates will be kept constant rather than decreased. A bearish expectation based on the announcement may be that the market will fall further because of the lack of a monetary stimulus. A bullish expectation may be that the market will rise because the Fed does not believe that a further monetary stimulus is necessary. Put yourself in the shoes of a bearish participant, and consider your reaction when a slew of new buy orders arrive on the market and prices start to rise. Would you reconsider your own assessment of the Fed's decision in light of how others have reacted? Anybody who would has adaptive valuations.

The divergence of expectations among investors and the adaptive nature of evaluations have major implications for the operations of a securities market. This explains why information change can lead to heavy trading. Namely, everyone does not react to new information identically, and, as prices adjust to news, some choose to buy while others decide to sell. Further, in an environment where expectations are divergent, share values cannot be determined at the desks of security analysts. Rather, prices must be set in the marketplace, where the buy and sell orders of a large set of participants are brought together and translated into trades. In other words, *price discovery* occurs in the marketplace.

As we will see in Chapter 3, "Liquidity," price discovery is a complex, dynamic process. Recognition of this has major implications for the role and development of good market architecture.

The Beauty Contest

Let's focus on the following: (1) Participants have divergent expectations, and (2) a stock's price reflects the desires of a broad spectrum of participants to hold shares. These two realities introduce another dimension into share valuation: Each individual considers what everyone else is thinking.

In recognizing this, John Maynard Keynes drew a colorful parallel between stock selection and a beauty contest:[9]

> ... *professional investment may be likened to those newspaper competitions in which the competitors have to pick out the six prettiest faces from a hundred photographs, the prize being awarded to the competitor whose choice most nearly corresponds to the average preferences of the competitors as a whole; so that each competitor has to pick, not those faces which he himself finds prettiest, but those which he thinks likeliest to catch the fancy of the other competitors, all of whom are looking at the problem from the same point of view. It is not a case of choosing those which, to the best of one's judgment, are really the prettiest, nor even those which average opinion genuinely thinks the prettiest. We have reached the third degree where we devote our intelligences to anticipating what average opinion expects the average opinion to be. And there are some, I believe, who practise the fourth, fifth and higher degrees.*

Keynes's analogy underscores the following. An investor hopes that the price of the shares that he or she owns will rise in the future so that the shares might then be sold at a profit. Whether it is because other investors think the shares are worth more, or because fundamental economic change has actually caused the shares to be worth more, is not, per se, relevant. What matters is only that the price does indeed rise. If some investors anticipate that other market participants will expect a price increase, they will buy shares, and the current market price of the stock will be bid up.

The beauty contest analogy is inadequate, however, as an expectations model. For one thing, share evaluation, unlike the assessment of beauty, is not a purely subjective matter—objective information is also taken into account. Furthermore, Keynes's analogy does not allow that the judges in the stock market contest can, with experience, learn how the process works.

Rational Expectations

The link between expectations and prices can be considered within the context of a specific model of expectation formation: a rational expectations model.[10] The model is structured as follows:

1. The stock market contest is played repetitively in consecutive periods. The outcome of each contest is given by the share assessments established at the end of each period. Each assessment reflects what investors, at the time, anticipate shares will be worth at the end of subsequent periods.

2. Investor assessments of share values are based, in part at least, on expectations concerning the future dividend payments they will receive, and the expected stream of future dividend payments depends on the future worth of the firm.

3. At the start of each period, investors can, at a cost, obtain additional information pertaining to the economic worth of the corporation as of the end of the period. Uncertainty is not eliminated, but investors who obtain the information do form more accurate expectations than uninformed investors of the future value of share price.

The presence of a meaningful informational signal and the absence of systematic mistakes are the essence of a rational expectations model. But there still is a beauty contest. All investors do not become informed each period (information is not costless), the uninformed still guess what the informed may have learned, and the informed anticipate what the uninformed will do. However, with informed investors, the current value of shares is linked to future economic worth. In addition, the uninformed investors learn with experience how the contest works, and knowledgeable judges do not make systematic mistakes.

Asymmetric Information and Price Signaling

Our previous classification of information as being either public, inside, or private enables us to classify investors in two groups: the informed (people possessing inside and/or private information) and the uninformed (people possessing public information only). When two participants, one of each type, meet as counterparties and enter into a bilateral trade, the informed participant profits from his or her informational advantage and the uninformed participant is hurt by the information asymmetry.

A large microstructure literature exists on the effect of asymmetric information on quote setting and trading, and we return to this issue in our discussion of order-driven markets (Chapter 6) and intermediated markets (Chapter 7).[11] Of interest in the current chapter is how the information possessed by informed participants can be transmitted to the uninformed through price. A landmark article by Grossman and Stiglitz shows how.[12] Their paper presents a rational expectations model that incorporates the following eight assumptions:[13]

1. There is a succession of investment periods of length T that are identical for all decision makers. Each investment period may be considered a contest period.

2. There are two assets, a risky asset and cash.

3. All informed investors at the start of each contest period possess some new information about the risky asset that the uninformed do not have that applies to that single period. The new information is obtained at a cost.

4. All informed investors assess the new information the same way (they have homogeneous expectations). When assessed, the information is given a dollar dimension, the expected value of share price as of the end of that period.

5. Uninformed investors have publicly available information, but do not know the new information that is possessed by the informed investors.

6. Share prices at the start of each contest period are determined in light of the information the informed participants possess along with other factors unrelated to information (such as the investors' liquidity needs).

7. Trades are made and share prices are set in a frictionless call auction.

8. The game is played repetitively so that all participants become thoroughly familiar with the processes and learn the statistical relationships between information and prices.

In this environment, if no trader were to become informed (being informed costs something), the market price would lose informational content. The situation is avoided, however, because the uninformed trader cannot infer information perfectly from the current market price for a reason that can be explained as follows. Factors such as changing investor liquidity needs that are not related to information also affect the desire of the informed to hold shares. Thus the uninformed investors, knowing neither the information nor the demand of the other investors with precision, cannot determine, on observing a price, that price's exact information content. In other words, a market price is a noisy signal.

In this rational expectations model, the uninformed participants make unbiased guesses about the expectations of the informed participants. While the inferences of the uninformed are accurate on average, in any specific period they are subject to uncertainty. Consequently, being informed gives a trader an advantage that compensates for the cost of becoming informed. Nevertheless, some of the knowledge of the informed is passed on to the uninformed through the signal that a stock's price conveys to the market. Further, because the informed and uninformed agents are all trading simultaneously at a single price, the uninformed are not hurt by the information asymmetry to the extent that they are in the bilateral trading models we discuss in Chapters 6 and 7.[14]

A simple example may clarify the Grossman-Stiglitz model. Assume that news is characterized in five ways: very bullish, bullish, neutral, bearish, and very bearish. Let the end of period price distributions associated with each of these five states be as follows:[15]

State	End of Investment Period Price
Very bullish	34, 35, 36
Bullish	33, 34, 35
Neutral	32, 33, 34
Bearish	31, 32, 33
Very bearish	30, 31, 32

To further simplify, assume that each of the five states is equally likely to occur and that each of the three outcomes for each state is also equally probable. The informed investors learn which of the five states applies for any specific investment period, and, given this knowledge, a current equilibrium price is set for each state, based on the demand to hold shares of both the informed and the uninformed investors. For each state, however, the current price can, with equal probability, have either of two values depending on the participants' liquidity positions: a high value (H) if liquid positions are high (perhaps participants just received an inflow of cash) or a low value (L) if liquidity positions are low (perhaps participants have just made some large cash payments). Assume that the start of period prices associated with each of the five states and two conditions are as follows:

Equilibrium Price at Start of Investment Period

State	Condition H	Condition L
Very bullish	34	33
Bullish	33	32
Neutral	32	31
Bearish	31	30
Very bearish	30	29

Before the market forms and a price is set, the uninformed, knowing neither the state that applies nor the start of period price, take the distribution of end-of-period prices as ranging from a low of 30 to a high of 36.[16] However, the uninformed are able to infer which state applies from the start of period prices. The inferences are:

Start of Investment Period Equilibrium Price	Inferred Distribution of End-of-Period Price
34	34, 35, 36
33	33, 34, 35, 36
32	32, 33, 34, 35
31	31, 32, 33, 34
30	30, 31, 32, 33
29	30, 31, 32

Because of the truncated nature of our example, at the extreme prices (29 and 34), the inferred distribution for the uninformed is as accurate as the known distribution of the informed. Of interest are the inferred distributions at the intermediate prices (30 to 33). Here, the knowledge inferred by the uninformed is not as precise as that possessed by the informed.

The less precise knowledge of the uninformed will affect their portfolio decisions. Namely, because they face a wider distribution of end-of-period prices, the uninformed will hold fewer shares of the risky asset. Further, they will submit a more complex order to the market. Namely, they would state the number of shares they would wish to own at each of the six prices from 29 to 34. Then, with the start of period price determined at the call, their order will execute appropriately. For instance, if the start of the period price is 34, they will wind up holding exactly the number of shares they wish to hold at 34. If the start-of-period price turns out to be 33, they will wind up holding exactly the number of shares they wish to hold at 33. And so on.

In sum, the uninformed face a more clarified distribution of end-of-period prices than they would have in the absence of price signaling, but a noisier distribution than that possessed by the informed traders. Interestingly, to benefit from the price signaling, the uninformed need not know the price before submitting their orders to the auction—they simply submit more complex orders that tell the auctioneer the exact number of shares they would each like to hold at each alternative price that might be established.

INFORMATIONAL EFFICIENCY, PRICES, AND RANDOM WALKS

The term *informational efficiency* refers to the accuracy with which prices that are set in a marketplace reflect the underlying information on which they are based. Prices should be efficient in the following five ways.

1. They should be appropriately set with regard to currently existing information.

2. An optimal amount of resources should be allocated to the production of information (research).

3. Equilibrium prices should represent an optimal transfer of information from informed to uninformed participants. They should also reflect an appropriate aggregation of diverse information bits that are possessed

by a broad spectrum of participants ranging from the relatively well informed to the relatively uninformed.

4. Market-clearing prices should be properly aligned with underlying equilibrium values.

5. We must also be concerned about the dynamic efficiency with which new information is disseminated and incorporated into prices. We discuss the five criteria in further detail in Appendix C, "Dimensions of Informational Efficiency." In this section of the chapter, we focus on tests of informational efficiency.

Examining whether or not traders can realize excess returns by trading on information is a test of the informational efficiency of a market. The null hypothesis, referred to as the *efficient market hypothesis* (EMH), is formalized as follows. Excess returns cannot be realized from information that is contained in:

- *Past prices.* This is referred to as *weak-form efficiency.*
- *Public information (including past prices).* This is referred to as *semistrong-form efficiency.*
- *All information (public plus inside information).* This is referred to as *strong-form efficiency.*

Weak-Form Tests

Weak-form tests of the EMH focus on the informational content of the previous sequence of stock price movements. How much information should these movements contain for a market to be informationally efficient? If the market is a frictionless environment, the answer is *none*. In informationally efficient markets, above-normal returns cannot be realized by using trading rules based on past price movements. Alternatively stated, weak-form efficiency requires only that past price changes cannot be used to improve predictions concerning the expected value of future price changes.[17]

When the expected value of a stock's price change is zero, and when successive price changes are statistically independent and identically distributed, the security's price is said to follow a random walk over time. Strict random walk is in essence a random number generator, but we use the term more broadly to characterize successive price changes that are statistically independent.[18]

The term *random walk*, and what it implies, has an interesting history. Assume one were to leave a drunk in the middle of a large field, let him stumble around for a while, and then, after some time has passed, go back and look for him. Where is the most efficient place to start looking? Because the drunk follows a random walk, knowledge of the direction of his or her last observed steps contains no useful information, and the best place to start looking is where the drunk was last seen.

Random walk was never the domain of the drunk alone. Bachelier reported evidence that the current price of a commodity is an unbiased estimate of the future price of the commodity.[19] Subsequently, other students of asset price movements have reported that prices change randomly over time.[20] The curious point is that the early findings presented evidence of random walk, but an understanding of why price changes would be uncorrelated in a frictionless, informationally efficient market was not forthcoming for many years.[21] The most comprehensive review of this early literature and a more comprehensive analysis is that of Fama.[22]

That prices are expected to follow a random walk in informationally efficient and frictionless markets is very important. Following the empirical demonstration that, by and large, markets are informationally efficient, we focus on deviations from random walk as evidence of operational inefficiency in nonfrictionless markets. Therefore, it is important first to understand why random walk would be evidence of informational efficiency. Of interest are price adjustments that result from changes in investor desires, information, and expectations. The question addressed is whether these price adjustments can be predicted or whether they are random.

Assume that some investors know that in one day other investors will discover something about a stock that will drive its price up 20 percent. Those who are currently in the know have an opportunity to capture the 20 percent increase for themselves and, in so doing, to make excess profits. As they do this by buying the stock at the lower price, the following happens:

- The price of the stock is bid up until these people no longer expect a further, abnormal price increase.
- The price increase that was expected in a day is realized in the current period.

The current adjustment of price to any change that is anticipated for the future means that, in equilibrium, all expectations are reflected in the current value of price. Accordingly, it is not possible to predict when, how, or by how much an equilibrium price will change in the future. This is because something that is *unanticipated* must occur in order for the equilibrium price to change. Therefore, in a market that is efficient in the sense that equilibrium prices are attained, prices follow a random walk over time.

The random walk can be pictured with reference to Exhibit 2.1. Let the market be in the initial equilibrium position shown in Exhibit 2.1(a), with the aggregate demand curve being D_0, the number of shares outstanding

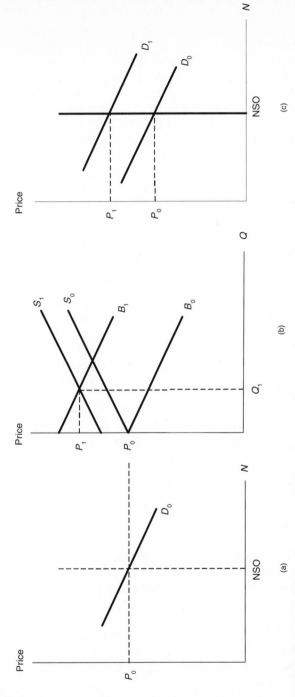

EXHIBIT 2.1 Effect of market demand shift on the price of an asset: (a) Determination of the initial equilibrium price P_0. (b) Shifts in the aggregate trade curves change the market price. (c) Contrast of the initial equilibrium price P_0 and the new equilibrium price P_1.

being NSO, and the market price being P_0. Then the associated trade curves will be B_0 (for buy orders) and S_0 (for sell orders), as shown in Exhibit 2.1(b). Until the demand curve shifts for at least some trader, the market price will remain P_0.

Assume that after some short period of time has passed, individual demand curves shift. Perhaps there has been a change in expectations, a change in the willingness of some investors to undertake risk, or a change in liquidity. Let the aggregate trade curves change to the lines labeled S_1 and B_1 in Exhibit 2.1(b). This shift causes the buy and sell curves to cross and results in Q_1 shares trading at a price of P_1. After the trade, market demand is the curve labeled D_1 in Exhibit 2.1(c), and the market-clearing price is P_1. Once again, the market will have achieved equilibrium. In summary, this is what happened:

The price change is $\Delta P = P_1 - P_0$.

The return is $r_1 = \Delta P / P_0$.

After the price change, the market is in equilibrium, as it was before demand shifted.

What will the next price change be? For the reasons just discussed, this cannot be predicted. Perhaps the next shift will change price from P_1 to some new value, P_2. The next return will then be $r_2 = (P_2 - P_1)/P_1$. Because the second return (r_2) cannot be predicted before it occurs, it must be independent of everything that preceded it, including r_1. That is, $r_2 \neq f(r_1)$.

Nonetheless, might information change in a correlated fashion that causes successive changes in the equilibrium prices to be correlated? Abstracting from issues of operational inefficiency in a nonfrictionless market, the answer is no. Information arrival may be correlated, but this does not imply that successive prices changes will be. Aside from drift, if the sequence of price changes is not independent, knowledge of past price changes could enable investors to predict future price changes. Trading on the basis of a predicted price change can be viewed as intertemporal arbitrage—shares are bought at one moment at a relatively low price and sold at another moment at a higher price (or vice versa). As is generally true with arbitrage trading, the very act of trading eliminates price patterns that can be profitably exploited. The point is, random walk is not caused by the pattern of information arrival, but by investor responses to information. Aside from long-run drift, a random walk is expected in a frictionless market that is informationally efficient.

Random walk is an elegant concept. It is also humbling because it implies that nobody armed only with publicly available information can have a crystal ball that will tell the future path that prices will follow. Yet the belief is widespread among many in the industry that information can be gleaned from charting price movements from the recent past (particularly trade-to-trade data from the current trading day) using techniques referred to as *technical analysis*. Academicians generally do not agree. One prominent academician, Burton Malkiel, wrote, "Technical analysis is anathema to the academic world. We love to pick on it. Our bullying tactics are prompted by two considerations: (1) the method is patently false; and (2) it's easy to pick on."[23] We comment further about technical analysis later in this chapter in the section, "Prices and Markets," and again in Chapter 4, "What We Want from Our Markets."

Semistrong-Form Tests

Semistrong-form tests focus on the speed with which specific pieces of public information are reflected in stock prices. The announcement of a piece of information is considered an event, and the studies are commonly referred to as *event studies*.

One early event study established the methodology that has subsequently been used by many others: Fama, Fisher, Jensen, and Roll's (FFJR) analysis of the effect of stock splits on share price.[24] Stock splits are expected to increase the total value of shares because they convey a bullish signal to shareholders (since stock splits have historically been associated with strong earnings growth and increased dividends). Fama et al. report that, for 940 splits for NYSE stocks between 1927 and 1959, over two-thirds were followed by the announcement of a dividend increase.

The FFJR study examined the pattern of price changes observed in the months preceding and following splits. Specifically, Fama et al. considered the difference between the actual return on a stock and the return that is expected, given the return on the market.[25] This difference is referred to as the *abnormal return*. They found for a sample of 622 stocks that abnormal returns tend to be considerably higher in the months preceding a stock split, that these returns continue to be somewhat higher in the months following a split for companies that do increase their dividends, and that they are somewhat lower in the months following a split for companies that do not increase their dividends.

Fama et al. captured these effects with the following procedure. For each stock in their sample, the month of the split was defined as month zero,[26] the last month before the split as month –1, the first month after the split as month +1, and so on, for a time span extending from month –29 to month +30. The abnormal return was then computed for each stock for each month. The month –29 abnormal returns were then averaged across the stocks, as were the month –28 abnormal returns, and so forth. The average abnormal returns were then cumulated, starting at month –29 and extending to month +30. A stylized representation of the resulting cumulative average for all stocks is shown in Exhibit 2.2. Notice that the cumulative average rises in the months preceding the split and is flat in the months following the split.

The considerably greater than expected returns before the split dates show that prices are adjusted upward on the basis of the optimistic signals that the stock splits convey. It is also likely that the companies were enjoying above-average and unsustainable prosperity in the two years before the split and that the effect of this is also observed in the pattern of the residuals. The somewhat greater than expected returns after the split dates for companies that increased their dividends show the positive price responses that result when the bullish signal is confirmed. The lower-than-expected returns after the split dates for companies that do not increase their dividends are evidence of the negative price adjustments that occur when a bullish expectation turns out to have been overly optimistic.

For a large sample of stocks, the FFJR findings show that prices adjust to news before an event has occurred (for instance, before the dates of the stock splits). Therefore, profitable trading strategies cannot be developed in relation to an event after it has occurred. A sizable number of other, more recent event studies have substantiated the informational efficiency of the market in the semistrong form of the hypothesis.

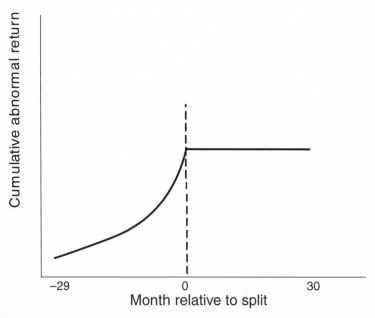

EXHIBIT 2.2   Cumulative abnormal return before and after stock splits.

The tests of semistrong-form efficiency have not, however, addressed the question of dynamic efficiency. As discussed in Appendix C, "Dimensions of Informational Efficiency," information may be quickly reflected in prices, but some investors may nevertheless have a preferential position vis-à-vis the information flow. If so, these investors might receive and act on information first, and they may receive excess profits.

Dynamic efficiency is particulary difficult to test, largely because price adjustments do occur rapidly. One might not expect to observe dynamic inefficiency in monthly price data as were used by Fama et al. and in many other studies. Rather, intraday prices could reveal a far more telling story. Dann, Mayers, and Raab, in their examination of the effect of block sales on transaction-to-transaction price movements, for instance, found that the price pressure caused by these sales does allow the formulation of profitable trading rules.[27] To earn a profit, however, an investor must make a purchase within *5 minutes* of the block transaction, because within *15 minutes* of the transaction, prices appear to have adjusted completely to their previous levels.[28]

Given the speed with which price adjustments are made in the equity markets, one might question the inferences concerning market efficiency that have been drawn from studies based on monthly prices. If the studies had shown positive evidence of inefficiency, the results would have been striking. Unfortunately, the failure to demonstrate inefficiency does not carry as much conviction.

Strong-Form Tests

As noted, the weak form of the EMH refers to public information that is contained in prior stock price movements, the semistrong form refers to all news that is publicly available, and the strong form refers to everything, including inside information and that which can be dug out by superior security analysis. Unfortunately, academic researchers are not as a rule privy to such information. Therefore, researchers have attempted to draw inferences concerning strong-form efficiency by testing whether investors who are most apt to enjoy this informational advantage do in fact realize excess returns.

Finding that the better informed do not make excess profits would be evidence in support of the EMH. On the other hand, observing that certain classes of investors make excess profits net of information costs may not be evidence against the EMH. The reason is twofold:

1. As discussed previously, informational efficiency requires that the marginal return to information equal the marginal cost of obtaining it. However, decreasing average and marginal returns and increasing

average and marginal costs result in average returns exceeding average costs when marginal returns equal marginal costs.[29] Hence, excess profits—such profits are sometimes referred to as *economic rent*—can be realized by some decision makers. Decision makers who undertake their own research are both producers and consumers of information. As producers they may face increasing average costs, and as consumers they may realize decreasing average returns.

2. As indicated previously, some investors do better than others simply because of luck. Therefore, larger realized returns *ex post* do not necessarily indicate that better decisions were made *ex ante*. For this reason, excess *ex post* returns are not themselves evidence against the strong form of the EMH. Rather, to reject the hypothesis, one must demonstrate that excess returns accrue to one individual persistently (and thus are not explained by chance).

The empirical evidence shows that professional investment managers do not consistently realize superior portfolio returns. Mutual funds have been the most frequently studied of the institutions. Some of the first and best-known studies showing that the funds do not outperform the market include those of Friend, Brown, Herman, and Vickers,[30] Sharpe,[31] and Jensen.[32]

Insider Trading   The strong form of the EMH also refers to information possessed by insiders. Much evidence indicates that this aspect of strong-form efficiency is violated, that insiders can realize abnormally high returns from trading on information that they alone possess.

Insiders have an advantage vis-à-vis the information flow and can manipulate it. Further, they are able to produce information. For example, the management of a profitable corporation could, if unrestricted, realize personal gain by selling shares short while jeopardizing the profitability of the firm. Consequently, insider trading must be regulated. We consider insider trading in greater detail in Chapter 11, "Regulation."

PRICES AND MARKETS

Thus far we have considered the relationship between information and prices without taking much account of the realities of a marketplace where orders are submitted and prices determined. Much standard economic analysis is based on the assumption of frictionless trading in a perfectly competitive environment. *Frictionless* means that there are no transaction costs, restrictions, or other blockages. *Perfect competition* means that, for a homogeneous resource, the number of buyers and sellers is sufficiently large so that no trader is big enough relative to the market to affect the resource's price. Price takers make only one decision with respect to a resource: the quantity to buy (demand) or to sell (supply) at a price that is determined by market forces. *Market forces* is an abstract concept meaning that if demand exceeds supply, then competition among buyers will cause prices to rise, and if supply exceeds demand, then competition among sellers will cause prices to fall. Problems concerning market operations do not exist in this environment.

A market center such as the New York Stock Exchange (NYSE) is sometimes cited as an example of a perfectly competitive environment. Standardized units are bought and sold at the NYSE, and any share of, for instance, IBM common, is like any other share of IBM common. A large number of investors own and trade shares of IBM. The company reported that, as of the end of 2003, it had 671,610 registered owners and another 1.9 million stockholders who owned shares through banks, brokerage houses, and other financial institutions. Therefore, one might expect the price of IBM shares to be determined by market forces. So they are, but much more is involved. Some investors (predominantly the institutions) are large enough to have market power. And, of course, the Big Board is not a frictionless market. Both of these realities affect the efficiency with which information is translated into prices.

In this chapter we have considered the enormous complexity of the information set and the extensive requirements for informational efficiency. In the process, we have focused on expectations formation and have paid particular attention to the fact that market participants have divergent and interdependent (adaptive) expectations. The discussion suggests that informational efficiency may not be readily achieved.

In recent years, high-frequency (intraday) data on quotes and transaction prices that have become widely available have enabled researchers to probe far more deeply in their assessments of informational efficiency and random walk. Increasingly, evidence is building that intertemporal returns dependency exists, and on all three levels of efficiency (weak, semistrong, and strong), questions can be raised about the speed and the accuracy with which new information is incorporated into share values.

We attribute the complexity of price determination to two factors in particular: (1) Investors possess private information and interpret public information differently (i.e., they have divergent expectations), and (2) trading is not a frictionless process. When these factors are taken into account, analyzing the dynamic process of price formation becomes considerably more complex, technical analysis cannot be quickly dismissed as baseless, and conclusions about market efficiency become less certain.[33]

Technical analysis involves using a recent history of realized prices to predict future values. While future prices are unknown, current prices are typically assumed to be determinate and known (this conceptualization is consistent with standard analyses of stock selection and portfolio formation). The orientation changes, however, if account is taken of the realities of a marketplace where prices are discovered while trading takes place. When faced with the uncertainties of price discovery, values at which participants transact in the current period depend on the participants' strategic trading decisions (how they price, size, time, and otherwise condition their orders). In this context, technical analysis may be viewed, not as a way of predicting values that can be realized in future trading sessions, but as a technique for assessing price movements that are likely to occur in the current session as the broad market proceeds with its search for appropriate consensus values.[34]

What about the efficient markets hypothesis? Lawrence Summers shows that an inability to reject the EMH is not a sufficient basis for accepting it, citing evidence provided by Modigliani and Cohn, by Shiller, and by Arrow, among others, that "certain asset prices are not rationally related to economic realities."[35] In light of his demonstration that large valuation errors need not be reflected in significant correlation patterns, Summers writes,

> *The standard theoretical argument for market efficiency is that unless securities are priced efficiently, there will be opportunities to earn excess returns. Speculators will take advantage of these opportunities by arbitraging away any inefficiencies in the pricing of securities. This argument does not explain how speculators become aware of profit opportunities. The same problems of identification described here as confronting financial economists also plague "would be" speculators. If the large persistent valuation errors considered here leave no statistically discernible trace in the historical patterns of returns, it is hard to see how speculators could become aware of them.*

Our own current analysis is more oriented to the very short term, dynamic process of price formation in the marketplace than these earlier studies, but our conclusions are compatible. If price discovery works itself out dynamically during the course of a trading session, then prices cannot fully reflect all existing information at any specific moment in time. Further, as we have noted, with the advent of high-frequency data, evidence has strengthened that dependency patterns do exist in stock returns. In short, the EMH does not appear as stellar as it once did. On the contrary, shortly after the market crash on October 19, 1987, Lawrence Summers was quoted as saying that the efficient market hypothesis is "the most remarkable error in the history of economic theory."[36]

The good news is that markets are a great deal more interesting to study when they are recognized as being less than perfectly efficient. The link between market architecture and price determination is important precisely because trading is a costly activity. Alternatively stated, the rules and protocols that determine how orders are handled and translated into trades and transaction prices matter when markets are not perfectly efficient.

When considering actual markets replete with their trading costs and other frictions, our focus turns to another variable that we have not thus far given much attention to—liquidity. What is the interaction between liquidity, market structure, and trading? How does liquidity's converse, illiquidity, impact portfolio formation, investment returns, and the efficiency with which information is translated into prices? We turn to issues concerning liquidity in the next chapter.

NOTES

1. Harry Markowitz, "Portfolio Selection," *Journal of Finance*, vol. 7, no. 1, March 1952, pp. 77–91. His further well known contributions include *Portfolio Selection: Efficient Diversification of Investments*, Yale University Press, 1959, and *Mean-Variance Analysis in Portfolio Choice and Capital Markets*, Basil Blackwell, 1987.

2. William F. Sharpe, "Capital Asset Prices: A Theory of Market Equilibrium," *Journal of Finance*, September 1964, pp. 425–442; John Lintner, "Security Prices and Maximal Gains from Diversification," *Journal of Finance*, December 1965, pp. 587–615 and "The Valuation of Risky Assets and the Selection of Risky Investments in Stock Portfolios and Capital Budgets," *Review of Economics and Statistics* 47, February 1965, pp. 13–37; and Jan Mossin, "Equilibrium in a Capital Asset Market," *Econometrica* 35, October 1966, pp. 768–783. Our presentation of CAPM in Appendix B most closely follows Sharpe (1965).

3. More specifically, returns are taken to be lognormally distributed.

4. Investor expectations of a stock's future share price are translated into expected returns for the stock by dividing the expected future share price by the known, current share price.

5. The *crowd* refers to floor traders on an exchange who have come together to trade, on either an agency or a proprietary basis. A floor trader typically does not reveal an order to the market until, in response to current market conditions, he or she steps forward with a piece or all of the order and participates in a trade. In an electronic environment, the concept of a crowd can be applied more generally to participants who use computer technology to work their orders.

6. *Price* is simply a monetary measure. Specifically, it is the exchange rate (e.g., in dollars, euros, or Swiss francs) at which shares can be bought or sold. If the transaction takes place at an exchange, it does so at an *official price.* In contrast, *value* reflects the worth of a share to a specific investor. Investors generally differ in their private assessments of share value. In some cases, however, investors can agree on share value. If value is linked totally to underlying fundamentals (e.g., the value of an option depends on the terms of the instrument and the nature of the security that it is written on), then all investors have the same assessment of value, and therefore the worth of that security can be considered an *intrinsic value.* The term *value* can also be used to describe a consensus market assessment (e.g., an *equilibrium value* or *consensus value*).

7. Peter Landers, "Drug-Data Chasm Punishes Small Investors," *Wall Street Journal,* October 6, 2003, p. c1, and "Heard on the Street, Small Investors Face Handicap in Drug Sector," *Wall Street Journal Europe,* October 6, 2003.

8. The data were "culled from thousands of pharmacies nationwide to give subscribers day-by-day tallies of the number and sales value of prescriptions filled."

9. J. M. Keynes, *The General Theory of Employment, Interest and Money,* New York: Harcourt, Brace, 1958, p. 156.

10. For further discussion, see S. Grossman and J. Stiglitz, "Information and Competitive Price System," *American Economic Review,* May 1976.

11. The first microstructure paper that dealt with asymmetric information is W. Bagehot (pseudo.), "The Only Game in Town," *Financial Analysts Journal* 27, 1971, pp. 12–14, 22. Other early contributors to this literature include T. Copeland and D. Galai, "Information Effects and the Bid-Ask Spread, *Journal of Finance* 38, 1983, pp. 1457–1469, and L. Glosten and P. Milgrom, "Bid, Ask and Transaction Prices in a Specialist Market with Heterogeneously Informed Traders, *Journal of Financial Economics,* 13, 1985, pp. 71–100. For discussion and additional references, see M. O'Hara, *Market Microstructure Theory,* Blackwell Business, 1995.

12. S. Grossman and J. Stiglitz, "Informational and Competitive Price Systems," *American Economic Review,* May 1976.

13. We have made a few simple, innocuous changes in their model description to facilitate our intuitive presentation of it.

14. For further discussion of the Grossman-Stiglitz model, see Robert A. Schwartz, *Reshaping the Equity Markets: A Guide for the 1990s,* Harper Business, 1991.

15. The end of period price that comes to prevail reveals the true share value.

16. Although this is inconsequential for our demonstration, note that the probabilities for this distribution are not equal.

17. Price changes that follow a *martingale process* satisfy this requirement.

18. Price changes are expected to exhibit upward drift, because investors demand a positive expected return. The upward drift would be slight in short-period (for instance, daily) intervals, and we ignore it to simplify the discussion. A return of 36 percent a year is associated with a price change of less than 0.1 percent per day.

19. L. Bachelier, *Théorie de la Spéculation*, Paris, France: Gauthier-Villars, 1900.

20. See, for instance, M. Kendel, "The Analysis of Economic Time Series," *Journal of the Royal Statistical Society*, Series A, 1953; H. Roberts, "Stock Market 'Patterns' and Financial Analysis: Methodological Suggestions," *Journal of Finance*, March 1959; M. F. Osborne, "Brownian Motion in the Stock Market," *Operations Research*, March/April 1959; C. Granger, "Spectral Analysis of New York Stock Market Prices," *Kyklos*, January 1963; and S. Alexander, "Price Movements in Speculative Markets: Trends or Random Walks," *Industrial Management Review*, May 1961.

21. See P. Samuelson, "Proof That Properly Anticipated Prices Fluctuate Randomly," *Industrial Management Review*, spring 1965; B. Mandelbrot, "Forecasts of Future Prices, Unbiased Markets, and 'Martingale' Models," *Journal of Business*, January 1966; E. Fama, "The Behavior of Stock-Market Prices," *Journal of Business*, January 1965; and Fama, "Efficient Capital Markets," *Journal of Finance*, May 1970.

22. See E. Fama, "Efficient Capital Markets: A Review of Theory and Empirical Work," *Journal of Finance*, May 1970.

23. Burton Malkiel, *A Random Walk Down Wall Street*, first edition, W.W. Norton & Company, Inc., 1973, p. 116.

24. E. Fama, L. Fisher, M. Jensen, and R. Roll, "The Adjustment of Stock Prices to New Information," *International Economic Review*, February 1969.

25. We discuss the relationship between the return on a stock and the return on the market in Appendix B (see the section, "The Market Model").

26. Month zero is not, therefore, the same calendar month for the different stocks in the sample.

27. L. Dann, D. Mayers, and R. Raab, "Trading Rules, Large Blocks and the Speed of Price Adjustments," *Journal of Financial Economics*, January 1977.

28. Note that Dann, Mayers, and Raab's study was published in 1977. We expect that the adjustment window is appreciably shorter in today's electronic environment.

29. The reason is that a marginal value is less (greater) than an associated average value for a decreasing (increasing) average value function.

30. I. Friend, F. Brown, E. Herman, and D. Vickers, *A Study of Mutual Funds*, Government Printing Office, 1962.

31. W. Sharpe, "Mutual Fund Performance," *Journal of Business*, supplement, January 1966.

32. M. Jensen, "Risk, the Pricing of Capital Assets, and the Evaluation of Investment Portfolios," *Journal of Business*, April 1969.

33. Behavioral economics offers an alternative approach to substantiating and explaining the existence of market inefficiency. For a review of the literature, see Nicholas Barberis and Richard Thaler, "A Survey of Behavioral Finance," in *Handbook of the Economics of Finance*, edited by G. M. Constantinides, M. Harris, and R. Stulz, 2003, Elsevier Science B.V.

34. For instance, one common practice of technical analysts is to locate a support level (a lower bound) and a resistance level (a higher bound) for a stock, based on the issue's recent trading range. If either of these bounds is approached, a technical analyst might expect the stock's share price to reverse course and to stay within the trading range. However, if either of these bounds is pierced, a strong signal is sent that the stock's value has indeed shifted to a new level. These bounds, of course, are not readily apparent but are assessed based on the skill and experience of the technical analyst. The technical analyst might attempt to profit by using a reversal (contrarian's) strategy if price appears to be fluctuating between the two bounds, and a momentum strategy if a support or resistance level is crossed.

35. Lawrence H. Summers, "Does the Stock Market Rationally Reflect Fundamental Values?" *Journal of Finance*, XLI, no. 3, July 1986, pp. 591–601; Kenneth J. Arrow, "Risk Perception in Psychology and Economics," *Economic Inquiry* 20, January 1982, pp. 1–9; Franco Modigliani and Richard Cohn, "Inflation, Rational Valuation and the Market," *Financial Analysts Journal* 35, March/April 1979, pp. 24–44; and Robert Schiller, "Do Stock Prices Move Too Much to Be Justified by Subsequent Changes in Dividends?" *American Economic Review* 71, June 1981, pp. 421–436.

36. *Wall Street Journal*, October 23, 1987.

CHAPTER 3

Liquidity

In the previous chapter, "From Information to Prices," we considered the perfectly frictionless environment of the capital asset pricing model (CAPM).[1] Trading is costless and price discovery trivial in this setting. The price of the market portfolio is readily determined, and so, too, is the price of each stock given the correlation of its returns with the returns on the market portfolio. This does not mesh with the realities of an actual marketplace. The CAPM world is far too sparse for our purposes. Simply stated, it is two-dimensional, while actual markets are three-dimensional. That is, CAPM encompasses just two variables, risk and return.[2] In actual markets, liquidity enters as an important third dimension. Liquidity does not have a role to play in CAPM because of the simplifying, frictionless world assumptions on which the formulation is based.[3]

In actual markets, trading is a complex activity that is distinct and separable from investing. *Investment decisions* involve portfolio formation and stock selection with respect to longer-term risk and return relationships in an environment where participants have imperfect information, *diverging expectations*, and *adaptive valuations*.[4] Trading involves implementation of the investment decisions. It also involves buying and selling to exploit short-run price swings and arbitrage possibilities in an environment replete with liquidity considerations, transaction costs, price discovery noise, and various other trading restrictions and blockages. Unlike in the frictionless environment of the previous chapter, in real-world markets characterized by divergent expectations (1) perfect substitutes do not exist for individual stocks, (2) the demand to hold shares of an individual stock is not horizontal (infinitely elastic) at some intrinsic value, and (3) the price

59

of each individual issue can be found only in the marketplace where its shares are traded.

Some excellent investment managers would make poor traders, and vice versa. Successful trading requires special analytical skills, emotions, and attitudes. Good traders can sense a market, spot pricing discrepancies, and make lightning-fast decisions. The long run for an investment manager may be the better part of a year or more. The long run for a trader, as of 9:30 A.M., is noon. Trading involves strategy and tactics. Traders do not want to pay more than necessary for a purchase or accept less for a sale. At the same time, they do not want to miss a trade because they have bid too low or offered too high. Optimal order placement in a nonfrictionless market depends on a participant's demand to hold shares of a risky asset, on his or her expectations of what the market-clearing price will be, and on the design of the trading system.[5] In this chapter, we turn to issues concerning how orders are submitted and translated into trades in markets that are less than perfectly liquid.

Nevertheless, the simple solutions obtained for the frictionless environment are elegant, and an analogy may suggest their importance. While negotiating high wind, currents, and waves in a stormy ocean crossing, the captain of a vessel must continue to know wherein lies true north.

DEFINING LIQUIDITY

As we have noted, three characteristics of assets and portfolios are relevant to a portfolio manager: return, risk, and liquidity. Return is easily defined and measured. Risk, although more difficult to measure, is also an operational concept. It is typically measured by the variance or standard deviation of returns. In the context of CAPM, systematic risk for a stock is measured by beta.[6]

How might one define and measure *liquidity?* The typical dictionary definition of a liquid asset is "one that is in cash or that is readily convertible into cash." This does not help much. "Readily" refers to the time required to convert into and out of cash and to the dollar cost of the conversion. But how are time and cost measured, and what are reasonable values to look for? A better approach may be to focus on the attributes of liquidity, such as the depth, breadth, and resiliency of a market:

> *Depth and breadth.* A market has depth and breadth if orders exist at an array of prices in the close neighborhood above and below the price at which shares are currently trading and if the best buy and sell orders exist, in total, in substantial volume (i.e., if the sum of

the orders at each price is sufficiently large). Bid-ask spreads are tighter and market impact slighter when a market has depth and breadth.

Resiliency. A market is resilient if temporary price changes due to temporary order imbalances quickly attract new orders to the market that restore reasonable share values. Trades are less apt to be made at inappropriate prices when a market is resilient.

Liquidity can also be measured by the tightness of bid-ask spreads (the difference between the lowest price at which anyone has stated a willingness to sell and the highest price at which anyone has stated a willingness to buy). The liquidity of a market may also be proxied by the frequency with which an asset trades and by the magnitude of an asset's short-period price instability. We discuss short-period instability in the next chapter, "What Do We Want from Our Markets?"

Each of the aforementioned attributes can be measured, but how should the individual measurements be combined into a single index of liquidity? The set of attributes, viewed comprehensively, can lead to conflicting assessments (e.g., a market may have depth and breadth but lack resiliency). Thus we do not have an unambiguous, operational definition of liquidity. Nevertheless, measures such as an asset's average bid-ask spread or short-period price volatility may be used as proxies in statistical analyses.[7] Measures of market thinness (e.g., the value of shares outstanding or average daily trading volume) may also be used as proxies.

The cost of illiquidity is that, if a price concession has to be paid to execute an order quickly, buyers incur higher prices, and sellers receive lower prices when they initiate trades. No concession would be necessary in a frictionless environment in which all markets and assets are equally and perfectly liquid. In other words, execution costs are attributable to illiquidity. Accentuated short-period (e.g., intraday) volatility also reflects trading costs that are attributable to illiquidity. For this reason, the accentuation of volatility in short periods is a promising measure of liquidity.

Illiquidity and Market Size

Large markets are said to be *deep* and small markets are said to be *thin*. For the spectrum of firms arrayed by size, market size and liquidity go hand in glove. In fact, a measure of market size for a stock can be used to proxy the stock's liquidity: its market capitalization (the number of shares outstanding times the price per share), number of shareholders, or average daily trading volume.

It is important to recognize, however, that even when a large number of individuals have invested in a company (as is the case with many firms whose shares are traded in a major market center), the market for a company's stock is commonly thin (even for the larger companies). This is because, during any trading session, only a small percentage of individuals may actually be seeking to trade. The problem can be particularly acute within a trading day as, at any specific moment in time, only a handful of individuals (if any) may be actively looking to buy or to sell shares.

Markets are thin because most investors seek to trade only when they are sufficiently dissatisfied with their portfolio holdings to incur the costs of a transaction. This is in contrast with the markets for most goods and services, where an individual must periodically make purchases in order to consume a resource (for instance, someone who drinks five cans of beer a week must, on average, buy five cans of beer a week). A market may also be thin because large, institutional orders are commonly worked quietly and, when not revealed to the market, can represent a substantial, latent demand to trade. We discuss this further in Chapter 5, "Institutional Order Flow."

Professional traders are well aware that an important influence on a stock's price behavior is its size, and the effect of thinness on the trading characteristics of individual securities has been well documented empirically. This would not be the case in the absence of transactions costs. In a frictionless environment, thinness would not matter.

MISCONCEPTIONS CONCERNING LIQUIDITY

Liquidity can easily be misunderstood and/or erroneously measured. In this section, we consider three common misconceptions. The first involves a liquidity ratio; the second two pertain to market power and price uncertainty.

The Liquidity Ratio

A common measure of liquidity relates the number or value of shares traded during a short time interval to the absolute value of the percentage price change over the interval. The larger the ratio of shares traded to the percentage price change, the more deep and liquid the market is presumed to be. This view underlies various measures of specialist performance that have been used by the stock exchanges, and this is the approach taken by some researchers to measure and to contrast the liquidity of different market centers.[8]

The liquidity ratio may not be meaningful because the advent of news also causes prices to change. If the separable impact of news is not taken into account, a large trading volume associated with small price changes need not be evidence of a liquid market. On the contrary, it could suggest that prices have adjusted inefficiently to informational change. This is because a bid that is too high attracts market orders to sell, and an ask that is too low attracts market orders to buy. Thus the slower the adjustment of the quotes after news, the larger is the number of shares that will trade during the price adjustment process. Consequently, to the extent that trading is triggered by information change rather than by idiosyncratic changes in investor demand to hold shares, the liquidity ratio is smaller (not larger) in a more efficient market.

Market Power

Another common misconception about liquidity concerns the market power of large traders. *Market power* is generally attributed to a seller who faces a downward-sloping demand curve or to a buyer who faces an upward-sloping supply curve. Institutional investors and other participants who are large enough to have a long-run effect on the price of a security may consider the market for that security to be illiquid for them. This is a misuse of the term: A market is illiquid only if, because of trading costs, orders execute at disequilibrium prices in the *short run*. If a 20 percent shareholder (or a subset of shareholders who in aggregate hold 20 percent of shares outstanding) decides to sell, the equilibrium price of a stock will likely change, regardless of the efficiency of the marketplace. Such a price change is not a manifestation of illiquidity.

Price Uncertainty

The third misconception about illiquidity concerns price uncertainty. Traders may consider the market for a security to be illiquid if they do not know the price at which shares of the asset may be transformed into cash at some future date. This view confuses illiquidity with uncertainty. Price uncertainty may be an attribute of a frictionless market; illiquidity is a property only of a nonfrictionless market. The concept of *illiquidity* is distinct from the concept of risk, and an investor's distaste for illiquidity is distinguishable from his or her distaste for risk.

LIQUIDITY AND TRANSACTION COSTS

In many respects, illiquidity and trading costs are two sides of the same coin. Trading is impeded by taxes and commissions; order handling, clearance, and settlement costs; trading halts, blockages, and other trading restrictions; and the potentially adverse price impact of a big order from a large trader in a relatively thin market. In this section, we take a closer look at the trading-cost side of the coin.

Transaction Costs

Transaction costs are classified as either *explicit costs* or *execution costs* (which are, by their nature, implicit). The explicit costs are visible and easily measured; they include, for example, commissions and taxes. Execution costs, on the other hand, are not easily measured; they exist because orders may, as a result of their size and/or the sparsity of counterpart orders on the market, execute at relatively high prices (if they are buy orders) or at relatively low prices (if they are sell orders).

As we will see in the next section, trading costs can appreciably reduce returns for investors. They also cause investors to adjust their portfolios less frequently and, accordingly, lead them to hold portfolios that would not be optimal in a frictionless environment. Pent-up demand increases the eagerness with which investors seek to transact when they eventually do come to the market. The more eager the trader, the more likely he or she is to place a market order (demand liquidity) rather than a limit order (supply liquidity).

Moreover, when trading is costly, participants do not generally reveal the number of shares that they would buy or sell at a *market-clearing price*. This is because net clearing prices are generally not known. When they write their orders (typically one quantity, at a single price), traders are uncertain about the prices at which their orders might execute. Consequently, as is not the case in the standard competitive model, investors use trading strategies. Understanding the existence, nature, and impact of the strategic trading decisions sheds much light on the behavior of the secondary markets and on the operations of its participants. With regard to market structure, the objectives of a trading system include (as we discuss in Chapter 1, "The Role of an Equity Market"), fair, cost-effective trade execution, and accurate price determination. Illiquidity makes these objectives a good deal more difficult to achieve.

Execution Costs

The following terms apply to our discussion of execution costs:

- *Quotation.* The price at which someone is willing to buy or to sell shares and the number of shares that he or she wishes to trade.[9]
- *Bid quotation.* The price at which someone is willing to buy shares. The highest posted bid on the market is the *best market bid.*

- *Ask quotation.* The price at which someone is willing to sell shares. The lowest posted ask on the market is the *best market ask.*
- *Market bid-ask spread.* The best (lowest) market ask minus the best (highest) market bid. The market spread is sometimes referred to as the inside spread or as the *best bid and offer* (BBO).
- *Individual bid-ask spread.* The difference between the bid and ask quote of an individual participant (typically a dealer) who will both buy and sell shares (i.e., make a two-sided market).
- *Market order.* An individual participant's unpriced order to buy or to sell a specific number of shares of a stock. Market orders to buy are typically executed at the best (lowest) quoted ask, and market orders to sell are typically executed at the best (highest) quoted bid.
- *Limit order.* An individual participant's priced order to buy or to sell a specific number of shares of a stock. The limit price on a buy limit order specifies the highest (maximum) price a buyer is willing to pay, and the limit price on a sell limit order specifies the lowest (minimum) price a seller is willing to receive. Limit orders that are posted on a market, if sufficiently aggressive, establish the best market quotes and thus the market's bid-ask spread.

To understand execution costs, it is helpful to distinguish between active and passive trading. In a market with continuous trading, an execution is realized when two counterpart orders cross. This happens if one of the following three conditions occurs:

1. One public trader posts a limit order, and another public trader submits a market order that executes against the limit order.

2. A market maker sets the quote, and a public market order executes against the quote.

3. Two or more public traders negotiate a trade. The negotiation may take place on the floor of the exchange, in the upstairs market, or via direct contact with each other.

In each case, one party to the trade may be viewed as the active trader and the other party as the passive trader. The one who is seeking to trade without delay is an active trader. Active traders are the public market order traders (cases 1 and 2) and the trader who initiates the negotiation process (case 3). Passive traders include the limit order trader (case 1), the market maker (case 2), and the trader who does not initiate the negotiation process (case 3).

Active traders generally incur execution costs; these payments are typically positive returns for passive traders. Passive traders, however, run the risk of delayed execution or of not executing at all. The execution costs include the bid-ask spread, market impact, and opportunity costs.

The Bid-Ask Spread   Because matched or crossed orders trigger transactions that eliminate the orders from the market, market bid-ask spreads are positive and, with discrete prices, must be at least as large as the smallest allowable price variation (currently one cent in the United States). The spread is the execution cost of a round-trip (e.g., initially buying at the offer and subsequently selling at the bid). An active trader typically buys at the offer and sells at the bid, and the bid-ask spread is the cost of taking a round-trip (buying and then selling, or selling short and then buying). Conventionally, half of the spread is taken to be the execution cost of either a purchase or a sale (a one-way trip). We discuss bid-ask spreads further in Chapter 6, "Order-Driven Markets."

Market Impact   Market impact refers to the additional cost (over and above the spread) that a trader may incur to have a large order execute quickly. It is the higher price that must be paid for a large purchase or the reduction in price that must be accepted for a large sale. Market impact may be thought of as a "sweetener" paid to induce the market to absorb a large order. Market impact also results when others, who learn that an order is in the offing or is being worked, "front-run" it (i.e., trade ahead of it, hoping to acquire a position quickly before the price moves, and then to flip out of the position at a better price).[10] Because of market impact, the effective spread is wider on average for a large order than for a small order.

Opportunity Cost   Opportunity cost refers to the cost that may be incurred if the execution of an order is delayed (commonly in an attempt to achieve an execution at a better price) or if a trade is missed. A buyer incurs an opportunity cost if a stock's price rises during the delay, and a seller incurs an opportunity cost if a stock's price falls during the delay.

TRANSACTION COSTS AND PORTFOLIO PERFORMANCE

The Plexus Group, a wholly owned subsidiary of JPMorgan Chase & Co., analyzes trading decisions and trading costs for an institutional customer base that currently accounts for approximately 25 percent of the worldwide exchange volume. Plexus has measured costs (including commissions) that average 1.57 percent, or 47 cents for a $30 stock. The breakdown is:

Commissions	17 bp[11]	5¢
Market impact	34 bp	10¢
Delay	77 bp	23¢
Missed trades	29 bp	9¢
Total	157 bp	47¢

Is 157 basis points (bp) a large amount?[12] The cost of a round-trip (buying and selling) is double, or 3.14 percent. To put this in perspective, consider a portfolio manager with a one-year holding period who is considering acquiring shares of a company with an expected return of 10 percent per year. If a cost of 157 basis points is incurred when the shares are acquired and then again when they are sold one year later, the return is knocked down to 6.86 percent. This is more than a 30 percent reduction! The percentage reduction in the risk premium for holding the shares (the expected return minus the risk-free rate) is even greater—if the risk free rate is 3 percent, the risk premium is reduced from 7 percent to 3.86 percent, a 45 percent reduction. This impact has led Wayne Wagner, chairman of the Plexus Group, to state that ". . . total transaction cost is the largest cost borne by investors over time, in most cases being a larger drag on performance than management and administrative fees. Yet these figures are never disclosed, and often are dismissed by a manager as merely 'part of the process.' "[13]

The Plexus numbers are based on a large sample of trades. As broad averages, they give a good picture of the magnitude of execution cost estimates. Execution cost measurements should, however, be accepted with caution. Particularly difficult has been measuring the execution costs of large trades and determining how these costs depend on the size of a trade, the difficulty of a trade, and the market center in which the trade is made. Capturing the market impact cost of a large order that has been sliced into smaller pieces for sequential execution over an extended period of time is even more difficult. Another problem in measuring execution costs is distinguishing between active and passive trades to obtain a targeted measure of execution costs for the active traders. Because trading is a zero-sum game for all participants, execution costs are underestimated if active and passive orders are not properly identified.

LIQUIDITY AND PRICE DISCOVERY

The term *price discovery* identifies the process by which a market finds a new equilibrium after a change in investor demand to hold shares. The process is inherently more difficult in illiquid markets. No one knows the equilibrium price of stock until orders are sent to a market and translated into trades. As we discuss further in Chapter 4, "What We Want from Our Markets," when trading is costly and a market is thin, transactions are commonly made at prices that deviate meaningfully from underlying but unobservable equilibrium values.

Only in recent years has awareness of the price discovery function of a securities market emerged, and efficient price discovery still remains an essentially unarticulated objective. In the United States, the Securities and Exchange Commission (SEC) has not taken much account of price discovery in the equity markets, although the Commodities Futures Trading Commission (CFTC) has recognized price discovery as an important function of the futures markets. A reason for the difference in regulatory focus is that, for the equity markets, it has not been clear how to assess realized prices because base values against which a contrast can be made are not observable. On the other hand, futures trading plays an important role in discovering prices for the cash market of the underlying asset on which the futures contract is written. This cash market price discovery role is particularly important for certain commodities that do not have well-organized cash markets. For instance, in the precious metals markets (e.g., gold, silver, and platinum), the futures price for the nearest futures contract (referred to as the delivery month) is typically used to set the spot price in the cash market for the physical underlying.[14]

Price discovery is a critical function of the equity markets particularly because, as we discuss in the previous chapter, participants have divergent expectations. Clearly, if everyone individually evaluates the equity of XYZ Corporation at $50 a share, price discovery is a no-brainer—XYZ shares will trade at $50. But what if individual share valuations differ?

Handa, Schwartz, and Tiwari (HST) have used a simplified environment to answer this question.[15] Following them, we can represent the divergence of expectations by dividing a set of participants into two groups. Let's call one group "the bulls" and the other "the bears." Let the bulls value XYZ shares at $55 and the bears value XYZ at $45. The bulls are the buyers, and the bears are the sellers. Let participants arrive sequentially in the market and either (1) post orders to buy or to sell or (2) trade immediately (at bid or offer prices established by limit orders that have previously been placed).

Handa et al. show that equilibrium bid and offer prices can be determined if one further piece of information is known—the percentage of participants who are bulls (denoted by k) and the percentage who are bears (denoted by $1 - k$). In this setting, the divergence of expectations among participants has two dimensions: (1) the magnitude of the difference between the high and the low valuations (in our case, $55 – $45) and (2) the distribution of investors between the two valuations.[16]

How do participants know or find out about the value of k? In the absence of a systematic pretrading communications system that they all participate in, the only way to find out how many are bulls and how many are bears is by observing the orders that are sent to the market. That is, through the orders that are revealed as trading progresses, participants discover the value of k. As they do, the price of XYZ shares fluctuates in response to changing perception of k. In the simplified HST environment, k discovery and price discovery are synonymous.[17]

In actual markets, participants' divergent expectations are distributed over a range of valuations and we cannot refer simply to Handa et al.'s variable, k. Nevertheless, the conclusion holds—when expectations are divergent, prices have to be discovered. The process is not simple. Roughly a quarter of a century ago, William Batten, who at the time was chief executive officer of the New York Stock Exchange, was considering with a small group of academicians the unique service that is provided by an exchange. After listening a while he commented, "We produce the price." The comment was prescient. The insight is of major importance.

PRICE INSTABILITY

Two attributes of an illiquid market, execution costs and errors in price discovery, translate into accentuated short-period price volatility. Because the accentuated price changes are a short-run phenomenon, returns must be analyzed over brief intervals (e.g., intraday) to observe them. Execution costs accentuate short-period price volatility as transaction prices bounce between the higher values paid by eager buyers and the lower values received by eager sellers. Price fluctuations that characterize the price discovery process can be further destabilizing if they cause investors to lack confidence that a price level is reasonable. At times, if some participants rush their sell orders to market and others step away with their buy orders, price can drop precipitously. At other times, some may rush their buy orders to market while others step away with their sell orders, and price can rise precipitously. When this happens, an extreme bout of volatility can occur.

Because the volatility accentuation is largely a short-run phenomenon, short-run volatility is a good (inverse) proxy for liquidity. We return to this thought in Chapter 4, "What We Want from Our Markets." Also important to note is that short-run volatility that is reflective of execution costs and the complexities of price discovery can be most effectively brought under control by improving the systems used for handling orders and translating them into trades. Alternatively stated, the liquidity of a market depends not only on the characteristics of an asset being traded (e.g., its market cap, number of shareholders, and exposure to informational change), but also on the structure of the marketplace where the asset is traded.

THE ORIGINS OF LIQUIDITY

Where does liquidity come from? Ultimately, a market is liquid because some participants are seeking to buy shares at the same time that others are looking to sell shares. Just how the orders of the various participants are brought together and translated into trades depends on the architectural structure of a market. The two primary market structures are *order-driven* and *quote-driven*. Order-driven markets are further classified as (1) continuous trading environments and (2) periodic call auctions.

Continuous Order-Driven Markets

The sole traders in a pure order-driven market are the investors who are seeking to buy or to sell shares for their own portfolio purposes. They are sometimes referred to as "the naturals." The two basic order types used by naturals in this trading environment are (1) *limit orders* (a maximum price limit is placed on a buy order and a minimum price limit is placed on a sell order) and (2) *market orders* (the instruction on a market order is simply to buy or to sell "at market").

The limit orders, which are entered into a *limit order book*, establish the prices at which the market orders will execute.[18] The market is order-driven precisely because the limit orders placed by some participants set the values at which others can trade by market order. In this environment, the limit order placers are the liquidity suppliers, and the market order traders are the liquidity takers. In an order-driven market, liquidity builds as limit orders are entered in the book, and liquidity is drawn down as market orders trigger trades that eliminate limit orders from the book.

Some participants are motivated to be liquidity providers because, whenever a trade is made, the transaction price typically favors the limit order placer. For instance, assume that the best bid set by a limit order placer seeking to buy is $50.00 and that the best offer set by a limit order placer seeking to sell is $50.05. If a market order to buy arrives, it will execute at $50.05, or 5 cents more than the limit order buyer would pay if his or her limit order were to execute. Similarly, if a market order to sell arrives, it will execute at $50.00, or 5 cents less than the limit order seller would receive if his or her limit order were to execute. On the other hand, while the market order trader pays more for a purchase or receives less for a sale, he or she benefits from trading with certainty and immediacy.

Two conditions must be met for an order-driven market to function: (1) As we have noted, some participants must be looking to buy at a time when others are looking to sell, and (2), on each side of the market, some participants must choose to place limit orders while others must select the market order strategy. In Chapter 6, "Order-Driven Markets," we consider the economic forces that result in a population of investors naturally dividing into these two groups—the limit order placers and the market order placers.

For an effective creation of liquidity, intermediaries who operate as brokers are also needed in a pure order-driven market. A broker handles an order for a customer but, unlike a dealer or market maker, does not trade with the customers. Brokers typically submit customer orders to the market, although, with computerized trading, direct access by a customer is technically possible. Additionally, exchange personnel are required to operate the market and to maintain the limit order book.

Periodic Call Auctions

As noted, an order-driven market can be structured in two ways: (1) as a continuous market and (2) as a call auction. In our preceding discussion of the order-driven market, we implicitly assumed a continuous trading environment. With a continuous trading environment, a trade is made at any moment in *continuous time* that the market is open and a buy order meets a sell order in price (as occurs when a market order executes against a limit order that has been placed on the book). Continuous order-driven markets are open for a *trading day* (e.g., 9:30 A.M. to 4:00 P.M. for the U.S. markets).[19] With a continuous trading order-driven market, orders placed in the limit order book enable buyers and sellers to meet in time.

In a call auction, trades are made at preannounced moments in time (e.g., at the 9:30 A.M. open or at the 4:00 P.M. close). Orders entered for a call are held until the call, at which time they are batched together for a simultaneous execution at a single price. A call is to continuous trading as a train is to a car. A commuter from the suburbs has the choice of traveling to the city by train or by car. With a car, the commuter has the freedom to leave home whenever he or she decides in continuous time. With a train, the commuter is pooled together with many other people according to a timetable that is set by the railroad. Similarly, a call, by pooling many orders together, focuses liquidity at predetermined points in time. We consider the call auction in greater detail in Chapter 6, "Order-Driven Markets."

Quote-Driven Markets

For a transaction to be made, a buy and sell order must meet each other in two ways: (1) in price and (2) in time. With regard to price, in the continuous order-driven market, a limit order placer sets a price (his or her quote), and a transaction is realized if a market order placer accepts the price. With regard to time, in the continuous order-driven market, the limit order placer waits patiently, with his or her order sitting on the book, for a market order placer to arrive. Consequently, it is the limit order placer's patience and the limit order book that enable a buyer and a seller to meet in time. This liquidity-producing procedure, unfortunately, does not work effectively under all conditions.

If a market is thin and order arrival infrequent, if some participants (e.g., institutional customers) have very large order size, and/or if a market is under particular stress (e.g., due to a news release), the order-driven market can break down. In these cases, structure beyond the limit order book is needed. Additional structure may be provided by intermediaries who are market makers. Unlike brokers who only handle customer orders on an agency basis, market makers trade as principals with their customers.

In a pure quote-driven market, prices are set only by dealer quotes (hence the term, *quote-driven market*). The quote-driven market is a very different alternative to the pure order-driven market where there are no market makers at all. A market maker buys shares when public participants wish to sell and sells shares when public participants wish to buy. At any moment, a market maker's bid quote is lower than his or her offer (ask quote), and the market maker attempts to profit from buying shares at prices that are lower than those at which he or she will sell.

By posting quotes, a market maker brings capital to the market that enables public customers to trade with immediacy. This does not mean, however, that market makers are the fundamental source of liquidity. As is true for an order-driven market, the fundamental source of liquidity for public buyers is public sellers, and the fundamental source for public sellers is public buyers. A market maker simply helps transmit shares from sellers to buyers by interceding in the trades.

After buying shares to accommodate a seller, the market maker has to reliquify his or her position by selling the shares. Similarly, after selling shares to accommodate a buyer, the market maker has to reliquify by buying shares. The reliquification of a position after buying from or selling to customers is part of a market maker's inventory control. We consider these operations in greater detail in Chapter 7, "Intermediated Markets."

Hybrid Markets

Liquidity provision is handled differently in each of the three generic structures that we have just considered: continuous order-driven, period call, and quote-driven. In recent years, it has become apparent that these generics are not alternatives, but should be offered simultaneously in hybrid market structures. The hybrids give customers the flexibility to choose just how they either supply liquidity (and are compensated) or receive liquidity (and pay for it).

Most markets have long had hybrid structures. The New York Stock Exchange, for instance, has historically included a specialist who maintains a limit order book and who also participates in trading as a principal.[20] Large trades for NYSE issues can be negotiated upstairs and brought to the exchange's trading floor for execution. Upstairs market makers also provide dealer capital for NYSE block transactions. The continuous order-driven electronic trading platforms in Europe include market makers on both contractual and voluntary bases. The NYSE opens and closes trading with a call auction, as do the European markets. Historically, Nasdaq and the London Stock Exchange were competitive market-maker markets, but both have altered their systems to include the public display of customer limit orders (London with the introduction of SETs in 1997, and Nasdaq with the introduction of SuperMontage in 2002). Like the other exchanges in Europe, London now opens and closes its market with a call auction, and currently Nasdaq is implementing plans to do the same.

Innovation in market structure is continuing. Increasingly, attention is shifting from building better generics to building more effective hybrids. Combining alternative systems is a complex task, but only when this is effectively accomplished will participants receive the liquidity that they may reasonably come to expect.

LIQUIDITY AND RANDOM WALK

In Chapter 2, "From Information to Prices," we established that prices are expected to follow random walks in frictionless, perfectly liquid markets. We now show why price changes are not random, but are intertemporally correlated when markets are less than perfectly liquid.

The term *intertemporal* refers to events that occur in different time periods. For instance, if the price change for a stock in one period is correlated with the price change for that same stock in another period (e.g., one hour or one day later), the stock's returns are *intertemporally correlated*. When the return is for the same stock, this intertemporal correlation is referred to as *autocorrelation* or *serial correlation*.

Returns are positively autocorrelated when positive returns are more likely to be followed by other returns that are positive and when negative returns are more likely to be followed by other returns that are negative. Therefore, if returns are *positively autocorrelated*, a series of price changes includes a larger number of *price continuations* (upticks followed by other upticks or downticks followed by other downticks) than would be expected in a random sequence of price changes. If, on the other hand, returns are *negatively autocorrelated*, a series of price changes includes a larger number of *price reversals* (an uptick followed by a downtick or a downtick followed by an uptick) than would be expected in a random sequence of price changes.

The intertemporal correlation need not be between sequentially adjacent returns. With inaccurate short-run price adjustments, for instance, the return in one period may be correlated with the return two or more periods later. The correlation between sequentially adjacent returns is *serial correlation*, or *first-order autocorrelation*. The correlation between nonadjacent returns is called *higher-order autocorrelation*. The term *autocorrelation* simply means that the returns for an issue are autocorrelated, although not necessarily of first order.

The return on one stock in one period of time may also be correlated with the return on another stock (or stock index) in another period of time. This is *serial cross-correlation*. Serial cross-correlation exists when different stocks do not adjust simultaneously to common information change.

Positive Intertemporal Correlation

Four factors can cause the returns for a security to be positively autocorrelated: (1) sequential information arrival, (2) the limit order book, (3) market-maker intervention in trading, and (4) noninstantaneous price discovery after change in investor demand.

Sequential Information Arrival Copeland[21] has shown that the sequential arrival of information (or, equivalently, the sequential adjustment of expectations) can cause a security's returns to be positively autocorrelated.

The Limit Order Book If orders on the book are not quickly revised after informational change, new orders based on the information transact at prices set by existing limit orders. As a series of such transactions eliminates the older orders sequentially from the book, a security's transaction price rises or falls in increments to a new equilibrium value.

Market Maker Intervention The affirmative obligation of stock exchange specialists leads these market makers to intervene in trading when transaction-to-transaction price changes would otherwise be unacceptably large. This can cause a security's price to adjust in increments to a new equilibrium value after the advent of news.

Inaccurate Price Discovery Price discovery is inaccurate when new equilibrium values are not instantaneously achieved. Price discovery is inaccurate because investors do not instantaneously transmit their orders to the market, because orders left on the market are not continuously revised, and because, when they write their orders, investors do not know what the equilibrium prices are or will be. With inaccurate price determination, actual prices differ from equilibrium values. Some price changes are too small (they underadjust to news), and other price changes are too large (they overadjust to news). *Ceteris paribus*, if inaccurate price determination that involves partial adjustment (undershooting) predominates, returns will be positively autocorrelated.

Negative Intertemporal Correlation

Three factors may cause negative intertemporal correlation in security returns: (1) the bid-ask spread, (2) the temporary market impact exerted by large orders, and (3) noninstantaneous price discovery after changes in investor demand propensities.

The Bid-Ask Spread With a spread, orders to sell at market execute against the bid, and orders to buy at market execute against the ask. In the process, the transaction price moves between the bid and the ask. The bid and ask quotes themselves change over time with the arrival of new orders and the elimination of old orders (that either execute or are withdrawn). Nonetheless, the bouncing of transaction prices between the quotes causes transaction-to-transaction price returns to be negatively autocorrelated. To see this, assume the quotes are fixed. Then, if at some moment in time the last transaction in a particular stock is at the bid, the next transaction that generates a nonzero return must be at the ask, and a positive return (price change) is recorded. If the quotes remain unchanged, the next nonzero return must be negative (when a market sell once again executes at the bid). Thus price reversals occur as the transaction price moves back and forth between the bid and the ask. Even if the quotes change randomly over time, the price reversals attributed to the spread introduce negative intertemporal correlation in transaction price returns.

Market Impact Effects The effective spread is expected to be greater for larger orders. Assume the arrival of a large sell order, for instance. If the book is relatively sparse and the effective spread large at the time of the order's arrival, the transaction price will be depressed so that the order may be absorbed by the relatively thin market. In this case, the lower price itself attracts new buy orders to the market and price once again rises. Therefore, the initial price decrease is followed by a reversal (an increase).

The reverse pattern would be caused by the arrival of a large buy order. Either way, the successive price changes are negatively autocorrelated.

Inaccurate Price Discovery   As we have noted, with inaccurate price discovery, actual prices wander about their equilibrium values. If inaccurate price determination that involves overreaction to news (overshooting) predominates, returns are negatively autocorrelated. Further, Goldman and Beja have shown that returns are negatively autocorrelated if the equilibrium price changes randomly over time and if the transaction price wanders randomly about its equilibrium value.[22] The intuition behind this result is that the equilibrium price pulls the transaction price back to itself whenever the transaction price wanders away. Thus, even if the equilibrium price is following a random walk, the price discovery process causes reversals and hence negative correlation in transaction price returns. This can be understood intuitively with the aid of the following visualization. Picture a man walking his dog on a leash across a field, with the dog racing randomly about the man, but never straying too far because of the leash. If the man follows a random path, the leash causes reversals in the dog's path, and thus the animal's movements are negatively autocorrelated.

Serial Cross-Correlation

The returns for two different securities are serially cross-correlated if the price adjustments generated by a causal factor (e.g., the advent of a new industrywide regulation) do not occur at the same moment in time for different firms in the same industry (i.e., if they are nonsynchronous).

If all price adjustments were instantaneous for all securities (as would be the case in a frictionless market), the price adjustments across the different securities would be synchronous. However, the factors that we have discussed in relation to returns autocorrelation also cause price adjustment delays, thus nonsynchronous adjustments across stocks, and hence serial cross-correlation. Assume, for instance, that a news bit arrives that implies a 2 percent upward revision in the price of two stocks, Podunk Mines and Liquidity Inc. In the very short run, any or all of the following may happen, thereby causing the short-run price movements to be different for the two securities:

- A large investor in Liquidity Inc. has been trying to liquidate her position for strictly personal reasons. On the other hand, a large buyer has suddenly, and for reasons known only to him, decided that Podunk shares must be included in a well-structured portfolio.
- The last trade in Podunk occurred at the bid; the last trade in Liquidity occurred at the ask.

- The book in Podunk happens, by chance, to be unusually deep; the book in Liquidity is relatively sparse.
- Investors in Liquidity Inc. happen to be relatively conservative; initially they believe the news will induce only a 1.5 percent appreciation in the share price. Investors in Podunk Mines are more optimistic; initially they anticipate a price change of 2.5 percent.
- Many investors in Liquidity Inc. happen to be otherwise occupied when the news bit arrives; many investors in Podunk Mines are watching the broad tape when the news is publicly announced.

After the dust has settled, the prices of the two stocks are once again aligned. However, the paths the price adjustments follow are disparate and, in fact, largely uncorrelated.

The prices of some securities tend to adjust faster than others to changing market conditions. One would expect the large, intensely watched issues on average to lead the market and the smaller issues to lag behind. This gives rise to a pattern of serial cross-correlation where price adjustments for securities such as IBM and Exxon precede price adjustments for thinner issues such as Liquidity Inc. and Podunk Mines. Serial cross-correlation patterns, however, are no doubt diffuse, complex, and not readily subject to exploitation by a clever trader. The reason is twofold: the time lags involved are not stable, and imperfect price discovery may entail both overshooting and undershooting.

DISCUSSION

Liquidity is indeed a difficult variable to deal with. As we have discussed, its very definition is multifaceted and its empirical measurement elusive. How is the liquidity of individual assets related to the liquidity of a portfolio? To what extent is an asset's liquidity determined by its attributes and the characteristics of its investors? How do transaction costs and dynamic price discovery, both individually and collectively, relate to the liquidity of a market? To what extent is liquidity determined by the characteristics of the marketplace where the asset is traded?

These are not simple questions to answer. Difficulties in defining, measuring, and analyzing liquidity largely explain why this attribute of financial assets and markets has not thus far been incorporated in formal stock evaluation and selection models. Nevertheless, from brokerage firm operations to market center operations, the jobs that people perform and the institutional structures that they work within are deeply influenced by the realities of illiquidity, the instability of illiquidity, and by the fact that actual markets are not frictionless environments.

Recognizing that markets are not frictionless environments, we can revisit the efficient markets hypothesis that we have discussed in the previous chapter. The EMH addresses the issue of informational efficiency (i.e., whether profitable trading strategies can be formulated on the basis of available information). The EMH has been widely tested by, among other things, searching for serial correlation patterns in stock returns. Historically, many tests have led to the conclusion that the hypothesis is substantiated. Yet we have noted how trading costs and the complexity of price discovery can be manifest in serial correlation. Why is it that these patterns are so difficult to detect? In brief, our answer is that the coexistence of both positive and negative serial correlation, and of both first and higher orders of correlation, and the shifting patterns of correlation, render them very difficult to detect by tests designed to capture relatively simple and stationary patterns.

What might the presence of serial correlation suggest about the operational efficiency of a market? In brief, our answer is that the potential exists for making markets more operationally efficient by designing superior trading systems. To this end, technology has greatly expanded the possibilities. But, securities markets are highly complex institutions, and good, implementable economic answers regarding market design are not readily come by.

Finally, one might question the role that public policy should play in leading our markets in the direction of greater efficiency. Some students of the market look to governmental regulators to play a proactive role in influencing market design, both for individual markets and on the national level. Others believe that markets should be allowed to evolve naturally in a free market environment. We consider this controversy in greater detail in Chapter 11, "Regulation." First, it is important to understand just what we want from our markets. This is the issue to which we next turn.

NOTES

1. We derive and further analyze the CAPM in Appendix B, "From Portfolio Decisions to Trading in a Frictionless Environment."

2. We note, however, that risk itself is a multidimensional concept.

3. The relationship between liquidity and asset prices has been studied by a number of authors (e.g., Amihud and Mendelson, "Asset Pricing and the Bid-Ask Spread," *Journal of Financial Economics* 17, pp. 223–249, 1986; Easley, Hvidkjaer, and O'Hara, "Is Information Risk a Determinant of Asset Returns?" *Journal of Finance*, 2002; Brennan and Subrahmanyam, "Market Microstructure and Asset Pricing: On the Compensation for Illiquidity in Stock Returns," *Jour-*

nal of Financial Economics 41, pp. 441–464, 1996; Pastor and Stambaugh, "Liquidity Risk and Expected Stock Returns," working paper, University of Chicago, 2001; and Jones, "A Century of Stock Market Liquidity and Trading Costs," working paper, Columbia University, 2002). A comprehensive understanding of the impact and determinants of liquidity is, however, still lacking.

4. We discussed both of these terms in Chapter 2, "From Information to Prices." In brief, *diverging expectations* means that participants do not have *homogeneous expectations* (i.e., that they disagree), and *adaptive valuations* means that these participants modify their expectations when they learn about each others' assessments.

5. When multiple assets are involved additional considerations can come into play. For instance, the demand for immediacy is important when baskets are traded, and hedging becomes a factor when derivative markets are taken into account.

6. Beta for a stock is the covariance of its return with the return on the market portfolio divided by the variance of returns for the market portfolio.

7. Amihud and Mendelson (1986) used the bid-ask spread as a liquidity measure in their analysis of the relationship between liquidity and stock returns. For a discussion of short-period volatility, see Hasbrouck and Schwartz (1988) and Ozenbas, Schwartz, and Wood (2002).

8. See K. Cooper, J. Groth, and W. Avera, "Liquidity, Exchange Listing, and Common Stock Performance," *Journal of Economics and Business*, February 1985, and B. Hui and B. Heubel, "Comparative Liquidity Advantages Among Major U.S. Stock Markets," DRI Financial Information Group Study Series no. 84081, 1984.

9. Quotes can be either *firm* or *indicative*. If firm, the participant setting the quote is obliged to honor it if a counterpart arrives. If indicative, the quoting participant is not obliged. During normal business hours, quotes set by market makers and limit order placers are generally required to be firm.

10. It is not legal for a broker-dealer to front-run a customer order. However, it is legal to trade on the expectation (as distinct from the "knowledge") that a customer might be seeking to buy or sell shares. Such expectations are common in an environment where large institutions break up their orders and present them to the market in smaller tranches over a period of time.

11. One basis point (bp) is one one-hundredth of 1 percent.

12. The category "missed trades" is not relevant when a trade does in fact occur. Thus, for our purposes, the 29 bp should perhaps be eliminated from the total. However, the category is relevant at the end of a holding period when the portfolio manager (PM) seeks to unwind the position but fails to do so. In any event, one could recalculate the total as wished, but we have chosen to stay with the total as reported by Plexus.

13. Testimony of Wayne H. Wagner, House Committee on Financial Services, March 12, 2003.

14. This is true for many futures markets, including agriculture, currency, and a variety of financial futures.

15. Puneet Handa, Robert A. Schwartz, and Ashish Tiwari, "Quote Setting and Price Formation in an Order Driven Market," *Journal of Financial Markets* 6, 2003, pp. 461–489.

16. For a given difference between the high and the low valuations, the divergence of expectations is at a maximum when k is 0.5 and disappears as k approaches its extreme values of 0 (everyone is a bear) and 1 (everyone is a bull).

17. This environment has been modeled by Jacob Paroush, Robert A. Schwartz, and Avner Wolf, "Dynamic Price Discovery in a Divergent Expectations Environment," Baruch College working paper, 2004.

18. Limit orders at the New York Stock Exchange used to be literally handwritten in a book. This practice ended with the introduction of electronic order management, but the term *book* is still widely used. The first electronic display book was introduced in 1983 to facilitate a huge surge in trading in seven Baby Bell stocks following their divestiture from AT&T. Over the next several years, the electronic display book was introduced for more stocks until, by 1988, they were being used for 1,100 stocks in 361 workstations.

19. In addition to the official trading day, executions are realized in *after-hours trading* and *preopen trading*.

20. We discuss the specialist's role further in Chapter 8, "The Evolving Scene in the United States."

21. Thomas Copeland, "A Model of Asset Trading Under the Assumption of Sequential Information Arrival," *Journal of Finance*, vol. 31, no. 4, 1976, pp. 1149–1168.

22. M. Barry Goldman and Avraham Beja, "Market Prices vs. Equilibrium Prices: Returns Variance, Serial Correlation, and the Role of the Specialist," *Journal of Finance*, June 1979.

CHAPTER 4

What We Want from Our Markets

Markets are complex, and exchanges are complex institutions. After decades of debate, opinions remain sharply divided about many key issues concerning market design. Various constituents, from institutional buy side traders to sell side market makers, have different needs and diverging agendas. The very term *market quality* means different things to different people. Achieving a highly efficient structure for the broad market is indeed a challenge.

Before understanding the operations of an exchange, we must first identify what a market center does. At the heart of a market center's operations are the containment of transaction costs and the provision of good price discovery. The two are closely related. Price discovery is a complex process that is perturbed by trading costs, incomplete information, and other frictions in the marketplace. When a market is under stress, accurate price discovery can break down. Stress is not a phenomenon that occurs every couple of years or so. It characterizes markets on a daily basis. Market openings and closings are periods of stress. News releases create stress. The arrival of a 500,000-share order for a stock that, on average, trades 300,000 shares a day produces stress. Momentum trading causes stress. And so on.

The quality of a market center depends on a broad array of exchange functions that pertain to trading costs and price discovery. These include market surveillance, the provision of adequate liquidity, the rule book that determines how orders are handled and translated into trades and transaction prices, and the technology used for order handling and information display. In viewing this set of functions comprehensively, it is clear that strong market centers, if appropriately structured, have an important role to play in the marketplace of the future. A critical requirement, however, is that competition be strong enough, today and in the future, to keep pushing the market centers forward.

Tremendous structural change has characterized the U.S. and European markets in recent years, and an equity culture is becoming far more extensive in many countries around the world. Nevertheless, market structure is still a work in process, and further improvements are needed. We start our analysis by considering the meaning of the term, *market quality*.

MARKET QUALITY'S MANY FACES

Market quality is an inherently amorphous concept. The attributes of market quality include transparency, reliability, consolidation of the order flow, and easy access to a market, all of which directly affect liquidity and trading costs. Trading costs include bid-ask spreads, market impact, opportunity costs, and commissions. These costs are difficult to define and elusive to evaluate empirically.

Liquidity (the subject of Chapter 3), transparency, order flow consolidation, and access are all complex items. Questions of measurement aside, how does one determine just what values to shoot for? Complete transparency is certainly not an objective. As we discuss in Chapter 7, "Intermediated Markets," too much transparency can discourage the provision of dealer capital and, in so doing, cause a market to be less liquid. In the opinion of many, total concentration of the order flow should not be an objective. Too much concentration can result in monopoly power and technological inertia that would undermine a market's incentive to innovate and to adopt new technologies. Even "easy access" is not a simple concept. Currently, access is generally obtained through an intermediary. However, direct access, for some participants and some trades at least, is possible. Can it be appropriately provided? Orders can be sent to a market either directly or via another market through linkages. Which works best? How does one even quantify the quality of "access"?

Trading costs, being higher in less liquid markets, are a bottom-line reflection of market quality. How readily can they be quantified? Commissions are most easily measured, but even they are not straightforward because of the widespread use of soft dollars (referred to as *soft commissions* in Europe). Bid-ask spreads are observable but may be misleading because trades are commonly made within the spread as orders are price-improved. The other two implicit costs of trading (market impact and opportunity cost) are the most important for large traders,

but they are far more difficult to quantify, especially for orders that a
re broken into smaller tranches and executed over an extended period
of time.

In light of the difficulties encountered in dealing with the various
aspects of market quality, the final section of this chapter gives special
focus to one measure in particular—price volatility. We assess intraday
price volatility patterns over half-hour intervals and contrast daily volatility
with volatility measured over one- and two-week periods. For two U.S.
markets (NYSE and Nasdaq) and three European markets (Deutsche
Börse, Euronext Paris, and the London Stock Exchange), an accentuation
of volatility characterizes short trading intervals in general and the first
half hour of the trading day in particular. The analysis is insightful for two
reasons:

1. Short-period (e.g., half-hour) volatility tends to be more accentuated
   when markets are relatively illiquid, spreads are wide, market impact
   is high, and/or price discovery is more difficult. Accordingly, the level
   of intraday volatility comprehends the other determinants of market
   quality.
2. It is more meaningful to assess market quality when a market is under
   particular stress (many boats float when the sea is calm). On a daily
   basis, the first half hour of the trading day is a period of particular
   stress.

MARKET QUALITY AS AN OBJECTIVE OF MARKET DESIGN

For the listed companies, maximizing market quality should unquestion-
ably be the single objective of market design. Enhanced market quality
means lower trading costs and sharper price discovery for the broad market. For a listed company, both improvements go straight to the bottom
line: They lower the cost of equity capital. Maximizing market quality
should also be the goal of public policy. Indeed, regulatory involvement in
market structure issues has typically been justified in terms of the benefits
of lower trading costs and generally better executions for investors. If a
country's capital markets are able to lower the cost of capital for their companies, that country is benefited in a number of ways, including enhanced
job creation and increased wealth formation.

Turning to portfolio managers, for any individual PM, improved market
quality feeds into lower trading costs and thus improved portfolio performance. But some funds can actually benefit from market imperfection.

Hedge funds in particular can find and exploit profit opportunities created by mispricing that occurs in fast-moving, nonfrictionless markets. Some mutual funds (those with superior technology and sophistication) can outperform their competitors by achieving lower trading costs, which translates into higher relative performance rankings and greater success in gaining customers. Improving market quality will undoubtedly change relative performance measures, and consequently may not be a net benefit to all mutual fund managers.

Further, minimizing trading costs is not necessarily a portfolio manager's primary goal. This is because, by paying higher commissions to broker-dealer intermediaries and receiving soft-dollar rebates, expenditures for trading services are united with payments for research, computer systems, and other services that a fund manager has outsourced. The procedure keeps research costs and other expenditures unobservable to the fund's investors. Consequently, it may not be in the portfolio manager's interest to have market quality improved if the improvement would involve a disintermediation of trading and lower commissions. We discuss this issue further in Chapter 5, "Institutional Order Flow."

Professionals at the trading desks have their own agendas. New technology that disintermediates the sell side trader will be resisted by that trader, regardless of the innovation's impact on market quality. Sell side traders are compensated because their services are valuable, and their services are more valuable when trading is more complex (which is the case when market structure is not of the highest quality).

Buy side traders may share this view, and for much the same reason. Currently, the advent of sophisticated electronic order handling systems that enable sell side disintermediation have increased the importance of traders on the buy side desks. Curiously, as this development continues, technology innovation that enhances market quality for the broad market may also disintermediate some buy side traders and, increasingly, meet with resistance from the buy side. Either way, the needs of portfolio managers will not, in aggregate, be maximally met.

Because of switching costs and franchise protection, it has historically been, and remains, extremely difficult for market centers to make structural innovations. In this context, the relative ability of membership organizations and for-profit organizations have been questioned. Major exchanges around the world have now privatized, and perhaps they will be in a better position to innovate. In Europe, the major primary market centers are now equity-based, for-profit institutions. In the United States, Nasdaq is moving in this direction, while, thus far, the NYSE is retaining its membership structure.

Whatever the organizational structure of a market center, it is desirable that it continue to perform some of the functions of a membership organization. Consequently, the ultimate impact that the transformation in exchange governance structure will have on market quality is not clear. Competitive forces are driving the equity markets toward greater efficiency and higher quality, but there continues to be a good deal of friction along the way.

BENEFITS OF A STRONG CENTRAL MARKET

Three factors in particular explain the desirability of having a strong central market: (1) Markets are characterized by network externalities. (2) Market making has public goods characteristics. (3) A market must be able to maintain reasonable quality during periods of stress. We consider each of these in this section of the chapter.

Network Externalities

Markets are networks of participants who come together to trade. The larger a network, the greater the value it offers participants. Fax machines provide a good example: Each user's machine is more useful if more people have one, because there are more people to whom faxes can be sent and from whom faxes can be received. A large number of people using the same text editing software also comprise a network; people benefit from the ability to pass files back and forth to each other in a standardized language and format. Similarly, an equity market is a network: As more orders converge in a marketplace, the orders provide greater liquidity to each other and better price discovery for the broad market.

No one individual in a network, however, is rewarded for providing the benefits that he or she conveys to others by joining the network (e.g., by buying a fax machine, by using standardized software, or by sending orders to a market center). Hence the term, *network externalities.*

An adage in the securities industry reflects the positive force that network externalities exert: "Order flow attracts order flow." It does so because larger markets are more liquid, generally offer tighter spreads, and tend to produce more reliable price discovery. Because of this centralizing force, the network developed by a national exchange may, in a free market environment, come to dominate smaller exchanges. Only by offering a clearly differentiated product (e.g., a better technology or a better service for local clientele) may a competitor be able to survive. What follows is that, in order to enjoy fully the benefits of network externalities, we may have to live with a public utility that has monopoly power.

The force of competition should not be underestimated, however. Niche firms arise to offer differentiated products. In today's technologically advanced environment, cross-border competition is a formidable force and one that is intensifying. Moreover, while network externalities can be enjoyed with respect to the order flow for individual securities, competition for the listings can still exist between alternative market centers. Further, network externalities can be realized, to some extent, by linking competing market centers informationally.

While order flow does attract order flow, a countervailing power also exists: free riding on price discovery. That is, in a free market environment, participants can meet and trade among themselves at prices established on the main market without incurring the potentially higher costs of going to the main market and without having to abide by the main market's order execution rules. Interestingly, the bigger, more liquid, and more transparent is the central market, the easier it is for subsets of participants to free-ride on its price discovery. For this reason, a central market has an incentive to impose an order consolidation rule on its members. Euronext Paris has such a rule, as did the New York Stock Exchange until, under pressure from the U.S. Securities and Exchange Commission, the Big Board abolished its order concentration Rule 390 in December 1999.

Public Goods

The classic example of a public good is the lighthouse in the harbor. Three attributes describe a public good: (1) There is one amount available for all (there is but one light from the lighthouse), (2) one person's consumption of the good does not reduce the amount available for others (one ship seeing the light does not result in less light being available for other ships to see), and (3) nonpayers cannot be excluded from consuming the good (any ship in the area can see the light).

Several exchange products have public goods characteristics. Price discovery is a good example. In certain respects, transaction prices resemble the beam from a lighthouse: Both signal important information to a broad array of recipients.[1] The quality of prices set in the central market depends on the systems, procedures, and protocols used to handle orders and translate them into trades and on how the exchange discharges its self-regulatory organization (SRO) obligations.

SRO operations and the provision of supplemental liquidity are other examples of exchange-produced public goods. As with price discovery, for both of these services there is just one amount provided for the broad market, one person benefiting from these services does not reduce the amount available for others, and nonpayers cannot be excluded from benefiting from them. Because nonpayers cannot be excluded, these services will be undersupplied in a freely competitive environment (as is the case with all public goods). This points out an important benefit of having one strong central market that operates as a quasi-public institution.

Markets under Stress

A market under stress can lose the ability to discover prices with reasonable accuracy. When, for instance, prices start to drop, natural buyers tend to pull back and natural sellers rush forward to trade. Both reactions accentuate the fall. Special procedures such as circuit breakers and supplemental liquidity provision are needed to ensure the continuance of market quality under such conditions.

Supplemental liquidity provision and price stabilization have public goods characteristics. Both call for a commitment of resources that are not freely forthcoming in a private market environment. Both convey benefits to the broad market. Both must be the responsibility of a single, designated market maker (like the specialist in the U.S. exchanges or the designated market maker in the European exchanges).

In the U.S. exchanges, trading is structured around the specialist, a market professional who functions as both principal (dealer) and agent (broker's broker). Specialists have an affirmative obligation to make a "fair and orderly market" for the stocks assigned to them. "Fair and orderly" is viewed as the absence of excessively large and erratic price changes. This means that the specialist must intervene in trading (provide supplemental liquidity) to keep price changes acceptably small by buying for and selling from his or her own account against a prevailing market trend. We discuss specialist operations in greater detail in Chapter 8, "The Evolving Scene in the United States."

Supplemental liquidity is provided in the French and German markets by agents called *liquidity providers* (in France) and *designated sponsors* (in Germany). These agents play a special role with regard to less liquid equities, exchange-traded funds, and warrants. They facilitate price discovery and help to create a smoother, more orderly market. The agents' direct responsibility for less liquid stocks and special products includes their being present at all times to keep spreads below maximum allowable levels and quantity above minimum levels. These agents have contracts with the listed companies whose shares they handle.[2]

Price stability is also further enhanced in London, Paris, and Frankfurt by the use of volatility interruptions (a form of circuit breaker) that halt trading for short periods when intraday price changes exceed certain critical thresholds. A volatility interruption in Germany's Xetra lasts for between 2 and 2½ minutes (the specific ending within the last 30 seconds is determined by random draw). The brief halt provides a check against errors in order entry, defuses momentum trading, and enables liquidity to be focused and price discovery sharpened when the halt ends. At the end of the halt, the market reopens using the call auction procedure.[3]

MARKET STRUCTURE ISSUES

We next address a variety of more specific issues that pertain to exchange operations. In certain respects, these issues relate to the three concepts we have just discussed: network externalities, public goods, and markets under stress.

Order Flow Fragmentation

Competition for order flow from alternative markets is both a reality and desirable. It pressures all competitors to be more efficient. But this benefit comes at a cost. Market quality may be impaired in a fragmented environment in several ways: Price discovery is more difficult, the supply of supplemental liquidity may be insufficient, and so forth. Further, the liquidity available in alternative markets may not be available to all market participants. Additionally, fracturing exchange revenues can result in an undersupply of public goods types of services.

It is useful to distinguish between competition among qualitatively different markets (e.g., exchanges and various alternative trading systems, or ATSs), and competition among essentially similar markets (e.g., a national market and various regional exchanges). Both can exert pressure on a market center to become more efficient but, in so doing, the former offers participants a greater range of selection than the latter. It is also important to distinguish between fragmentation among markets (and across national boundaries) and fragmentation of the order flow. In Europe, for instance, there are many markets and they are fragmented, but for the most part the order flow is not. The reason is that there is generally but one stock exchange in each country, and national stocks trade predominantly in their home markets (e.g., Italian stocks trade in Milan, and German stocks trade in Frankfurt). Thus liquidity tends to build on a single trading platform. Every European national market is a world champion in its own national stocks (this is known as the *home markets principal*).

Interestingly, as market centers consolidate across Europe, increasing fragmentation may result as the various centers compete for the order flow for a common set of stocks. The London Stock Exchange, virt-x, Deutsche Börse, and Euronext all compete in this arena. This fragmentation of the order flow will occur predominantly for the European blue chips, however, as trading in the mid- and small-cap stocks will continue to remain local. Fragmentation of the blue-chip segment creates a need to consolidate. Stock exchange customers all want one market with one set of rules and regulations for the blue chips. Further, investors want to be able to trade baskets quickly at reasonable cost, issuers want a unified

European platform to facilitate capital raising, and members want a unified technology and regulation to streamline their operations and risk management.

Free Riding

When markets are fragmented, free riding is expected. Free riding can occur when trades are made in satellite markets, in the "upstairs" markets of banks and brokerage houses, or among participants meeting directly without the services of an intermediary. Commonly, the contribution of these trades to price discovery is minimal. In the U.S. listed market, the NYSE is the facility where prices are discovered. In Germany, seven regionals and the Frankfurt floor look to Xetra as the main price discovery mechanism.

Free riding can be problematic. Limit orders that have been placed in the main market (and that have contributed to price discovery) may remain unexecuted as trades occur off-board at equivalent prices. This discourages the placement of limit orders in the central market, thereby decreasing liquidity and obfuscating price discovery.

On the other hand, off-board trades provided by alternative systems such as Instinet, Posit, and Liquidnet can enhance market quality by enabling large, institutional orders to meet in a more orderly fashion and at lower cost. This can result in lower market impact and in fewer unsold or unbought shares left overhanging the market. For this reason, the crossing networks can help diffuse intraday price volatility and sharpen price discovery for the broad market.[4]

France has an order consolidation rule to counter fragmentation. Germany has a weaker requirement: If a customer does not explicitly say that an order is to be routed to some other venue (e.g., to an ECN or a market maker), it must go to an exchange. London does not have an order consolidation rule. The London Exchange's expressed desire is to offer a facility that customers will freely want to use. The NYSE had a rule (Rule 390) that precluded the in-house execution of customer orders by requiring that member firms bring customer orders to an exchange for execution. Under pressure from the U.S. SEC, the exchange eliminated the rule in December 1999. We discuss this further in Chapter 11, "Regulation."

Systemic Problems

Market failure can occur in several ways. Disruptions in some segment of the market (e.g., equities) can spread to other segments (e.g., options). Clearing and settlement problems can trigger a broad market collapse. A most serious systemic problem is liquidity drying up in a market under stress. When this occurs, the ability to discover price with reasonable accuracy breaks down. The fragmentation issue should be revisited in this light: Fragmented markets may be less resilient under crash conditions.

Preventive devices are needed to protect against crash conditions. Two such measures that we have discussed with regard to price stabilization—circuit breakers and supplemental liquidity providers supplying risk capital—appear to work well, although thus far their effectiveness has not been tested by a major market downdraft.

Price Discovery

As we discuss in several places in this book, price discovery is one of the major services produced by an exchange. Prices "discovered" in a market should be *consensus values* (values that reflect the broad market's desire to hold shares). The quality of price discovery depends on the structure of a marketplace. For instance, price discovery is inherently more difficult in fragmented markets.[5] For reasonably accurate price discovery, the entire order flow should be viewed comprehensively.

More than one trading mechanism is needed for efficient price discovery. Along with continuous trading, call auctions should be used to focus liquidity at critical points in time during the trading day. Importantly, calls are now being used to open and to close the markets in London, Frankfurt, and Paris. This focusing of the order flow is particularly important for less liquid securities. Comprehensively viewed, call auctions in Europe are thought to be working well. Thus far in the United States, however, the call auction has played no meaningful role aside from the NYSE's use of a not fully electronic call to open and to close the market for its listed securities. At the time of this writing, Nasdaq has introduced a fully electronic call auction for closings and anticipates doing the same for openings. We discuss call auctions in greater detail in Chap-ter 6, "Order-Driven Markets."

Price discovery should be the product of the broad market, as orders from all sources interact to set prices and generate trades. But one group of participants, because their view of the order flow is generally more comprehensive, plays a special role with regard to price discovery: the market makers. No other single market participant wishes to have any responsibility for price discovery, and institutional participants in particular want to stay as far away from price discovery as possible.

In Europe, one kind of market maker in particular, referred to as *designated market maker* (in Germany) and *liquidity provider* (in France), plays a particularly important price discovery role for the less liquid securities. However, these agents play no role at all for the large-cap securities, as the CAC 40 and DAX 30 stocks are thought to be sufficiently liquid without them. To further facilitate price discovery, Deutsche Börse currently runs three call auctions a day in Xetra: one at the open, one at the close, and one intraday. The London Stock Exchange and Euronext have two call auctions a day: one at the open and one at the close.

Hybrid Market Structure—Special Facilities

"One size does not fit all" is a well-established adage in the equity markets. Different trades require different kinds of facilities, depending on the difficulty of a trade as determined by the size of the order, the depth of the market for a stock, and the needs of a trader for low execution cost, speed, control, anonymity, and so forth. To offer the range of options that participants need, a market center must have a hybrid structure that combines continuous order-driven, quote-driven, and periodic call auction features. Currently, good market designs exist for each of the generic structures (i.e., order-driven, quote-driven, and periodic call). The challenging problem in market architecture is integrating the separate facilities into an efficient hybrid structure. As we have previously discussed in this chapter, the hybrid structure must also include special facilities, such as volatility interruptions, to cope with the problem of markets under stress.

The most complex integration to achieve is the inclusion of public limit orders in a primarily quote-driven market (as is currently being done in Nasdaq's SuperMontage). This integration is particularly difficult in a computerized environment, where the details of order handling and trade execution must be spelled out fully, in precise detail, and with strict reference to a clock that measures time in nanoseconds. The inclusion of market maker quotes in a primarily order driven market is considerably less difficult to accomplish.

In the United States, the integration of the order-driven and quote-driven environments has evolved naturally on the New York Stock Exchange, a floor-based market that includes a public limit order book, a designated market maker (specialist), additional broker-dealer floor traders, and upstairs market makers. Nasdaq, on the other hand, has had a more difficult problem integrating public limit orders into its predominantly quote-driven market. Nasdaq's current initiative designed to accomplish this, SuperMontage, started operations in fall 2002.

Another dimension of the hybrid market structure is the inclusion of crosses and price discovery call auctions along with continuous trading. This integration is relatively straightforward and far more readily accomplished than the simultaneous inclusion of dealer quotes and public limit orders in a continuous trading environment.

Appropriate Intermediary and Market Center Profitability

Broker-dealers and market centers supply various important services, including order handling, the provision of dealer capital, and price discovery. For these services to be forthcoming, the sell side must be appropriately compensated. However, many questions arise regarding this issue.

Broker-dealer firms provide a package of services (trading, research, etc.). Should the package be unbundled? What effect does commission bundling and soft-dollar practices have on the efficiency with which orders are handled and translated into trades?[6] How should broker-dealers best be brought on board so that they will not resist much-needed market structure innovation and change? What is the best way to structure the integration of dealer quotes with order book prices? What is the best way for broker-dealers to compete with an order book? How should markets be run to generate appropriate revenues for broker-dealer services? For exchanges, is the private, for-profit approach a good model, or is the public utility model a better one?

Widely accepted answers do not exist for these important questions. Fathoming sell side remuneration has been further complicated by the rapid increases in network capacity, trading software, and computer power that make finding the contra side of a trade ever easier. The technological innovations have in recent years decreased the need for intermediation and the cost of performing intermediation services. Yet the intermediaries remain vitally important for the quality of markets. They should be appropriately compensated.

Proper Handling of Institutional Order Flow

Institutional order flow presents one of the most challenging problems faced in market design. The reason is that large orders incur high trading costs. How, for instance, does one handle a 500,000-share order for a stock that, on average, trades 300,000 shares a day?

If the large orders are traded slowly over an extended period of time, opportunity costs may be incurred. However, relatively fast, intermediary-facilitated executions can be expensive in terms of spreads, market impact, and commissions. Further, institutional orders are commonly front-run by others, which largely explains why market impact costs are high. We discuss this and related issues further in Chapter 5, "Institutional Order Flow."

Proper Identification of Customer

As we discuss in Chapter 1, "The Role of an Equity Market," Exchanges have three constituents—broker-dealer intermediaries, natural buyers and sellers (the investors), and the listed companies. These constituents have different objectives, needs, and agendas. How does an exchange prioritize between them?

Historically, exchanges have been membership organizations, and for a membership organization the answer is straightforward: The broker-dealer intermediaries, who are their members, are their primary customers. With a membership organization, the other two constituents (investors and the listed companies) are important primarily because they are critical for the profitability of the members. Nevertheless, the bottom line is, with a membership organization, the interests of the intermediaries come first.

Particularly in an environment of technological change and disintermediation, this orientation may not lead to decisions that are optimal from the viewpoint of investors and listed firms. Today, the traditional view is changing and the interests of investors are moving closer to center stage. The reasoning is that, if a market center meets the needs of the investors, it will retain its listings, and if it has the investors and the listings, the intermediaries will be better off.[7] Nevertheless, conflict continues. Decisions that may be desirable from the viewpoint of investors but that are not embraced by the sell side are still not easily made.

INTRADAY VOLATILITY

As noted at the start of the chapter, market quality refers to the magnitude of trading costs and the accuracy of price discovery, both of which are linked to an accentuation of short-period (i.e., intraday) price volatility. Consequently, an analysis of intraday volatility provides important insight into market quality. This section of the chapter is devoted to this analysis.[8]

Volatility is like cholesterol—some is good and some is bad. Good volatility characterizes price adjustments that are attributable to news concerning fundamental values. We refer to this as *fundamental volatility*. Bad volatility, which is process-driven, characterizes price changes that are attributable to transaction costs. We refer to this as *technical volatility*. Technical volatility is manifest in accentuated price swings, the runs and reversals that occur over relatively brief trading intervals in response to the arrival of buy and sell orders in the market. We suggest that an objective of market structure is to control technical volatility. However, as we explain in Chapter 6, "Order-Driven Markets," it should also be recognized that, to some extent, short-run volatility must be accentuated to appropriately compensate liquidity providers (i.e., limit order trades and broker-dealer intermediaries).

In this section of the chapter, we assess short-period volatility in five major market centers—the New York Stock Exchange and Nasdaq in the United States, and the London Stock Exchange, Deutsche Börse, and Euronext Paris in Europe. The five-country analysis underscores the pervasiveness of the relationship between short-period volatility, trading costs, and the accuracy of price discovery.[9] We give major emphasis to volatility measured over half-hour intervals. For the set of days in our sample period (all trading days in 2000), we separately consider the set of first half-hour returns (e.g., 9:30 to 10:00 for the U.S. markets), second half-hour returns, and so on, through the last half-hour returns.

This methodology contrasts with two more traditional approaches. One, which uses the series of consecutive short-period returns (e.g., Hasbrouck and Schwartz[10] use half-hour intervals, and Andersen, Bollersley, and Das[11] use five-minute intervals), focuses on the effect of differencing interval length without considering time-of-day effects. The other approach, which uses 24-hour periods that start at different times of the day (e.g., Amihud and Mendelson[12] and Gerety and Mulherin[13]), captures time-of-day effects without considering the effect of differencing interval length. Our approach seeks to achieve both objectives simultaneously. Regarding the time-of-day effects, we pay particular attention to the opening and closing half-hour periods, because these are times of heightened stress for the markets.

We have a further reason for this methodology. When the returns measurements are contiguous and the returns are negatively autocorrelated, short-period volatility is accentuated relative to longer-period volatility. Alternatively, when the returns measurements are positively autocorrelated, short-period volatility is dampened relative to longer-period volatility.[14] Consequently, to the extent that negative and positive autocorrelation coexist, the offsetting correlations tend to render each other invisible, which undermines the efficacy of variance analysis.[15] Treating noncontiguous returns helps to solve this problem. With our methodology, a momentum move in one direction on one day, matched with a momentum move of opposite direction on another day, maps into accentuated volatility.[16]

An array of factors may cause the accentuation of intraday volatility to differ across markets. These include:

- The architectural structure of a market.
- Patterns of news release (e.g., whether corporate and government announcements tend to be made in the overnight halt or during the trading day).
- Investor characteristics (e.g., whether the market is predominantly institutional or retail).
- Intraday trading patterns of institutional investors (e.g., whether or not the big players tend to avoid trading at the open).

- The cross-listing of stocks in markets with overlapping time zones (e.g., a British company listed both on the London Stock Exchange and in the U.S. market as an ADR).
- The amount of after-hours and preopen trading.

Our goal is not, however, to contrast or to explain volatility differences across the five markets, but to establish that accentuated short-period volatility is a phenomenon that is common to all.

Volatility analysis has implications for market structure. By paying particular attention to the more challenging times of the trading day (the first and the last half-hour of trading), we are able to detect imperfections in price discovery that may not be as apparent in the rest of the day. Our findings suggest that price discovery at market openings and closings needs to be improved in each of the five markets.[17] This underscores the importance of making the trading systems more efficient.

Participant Attitudes toward Accentuated Intraday Volatility

To the extent that accentuated intraday volatility reflects trading costs, one might presume that participants would find elevated volatility undesirable. This is not necessarily the case. There is, of course, a net loss for the market in aggregate to the extent that high costs and high volatility discourage trading.[18] Aside from this loss, trading is a zero-sum game: What one participant loses, another gains (i.e., one participant's cost is another's return).[19] Consequently, participant attitudes toward high intraday volatility depend on how the individuals cope with the volatility and on whether it is predominantly their revenue or their cost that is increased by it.

Generally, the passive side of the market—market makers and public traders who use limit orders—benefit from accentuated volatility. A trader can capture the accentuated volatility by (1) posting a quote or placing a limit order, (2) next, buying at a relatively low price or selling at a relatively high price, and (3) then having price revert to its previous level. In fact, intraday volatility must be accentuated in order to compensate dealers and limit order traders for the risks they take when setting the prices at which others can trade.[20] Further, in the opinion of one sell side participant, Henry Paulson Jr., chairman and chief executive of Goldman Sachs Group, intraday volatility also generates a need for broker-dealer services. Paulson put it this way: "Volatility is our friend. . . . If it wasn't for volatility, why should you need Goldman Sachs?"[21]

Technical analysis is widely used by participants on both the sell side and the buy side. While generally looked down on in academic circles, technical analysis, in principle at least, has a valid role to play.[22] Though rarely stated this way, technical analysis can be thought of as an approach to inferring where a stock's price is relative to an unobserved consensus (equilibrium) value. Any participant who, either through technical analysis or by any other means, can properly time his or her orders in a volatile market will have a positive attitude toward the volatility.

Notwithstanding, the active participants in the market—those who step forward with market orders and trigger trades—generally pay the cost implied by the accentuated volatility. They pay it in terms of the spread and market impact. They pay it in the form of the risk they incur as momentum players. And, when a temporary buy-sell imbalance pushes price up too high or down too low, traders on the "heavy" side of the market (those whose orders have collectively caused the price move) bear the cost of having chased liquidity rather than having supplied it.

High intraday volatility is costly for the market in aggregate. It discourages trades and makes portfolio returns more uncertain. A portfolio manager who receives high scores for asset selection can see his or her returns seriously eroded by trading costs. Most portfolio managers view trading costs as such, and few count on enhancing their performance by turning trading costs into returns (except, that is, for some hedge funds and some of the more technologically sophisticated fund managers who have discovered that they can earn the spread rather than pay it). Accordingly, while they should accept some accentuation of intraday volatility as inevitable, fund managers, by and large, find it undesirable.

The Link between Volatility, Trading Costs, and Price Discovery

We use a simplified, stylized representation to establish the link between trading costs and accentuated short-period price volatility.[23] First, we define some terms. The discussion makes reference to the ledger presented in Exhibit 4.1.

The implicit transaction cost, per share, of buying or selling a stock is C. The implicit cost is embedded in the price of a transaction. It includes the bid-ask spread and market impact, but not commissions. For simplicity, let C have the same value for all trades.

The doughnut shape represents a transaction price that is observed when the transaction has been triggered by a buy order. A buy-triggered transaction price reflects the bid-ask spread (i.e., an offer price that is higher then the bid), the market impact, and/or whatever else might be pushing up price.

The triangle shape represents a transaction price that is observed when the transaction has been triggered by a sell order. A sell-triggered transaction price reflects the bid-ask spread (i.e., a bid price that is lower then the offer), market impact, and/or whatever else might be pushing down price.

The length of the vertical line represents the magnitude of C.

P^* is a value for a stock that we cannot see but that can nevertheless be conceptualized. It is an unobservable, costless trading price that might be viewed as a consensus value (or an equilibrium value).

Let's start with P^*. Exhibit 4.1 shows how P^* may evolve over the course of a trading day. The consensus value for the stock fluctuates with change in the fundamental desire of investors to hold shares of the stock in their portfolios. Informational change (news) is the simplest factor to point to.

Exhibit 4.2 adds transaction prices to the picture. In the exhibit, each transaction price is P^* plus C for a buy-triggered trade, or P^* minus C for a sell-triggered trade. In the exhibit, the first trade of the day was triggered by a buy order that arrived early in the morning, and the first transaction price is represented by the first doughnut. The second trade of the day was triggered by a sell order, and the first triangle identifies the price of that trade.

The trading day continues. There are more trades and transaction prices, more doughnuts and triangles. In Exhibit 4.3, we connect the transaction prices with dotted lines to indicate the returns. Volatility is measured by the variance, or standard deviation of returns.[24] The returns are the slopes of the dotted lines. Sometimes the dotted lines slope upward, sometimes they slope downward. Sometimes they are relatively flat. What is the volatility implied by this set of transaction prices? How does this volatility compare with the volatility of P^*? Shortly, we will consider the volatility measures. For now, it is important to get a more intuitive feel for the issue.

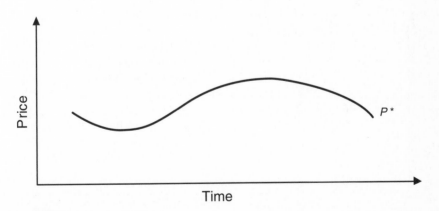

EXHIBIT 4.1 Evolution of the unobserved, costless price, where P^* = unobserved, costless trading price.

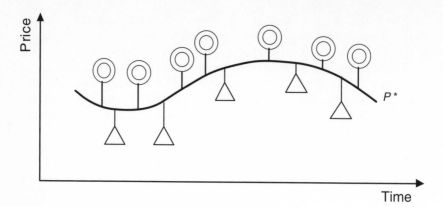

EXHIBIT 4.2   Evolution of the transaction price, where
◎ = transaction price (triggered by buy order)
△ = transaction price (triggered by sell order)
| = magnitude of *C*, implicit transaction cost of buy or sell

Exhibit 4.4 is the same as Exhibit 4.3, but with the price path for $P*$ restored. Notice that the realized transaction prices jump around more than $P*$. This is because of implicit transaction costs. The costs raise the prices paid by buyers when their buy orders trigger trades, and they lower the prices received by sellers when their sell orders trigger trades. The sizes of the jumps depend on the changes of $P*$ and the length of the vertical cost lines.

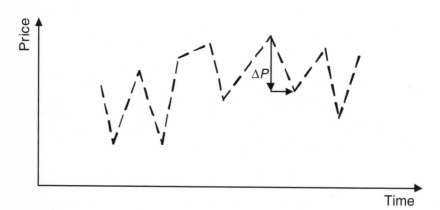

EXHIBIT 4.3   Evolution of the transaction price and returns.

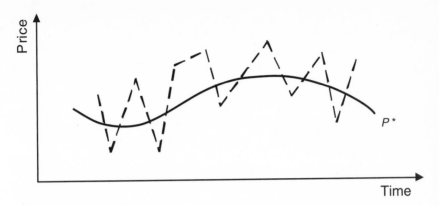

EXHIBIT 4.4 Which is more volatile, *P** or the transaction price?

Two implicit costs are clearly represented by the length of the vertical cost line:

1. *Bid-ask spread.* Even if the quotes are constant over a period of time, transaction prices will bounce between the bid and the offer, with the staggered arrival of market sell orders that execute at the bid and the arrival of market buy orders that execute at the offer. This effect is likely to be minimal with the current small tick sizes.
2. *Market impact.* A large buy order pushing the transaction price above the posted offer, or a large sell order pushing the transaction price below the posted bid, means that the effective bid-ask spread is wider for larger orders, particularly when the buy-sell programs are undertaken by impatient traders who, just possibly, are informed.

Two other market process factors also account for short-period volatility accentuation:

1. *Price discovery.* As discussed in Chapter 3, the process of price discovery is the search for a stock's consensus price—the value that reflects the broad market's willingness to hold shares, given the new information and the divergent expectations of investors based on the news. During the search process, a stock's price will sometimes run up too far, while at other times it may fall too low.

   En route to finding its consensus value, lows and highs emerge that are commonly associated with support and resistance levels.[25] With divergent expectations, a support level may be associated with the bearish end of the expectations spectrum, and a resistance level may be associated with the bullish end. Bouncing between a support level and a resistance level has the same effect (although it is likely stronger) as bouncing between a bid and an offer quote. Both the bid-ask bounce and the high-low bounce translate into accentuated intraday price volatility.[26]

2. *Momentum trading.* Protracted buying or selling pressures can develop when large, institutional participants and/or informed traders, in an attempt to control market impact costs, break up their trading in a stealthy fashion for partial execution over a series of trades. Price discovery in a nonfrictionless trading environment where participants have different beliefs about a stock's value may also result in periods of protracted buying or selling pressure. The protracted pressures lead naturally to momentum trading.

When participants buy simply because the sequence of recent price changes has been predominantly positive, a stock's price is apt to be pushed up too far. Similarly, when participants sell simply because the sequence of recent price changes has been predominantly negative, a stock's price is apt to be pushed down too far. A stock's price running up too high and/or down too low translates into accentuated intraday volatility.

All four factors—the bid-ask spread, market impact, momentum trading, and imperfect price discovery—are costs, but they also exist because markets are not perfectly liquid, frictionless environments. Bid-ask spreads and market impact exist because orders do not interact with each other in a perfectly liquid, frictionless environment.[27] With momentum trading, when prices are rising, more traders hop on the bandwagon and buy. This implies that these traders do not have confidence in the current price. They think that price is going to a new level. But, one might ask, why isn't price already at the level that it seems to be heading toward? Because of costs. Because trading is a friction process. Because price discovery is not simple, and no one can see $P*$.

The four phenomena—spreads, market impact, momentum trading, and imperfect price discovery—have something else in common. They all result in prices bouncing between two values, one high and the other low. Price bouncing between two values translates into accentuated volatility. With a bid-ask spread, price bounces between the higher offer and the lower bid. The same is true with market impact—price is effectively bouncing back and forth across a larger spread. If it is a momentum move, price went down too low or rose up too high. Either way, price is swinging too far and, as it bounces back, the last momentum trader always gets killed. Price discovery can also be viewed in this context. One of the basic patterns looked for by technical analysts (chartists) is support and resistance levels.

We can extend the notion of the bounce to include price swinging between a lower support level and a higher resistance level. All of these—the bid-ask bounce, market impact bounce, momentum bounce, price discovery bounce, and any combination thereof—result in accentuated intraday volatility.

Returning to Exhibits 4.1 to 4.4, we can now better understand the sense in which intraday volatility is accentuated. If we were to extend the price charts out over a far longer interval of time, changes in P^* would become increasingly appreciable relative to the magnitude of the implicit trading costs. This is because the collective impact of information change cumulates over time, while the length of the vertical cost lines remains constant. Consequently, the relative impact of the vertical cost lines on returns becomes increasingly less important as the period over which returns are measured is lengthened. An interesting thing occurs as the differencing interval (the length of time over which returns are measured) is lengthened: The volatility of observed transaction prices converges on the volatility of P^*. Because these two volatilities converge for longer-period returns, we are able to infer the intraday volatility of P^*. This inference enables us to assess the intraday volatility accentuation and hence the magnitude of implicit trading costs.

The volatility accentuation can be captured as follows. As we discuss in Appendix A, "Prices and Returns," in a perfectly frictionless, random-walk world, volatility is the same for all differencing intervals if the volatility measure for each is adjusted to reflect the length of the differencing interval. That is, if we look at half-hour returns, hourly returns, daily returns, weekly returns, or whatever, the volatility for all of these, adjusted for the length of the differencing interval, should be the same. The adjustment is simple. To normalize all measures to a one-day volatility, for instance, simply divide a two-day measure by 2, a one-week measure by 5, and, more generally, an n-day measure by n. In other words, simply divide by the relative length of the differencing interval.[28] If prices follow a random walk, the normalized values will all be the same.

On the other hand, normalized volatility is not the same for all differencing intervals if prices do not follow a random walk. The price-bouncing (mean-reverting) phenomena that we have just attributed to implicit trading costs, momentum moves, and imperfect price discovery, all represent deviations from random walk. They all introduce negative correlation in short-period price movements, and consequently they all result in accentuated short-period volatility.

Empirical Findings

Ozenbas, Schwartz, and Wood have assessed half-hour volatility for five markets—the New York Stock Exchange and Nasdaq in the United States, and the London Stock Exchange, Euronext Paris, and Deutsche Börse in Europe—using transaction prices for the year 2000.[29] The return for each half-hour interval in the sample was the price change from the first trade in an interval to the last trade in the interval. Their study considered the largest stocks in each market, assessed each stock individually, and broke the sample for each market into two time periods, each approximately half a year in length. For each stock and time segment, volatility was computed by taking the standard deviation of the logarithmic returns for each measurement interval and dividing by the square root of the measurement interval's length.[30]

To further analyze the intraday half-hour volatility patterns, Ozenbas, Schwartz, and Wood separated the half-hour intervals into four groups: the first half hour, the second half hour through the second-to-last half hour, the last half-hour, and, where applicable, the brief period between the close of the continuous market and the closing call auction (labeled "Closing call"). The average of the set of half-hour volatilities for the second half-hour interval through the second-to-last half-hour interval was used as a base against which to assess the volatilities for the first and last half-hour periods. The results are shown in Exhibit 4.5.

To illustrate, in Exhibit 4.5, for the NYSE first period (the first half of 2000), for the first half hour, the value of 1.78 indicates that this volatility is 78 percent higher than that of the average of the 11 midday, half-hour volatilities.

The story told by Exhibit 4.5 is clear. The volatility spike for the first half hour is substantial for all five markets in each of the two calendar periods. If news alone caused the price changes, the intraday volatility pattern should reflect the intraday pattern of news releases. If news releases are more prevalent for some half-hour intervals than for others, the half-hour volatility should be highest for those intervals that experience the most news releases. Or, if news releases have no systematic intraday pattern, then the intraday volatility pattern, including the first half-hour interval, should be flat. However, the first half hour of trading is a relatively informationless period (as a rule, controllable information releases, such as earnings announcements, are not made in the opening half hour of trading). Nevertheless, for the London Stock Exchange, volatility in the first half hour is roughly three times the average of the other periods (excluding the opening and closing half-hour periods), whereas for the other European and two U.S. exchanges it is about double.

Don't overnight news events have relatively large price impacts at the open? They do, but the point is, this will not affect the first half-hour returns if the opening transaction prices are accurately established. The reason is that the first recorded *price change* that we analyze does not include the overnight price change. Rather, it is the difference between the

	NYSE		Nasdaq		London Stock Exchange		Euronext Paris		Deutsche Börse	
	First Period	Second Period	First Period	Second Period	First Period	Second Period	First Period	Second Period	First Period	Second Period
First ½ hr	1.78*	2.04*	1.87*	1.91*	3.12*	3.11*	1.75*	1.78*	1.76*	1.96*
Last ½ hr	1.18†	1.10	1.55*	1.32*	1.64*	1.53*	1.45*	1.31*	1.17†	1.15†
Closing call	NA	NA	NA	NA	NA	1.50*	1.09	1.00	0.91	0.63†
Open-to-close	1.14	1.13	1.14	1.13	1.18†	1.20†	1.00	1.05	1.00	0.99
1 day	1.26*	1.30*	1.21†	1.24*	0.98	1.10	1.12	1.00	1.09	1.10
1 week	1.14	1.29*	1.04	1.16†	0.94	0.88	0.98	0.87	0.91	0.84†
2 weeks	1.12	1.23†	1.06	1.05	0.84†	0.81†	0.93	0.82†	0.89	0.85†

*Indicates significantly different than unity at the 1 percent confidence level.
†Indicates significantly different than unity at the 5 percent confidence level.

EXHIBIT 4.5 Normalized price volatilities. Price change in each half-hour segment is measured as the natural logarithm of the last price divided by the first price in the segment. The half-hour price changes are then divided into separate sets: the first half hour of the day, the second half hour, and so on through the final half-hour interval of the trading day. Half-hour volatility is then computed for each stock for each of the intraday segments by taking the standard deviation of the series of price changes recorded for each of the segments. The volatility for each market, for each half-hour segment in the day, is computed as the equally weighted average volatility across all of the stocks in our sample for that market and for that interval. The reported volatilities are then normalized by dividing them by the average of the volatilities from the second half-hour segment to the second-to-last half-hour segment. Hence, the reported volatilities are scaled by dividing them by the mean midday volatilities.

last price in the first half-hour interval and the *price at which the market opened*. Thus, because of how we have measured it, the accentuation of first half-hour volatility is not attributed to overnight news per se, but to opening prices not reflecting accurate adjustments to the news. As such, the accentuated first half-hour price volatility is evidence of price discovery being a protracted process that extends into, and perhaps beyond, the first half-hour period. Fleming and Remolina,[31] in their study of the U.S. Treasury market, have also underscored the difficulty of achieving accurate price discovery by demonstrating that protracted surges in intraday volatility attend the release of major macroeconomic news announcements. The bottom line is that the volatility spike for the first half hour in each of the five markets is a particularly meaningful, inverse measure of market quality.

Volatility at the close is also accentuated, although less so than at the opening. As shown in Exhibit 4.5, volatility over the last half hour is more than 50 percent greater than the midday volatility for the London Stock Exchange in both subperiods, and over 30 percent greater for Euronext Paris. Volatility at the close is 17 percent more for Deutsche Börse in the first period and 15 percent more in the second subperiod. Nasdaq closing volatility is 55 and 32 percent higher for the first and second periods, respectively, while the NYSE's closing volatility is 18 and 10 percent higher. The volatility spike at the close may be attributed to traders rushing to complete their executions as the end of a trading session draws near.

Also of interest in Exhibit 4.5 is the volatility between the close of the continuous market and the closing call auction (Closing call).[32] The relative volatility numbers presented in Exhibit 4.5 show that, for the three European market centers, some price volatility exists between the close of the continuous market and the closing call. The normalized volatility ranges from 1.00 to 1.09 for the continental European exchanges. Period 2 for the London exchange yields a normalized volatility of 1.50.[33] This volatility spike at London's closing call may be attributed to meaningful price discovery taking place in the closing auction. Interestingly, for the second period for Deutsche Börse, the call auction volatility is only 63 percent of the midday volatility at the 5:30 P.M. call, while it is 14 percent greater than the midday volatility at the 8:00 P.M. call.[34] Apparently, with trading activity being relatively low between 5:30 P.M. and 8:00 P.M., meaningful price discovery does occur at the final call.[35]

Exhibit 4.5 also shows the normalized open-to-close volatilities. The values for open-to-close volatilities range from 0.99 to 1.20. While they are predominantly greater than unity, only the London values are significantly greater. Open-to-close is highest for the London Stock Exchange, standing at 1.18 and 1.20 for the first and second periods, respectively. For Euronext Paris, open-to-close volatility is 1.00 for the first period and 1.05 for the second period. For Deutsche Börse, open-to-close is also 1.00 for the first period and 0.99 for the second period.[36] Open-to-close volatilities for the two U.S. markets in both periods are tightly grouped at 1.13 and 1.14. However, because of the general lack of significance, interpreting these results as evidence of reversals behavior may be misleading. Values of open-to-close that are not significantly greater than 1.00 (which, except for London, we have observed) suggest that price dislocations attributable to the four market process factors (spreads, market impact, dynamic price discovery, and momentum trading) may have been partially repaired by price reversals that have occurred by the end of the trading day, but reversal behavior may not be confined to a single trading day—it could extend into next-day price behavior (and perhaps beyond).

The longer-period normalized volatilities displayed in Exhibit 4.5 are for three measurement intervals—one day, one week, and two weeks. The one-day interval (the volatility of close-to-close returns) captures the price change from the closing trade on one trading day to the closing trade on the next trading day. The one-week interval captures the price change from the closing trade on one trading day to the closing trade five trading days later. The two-week interval captures the price change from the closing trade on one trading day to the closing trade ten trading days later.

Each of these longer-period measures encompasses overnight (and over-weekend) price changes. The overnight price changes reflect x-dividend price behavior and stock splits, along with overnight news releases, all of which make the recorded price changes more volatile.[37] For this reason, any diminution of volatility as one progresses from the intraday to the one-day to the one-week and, finally, to the two-week measurement interval is particularly strong evidence of reversal behavior in stock price changes.

The first contrast of interest in Exhibit 4.5 is between open-to-close and one-day intervals. For the NYSE and Nasdaq, one-day is greater than unity with statistical significance, while open-to-close is statistically indistinguishable from 1 for both markets. For London, on the other hand, open-to-close is statistically different from 1, while one-day is indistinguishable from 1. Thus, while the U.S. markets reflect substantial volatility from the prior day's close to the subsequent open, the London market reflects substantial mean reversion during the overnight period. For Euronext Paris and Deutsche Börse, both the one-day and open-to-close measures were indistinguishable from unity for the two study periods.

Generally, for all five markets, the normalized volatility successively declines as we move from one day to one week to two weeks.[38] This finding may reflect, at least in part, the diminishing influence of the bid-ask bounce and market impact as the horizon is lengthened. This could also reflect the fact that, over an extended period, errors in price discovery are largely repaired by reversals that bring prices back toward equilibrium. Note also in Exhibit 4.5 that the levels of the one-day ratios in the U.S. markets are higher than unity, whereas those in European markets generally are not. These differences could reflect the relative practices of intraday news release in the United States and Europe.[39]

Across the five markets, the values for two weeks are generally somewhat less than those for one week. However, the one- and two-week values are similar, and it appears that much of the reversal behavior is captured by the one-week measure.

UNANSWERED QUESTIONS

The picture that emerges for each of the five markets considered in the volatility study is one of accentuated short-period volatility, especially at market openings.[40] Daily opening prices are particularly volatile in the heavily institutional British market. We are unable to explain this result fully, but note that trading volume at the open is low for London.[41] The lower volume indicates that institutional investors in London tend to avoid trading at the open. While institutional traders in the United States may also tend to avoid the open, retail trading interest in the United States (and in continental Europe) provides ample volume at the open and, in so doing, may lead to better price discovery. Additionally, Werner and Kleidon[42] suggest that the extensive trading of London stocks in the United States alters their trading behavior in the United Kingdom.

In establishing these findings, we have not focused on the actual *levels* of volatility in the various markets studied. Intermarket differences in underlying volatility levels could be attributed to the different characteristics of the stocks traded in the various markets, to different inherent levels of risk and uncertainty in the various countries in which the shares are traded, and possibly to other factors that were not taken into account by the analysis and that have little to do with market structure per se. Rather, the key volatility measures are expressed in *relative* terms (i.e., relative to midday volatility). Doing so provides a cleaner picture of the volatility patterns over the course of a trading day, across measurement intervals of differing length, and across different market structures.

The five exchanges considered represent very different market structures. The NYSE is an order-driven market that includes market makers (each of the listed companies is allocated to a single specialist). Nasdaq in the year 2000 (the test year for the study) had predominantly a dealer market structure (albeit with some characteristics traditionally associated with order-driven markets). Paris, London, and Frankfurt use automated (i.e., not floor-based) order-driven trading platforms.[43] Given the architectural diversity of the trading systems and the similarity of the findings, accentuated volatility, especially at the open, cannot simply be ascribed to a specialist taking into account his or her own inventory considerations, or to order flow being fragmented in a competitive dealer market, or to the attributes of an electronic platform.

A number of questions concerning market quality/efficiency on both sides of the Atlantic can be raised in light of the magnitude of the observed volatility relationships. Volatility spikes ranged from 76 percent to 212 percent for the first half hour of trading, and volatility spikes at the close ranged up to 64 percent. What accounts for this? At each opening, information that has been released since the previous close must be incorporated into prices. In the process, conflicting opinions held by traders have to be resolved quickly, in an orderly manner, and with a high degree of accuracy. Not surprisingly, opens are typically periods of serious buy-sell imbalances that result in transaction prices being imperfectly aligned with their consensus values.

It is not normally the case that extensive information is released at the close, and one would expect price discovery to be sharper after a full day of trading. The volatility spikes at the close, in part at least, result from the price pressures caused by agents cleaning up orders that must be completed within the day and from traders unwinding their positions to end the day flat.

One market structure innovation that could alleviate price pressure at the close is the closing call auction that has now been incorporated into each of the three European markets included in the study. Pagano and Schwartz[44] found that introduction of a closing call in the Paris market has resulted in more efficient price behavior, both in the closing call itself and in the last 15 minutes of the continuous market. They posit that availability of the closing call auction makes it safer toward the end of the continuous market for participants to be liquidity providers (i.e., to place limit orders) than to be liquidity demanders (i.e., to place market orders). This is because limit orders that do not execute in the continuous market can be rolled into the call. Consequently, following the introduction of the closing call, books became deeper in Paris and price volatility has been better controlled in its continuous market.

On the other hand, for the five markets included in the study, the first half-hour volatility measures show that the three European markets that open with fully electronic calls perform no better by this metric than the two U.S. markets that do not (the NYSE's call is not fully electronic, and Nasdaq, at the time of the study, had no formal opening procedure). However, as previously stated, one must be cautious about making cross-market comparisons. For the London market, as we have noted, the particularly sharp volatility accentuation at the open could be attributed primarily to its heavily institutional nature and to the fact that the U.K. institutional investors tend to shy away from trading at the open. In any event, we anticipate that, for any given market center, proper design and implementation of an electronic call would improve market quality, especially if it is structured to provide the appropriate incentives for participants to use it. Further investigation of the issue would be desirable.

Research into market quality could be extended in a number of other ways. The analysis should be applied to small-cap and mid-cap stocks, in addition to the large caps focused on in the findings presented here. Attention could also be given to the effect of preopening trading on first half-hour volatility. The trading behavior of institutional investors, and its effect on the intraday patterns of volatility and volume, needs to be examined. The relationship between volatility and trading volume should be revisited with reference to the intraday patterns discussed in this chapter. Of further interest would be an analysis of how the intraday volatility metric has evolved in recent years, a period that has seen extensive change in the structure of the equity markets. Of particular importance would be an examination of the effect that the conversion to decimals in the United States (completed in 2001) had on the U.S. markets; one might anticipate a volatility effect to the extent that introduction of the penny tick has affected the liquidity suppliers (market makers and limit order traders). Finally, matched samples and multivariate statistical techniques should be used so that meaningful cross-country comparisons can be derived from the intraday volatility metric.

One conclusion is clear, however. Market quality—the magnitude of trading costs and the accuracy of price discovery—is a complex, subtle subject. Much is not known about how best to measure it and, even more important, about how to control it through superior market design. In the next chapter, we turn to a consideration of market quality from the point of view of institutional investors. How best to cope with their large orders is one of the most difficult issues in market design. By focusing on this issue, we will be flying into the eye of the storm.

NOTES

1. Exchanges do, of course, sell their trade and quote data, and nonpayers are commonly denied immediate receipt. Further, the question of who owns the quotes (the trader whose order has established a price or the exchange to which the order has been sent) has been widely debated. In general, investors

who place limit orders that set prices and who submit market orders that trigger trades do so because of their own desire to trade, not because the information they are generating is valuable to others. For them, the value of the information to others is an externality (i.e., they are unaffected by the benefits conveyed to others, and consequently the order placers do not take the benefits to others into account when making their own decisions).

2. In return, the special liquidity providers receive direct compensation in the form of having their trading fees waved. In Germany, the companies pay directly for the service; in France they do not, but the companies make shares available to them. In France, "implicit" liquidity providers also improve market quality for the CAC 40 stocks. Here, their compensation is indirect; they earn the spread, but have no explicit privileges.

3. In the United States, the Brady Commission task force, which was established following the market crash on October 19, 1987, concluded that the only way panic could have been avoided on October 19 was by halting trading and reopening the market with a call.

4. Nevertheless, the crossing systems are using mid-spread values to price their crosses, and thus are indeed free-riding on the price discovery provided in the central market. If a crossing system gains a large enough share of the order flow, this free riding will undermine the very thing that it depends on—price discovery in the central marketplace that their customers can have confidence in.

5. Note that, in the United States, the ECNs are informationally linked even though they are separate venues. The informational linkages can offset some of the potential loss of price discovery due to competing venues.

6. For further discussion, see "Institutional Investment in the United Kingdom: A Review," by Paul Myner (the Myner Report), March 2001. Also see Robert A. Schwartz and Benn Steil, "Controlling Institutional Trading Costs: We Have Met the Enemy, and It Is Us," *Journal of Portfolio Management*, 2002.

7. This line of reasoning has been articulated in the United States by officials of the Nasdaq Stock Market.

8. Parts of this section have been adapted with permission from Schwartz, Byrne, and Colaninno, eds., *A Trading Desk's View of Market Quality*, Kluwer Academic Publishers, 2004, forthcoming, and Ozenbas, Schwartz, and Wood, "Volatility in U.S. and European Equity Markets: An Assessment of Market Quality," *International Finance*, Blackwell Publisher, volume 5, no. 3, winter 2002, pp. 437–461.

9. Also see I. Werner and A. Kleidon, "UK and US Trading of British Cross-Listed Stocks: An Intra-Day Analysis of Market Integration," *Review of Financial Studies* 9, 1996, pp. 619–664. Werner and Kleidon use 15-minute intervals, but for a different purpose than ours. They do not investigate intraday volatility as an inverse measure of quality and do not focus on the opening and closing periods of a trading day as moments of particular stress.

10. J. Hasbrouck and R. Schwartz, "Liquidity and Execution Costs in Equity Markets," *Journal of Portfolio Management*, spring 1988, pp. 10–16.

110   EQUITY MARKETS IN ACTION

11. T. Andersen, T. Bollerslev, A. Das, "Variance-Ratio Statistics and High-Frequency Data: Testing for Changes in Intraday Volatility Patterns," *Journal of Finance* 56, 2001, pp. 305–327.

12. Y. Amihud and H. Mendelson, "Trading Mechanisms and Stock Returns: an Empirical Investigation," *Journal of Finance* 42, 1987, pp. 533–555.

13. M. Gerety and H. Mulherin, "Price Formation on Stock Exchanges: The Evolution of Trading Within the Day," *Review of Financial Studies* 7, 1994, pp. 609–629.

14. This can be shown with the use of the following variance ratio equation (for more detail see Appendix A, "Prices and Returns," and Hasbrouck and Schwartz op. cit.:

$$\text{VR(m)} \equiv \frac{m \text{Var}[r_t(1)]}{\text{Var}(r_t(m))} = \left[1 + 2 \sum_{k=1}^{m-1} \left(\frac{m-k}{m} \right) \rho(k) \right]^{-1}$$

where the numerator on the left-hand side is the short-period variance times m, the denominator on the left-hand side is the long-period variance, and m is the ratio of the long-period differencing interval to the short-period differencing interval. The right-hand side is the inverse of unity plus two times the summation of autocorrelation factors. The formula shows that, if the autocorrelation factors are predominantly positive (negative), short-term volatility is dampened (accentuated) relative to long-term volatility.

15. Positive and negative correlation can coexist for two reasons. First, in some periods (perhaps when there is little news), returns may be dominated by reversal behavior (e.g., the bid-ask bounce), while in some other periods (perhaps following the advent of new information) trending might predominate. Second, first-order correlation that is positive can coexist with higher orders of correlation that are negative (e.g., when a trend is followed by one reversal and then a trend in the opposite direction).

16. Alternatively stated, with negative first-order autocorrelation alone, short-period volatility is accentuated, and with positive first-order autocorrelation alone, short-period volatility is dampened. If prices tend to run in one direction and then reverse, positive first-order autocorrelation coexists along with higher orders of correlation that are negative, and the accentuation of short-period volatility is more effectively captured using noncontiguous returns.

17. Price volatility at the open is accentuated by the difficulty of finding appropriate share values after the overnight trading halt, while price volatility is accentuated in the last half hour of trading, primarily because traders come under increasing pressure to close out their positions as the overnight halt draws near. With respect to both periods, a more efficient market mechanism would facilitate order interaction and price determination, and thus mitigate volatility at these critical times in the trading day.

18. On the other hand, inefficient price discovery may generate excessive trading. For discussion and further references see Barber and Odean (2000).

19. By *zero-sum game*, we mean that the trading costs (e.g., bid-ask spread and market impact costs) paid by one participant (generally the liquidity demander) are another participant's returns (generally the liquidity supplier). We do not mean to imply that both participants in a trade cannot mutually benefit. On the contrary, it is well established in economics that the gains of trade involve consumer surplus on the buyer side and producer surplus on the seller side. In a security transaction between a natural buyer and a natural seller, the surplus that each participant receives from a trade is attributable to the portfolio rebalancing that the participant wishes to achieve for longer-run investment purposes.

20. We discuss this further in Chapter 6, "Order-Driven Markets." Also see Handa and Schwartz, "Limit Order Trading," *Journal of Finance*, 1996, pp. 1835–1861.

21. See Neil Weinberg, "Fear, Greed and Technology," *Forbes Magazine*, May 15, 2000.

22. We discuss this further in Chapter 2, "From Information to Prices." Academic studies that provide theoretical justification for the use of technical analysis include Blume, Easley, and O'Hara ("Market Statistics and Technical Analysis: The Role of Volume," *Journal of Finance*, vol. 49, no. 1, 1994, pp. 153–181), and those that provide empirical support include Lo, Mamaysky, and Wang ("Foundations of Technical Analysis: Computational Algorithms, Statistical Inference, and Empirical Implementation," *Journal of Finance* 55, 2000, pp. 1705–1770).

23. The relationship between short-term volatility and trading costs has been extensively analyzed in the microstructure literature. Schwartz and Whitcomb ("The Time-Variance Relationship: Evidence on Autocorrelation in Common Stock Returns," with David Whitcomb, *Journal of Finance*, 1977, pp. 41–55) and Lo and MacKinlay ("Stock Market Prices Do Not Follow Random Walks: Evidence from a Simple Specification Test," *Review of Financial Studies* 1, 1988, pp. 41–66) use variance analysis to establish that short-term volatility is accentuated compared to longer-term volatility. Hasbrouck and Schwartz ("Liquidity and Execution Costs in Equity Markets," *Journal of Portfolio Management*, spring 1988, pp. 10–16), Stoll ("Friction," *Journal of Finance* 4, 2000, pp. 1479–1515), Bessembinder and Rath ("Trading Costs and Return Volatility: Evidence from Exchange Listings," working paper, University of Utah, 2002), and Ozenbas, Schwartz, and Wood ("Volatility in U.S. and European Equity Markets: An Assessment of Market Quality," *International Finance*, vol. 5, no. 3, winter 2002, pp. 437–461) are some of the studies that find evidence of a link between accentuated volatility and heightened transaction costs. Werner and Kleidon ("UK and US Trading of British Cross-Listed Stocks: An Intra-Day Analysis of Market Integration," *Review of Financial Studies* 9, 1998, pp. 619–664) have analyzed intraday volatility patterns for the NYSE and London cross-listed stocks to assess the extent to which price discovery is integrated across markets. In their study of the U.S. Treasury market, Fleming and Remolina ("Price Formation and Liquidity in the U.S. Treasury Market: The Response to Public Information," *Journal of Finance* 54, 1999, pp. 1901–1915) have further underscored the difficulty of achieving accurate price discovery by demonstrating that protracted surges in intraday volatility attend the release of major macroeconomic news announcements.

24. For further discussion, see Appendix A, "Prices and Returns."

25. "Support and resistance levels" is part of the terminology of technical analysis. A support (resistance) level denotes a lower (higher) reflecting barrier that price is not apt to penetrate in the absence of informational change.

26. The level of volatility resulting from price discovery will vary across markets (and stocks) depending upon the design and regulation of a market, as well as upon the skill of its traders.

27. See Cohen, Maier, Schwartz, and Whitcomb for an analysis of the existence of bid-ask spreads in an order-driven market and theoretical proof that, in this environment, spreads exist because trading is not a frictionless process.

28. The procedure of dividing by the relative length of the differencing interval holds when logarithmic returns are used to compute a variance. If the standard deviation of logarithmic returns is being taken to measure volatility, then the square root of the differencing interval should be used.

29. Ozenbas, Schwartz, and Wood, op. cit. The sample stocks are those that make up the major index for each of the countries: the S&P 100, the Nasdaq 100, the CAC 40, the DAX 30, and the FTSE 100. We use the TAQ database of the New York Stock Exchange, the BDM database of Euronext Paris, the Transaction Data Service database of the London Stock Exchange, and Deutsche Börse's Transactions Database.

30. We have stated that variance is normalized by dividing by the length of the measurement interval. Equivalently, the square root of the measurement interval is used to normalize the standard deviation of logarithmic returns.

31. M. Fleming and E. Remolina, "Price Formation and Liquidity in the U.S. Treasury Market: The Response to Public Information," *Journal of Finance* 54, 1999, pp. 1901–1915.

32. The interval from the close of the continuous market to the closing call was treated as if it were another half-hour period. The treatment is conservative in that the actual time to the closing call is roughly five minutes.

33. London introduced its closing call on May 30, 2000.

34. The 14 percent figure is not shown in Exhibit 4.5.

35. This is consistent with Pagano and Schwartz's finding that the introduction of the closing call by Euronext Paris in 1996 (thinner stocks) and 1998 (extended to all stocks) did increase the quality of price determination in that market. See M. Pagano and R. Schwartz, "A Closing Call's Impact on Market Quality at Euronext Paris," *Journal of Financial Economics* 68, 2003, pp. 439–484.

36. Interestingly, when for the second period the analysis is extended to the 8:00 P.M. close, open-to-close volatility increases to 1.07.

37. The authors accounted for stock splits and dividends by eliminating the extreme results that stem from such events. The price series could, of course, be adjusted for cash and stock dividends and for stock splits, but the adjustment factors were not available to the authors for the study.

38. This decline is more pronounced (and has higher statistical significance) for the European markets.

39. It is further interesting to note that all of the one-week and two-week estimates for the European exchanges are less than 1 and that some of these deviations are statistically significant. This means that the adjusted volatility of these longer-period returns is less-than-average midday volatility, and this can be taken as evidence of more accentuated midday reversal behavior and/or more protracted short-term trending in the European markets.

40. This section is adapted from Ozenbas, Schwartz, and Wood, op. cit.

41. Volume data are presented in D. Ozenbas, "Intra-Day Price Volatility: A Reflection of Trading Friction," Ph.D. dissertation, August 28, 2002.

42. I. Werner and A. Kleidon, "UK and US Trading of British Cross-Listed Stocks: An Intra-Day Analysis of Market Integration," *Review of Financial Studies* 9, 1996, pp. 619–664.

43. Frankfurt still has a trading floor, although much of the activity has migrated to its electronic platform, Xetra. Trading on the floor starts at 9:00 A.M., the same time the electronic market opens, and both venues open with a call auction. Because the call is electronic on the electronic platform but not on the floor, it is possible for the floor traders to see the opening price on Xetra, but prices set on the floor openings are not known at the time of the Xetra call.

44. M. Pagano and R. Schwartz, "A Closing Call's Impact on Market Quality at Euronext Paris," *Journal of Financial Economics* 68, 2003, pp. 439–484.

CHAPTER 5

Institutional Order Flow

For roughly two decades, equity markets on both sides of the Atlantic have been experiencing remarkable technological developments, major shifts in their regulatory environments, and the growth of institutional investing. All of the major market centers in Europe now have fully electronic trading platforms. Currently, we are entering an era of global markets. In recent years, the pace of change has accelerated. This might leave us all breathless, but is further development still needed? Yes. The major problem is that market structure does not cater adequately to the needs of institutional customers. An array of commonly debated issues, such as transparency, consolidation, connectivity, the timeliness of executions, and the provision of reasonable liquidity at reasonable cost, should all be dealt with specifically in the context of institutional investors.

Starting in the 1970s, a time when the markets were far less dominated by institutional order flow than they are today, and continuing through to the current period, a major regulatory objective in the United States has been the protection of retail investors.[1] The belief has been that retail investors need to be protected from the presumably more knowledgeable and powerful institutional investors. Academic interest in security market microstructure, which dates back to the 1970s as well, has also had a

Major portions of this chapter have been adapted with permission from Schwartz and Steil, "Controlling Institutional Trading Costs: We Have Met the Enemy, and It Is Us," *Journal of Portfolio Management*, vol. 28, no. 3, spring 2002, pp. 39–49, and Schwartz and Wood, "Best Execution: A Candid Analysis," *Journal of Portfolio Management*, vol. 29, no. 4, summer 2003, pp. 37–48.

strong focus on retail order flow. In part, this is because an environment consisting of a large number of small (atomistic) competitors is far more easily modeled than one where some customers have market power.

Consequently, the debates have largely centered on retail investors, and a market structure has evolved that deals far more effectively with retail than with institutional order flow. One sell side participant, Natan Tiefenbrun of Instinet, stated this outright: "These (order handling) rules were a good thing for the retail investor. But I do not think that the SEC put serious thought into how the rules would affect the institutional community." An institutional investor, Chris Killeen of TIAA/Cref, put it this way: "Our problem is that we have these institutional sized orders in a market that has been designed for retail investors. . . . I search for liquidity because the market is not built for trades of hundreds of thousands of shares."[2]

Even from the point of view of the retail customers, it is advisable to pay more attention to the needs of the institutional investors. Their needs cannot be appropriately met if institutional customers cannot get their orders executed at reasonable prices. All market participants face the same quotes and transaction prices, and all suffer the consequences of destabilized prices. If large orders have bigger price impact, then the *location* of the quotes will be less stable for the retail customers.

Handling huge orders will forever be complex, and an ideal system may never be implemented. But we are far from perfection. Much is not known about how best to handle the big orders. For a major market center, vested interests and technological inertia stymie the introduction of meaningful design change. Change can also come from the outside, but any new trading venue faces the daunting challenge of achieving critical-mass order flow. Further, as we discuss in the last section of this chapter, the institutions themselves share responsibility for the high trading costs they incur. Portfolio managers often have insufficient knowledge of the trading process, which makes it more difficult for them to evaluate how well their trading desks are handling their orders. More critically, trading costs are inflated because of the buy side's practice of using commissions to pay for research, computer systems, and various other services that they have outsourced. Because trade execution is only part of a bundle of services, institutional orders are not necessarily routed to the brokers who will give the best trade execution services.

INSTITUTIONAL ORDER SIZE

Institutional orders are commonly huge, because many of the institutions are enormous. This is not a new phenomenon. According to *Business*

Week, December 25, 1995, "With $367 billion in assets under management, Fidelity holds, at one time or another, nearly every publicly traded stock. As of September 30, Fidelity owned 5% or more of 863 outfits and 10% or more of 330 more companies."

As of August 11, 2003, the two largest U.S. funds ranked by net assets were the Vanguard 500 Index fund ($63.19 billion), and Fidelity Magellan ($61.94 billion). The big players have big holdings of individual stocks. For instance, on August 11, 2003, Vanguard 500 Index Fund had 3.28 percent of its portfolio ($2.07 billion) in Microsoft. This investment translated into 80.58 million Microsoft shares and 0.75 percent of Microsoft's market cap. Also on that date, Fidelity Magellan had 4.02 percent ($2.60 billion) of its funds invested in Citigroup. This investment represented 58.38 million Citigroup shares and 1.13 percent of Citigroup's market cap.

Institutional trading volume is big relative to aggregate market volume. The numbers are not readily come by, but Becker and Angstadt have estimated that, in 1994, institutional trading accounted for between 75 and 80 percent of NYSE volume.[3]

Institutional orders are large. Wagner has estimated that about 80 percent of U.S. institutional orders exceed half of the relevant stock's average daily trading volume.[4] Chan and Lakonishok (1995) find that only about 20 percent of the value of institutional buy orders is completed within a day, and less than half within four days. Phinney and Wagner have illustrated the nature of a large trade with a particularly insightful example:[5]

> *A client provided us with the complete trading records for a trade in Oracle that was made on August 15th, 2002. A momentum manager had sent a 1.8 million share buy order for Oracle to his trading desk, and the process unfolded as follows. The order was fed to the Bloomberg B-trade automated trading system. Trading began at 9:53 in the morning and the order was completely executed within 51 minutes. It required over 1000 separate executions to complete that order. The average execution size was 1700 shares. The single largest execution was 64,000 shares. That large trade occurred in a cluster of rapid executions when almost 190,000 shares were executed in less than one minute. The smallest execution in the block was for 13 shares. 17% of the executions were for 100 shares or less, and 44% of that total order was executed in pieces of less than 1000 shares. In total, 61% of the shares were executed in pieces less than 1000 shares per execution. There were up to 153 executions per minute.*
>
> *We can put some context around this trade by looking at Oracle trading on that day. The total share volume for the day was 59 million shares. Thus this particular trade represented less than 3% of*

total volume. After the trading was completed for the block, the price of Oracle rose to $11.46. In trading parlance, this would be referred to as a "DFT," otherwise known as a "Damn Fine Trade."

Let us take a peak at exactly why it was a DFT. First, the delay cost, *computed as the difference between the opening price and the price of the first trade done, was 8 cents. The* market impact, *computed as the average execution price less the first trade price was only 7 cents per share. The* captured value *for that particular trade for that day of almost 45 cents represents the difference between the closing price and the average execution price. Thus, over the very short term, it looks like a most successful trade in terms of captured value versus cost of acquiring. It was a success from the perspective of the broker, the trade desk and especially the portfolio manager.*

It is common for institutions to break their orders into smaller tranches that are fed to the market over an extended period of time. However, when they do, they run the risk of being front-run on the one hand and of incurring opportunity cost on the other. This slice-and-dice procedure can be achieved in a different way on Euronext and Xetra, as the order books of these European markets accept what is known as *iceberg orders* (London does not have this order type). With an iceberg order, only a small part of an order is shown in the exchange's open limit order book, while the larger part is hidden. As executions are realized, successive parts of the iceberg order are entered in the open book. Institutions can also trade directly with each other.

Institutions attempt to minimize their trading costs by revealing minimal information about their trading intentions to the market. The big traders want more than anonymity—they want virtual invisibility. However, a black-box approach does not work, either, because participants have no way of knowing what market impact their orders will have. In other words, while the individual institutions do not want their own orders to be seen, all want very much to see the orders of everyone else.

As the elephants tiptoe into the continuous market to trade, their orders can be broadly disruptive. The market impact they cause accentuates intraday price volatility, and their unexecuted orders create market overhang that sets the stage for momentum trading. The momentum trading, in turn, further undermines price discovery. This is widely disruptive, for both retail investors in particular and the broad market in general. Developing systems to deal effectively with institutional order flow while at the same time achieving a reasonable integration of institutional and retail order flow represents a formidable challenge for market design. Unfortunately, problems involved in handling huge institutional orders are more easily recognized than they are solved.

PRICE AND QUANTITY DISCOVERY

A well-functioning equity market should provide reasonable price and quantity discovery for all participants. The task is not simple. One reason is that institutional investors are reluctant to participate actively in price discovery. Instead, as we have noted, they seek invisibility in the marketplace. As a consequence, they hold back orders, even at prices that would be market-clearing values.

Institutional customers have several reasons to avoid active participation in price discovery. For one thing, unlike retail customers, who typically do not give the possibility much thought, large traders know that their orders can impact market prices.[6] As Bruce Turner, who at the time was at Nasdaq, explained, "We are all playing poker, and we all keep our cards close to our chests." Andy Brooks of T. Rowe Price put it this way: "How confident are you of what you really think is going on in terms of supply and demand that has not come to the market? I am referring to the latent trading interest of those who are just looking. You know, those people who are staying out of the opening and who might show up at 10:30."[7]

No buy side equity trader wants to purchase 30,000 shares of a stock at $50 and then see price drop to $49.75 on a 500-share sell order. If price is not maintained, as Brooks has pointed out, "they could immediately look stupid."[8] Not looking stupid is a compelling reason for institutions to avoid playing a leadership role with respect to price discovery. Consequently, many institutional investors shy away from active price discovery and, collectively, the retail order flow has a disproportionate effect on price determination. If institutional and retail demands are different (which is generally the case), equilibrium values cannot be properly discovered, and quantity discovery is perturbed.

What can be done to ensure better price and quantity discovery for the broad market? The integration of small (retail) and large (institutional) orders is key. That integration serves the interests of both retail and institutional customers.

To some extent, however, separate order handling may be unavoidable. This is certainly the case, for example, in the NYSE's trading environment. Namely, small retail orders are typically sent electronically by SuperDot to specialist posts, and large orders are commonly worked by floor brokers on a *not-held* basis or are negotiated in the upstairs institutional market.[9] These procedures, however, are coordinated and the exchange's order flow is reasonably well integrated.[10] This is of critical importance because price discovery should reflect the desires of the broad market to hold shares of a stock.

Integration of retail and institutional order flow does not imply that the needs of retail customers are sacrificed to the needs of institutional customers. The quotes and transaction prices established in the market apply to all participants. All participants are effectively in the same boat. As we have noted, if prices are destabilized for one, they are destabilized for all. Consider, for instance, the consequence of the reductions on the NYSE and Nasdaq of the minimum price variation from an eighth to a sixteenth in 1997 and then, in 2000 and 2001, to a penny. The reductions were instituted with the aim of narrowing spreads for retail customers. Spreads have tightened, but the liquidity available for institutional-sized orders has also fallen. Consequently, the *location* of the quotes has become less stable for the broad market. The bottom line is, when the institutions cannot get their orders executed at reasonable prices, retail customers are also hurt.

INTERACTION OF LARGE ORDERS

We next consider a critical issue concerning the interaction of large institutional orders: the extent to which institutional order flow is two-sided. How commonly are some institutions seeking to buy shares at times when others are looking to sell?

If only news triggers institutional order flow, and if portfolio managers all interpret information identically, institutional order flow would be one-sided. Bullish news would send all of the big players to the market as buyers, and bearish news would send them all to the market as sellers.

But institutional investors seek to trade for a variety of reasons. Liquidity motives (cash inflows and cash outflows) is one of them. The need to track an index is another. Hedge funds seek to exploit momentum moves and to arbitrage price discrepancies. Most important, institutional investors (much like retail customers) interpret news differently and have different opinions about share valuations. In other words, the world of investing is characterized by divergent expectations, as discussed in Chapter 2, "From Information to Prices." These realities would all lead to two-sided institutional order flow.

Sarkar, Schwartz, and Wolf[11] have studied the two-sidedness of institutional order flow. They have analyzed the arrival of large orders in half-hour trading intervals during three months in 2003. Their (matched) sample included 41 large-cap NYSE issues and 41 large-cap Nasdaq issues. Each trade in each of the intervals was identified as either a buy trade or a sell trade. It was identified as a buy trade if the transaction price was either at the offer or closer to the offer than to the bid. Similarly, it was identified as a sell trade if the transaction price was either at the bid or closer to the bid than to the offer.[12] If markets are predominantly one-sided, one would expect to see predominantly buy trades or predominantly sell trades within each of the half-hour intervals. If markets are predominantly two-sided, buy and sell trades would both be observed in half-hour intervals.

Sarkar, Schwartz, and Wolf found that institutional order flow is commonly two-sided. Further, they observed that institutional trades tend to cluster in time. An important implication follows from each observation.

- Because the order flow is two-sided, institutions can potentially provide liquidity to each other if the market structure allows for it. The trick is for the big traders to find each other.
- The fact that institutional trades cluster in time suggests that the trades are portable in time. Portability indicates that institutions time their orders (i.e., that they use trading tactics when submitting their orders). Apparently, something must occur to make the trades happen. Further, the natural clustering that occurred in the continuous market suggests that institutions would be willing to wait to meet each other in a multi-lateral call auction.

INSTITUTIONAL TRADING NEEDS

Our discussion in this section focuses on institutional investor attitudes toward volatility, transparency, consolidation of order flow and information, and immediacy.

Volatility

In our consideration of volatility in Chapter 4, "What We Want from Our Markets," we noted that, over reasonably long periods of time (e.g., a week or more), share prices change largely in response to changes in the fundamental determinants of share value. Over relatively brief intervals (e.g., intraday), volatility is accentuated and, intraday, the accentuation is most pronounced in the first half hour and the last half hour of trading, times when markets, on a daily basis, are under particular stress.[13] The accentuation can be attributed to trading costs (e.g., the bid-ask spread and market impact) and to the dynamic process of price discovery. The complexities of price discovery at market openings, in particular, appear to account for the daily opening half-hour volatility spike.

With the exception of some hedge funds, few buy side traders are able to profit from the volatility accentuation. On the contrary, they find it challenging to cope with. As Andy Brooks stated at the 2002 Baruch conference, "Intra-day volatility is really making our jobs very difficult. It is making it very hard to trade, and our orders are indeed large." He went on to add, ". . . intra-day GE's volatility is 5%. Knowing this, do I want to have completed my 100,000-share order at 9:37? I had better have a pretty strong feeling to do so."[14]

Seth Merrin of Liquidnet explained intraday volatility as follows: "The problem is that because institutions hold their orders so close to the vest, the supply and demand of the institutions is not represented on the exchanges. Only retail supply and demand is represented. This leads to a tremendous amount of volatility because, ultimately, the institutional demand goes against the retail supply. You are bumping two different sizes together. There has to be volatility. And it is this volatility that leads to a 47 cents cost per share, on average, every time these big guys go into the market."[15]

Transparency

A commonly discussed attribute of a market is the degree to which it is transparent. But a conundrum exists with regard to transparency. Bruce Turner stated it as, "Everyone wants to see the liquidity, but no one is actually going to put his or her order out there. Everyone wants markets to be transparent, but nobody wants anyone else to know what they themselves want to do."[16] Seth Merrin described the problem as follows:[17]

The way that our markets are structured today, going out and searching for liquidity means giving up information. As far as I can see, two major factors move market prices against the institutions. Number one is information dissemination. A broker gets an order and tries to find the natural other side. This should be good for an institution because presumably there would be less market impact. So the broker calls up other institutions, advertises on AutEx, and/or sends out FIX indications of interest. These are nice gadgets. The problem is, according to the New York Stock Exchange (I don't have the figures on Nasdaq), the process works only about 30% of the time, and that 30% is when the order is crossed upstairs. The other 70% of the time, the procedure works to the disadvantage of the institution by informing the rest of the marketplace that there is a large buyer or seller out there. The other major market mover is size disparity. The average order size for institutions is now well over 250,000 shares. At the same time, average execution size is 670 shares for

New York, 605 shares for Nasdaq, and 300 shares for the ECNs. Whenever you have that kind of size disparity, there will be market movement. There is no way to fill that square hole with that round peg. . . . Our current market structure is no longer working for institutional participants.

Research that leads institutional traders to trade is pilfered by day traders, hedge funds, market makers, and others who undertake no research on their own, but who carefully study the tape for signs of latent trading interest.[18] Consequently, large institutions that trade on the basis of research must seek to cover their footsteps. To do so, the big players need virtual invisibility. To get it, they keep large parts of their orders hidden, and, in good part, their demand to trade remains latent. It will never be possible to force them to disclose their intentions fully. Nevertheless, as institutions slowly meter trades into the market, they leave tracks that cannot be totally obscured from prying eyes. The result is that prices move ahead of institutional trading. The only viable answer is for a market structure to develop within which institutional participants will feel it safe to show their hand. Their latent demand should be brought in from the cold.

Consolidation of Order Flow and Information

Consolidation typically refers to the geographic pooling of order flow in one market center. The term also refers to the pooling of information. With regard to both, consolidation is desirable. It increases order interaction, concentrates liquidity, and sharpens the accuracy of price discovery. A marketplace made up of multiple trading facilities is effectively consolidated if:

- Information in the separate books is widely available.
- Access to the various trading facilities is widely available and fast.
- Arbitrageurs are present.

Increasingly, information technology, order routing systems, and smart order management systems are making this possible. When these three conditions are met, the major missing item in the "spatially fragmented" environment is the ability to impose a secondary priority rule of order execution (such as time priority) across all orders in all markets.

Nevertheless, problems concerning fragmentation have increased in the current environment in the United States. The Securities and Exchange Commission (SEC) has paid particular attention to them in two releases. In a February 23, 2000, release on Market Fragmentation, the commission expressed the concern that "customer limit orders and dealer quotes may be isolated from full interaction with other buying and selling interest in today's markets."[19] In a December 10, 1999, release on the Regulation of Market Information Fees and Revenues, the commission emphasized that retail investors must have access to market information, that the information must be consolidated, and that transparency must be enhanced.[20]

But information cannot be consolidated and transparency enhanced if, because of inadequate market structure, large orders are being chopped into tiny pieces for sequential execution over extended periods of time in a multiplicity of trading vehicles. Only if trading interests are revealed can information be consolidated, and only good market structure, not regulation, can turn latent demand into openly expressed interests to trade.

It boils down to this. *Spatial* fragmentation is not the only serious aspect of the consolidation problem. The other major concern is the *temporal* fragmentation of order flow. Temporal fragmentation occurs because, in a continuous trading environment, orders can fail to meet simply because they arrive at the market at different moments in time. The temporal dimension is particularly troublesome in the current environment because of the prevalence with which institutional investors break their large orders into smaller tranches. As a consequence of this slicing and dicing (some are now using the term *shredding*), quantity discovery is in disarray, price discovery is perturbed, and intraday price volatility is inflated.

Temporal fracturing of the order flow can be countered with the use of periodic call auction trading, a facility that we consider in Chapter 6, "Order-Driven Markets."[21] Calls could be held several times a day: at the open, at the close, and perhaps multiple times in between. Because they pool liquidity temporally, calls facilitate trading institutional-sized orders. With them, institutions could, in fact, get the job done more quickly.

For an intraday call to be successful, participants would have to choose to wait for their orders to be executed. Will they? This depends on their demand to trade with immediacy, the topic to which we next turn.

Immediacy

Our continuous trading systems are designed to provide immediacy. For large-cap stocks at least, they deliver it for retail customers. But the story is different for institutional customers. As we have noted, a large institution typically slices its orders into smaller tranches, which it submits to the market over an extended period of time (commonly up to a day or even several days). The process, as described by Harold Bradley of American Century Asset Management, works as follows: "Orders travel from investor to specialist with successively smaller order amounts passing from trader to trader within this sort of 'bucket brigade.' . . . After an investor gives the institutional trader 500,000 shares to trade, that institutional trader gives the sales trader 250,000 shares to trade. The sales trader gives the upstairs trader 125,000 shares to trade, and the upstairs trader, through the floor broker, tells the specialist to post 25,000 shares. With such a system, no wonder traders believe that trading is a win-lose function."[22]

Four studies of equity trading practices conducted in the second half of the 1990s found that institutions commonly do not have a non-trading-related reason to trade quickly and that they do not, in fact, receive immediacy when they go to the market to trade: Economides and Schwartz's survey of U.S. investors; Schwartz and Steil's survey of British and Continental European investors; Demarchi and S. Thomas's survey of French investors; and Douglas and C. Thomas's survey of Australian investors.[23]

The survey findings for very different populations portray a remarkably consistent picture. Across the board, many buy side traders are typically given more than a day by their portfolio managers to work a large order, they frequently delay their trades in an attempt to lower trading costs, they commonly break up their large orders, and they regularly take more than a day to execute all the pieces of their large orders.

Nevertheless, large investors also seek rapid implementation of their portfolio decisions, and it is interesting to know why. We return to this important question later in the chapter (see the section, "Controlling Institutional Trading Costs"). At this point, let's simply consider two quotes that suggest a reason. According to Seth Merrin:[24]

> *This is the way the market structure works. You pick up the phone and call a broker. You hang up the phone and have lost all control over where that information goes. The broker is obviously incented to try and find the other side. The broker uses a shotgun approach by making phone calls, advertising on AutEx, and sending FIX indications of interest to pretty much anybody who would accept them. As a result, with most of the orders that you give to traditional brokers, a lot of information runs away from you.*

According to Sanjiv Gupta of Bloomberg Tradebook:[25]

> *To not know what has happened to your order is trouble. You look up at the screen and see a 50,000 share offer, you route your order, and you may even get there first. Then, in the auction, the specialist interacts with the crowd, and you haven't heard back, and then you still haven't heard back. Thirty seconds later, you see the quote move, and suddenly the specialist bid is a penny above your limit price. And you haven't got an execution yet. These are the problems.*

We conclude that institutional customers do demand immediacy, but for a poor reason. As they approach a market to trade, prices start to run away from them because of information leakage. This problem reflects a market's inability to meet institutional investors' trading needs.

BEST EXECUTION

Best execution is a hot topic.[26] Simply stated, a best-execution obligation refers to the responsibility of a broker-dealer intermediary or asset manager to execute customer orders at the best possible price with minimum broker-dealer intervention. The concept was set forth in the United States as a regulatory obligation in the Congressional Securities Acts Amendments of 1975. At that time, before the dramatic growth of the institutional presence, the U.S. Congress fashioned the best-execution obligation with a primary focus on retail orders.

The retail focus also characterizes the regulatory approach taken by the Financial Services Authority in London. In its Discussion Paper, the Financial Services Authority states, ". . . when dealing in securities traded on the Stock Exchange Electronic Trading System ('SETS'), to meet the best execution requirement, firms should achieve a price (whether on SETS or an alternative execution venue) which at least matches the best price available on SETS."[27] The statement is retail-oriented because only small orders can predictably execute fully at the best bid or offer.

The best execution obligation has been extended to institutional orders in recent years. For three reasons in particular, the extension is extraordinarily difficult to implement. First, execution quality depends on an array of trade characteristics. In addition to price, institutional investors also care about speed of execution, certainty of execution, and anonymity. As we have just discussed, immediacy matters largely because the mere knowledge that an order is being brought to market can move market prices.[28] The institutional investor faces a trade-off between (1) transacting with certainty at a current market price and (2) risking nonexecution in an attempt to get a better price (e.g., by placing a limit order). Anonymity (and, even more, invisibility) is required to contain market impact costs. The importance of each of these characteristics depends on the needs of the individual trader, the attributes of the specific stock being traded, and the motive for trading (e.g., information or liquidity reasons). Clearly, "one size does not fit all" is a reality that makes an objective definition of best execution very difficult to come by.[29]

A second reason why best execution is not subject to simple definition is that institutional customers typically break up their orders for execution over a series of trades over an extended period of time. As previously noted in this chapter, Wayne Wagner has reported that 80 percent of institutional orders are larger than half of a stock's average daily trading volume.[30] It is clear that the big funds are forced to reduce their trading interest to a size that markets can accommodate. That is, because of the difficulty of integrating large orders into a predominantly retail order flow, they slice and dice their orders. Consequently, best execution cannot simply be defined with regard to a snapshot picture of prices that are available at any given moment in time. Rather, it must include the optimal timing of orders over a series of trades. If a snapshot assessment is difficult, an assessment of a sequence of trades is close to impossible. What is needed is a benchmark, such as the volume weighted average price (VWAP), against which to assess a realized sequence of executions. Unfortunately, as we discuss subsequently, VWAP is a poor benchmark, and a good alternative is not readily available.

Third, a best-execution obligation cannot be reasonably imposed in any market where the structure is not working well for institutional investors. As we have stressed, today's markets are geared to accommodate retail-sized trades averaging less than 1,000 shares per execution, and the big traders are trying to fit their large pegs into these tiny holes. Moreover, the belief is widespread that the pegs are growing larger while the holes are shrinking. Because of the size and complexity of the job they are trying to accomplish, larger traders expect to incur higher transaction costs. The bottom line is, market centers share the best execution responsibility.

The responsibility for excessive trading costs also lies with the buy side participants themselves. This is because their focus on minimizing trading costs is undermined by soft-dollar arrangements. In the words of Harold Bradley, "Clearly, soft dollar agreements play an important role in the execution decision and are often in direct conflict with an investment firm's fiduciary duty to the client."[31] As we discuss further in the next section of this chapter, the problem is that, through soft-dollar arrangements, asset managers outsource research, computer systems, and other support services to the sell side and use client assets as payments.

Hopefully, with the increased attention currently being given to best-execution procedures and to the measurement and containment of transaction costs, the industry will be weaned from its soft-dollar practices. Theodore Aronson of Aronson + Johnson + Ortiz is optimistic that this will be the case. Referring to the Association for Investment Management and Research's (AIMR) task force on best-execution guidelines, Aronson stated, "It will change things significantly. For the first time in twenty seven years, there will be a significant decrease in the use of soft dollars, in the related sins of directed trading, and all that sort of stuff."[32]

Best Execution and Transaction Cost Analysis

Recent developments in computer technology, analytic skills, and data availability have facilitated transaction cost analysis and order management. An ability to quantify transaction costs and to use smart order routing systems, however, does not necessarily allow one to quantify and to obtain best execution. Transaction costs are typically measured ex post (i.e., after the trade), and smart order routing systems can only attempt to control transaction costs. Best execution depends on knowing ex ante (i.e., before the trade) what execution costs will be and, if taken literally, means that the very best of all possible trades has been made.

Best execution is a broader concept than transaction cost analysis. A best execution obligation carries with it a fiduciary responsibility. The AIMR report states:[33]

> *When one looks closely at the chain of responsibility as trades go from the idea to completion stage, it can be seen that responsibility for securing best execution is shared by many. These responsibilities can be thought of as being hierarchical: investment management traders operate within parameters established by managers, brokers follow instructions specified by investment management traders, and exchanges execute their procedures according to the submissions of brokers.*

We address issues concerning best execution, not transaction cost analysis per se. We underscore the virtual impossibility of quantifying best execution, and we reiterate that the responsibility for delivering it is shared with the exchanges and other providers of trading services.

Measurement Problems

Let us look more closely at the difficulties encountered when trying to apply the concept of best execution. We start by taking a simplistic view. Assume a market characterized by a sizable number of small, priced orders, and for a moment focus myopically on a single point in time when an incoming order arrives and triggers a trade. In this environment, best execution means that the incoming order executes at the best counterpart price available (i.e., that a sell order transacts at the highest posted bid and that a buy order transacts at the lowest posted offer). If all orders are consolidated on a single book, best execution is assured by the price priority rule of order execution (i.e., that the most aggressively priced orders trade first). If the marketplace is geographically fragmented, best execution requires that a newly arriving customer can, through intermarket linkages and/or integrated quotation displays, find and execute against the most aggressive counterpart quote in the broader market.

In the situation just described, a snapshot is taken to determine whether a participant has received best execution. The snapshot is the configuration of prices across markets at the specific moment when a trade is made. Emphasized in this picture is the size of the bid-ask spread and the depth of the book at the bid and offer quotes.

Let's move away from the static setting. Allow a participant to also decide just when to step forward with an order and trade. This is the dynamic environment within which professional buy side and sell side traders operate. Namely, they time their trades in accordance with current market conditions (as we discuss further in Chapter 7, "Intermediated Markets").

In the dynamic environment, bid-ask spreads and market impact effects continue to play a role, but, very importantly, there is a third factor: price discovery. To an appreciable extent, the accentuated intraday price volatility that we describe in Chapter 4, "What We Want from Our Markets," reflects the dynamic process by which a market searches for the price that best reflects the broad desire of participants to hold shares of a stock.

Price discovery, because it is a complex, dynamic process, makes best execution far more difficult to measure. The question is no longer one of simply obtaining the best possible price for an incoming order at the time of its arrival. The trader must also pick the best possible time to step forward with the order and trigger a trade. But what is the best time? Against what value should an execution be assessed? In a dynamic environment, a performance benchmark is required. With a benchmark, best execution does not mean getting the best price. It means matching or bettering the benchmark.

Performance Benchmarks

What should the benchmark be? Two are currently being widely used by traders in the United States and Europe: the volume weighted average price (VWAP) and the average of the low, high, open, and close prices (LHOC).[34] Both measures are averages. As averages, both are saying that the relevant benchmark is the price at which an average (representative) share has traded during a relevant interval of time (e.g., a trading day). According to the benchmark, any participant who bought below the average or who sold above the average has traded well.

Questions can be raised concerning these benchmarks. For one thing, a full-day price history is not applicable if, for instance, a buy side trader receives the order from his or her portfolio manager in the later part of the afternoon. Would it be better for the benchmark to reflect only the prices from the time the buy side trader has received the order until the end of the day? The problem then would be that the trader's own execution increasingly defines the average, as the window over which the average is computed tightens around the trader's order. The same problem exists when prices over the full day are used, but the market for the stock is thin and the trader's order is large. That is, the execution of a 500,000-share order for a stock that, on average, trades 300,000 shares a day, is bound to have a sizable impact on the benchmark against which it is being assessed.

Another problem with the performance benchmark is that it creates an incentive for traders to time their orders with respect to the benchmark, a practice that can lead to higher trading costs. For instance, a buyer, seeing that prices are rising toward the end of a day and knowing that continued purchases could drive his or her average buying price for the day above the performance measure, will wait for the next day before buying more shares. The next day prices may be even higher but, if so, so, too, will be the benchmark. Consequently, the trader can receive high scores on both days from the assessment system even though effective trading costs are higher. The same is true for a seller who sees prices fall as the day progresses. If the price decline continues into the next trading day, the seller may beat the benchmark on both days by postponing sales to the second day, even though he or she sells at lower prices on the second day than could have been obtained on the first.

A third problem exists. Roughly speaking, a trader cannot account for a substantial part of a day's market volume (e.g., a fifth or more) and not fall awry of VWAP. As we have noted, VWAP traders therefore hold back huge portions of their orders, filling them over several days, and often over a week or more, as a means of staying within or near the VWAP benchmark. When a large number of institutional traders in the market behave in this fashion, share prices naturally fail to reflect true levels of demand, and the relevance of VWAP as an indicator of demand is eliminated. VWAP merely reflects those small portions of various orders that are actually brought to the market each day, in the expectation that they are too small to affect the market price significantly.

A VWAP trader can therefore "chase a stock" several percentage points up or down over a period of days, appearing skillful against VWAP while often damaging the fund's performance. Chan and Lakonishok's (1995) finding that market impact costs are significantly higher when measured for trade *packages* rather than for individual trades underscores the flaws inherent in VWAP as a trading performance benchmark. American Century Mutual Funds reported finding that its broker who ranked best under a VWAP methodology ranked *worst* under a methodology that accounted for share price movements the day after the trades were made.

We have one other bone to pick with the VWAP and LHOC benchmarks. There is no reason to believe that an average realized transaction price in a continuous market, however that average is measured, reflects any consensus value that the market is trying to discover. Because of the vagaries of the order flow, a stock's share price may be higher than its unobservable consensus value at any given moment, and at some other moment the stock's price may be below its unobservable consensus value. Deviations can persist for some time. There is no reason to expect that, over the course of a trading day, the average realized trade price and the average consensus value will have converged.

Best Execution as a Procedure

Given the problem of finding a good benchmark against which to judge trades, attention has turned away from assessing best execution with reference to the transaction costs incurred for a trade to assessing the investment/trading procedures that have been followed. Ananth Madhavan has stated, "The bottom line is, the AIMR guidelines do not prescribe how firms should measure best execution. Rather, they focus on the procedures by which firms check that client portfolios are in fact being properly handled. It is not a trade-by-trade process. Rather, what AIMR is looking for is that managers, traders, and brokers put into place a set of processes that will ensure that considerations involving trading are carefully looked at during day-to-day operations."[35]

Natan Tiefenbrun of Instinet put it this way: "We (Instinet) have defined best execution as a very holistic term. This is all part of the best execution obligation. I think that is right. It should be a holistic term. This is what we should be very focused on—how to get a money manager to look at the entire process, from end to end. How do we minimize all of the frictions that exist between the portfolio manager and the trading desk, and between the trading desk and a broker? How do we mitigate the conflicts of interest that exist?"[36]

Viewing best execution as a procedure is a meaningful development, and some progress might be anticipated. However, problems still remain. In particular, the definition of best-execution procedures cannot be formulated without reference to the participants to whom they are applied. What is best is different for a buy side participant than for a sell side participant, for an active fund versus an index fund, for a broker-dealer intermediary versus a market center, and so forth.[37] Moreover, procedures should not be specified in such detail that agents are micromanaged. If agents are not given some leeway to make their own decisions, what is their value added?

Best Execution Advice for the Buy Side Trader

The landscape is changing rapidly for buy side traders. Market structures are evolving, and technological capabilities for connectivity and order management are exploding. In both the United States and Europe, transaction cost analysis is becoming considerably more prevalent and sophisticated. What implications does all this have for the buy side trader? Here are eight.

1. Minimization of trading costs has not been the only objective of institutional participants. The widespread practice of bundling trade execution services with soft-dollar products (such as research) that are paid for with commission dollars, in the opinion of many, has resulted in excessive execution costs and has imposed a competitive barrier for new, alternative trading facilities that offer lower trading commissions. Enforcement of best-execution practices may help to rectify these problems.[38] We consider the soft-dollar issue in more detail in the next section of this chapter.

2. The challenge of handling institutional-sized orders will continue to be formidable. Breaking into the flow of the continuous market and getting anything close to best execution will remain difficult. The very care that institutions take in approaching the market with their large orders makes it hard for them to meet and to provide liquidity to one another.

3. Star Wars technology in market centers and trading rooms is not a panacea. Electronic order book markets that are the main trading platforms throughout the European equity markets are very efficient at handling retail order flow for blue-chip issues. Gathering the liquidity that institutions require remains a challenge, however, particularly for the mid- and small-cap issues. Electronic linkages also accelerate the speed with which events can take place. This means that one trader's order can tap into a liquidity pool with lightning speed, but still lose out to a competing order that arrived a few nanoseconds ahead of it. Electronic connectivity enables buy side trading desks to access liquidity pools with minimal broker-dealer intermediation; nevertheless, intermediaries are still needed and liquidity pools are still fragmented.[39]

4. The proper timing of orders by a buy side trader can lead to less costly, more profitable trading. Conventional thinking among both practitioners and academicians is that some traders, being patient, are willing to be liquidity providers and place limit orders, and that others, being eager to trade quickly, place liquidity-demanding market orders. However, professional traders commonly use a switching strategy. Namely, the buy side trader, upon receiving an order from the portfolio manager, may initially be patient, hoping the market will come to him or her. However, if market conditions indicate that price is about to move away, the buy side trader will switch from being a liquidity supplier to being a liquidity demander. He or she will step forward with an order and trigger a trade. This is what market timing is all about, and the evidence suggests that it is profitable.

   As we discuss in further detail in Chapter 7, "Intermediated Markets," Handa, Schwartz, and Tiwari[40] used a 15-minute market imbalance measure (a ratio of buy triggered or sell triggered trading activity to total trading activity) to reflect current market conditions. They found, using data provided by the American Stock Exchange, that orders handled on a not-held (NH) basis by floor brokers are timed in relation to current market conditions and that this timing results in lower market impact costs.

5. As already discussed, institutional traders commonly break up their orders for submission to the market over an extended period of time. This creates overhang in the market and sets the stage for momentum trading. The net result is a diminution of order size and an acceleration of order arrival. The order flow may fracture and the market can become hypercontinuous. This disruption of price discovery makes the work of the buy side trader considerably more difficult.

6. Some institutional investors tend to avoid trading at, and close to, market openings. One can readily understand why: The big traders want to know the prices, not set them, and they have less confidence in the quality of price discovery at and near the opening. As discussed in Chapter 4, "What We Want from Our Markets," volatility in the first half hour of the day is strikingly high in the New York, Nasdaq, London, Frankfurt, and Paris markets. This is the time when markets are most apt to become hypercontinuous. Volume is strikingly low for the opening half hour in London, a market that is heavily institutionally dominated. We also note, however, that institutions are pressured to trade at and near market openings when seeking to obtain a VWAP price for the day.

A good picture of what can happen at the open is presented in Exhibit 5.1, which displays transaction information for the Nasdaq stock, Cisco, for the 9:00 A.M. to 10:00 A.M. interval on January 22, 2001.[41]

In Exhibit 5.1, order size is on the horizontal axis and the number of prints is given on the vertical axis. More than 2,500 prints of size 100 shares are shown as having been made in the interval, an average of one 100-share print every 1.4 seconds. During the period, nearly 8 million shares in total traded in nearly 10,000 trades, with an average trade size of 819 shares. Throughout the half-hour period, the spread was generally $\frac{1}{16}$ or $\frac{1}{8}$ of a point, and the difference between the 9:30 A.M. price and the 10:00 A.M. price was $\frac{1}{4}$ point. However, prices over the 30-minute interval ranged from a high of $40\frac{63}{64}$, to a low of 40, nearly a $1 (or 2 percent) swing. We interpret this as evidence of fractured price discovery that can occur when a market becomes hypercontinuous. Understandably, many buy side traders prefer not to navigate in these waters. When the currents become too treacherous, best execution ceases to be a viable goal.

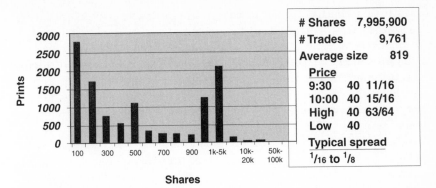

EXHIBIT 5.1 Trades of Cisco Systems between 9:30 and 10:00 A.M. on January 22, 2001.

Source: Global Instinet Crossing.

7. In the United States, the decline in tick size from eighths to teenies (sixteenths) in 1997, and especially the drop from teenies to pennies in 2000 and 2001, has dramatically impacted the amount of liquidity available from limit orders—and hence the trading strategies that must be employed to obtain best execution.[42] Small tick sizes result in smaller quantities being displayed by limit orders since they make it easier for participants to step ahead of limit orders on the book.[43] While the tick size has been small in Europe for some time, and the European markets have adjusted to this reality, the tick size reduction in the United States has been controversial.

8. VWAP and LHOC are fallacious benchmarks. Buy side traders and their portfolio managers should understand that trading practices designed to beat an erroneous benchmark can be costly. Further, they should recognize that price discovery can go awry, especially when a market becomes hypercontinuous. Buy side traders are understandably averse to discovering price. This aversion is reflected in the rapid growth of VWAP trading, a practice that, ironically, can increase their trading costs, as we have noted.

Thoughts for the Providers of Trading Services

Competitive and technological pressures are causing the landscape to change dramatically for exchanges and other providers of trading services. We offer nine thoughts relating to the development of market structure. These are formulated with a primary focus on the national market centers.

However, they also have implications for the operations of alternative trading systems (ATSs).

1. Improving market quality should be the overriding objective of a market center. The important question is how to implement the objective. It is inappropriate to focus myopically on a factor such as the bid-ask spread simply because it is readily measured. An assessment of intraday price volatility, a variable that may capture a broader array of transaction costs, is also advisable. Our discussion in Chapter 4, "What We Want from Our Markets," is focused primarily on the magnitude of price volatility during the first half hour and the last half hour of the trading day. On an ongoing basis, price discovery is particularly difficult during these periods, and an assessment of market quality is most meaningful at a time when the market is under stress.

2. A market center has its own best-execution obligation. Namely, it has the obligation to reduce trading costs for the broad spectrum of investors who are its customers. To meet this obligation, order flow from the disparate groups of investors who inevitably characterize a market must be appropriately integrated. As we have previously discussed in this chapter, only if this is accomplished will good price and quantity discovery be achieved.

3. The quality of price discovery and of quantity discovery should be assessed with regard to two variables: (1) the level of intraday price volatility and (2) institutional order size. The extent to which institutions show only small parts of their orders to the market should be closely monitored and assessed by the market centers. The coexistence of high intraday volatility and small institutional order size would indicate that market quality is low and that best execution is inordinately difficult to achieve.

4. Electronic limit order book markets are good trading platforms for the retail order flow of liquid, large-cap stocks. Unfortunately, the economic structure of a continuous, order-driven market breaks down when the order flow it receives is low (see the discussion in Chapter 7). Even for big-cap stocks, plain-vanilla electronic markets do not offer sufficient liquidity for large orders. While allowing for hidden orders helps, further market structure is needed for handling institutional order flow.[44] Additional structure is now provided in the U.S. and European markets by (1) the inclusion of crossing (either on an exchange as does Deutsche Börse or on an ATS such as POSIT, Instinet, or Burlington Capital Markets' BLOX); (2) the use of price discovery call auctions (predominantly by the European exchanges); and (3) new, electronic negotiation systems (such as Liquidnet and Harborside+).

5. The accelerating onslaught of technology could continue the trend toward hypercontinuous trading. With penny ticks in the United States, quotes are changing so rapidly in the most frequently traded stocks that the eye cannot follow them.[45] Providers of trading services need to offer technology that will accommodate strategies adapted to the environment of rapid quote changes. For example, smart limit orders can be configured to morph themselves automatically depending on market conditions. Such limit orders can be programmed to raise or to lower their bid or offer price, to change their size, or to convert into marketable limit orders or market orders, depending on changing market conditions.

6. Consolidation has two important dimensions. Along with the spatial integration of orders, good market structure also calls for an appropriate *temporal integration* of orders. Temporal fragmentation can be every bit as damaging to market quality as its spatial counterpart. The inclusion of predetermined meeting points in time, be they crosses or price discovery calls, enables participants in general, and institutional traders in particular, to meet in an orderly fashion and to provide liquidity to one another with minimal price dislocation.

   Our previous discussion of Exhibit 5.1, containing information about the first half hour of trading in Cisco on January 22, 2001, highlights a reality of the continuous market. Orders execute against each other at fluctuating prices in trades that are generally bilateral. When the trades are small and are separated from each other by only a second or so, the price fluctuations simply are not efficient adjustments to new information. Rather, they are a manifestation of chaos.

   During the opening 30 minutes of trading for Cisco on January 22, price discovery appears to have been in disarray. Far better would it have been for the traders in Cisco to have had the opportunity to meet at a single point in time so that their orders could be executed at a single price in one large, multilateral trade. Unfortunately, they were not able to do so because at the time there was no single price call auction facility in Nasdaq's market mechanism.[46]

   Multiple call auctions are now included in the European equity markets, and they are attracting meaningful order flow. Nevertheless, institutional participants continue to avoid trading in the opening minutes. Presumably, they prefer to wait until prices are more clearly established before stepping forward with their large orders. We suggest that continuing attention be given to the architecture of existing call auctions to assure that they have appropriate functionality for institutional investors.

7. As we have discussed, institutional investors in both the United States and Europe need a good benchmark against which to assess the qual-

ity of their trades. The standard benchmarks (VWAP and LHOC) do not do the job. Traders should not be assessed against an average of a day's worth of poorly discovered prices. Rather, well-discovered prices in which participants can have confidence are needed. Pooling multiple orders in a properly structured call auction is the best way to produce prices that are worthy of being used as benchmark values.

Interestingly, with the introduction of closing calls in the European markets, confidence is beginning to build in the closing price.[47] If this continues, more orders will be attracted to the closing auctions. In a virtuous circle, this will in turn reinforce the quality of price discovery at the close. At some point, the closing price may earn its status as a widely accepted benchmark. If volume also builds for the opening (and possibly intraday) auctions, these calls as well will produce values that could be used as benchmarks. The benchmarks produced in the call auctions could then be treated as "safe harbor" values for a best-execution obligation.

8. Currently, much attention is being given to the introduction of new electronic technology for order routing and information dissemination. This technology keeps making it easier to find the other side of a trade. Hence, the need for intermediaries is diminished. Nevertheless, intermediaries will continue to be needed to resolve imbalances, to facilitate handling large orders for big-cap stocks, to make the mid-cap and small-cap markets viable, and to play a special role for all stocks when markets are under stress.

9. Three trading modalities are required for an efficient market model: (1) the limit order book continuous market, (2) call auctions, and (3) a market maker, quote-driven component. Combining these three modalities into an efficient hybrid is far from simple. To some extent, the objective may be attained with ATSs providing separate modalities as niche players. Strong central exchanges can also provide the requisite interfaces and run the modalities. Whichever way, additional market quality improvements are needed and, for some time to come, achieving a maximally efficient hybrid marketplace will remain a challenge.

A Candid Look Back at Best Execution

Candide, portfolio manager for Voltaire's Best Possible World Fund, has just received several trade reports. First, 5,000 shares bought at $35.10 at a time when the market was offering 4,000 at 35, and another 1,000 were available at $35.10. "Excellent," she exclaimed. "Just think of all the free research I have received from that broker—not to mention those New York Knicks basketball tickets that he sent me." Second, 10,000 shares sold at

$28 at a time when the market was showing a bid for 8,000 shares at $28.30. "Wonderful," she bubbled forth, "I sold all those shares immediately." Third, 100,000 shares bought in 20 tranches over the course of five trading hours at an average price of $42.15 (the volume weighted average price for the period was $41.75). "I'm thrilled," Candide shouted, "just wait until you see what the VWAP will be tomorrow!"

Do these trades satisfy a best-execution criterion? What is "best" is in the eyes of the beholder. If you are like Candide, the answer is yes. But any criterion that can make a bad execution look good (or a good execution look bad) must be questionable. The bottom line is, best execution is a multifaceted concept that is difficult to define and even more challenging to measure. In large part this is because the quality of executions received by participants depends not only on their individual needs and trading decisions, but also on the characteristics of a specific trade or package, on the stock being traded, on the objective of the participant requesting the execution, and on conditions existing in the market as the order is being executed. Further, best execution also depends on the overall efficiency of market structure.

FUND MANAGERS' INCENTIVE TO CONTROL THEIR TRADING COSTS

The story line that one could infer from our previous discussion, as well as from a large and growing academic literature on institutional trading costs, is that (1) these costs are the bane of institutions, and (2) despite tireless efforts to reduce them, institutions face inefficient market structures manned by inefficient intermediaries who conspire to keep the costs high. Perhaps so, but a closer look at institutional trading practices suggests that fund managers are hardly passive victims of sell side structures and practices. If the buy side's goal were truly to minimize trading costs, then those investors would appear to be their own worst enemies. In this section of the chapter, we direct our attention to sources of systematic buy side trading underperformance that are attributable to buy side trading practices.[48]

The discussion in this section of the chapter draws on findings obtained from a survey conducted by Schwartz and Steil of chief investment officers (CIOs) and head equity traders at 72 major asset management firms in North America, Europe, and Australia.[49] These firms reported assets under management of $2.066 trillion in 1998, which at that time was equivalent to about 15 percent of world mutual and pension funds and 10 percent of total institutional assets.

Institutional Commissions and Commission Bundling

Institutional commission rates have been stagnant in recent years.[50] U.S. weighted average agency commission rates fell only 10 percent from 1994 to 1998, from 6.1 cents per share to 5.5 cents per share,[51] in spite of trading volumes rising fourfold over this same period.[52] Subsequently, they have ranged from about 5 cents down to 2 cents, depending on the type of trade (e.g., single stock versus a basket trade). This compares with nonintermediated electronic trading commissions of 0.25 to 2 cents per share in the U.S. market. Yet for NYSE-listed issues, there has been no mass institutional migration to electronic platforms. Currently, the Big Board is capturing about 80 percent of the volume for its shares. What accounts for the persistence of both traditional institutional trade intermediation and relatively high commission rates in the face of proliferating low-cost electronic competition?

We focus on two interrelated answers to this question. The first is that those in the best position to place orders in the market on the basis of cost performance (the traders) are frequently passive participants in the trading process. More than half of U.S. institutional commission payments are not actually controlled by those doing the trading, but by a combination of the institution's portfolio managers, analysts, and clients.[53] Some portfolio managers actually specify the broker to be used on the majority of their orders submitted to the trading desk, and some even indicate that their trading desk's choice of broker should reward good research on most transactions.

This leads to the second, more fundamental, explanation: Institutions are paying for services wholly unrelated to trade execution (such as company and macro research) via trade execution commissions. Institutional trading desks engaging in such *commission bundling* (buying non-trade-related services from broker-dealers with trading commissions) are not pursuing trading cost minimization as an overriding objective.

Exhibit 5.2 displays the factors driving the choice of a broker. The Schwartz-Steil survey asked institutional head equity traders how frequently their choice of broker *is driven* by the factors indicated and asked chief investment officers (CIOs) how frequently the trader's broker choice *should be driven* by these factors. As is apparent from the responses, factors other than minimizing execution cost are indeed significant. "Rewarding good research," which is wholly unrelated to seeking best execution, featured prominently. "Soft-commission obligations," which represents a binding prior commitment to pay for research-related services through trading commissions, was not dominant but nevertheless conspicuous.

Interestingly, traders from large institutions (over median sample asset size of $6.2 billion) placed considerably more emphasis on both execution

	All Traders	U.S. Traders	Larger Fund Traders	Smaller Fund Traders	All CIOs	U.S. CIOs
Lowest possible execution costs	3.53	3.76	3.70	3.18	3.39	3.61
Fastest possible execution	3.37	3.42	3.67	3.00	3.24	3.22
Rewarding good research	3.39	3.24	3.20	3.61	3.42	3.11
Soft commission obligations	2.45	2.87	2.59	2.21	2.44	2.44
Portfolio manager direction	2.39	2.24	2.37	2.41	N/A	N/A

Scale: 1 (*never*) to 5 (*very frequently,* or 75 to 100 percent of the time).

EXHIBIT 5.2 Factors determining how institutions choose brokers.

cost and speed than did traders from smaller institutions, who directed their commissions largely to pay for research services that they could not provide in-house. Traders in general also put slightly more emphasis on the trade-related factors of cost and speed than did the CIOs.

The survey further found that, on average, traders directed 26 percent of their order flow to specific broker-dealers as a means of payment for "research, trading, or information systems or third-party services." U.S. traders directed a considerably larger portion of their orders for such purposes (32 percent) than did traders in other major markets (e.g., Europe, 18 percent).

Soft Commissions

Over 70 percent of U.S. institutions engage in soft-commission business, guaranteeing broker-dealers minimum annual commission payments for various services, including IPO access.[54] Over half of all U.S. institutional commissions are actually targeted in advance, as an annual minimum commitment, to specific brokers to pay for a combination of:

- Research services from that broker.
- Third-party research acquired by the broker, as well as other soft services such as trading and analytic technology.
- Commitment to providing capital to facilitating trades.

The degree to which an institution provides research services internally or subcontracts them from broker-dealers is clearly a matter of business judgment. A problem of fiduciary accountability arises, however, when the cost of acquiring research services is embedded in the cost of

individual trade transactions. A fund manager's portfolio management services are contracted by fund holders—either individual investors or other
institutions, such as pension funds. An explicit management fee schedule is
associated with such services. Yet if the fund manager is dependent on brokers for research and other services necessary to manage client funds, and
if the fees for such services are embedded in trading commissions, it is
impossible for clients to observe the expenditure and to evaluate the efficiency with which their assets are being managed.

Among fund managers, views on soft commissions are quite diverse,
but generally positive. Schwartz and Steil report that 67 percent of institutional head traders believe it "appropriate for a fund management firm to
pay 'soft commissions' on trades as compensation for broker research."
Similarly, 61 percent believe that such payments are also appropriate "as
compensation for third-party services, such as computer information or
trading systems." On the other hand, a substantial 51 percent believe that it
is, in principle, desirable to unbundle payment for external research and
brokerage commissions. Views are split, however, on the degree to which
it is, as a practical matter, *feasible* to unbundle these services and to charge
for them separately, with 31 percent considering it feasible and an almost
identical 29 percent considering it infeasible.

Whatever their views on the matter, it is important to emphasize that
institutions have no financial incentive to support the unbundling of execution and research payments, since these are made directly out of *client
funds* rather than out of the institution's own capital. This is a principal-
agent problem in the operation of collective investment schemes, and it
acts to discourage efficient implementation of portfolio decisions taken on
behalf of fund holders.

Commission Bundling and Implicit Trading Costs

If paying higher institutional commissions results in lower implicit execution costs, there would be less reason to be concerned about the effects of
commission bundling on fund performance. The evidence, however, suggests the contrary. Keim and Madhavan[55] find a positive correlation coefficient between explicit and implicit costs of 0.14 for sells and 0.07 for buys.
The findings of Berkowitz, Logue, and Noser Jr.[56] and Domowitz and Steil[57]
are consistent.

Various studies have documented significant losses in trading performance specifically attributable to the inherent problems of incentive structure and monitoring in soft-dollar and directed brokerage arrangements.
Conrad et al. (2001) calculate that soft-dollar trade executions cost the
client an average of 0.29 percent more than discretionary executions for
buy trades and 0.24 percent more for sells. They found explicit costs on

soft-dollar transactions to be, on average, four times greater than those on nonintermediated electronic systems (0.278 percent versus 0.069 percent), while generating implicit costs three times higher (0.695 percent versus 0.233 percent). Glass and Wagner[58] report that money managers handling directed trades on behalf of plan sponsors frequently execute them after trades in the same stocks on behalf of other fund holders and that such "sequencing" practices can result in higher trading costs attributable to delayed execution.

Commission Bundling and the Demand for Immediacy

We now return to the question raised earlier concerning why fund managers value immediacy. Intermediated markets generate a demand for immediacy because of the effect of order revelation on prices. An institution trading in a dealer market, or human-intermediated order-driven market, must give up its identity when trading, thereby signaling to broker-dealers its *future* buying or selling intentions. An order to buy, for example, will often indicate more buying to come. When the order is from a large fund, the importance of the signal is correspondingly greater.

Such information leakage naturally induces a tendency to trade quickly, before intermediaries are able to trade or pass the information on to other clients. Agency brokers will frequently tip off one institutional client about another's trading interest, hoping to win more commission business as a reward. Knowing how this game is played, clients naturally try to execute their orders before others are offered the opportunity to trade ahead of them. This was particularly salient in London under its dealer structure, before the blue chips were moved to the exchange's SETS electronic auction platform in 1997. At the time, participants interchangeably used the terms *liquidity* and *immediacy* in that market, reflecting the critical importance of immediacy when information leakage is endemic to market structure.[59]

Institutional awareness that costs are implicit in human trade intermediation is reflected in the concern that CIOs express to have large orders traded quickly, without revealing information about either their identity or order size (see Exhibit 5.3). Awareness of the problem among buy side traders is reflected in their growing tendency to see broker-dealers as competitors[60] and in their identifying anonymity as a key attraction of nonintermediated electronic trading systems.[61] Dealers themselves are extremely concerned about the impact that revelation of their own trades can have on the value of their own proprietary positions. A remarkable 41 percent of North American buy side traders indicated that their dealers regularly delayed the publication of risk trades more

1. Little or no market impact	3.95
2. Speed	3.42
3. Not revealing the full size of order to market	3.40
4. Not revealing the identity of company or fund	3.21
5. Within the current market inside spread	3.06
6. Price better than the VWAP	2.93
7. Low or no commission	2.29

Scale: 1 (*not at all important*) to 5 (*very important,* or 75 to 100 percent of the time).

EXHIBIT 5.3   Factors important to CIOs in judging the quality of execution for large orders.

than \$5 million in size, in contravention of publication rules.[62] This highlights the significance of the interrelationship between market structure and trading practices.

Immediacy and Trading Costs

Trading styles vary widely across institutions, but a significant core considers it of great strategic importance to execute orders quickly once they have passed from the portfolio manager (PM) to the trader. For these institutions, the choice of broker is frequently driven by a demand for immediacy, with large-fund traders generally more trigger-happy than CIOs—and considerably more so than small-fund traders (see Exhibit 5.2). CIOs consider speed on large orders to be important, although they rank it well below market impact (see Exhibit 5.3).

Trading quickly may help to mitigate the costs of being front-run, but it still results in high market impact costs. Keim and Madhavan[63] document far higher trading costs for quick-trading technical investors than for patient-trading value investors, both on the NYSE and Nasdaq. Analyzing five years of implicit and explicit trading cost data from a large U.S. mutual fund, Domowitz and Steil[64] find sell trades (for which immediacy is more frequently demanded than for buys) to be on average 42 percent more expensive than buys for NYSE stocks and 523 percent more expensive for Nasdaq stocks. Using crossing systems (Instinet and POSIT) specifically for sells, which precludes immediacy, yielded considerable savings over continuous trading: 33 percent for NYSE stocks and 49 percent for Nasdaq stocks. As we discuss in Chapter 7, "Intermediated Markets," Handa, Schwartz, and Tiwari[65] find considerable trading cost savings when orders are timed with respect to buy-sell imbalances in the market rather than being reflexively executed on transmission from the PM to the trading desk.

Is the Observed Demand for Immediacy Accounted for by Opportunity Costs?

Opportunity cost is the loss of investment returns owing to an adverse price move between the time a portfolio decision is made and the time it is implemented. An opportunity cost is incurred when the following three conditions are met:

1. The price of a stock rises (falls) after an investor decides to buy (sell) shares, but before he or she is actually able to do so.
2. The price change is independent of the investor's decision.
3. The price change reflects a "permanent" shift in an underlying equilibrium (i.e., consensus) price.

When opportunity costs are present, fund managers clearly have a strong incentive to trade quickly before prices can fully adjust to the new information. Given that traders are widely observed to trade impatiently, their behavior is routinely ascribed by both economists and consultants to the prevalence of opportunity costs. But the empirical evidence on the significance of opportunity costs is minimal and mixed.[66]

It is not surprising that a portfolio manager would be worried about missing a price move. We find that CIOs, on average, indicate that the receipt of new company-specific information is a fairly frequent source of order generation (see Exhibit 5.4). However, such information ranks well below internally generated research, and not far above other factors such as cash flows, portfolio structure, external research, and re-evaluation (factors that should impose no need for immediacy).

Schwartz and Steil further find that PMs rarely wish to trade because they have company-relevant information to which the market would quickly react. The following responses are particularly fecund:

- When asked to indicate, in deciding whether to buy a stock, the weight they generally give to their estimate of a company's share price a day hence, 65 percent of CIOs said they give it "no weight" at all, and none said that they give it "very great weight." In contrast, 70 percent said they give "great" or "very great weight" to their share price estimates *two years* hence (see Exhibit 5.5).
- Only 9 percent of the respondents said that their buy orders are regularly generated from a decision process lasting under one hour, which

1. Internally generated company research	4.14
2. Receipt of new company-specific information	3.38
3. Cash inflows or redemptions	3.13
4. Reevaluation of portfolio structure	3.03
5. Externally generated company research	3.03
6. Profit taking	2.71
7. Receipt of new marketwide economic or political information	2.61
8. Desire to cut losses	2.43
9. Trading activity or order flow in the market (e.g., "merchandise" reported by the trading desk)	2.20
10. Need to track a market index	2.09

Scale: 1 (*never*) to 5 (*very frequently,* or 75 to 100 percent of the time).

EXHIBIT 5.4 Frequency with which orders are generated as a direct result of the conditions listed.

must be the case for information-driven trades, whereas 77 percent said that this is "never" or "infrequently" the case. In contrast, 48 percent said that the decision process is "regularly" or "very frequently" between a week and a month in duration, and 38 percent said it "regularly" or "very frequently" takes over a month (see Exhibit 5.6).

- When trading because they believe a stock is mispriced, only 5 percent said that they "regularly" or "very frequently" expect the price correction to take place within an hour, and 8 percent within an hour and a day. In contrast, 86 percent said that they "never" or "infrequently" expect the

	5	4	3	2	1	Mean
1. One day	0.0%	3.1%	12.1%	19.7%	65.1%	1.53
2. One week	0.0%	3.1%	20.0%	23.0%	53.8%	1.72
3. One month	0.0%	10.7%	32.3%	23.0%	33.9%	2.20
4. One quarter	6.2%	27.7%	29.2%	13.8%	23.0%	2.80
5. One year	34.3%	28.4%	20.8%	4.5%	11.9%	3.69
6. Two years or more	53.7%	16.4%	11.9%	6.0%	11.9%	3.94

Scale: 1 (*none*) to 5 (*very great*).

EXHIBIT 5.5 In stock purchase decisions, weight given to estimate of share price in given time periods.

	5	4	3	2	1	Mean
1. Less than one hour	3.1%	6.2%	13.8%	46.1%	30.8%	2.05
2. One hour to one day	7.7%	9.2%	41.6%	24.6%	17.0%	2.66
3. Over day to one week	10.7%	32.3%	27.7%	20.0%	9.2%	3.15
4. One week to one month	7.5%	40.9%	21.2%	18.2%	12.1%	3.14
5. Over one month	15.2%	22.7%	19.7%	24.2%	18.2%	2.92

Scale: 1 (*never*) to 5 (*very frequently,* or 75 to 100 percent of the time).

EXHIBIT 5.6 Time typically taken to make a buy decision.

correction within an hour, and 84 percent said the same for corrections within an hour and a day, whereas 51 percent "regularly" or "frequently" expect the correction to take over *one year* (see Exhibit 5.7).

Furthermore, CIOs do not believe that liquidity itself is a product of differential information—they believe that trading is far more likely to be driven by *different interpretations* of identical information, different portfolio objectives, and different cash flows (see Exhibit 5.8). This is consistent with Sarkar, Schwartz, and Wolf's finding that institutional order flow is typically two-sided (as discussed previously in the section, "Interaction of Large Orders").

To the extent that institutional demand for immediacy is rational, opportunity costs would appear to be a relatively insignificant source of the demand. Rather, it is primarily the information on their *identity* and *order size* that is captured by the prying eyes of others that triggers adverse price movements for institutions. Institutions are attempting to mitigate

	5	4	3	2	1	Mean
1. Less than one hour	1.6%	3.2%	9.5%	25.4%	60.3%	1.60
2. One hour to one day	3.2%	4.8%	7.9%	31.8%	52.3%	1.75
3. One day to one week	4.8%	11.1%	17.5%	41.3%	25.4%	2.29
4. One week to one month	1.6%	29.0%	32.3%	22.5%	14.5%	2.81
5. One month to one year	15.9%	36.5%	36.5%	4.8%	6.4%	3.51
6. Over one year	19.7%	31.2%	16.4%	22.9%	9.8%	3.28

Scale: 1 (*never*) to 5 (*very frequently,* or 75 to 100 percent of the time).

EXHIBIT 5.7 When buying or selling a stock believed to be mispriced, time expected for the price correction to occur.

Because buyers and sellers:	
1. Receive similar information but disagree in their interpretations	3.97
2. Have different portfolio objectives	3.65
3. Have different cash flows at a given point in time	3.31
4. Receive different information about stocks	2.79
Scale: 1 (*never*) to 5 (*very frequently*, or 75 to 100 percent of the time).	

EXHIBIT 5.8   Why CIOs believe that "markets are liquid."

these effects by transacting quickly. However, a more effective way to eliminate the market impact costs of information leakage is to transact *directly* and *anonymously*.

Soft Commissions and U.S. Market Structure

Domowitz and Steil (2001) found comparable trading cost savings for ECN trading of listed stocks (28 percent vis-à-vis the NYSE) as for Nasdaq stocks (33 percent vis-à-vis broker-dealers). Nevertheless, the use of electronic communication networks (ECNs) is low for NYSE-listed stocks (as noted, the NYSE currently is receiving about 80 percent of the order flow for its stocks). This contrasts with Nasdaq issues, where the use of ECNs is high (currently, less than 20 percent of trading in Nasdaq stocks goes through Nasdaq). What accounts for this difference? Soft commissions are likely an explanatory factor. Soft-commission obligations are fulfilled overwhelmingly on NYSE share trading, as Nasdaq broker-dealer trades are priced net of commissions. This produces a perverse effect whereby institutions frequently pay brokers for research on Nasdaq issues via executions in NYSE issues. This makes institutional trading of NYSE issues abnormally price-insensitive: An institution will pay 5 cents a share to a member firm rather than 1.5 cents or less to an ECN because it is actually buying items such as research and IPO access rather than execution.

Will Commission Bundling Persist?

Strong forces are at work to perpetuate commission bundling. The evidence suggests that investors tend to reward very high performance with greater cash inflows but fail symmetrically to punish lower performance through divestment.[67] The net effect is to encourage funds to take greater investment risks as a means of increasing the likelihood of exceptional returns while offering little incentive for ending commission bundling. Furthermore, many institutions use flawed benchmarks such as VWAP.

VWAP in recent years has taken on an enormous significance as a benchmark for evaluating trading performance. CIOs rank VWAP performance well above other criteria for evaluating how well their traders handle their orders (Exhibit 5.9). In the previous section of this chapter, we have stressed that VWAP is a poor benchmark. Unfortunately, a VWAP shop will fail to measure implicit costs accurately and therefore may fail to detect the performance damage caused by commission bundling.

Market forces on their own could unbundle the payments for trade execution from the payments for nonexecution services. This outcome could result for the following reasons.

- Institutions will certainly have to employ more accurate ways of estimating trading costs. Fortunately, these are now widely available, and knowledge of the techniques and service providers in the industry is growing. Larger funds are more likely than smaller funds to find external cost-measurement services cost-effective.
- The cost gap between bundled-commission trades and nonbundled trades is likely to continue to grow. This will make it cost-effective for more large-fund managers to provide research services internally and to hire the traders necessary to take fullest advantage of nonintermediated electronic trading systems. Given the growing complaints from institutions over the lack of objectivity in sell side research (due to conflicts of interest stemming from investment banking activity), we suspect that large funds will, in fact, move to insource more research.
- Large funds that can measure costs more accurately and insource more research and trading activity would lead the drive for unbundling. Interestingly, the economics of unbundling would also appear to favor funds operated by the sell side. Large investment banks, which already have significant in-house research capability and the most advanced trading desks, should be in the best position to exploit the growing cost

1. Execution price of order relative to VWAP	3.06
2. Speed of execution	2.76
3. Execution price of each trade relative to contemporaneous market price	2.69
4. Average daily execution price relative to the day's closing price	2.53
5. Commission cost	2.10
6. No evaluation made	1.88

Scale: 1 (*never*) to 5 (*very frequently,* or 75 to 100 percent of the time).

EXHIBIT 5.9 Criteria CIOs use to determine quality of trades.

benefits of disintermediation. Nevertheless, although banks have been making massive investments in building or buying asset management arms in recent years, so-called Chinese Walls between the asset management and brokerage divisions may severely limit the ability of banks to exploit growing economies of scope.

- The investor-protection rationale for maintaining Chinese Walls, which limits market intelligence or direct trading system access on the asset management side, needs to be revisited. In any event, the traditional division between buy side and sell side (as well as between investors and intermediaries more generally) has been rendered increasingly obsolete by advances in trading technology.

- Regulatory pressure on commission bundling will continue to grow. In the United States, the SEC's approach, based on obliging disclosure to fund holders, however, is unlikely to be effective, as nearly two-thirds of soft-dollar arrangements between brokers and fund managers are entirely undocumented.[68]

A far more radical approach recommended in the March 2001 U.K. Myners Report[69] would oblige fund managers to absorb all commission costs themselves. This would address the principal-agent problem more directly.[70] If implemented and enforced, fund managers would be encouraged to behave more like the profit-maximizing agents than trading cost literature has held them to be.[71]

LOOKING TO THE FUTURE

The perfect, frictionless marketplace will never be achieved, and handling the huge orders of giant institutional investors will forever be a challenge. But given the current state of the art, improvements are possible.

The need to deal with big orders more efficiently has clearly been perceived in the marketplace. The NYSE (with Liquidity Quotes and Direct+) and Nasdaq (with SuperMontage and its introduction of opening and closing call auctions) have both sought to improve their handling of institutional order flow, and alternative trading systems (ATSs) such as Instinet and Archipelago have presented good venues for the institutional players. Currently, crossing networks such as ITG's POSIT, Instinet's Crossing Network, and Burlington Capital Markets' BLOX, enable institutions to trade with no price impact in batched environments (crosses are made at prices established in the major market centers). Liquidnet, which initiated operations in the United States and has now entered Europe, and Harborside+, are helping institutional participants to meet anonymously and to negotiate their trades with virtual invisibility in an electronic environment that uses current quotes from the major markets as pricing benchmarks.

Nevertheless, institutions continue to find it difficult to have their orders executed with reasonable immediacy at reasonable cost. They pay high transaction costs because of fragmentation (both spatial and temporal). In nonelectronic environments in particular, they are hurt by a lack of transparency and by a loss of anonymity (which leads to front running). They lack confidence in the quality of price discovery and are wary of participating in trades that, with hindsight, will look bad.

Institutions want to trade at "validated" prices. Perhaps a portfolio manager would be willing to pay up to $45 to acquire shares of a stock if $45 were indeed the price at which shares are trading. But he or she would not be willing to pay $38 and, in a matter of minutes, see the stock trading at $35. The need for a validated price leads the institutions to crossing networks and to VWAP trading. With both, validation comes from the fact that enough other participants have traded at the price. However, there is no presumption that crossing benchmarks and VWAP values are well-discovered prices.

Further developments in market architecture will continue to be forthcoming in future years. Success on this front will be welcome, not just to institutions in particular, but to participants in general. As we have stressed, mishandling large orders blurs price discovery and inflates intraday volatility for all participants. It thereby increases trading costs for many.

For the benefit of the broad market, market architecture should be structured to integrate institutional and retail order flow more effectively. This need, which exists in some markets for the blue chips, is particularly acute for the mid- and small-cap segments. However, it is far easier to recognize problems than it is to solve them. Given the intricacy of the issues involved and our past experiences with the unintended consequences that can attend market structure change, we suggest that market structure development be the responsibility of the marketplaces and the innovators who inhabit them.

NOTES

1. The *Institutional Investor Study* (SEC, 1971) that was commissioned by the SEC led to the National Market System regulation. Although institutional dominance was far less in the early 1970s than today, it was enough to empower the NMS regulation and to spur deliberate attempts to level the playing field.

2. Tiefenbrun's and Killeen's remarks were made at the Baruch College Conference, *A Trading Desk's View of Market Quality*, April 30, 2002. The discussion is in Schwartz, Byrne, and Colaninno (2004a).

3. B. Becker and J. Angstadt, in R. Schwartz, ed., *Global Equity Markets: Techno-logical, Competitive and Regulatory Challenges*, Irwin Professional, 1995.

4. See W. Wagner, in R. Schwartz, J. Byrne, and A. Colaninno, eds., *A Trading Desk's View of Market Quality*, Kluwer Academic Publishers, forthcoming 2004.

5. Discussion by John Phinney and Wayne Wagner in R. Schwartz, J. Byrne, and A. Colaninno, eds., *Coping with Institutional Order Flow*, Kluwer Academic Publishers, forthcoming 2004.

6. Academic research in this area is considerable. Fang Cai, Gautam Kaul, and Lu Zheng ["The patterns of returns, raw returns and excess returns, before and after institutional trading are striking," *Institutional Trading and Stock Returns*, pp. 2–3, 6, 2000] show that excess returns to the portfolios before and after significant trading by institutions suggest that there is a run up (down) in returns before and during the major buying (selling) activity by institutions, but that any "excess" returns disappear soon after the peak in the trading activity. Kraus and Stoll ["Price Impacts of Block Trading on the New York Stock Exchange," *Journal of Finance* 27, pp. 569–588, 1972] find that institutional trading has a significant price effect: Price movement in a stock is positively related to contemporaneous herding, but negatively related to herding in the previous month. Nofsinger and Sias ["Herding and feedback trading by institutional and individual investors," *Journal of Finance* 54, 1999, pp. 2263–2295] and Wermers ["Mutual Fund Herding and the Impact on Stock Prices," *Journal of Finance*, April 1999] document a positive contemporaneous relationship between institutional trading and stock returns. Hong and Stein ["A Unified Theory of Under-Reaction, Momentum Trading and Overreaction in Asset Markets," *Journal of Finance* 54, 1999, pp. 2143–2184] show that as firm-specific information becomes gradually incorporated into stock prices and results in return momentum, increasing institutional trading speeds up the price adjustment to the new information and eliminates the abnormal returns. Further, recognizing that they are all working their orders carefully, institutional participants typically distrust the prices that they see in the market. Bradford J. DeLong, A. Shleifer, L. H. Summers, and R. J. Waldmab ["Positive feedback investment strategies and destabilizing rational speculation," *Journal of Finance* 45, 1990, pp. 379–395] and Bikhchandani, Hirshleifer, and Welch ["A theory of fads, fashion, custom, and cultural change as informational cascades," *Journal of Political Economy* 100, 1992, pp. 992–1026] argue that as one or a few institutions trade in certain stocks in response to some information, or for noninformational reasons, other institutions may simply follow the leaders under peer pressure. Sias and Starks ["Return autocorrelation and institutional investors," *Journal of Financial Economics* 46, 1997, pp. 103–131] show that the autocorrelations in daily returns of both NYSE portfolios and individual securities are an increasing function of the level of institutional ownership.

7. The remarks by Turner and Brooks were made at the Baruch conference, April 2002. See Schwartz, Byrne, and Colaninno (2004a, op. cit.).

8. Comment made at the Baruch conference, April 2002. See Schwartz, Byrne, and Colaninno (2004a, op. cit.).

9. *Not held* (NH) means that a broker working an NH order is "not held responsible" if, in the process of attempting to obtain a better price for a customer, the market moves away and the order is filled at a worse price than that which existed when the order was first delivered to the broker. The term is sometimes taken to mean that the broker is not being "held to the price" at which the order could have initially been filled.

10. The coordination can be seen as follows. Small orders are typically exposed to floor brokers in an effort to receive price improvement. Orders worked by floor brokers are typically brought forth and turned into trades in response to current market conditions as described by, among other things, the broad balance between buy and sell orders in the market and price momentum. Upstairs negotiations of large trades take account of conditions on the trading floor, and the blocks are typically priced with reference to recent trades and current quotes. Trades frequently involve retail customers, and the current quotes are commonly set by the small orders.

11. A. Sarkar, R. Schwartz, and A. Wolf, "On the Existence and Nature of Two-Sided Markets," Baruch College working paper.

12. Trades at midspread values were classified with reference to previous transaction prices.

13. The intraday volatility patterns have been documented and analyzed for five equity markets (the New York Stock Exchange, Nasdaq, the London Stock Exchange, Euronext Paris, and Deutsche Börse) by Ozenbas, Schwartz, and Wood, "Volatility in U.S. and European Equity Markets: An Assessment of Market Quality," *International Finance*, vol. 5, no. 3, winter 2002, pp. 437–461.

14. See Schwartz, Byrne, and Colaninno (2004a, op. cit.).

15. The remarks made by Killeen and Merrin were made at the Baruch conference, April 2002. See Schwartz, Byrne, and Colaninno (2004a, op. cit.). In Chapter 3, "Liquidity," we cite the Plexus cost estimate of 47 cents per share for a $30 stock.

16. See Schwartz, Byrne, and Colaninno (2004a, op. cit.).

17. See Schwartz, Byrne, and Colaninno (2004a, op. cit.).

18. Wayne Wagner, testimony before the House Committee on Financial Services, March 12, 2003.

19. SEC Release No. 34-42450; File No. SR-NYSE-99-48, p. 3.

20. SEC Release No. 34-42208; File No. S7-28-99. Notice the reference to "retail investors."

21. At each call, multiple orders are batched together, a single clearing price is determined, and buy orders at the clearing price and above execute, as do sell orders at the clearing price and below. For further discussion, see Economides and Schwartz, "Electronic Call Market Trading," *Journal of Portfolio Management*, 1995, pp. 10–18, and Schwartz, Byrne, and Colaninno, *Call Auction Trading: New Answers to Old Questions*, Kluwer Academic Publishers, 2003.

22. See Bradley, "Views of an 'Informed' Trader," reprinted by AIMR 2002 from the AIMR proceedings, *Organizational Challenges for Investment Firms* (Charlottesville, VA: AIMR, May 2002).

23. Economides and Schwartz (1995, reprinted in Schwartz, 2001), Schwartz and Steil (1996, reprinted in Schwartz, 2001), and Demarchi and S. Thomas and Douglas and C. Thomas in Schwartz (2001).

24. See Schwartz, Byrne, and Colaninno (2004a, op. cit.).

25. See Schwartz, Byrne, and Colaninno (2004a, op. cit.).

26. Material in this section has been modified with permission from Schwartz and Wood, "Best Execution: A Candid Analysis," *Journal of Portfolio Management*, vol. 29, no. 4, summer 2003, pp. 37–48. We also discuss best execution in Chapter 11, "Regulation."

27. Financial Services Authority (FSA), "Best Execution," discussion paper, London, April 2001, p. 13.

28. When traders receive an indication that a large order to buy (sell) is coming to the market, they may try to buy (sell) ahead of it. The practice is referred to as *front running*.

29. Sofianos ["Trading and Market Structure Research," Goldman Sachs, May 2001] presents a framework for evaluating and comparing the execution quality for large institutional orders. His analysis considers commissions, execution shortfall for filled orders, fill rates, opportunity costs for nonfilled orders, and information content.

30. See Wagner (Schwartz, Byrne, and Colaninno, 2004a, op. cit.).

31. See Bradley (2002, op. cit.). Bradley also made this statement in his testimony before the Congressional Subcommittee on Capital Markets, Insurance and Government Sponsored Enterprises, March 12, 2003.

32. See Schwartz, Byrne, and Colaninno (2004a, op. cit.).

33. Association for Investment Management and Research (2001, op. cit.).

34. We suggest that "LHOC" be pronounced "L HOCK" so that it rhymes with "AD HOCK." Parts of this subsection have been adapted from Schwartz and Steil, "Controlling Institutional Trading Costs: We Have Met the Enemy, and It Is Us," *Journal of Portfolio Management*, vol. 28, no. 3, spring 2002, pp. 39–49.

35. Comments made at the Baruch College Conference, *A Trading Desk's View of Market Quality*, April 30, 2002. At the same conference, Minder Cheng of Barclays Global Investors presented details of a specific assessment procedure that is used by his firm. The discussions are in Schwartz, Byrne, and Colaninno (2004a, op. cit.).

36. Remarks made at the Baruch College Conference, *A Trading Desk's View of Market Quality*, April 30, 2002. The discussion is in Schwartz, Byrne, and Colaninno (2004a, op. cit.).

37. Wayne Wagner, speaking at the April 30, 2002, Baruch College Conference, stated this as follows: "But it gets complicated. These decision processes are all very different. Consequently, what represents best execution for a hedge fund that wants immediate execution, may not apply to Minder (Cheng) who is mostly running index funds and therefore is interested in achieving lowest possible costs. It is also different for a momentum manager who simply has to get the shares that his portfolio manager has decided on into the portfolio, no matter what the cost." The discussion is in Schwartz, Byrne, and Colaninno (2004a, op. cit.).

38. Ted Aronson has stated that a decreased use of soft dollars will "be the most important result of the AIMR Task Force Guidelines." See Schwartz, Byrne, and Colaninno (2004a, op. cit.).

39. Wayne Wagner stated it this way: "Love them or hate them, institutional traders still need market makers. It is a relationship built upon mutual need: Searching for liquidity, bringing companies to market, providing research, referrals and soft-dollar services," Schwartz, Byrne, and Colaninno (2004a, op. cit.).

40. P. Handa, R. Schwartz, and A. Tiwari, "The Economic Value of a Trading Floor: Evidence from the American Stock Exchange," *Journal of Business* 77, no. 2, pt. 1, April 2004, pp. 331–355.

41. The figure was supplied by Global Instinet Crossing.

42. For further discussion, see Chakravarty, Wood, and Van Ness, "Decimal Trading and Liquidity: A Study of the NYSE," *Journal of Financial Research* 27, no. 1, spring 2004, pp. 75–94.

43. This point was first made by Larry Harris in "Minimum Price Variations, Discrete Bid/Ask Spreads and Quotation Sizes," *Review of Financial Studies, 1994* vol. 7, no. 1, pp. 149–178.

44. Hidden orders are orders that have been submitted to a market (e.g., an electronic limit order book) but that are not openly displayed at the trader's request. In Europe, hidden orders are commonly referred to as *iceberg orders*.

45. Chakravarty, Wood, and Van Ness (2002, op. cit.) find stock quote updates of up to 257 per minute for AOL following the introduction of decimal trading on the NYSE.

46. In April 2004, Nasdaq started to roll out a closing call in its market model. This is planned to soon be followed by the introduction of an opening call.

47. Pagano and Schwartz, ["A Closing Call's Impact on Market Quality at Euronext Paris," *Journal of Financial Economics* 68, 2003, pp. 439–484] found that the introduction of a closing call in the Paris market did improve the efficiency of price formation at the close.

48. The material in this section has been adapted with permission from Schwartz and Steil (2002, op. cit.).

49. Schwartz and Steil sent out 850 questionnaires, for a response rate of 8.5 percent; 54 percent were based in the United States, 19 percent in Canada, 11 per-

cent in Australia, 8 percent in the United Kingdom, and 7 percent in continental Europe. See Schwartz and Steil (2002, op. cit.).

50. Commission bundling, along with soft dollar payments, is also discussed in Chapter 11, "Regulation."

51. Greenwich Associates, "Advances and Anomalies in 'Nontraditional' Trading," A Report to Institutional Investors in the United States, 1999.

52. The value of shares traded in the United States rose from $3.56 trillion in 1994 to $13.15 trillion in 1998 (Securities Industry Association, 1999).

53. Greenwich Associates (1999, op. cit.).

54. J. Conrad, K. Johnson, and S. Wahal, "Institutional Trading and Soft Dollars," *Journal of Finance*, vol. 56, 2001, pp. 397–422.

55. D. B. Keim and A. Madhavan, "Transactions Costs and Investment Style: An Inter-Exchange Analysis of Institutional Equity Trades," *Journal of Financial Economics* 46, December 1997, pp. 265–292.

56. S. A. Berkowitz, D. E. Logue, and E. A. Noser, "The Total Cost of Transactions on the NYSE," *Journal of Finance*, 1988, pp. 97–112.

57. I. Domowitz and B. Steil, "Automation, Trading Costs, and the Structure of the Securities Trading Industry," Brookings-Wharton Papers on Financial Services, 1999, pp. 33–92.

58. S. Glass and W. Wagner, "The Dynamics of Trading and Directed Brokerage," *Journal of Pension Plan Investing*, 1988, pp. 53–72.

59. See, in particular, the testimony of London Stock Exchange Chief Executive Gavin Casey before the U.K. Treasury Committee on March 17, 1997 ("The Prospects for the London Stock Exchange").

60. Compared with five years prior to the survey, 43 percent considered broker-dealers to be acting more as "competitors" than as "agents," and 24 percent considered them to be acting more as "agents."

61. See N. Economides and R. A. Schwartz, "Equity Trading Practices and Market Structure: Assessing Asset Managers' Demand for Immediacy," *Financial Markets, Institutions and Instruments*, vol. 4, no. 4, 1995, pp. 1–4, and R. A. Schwartz and B. Steil, "Equity Trading III: Institutional Investor Trading Practices and Preferences," in B. Steil, ed., *The European Equity Markets: The State of the Union and an Agenda for the Millennium*, European Capital Markets Institute and the Royal Institute of International Affairs, London, 1996.

62. In Europe, where many major national markets have explicit rules to accommodate delayed publication of block trades, the figure was only 8 percent. The exact question in the Schwartz-Steil survey was, "When you trade a large block of shares (over $5 million) directly with a dealer, how often does the dealer 'stop' ('work' or 'protect') the order—that is, guarantee a price that he or she will try to improve on, but not print the trade until natural counterparties are found—or otherwise deliberately delay publishing the trade to the market?" The response "regularly" is defined as 50 to 74 percent of the time, while the response "very frequently" is defined as 75 to 100 percent of the time.

63. D. B. Keim and A. Madhavan (1997, op. cit.).

64. I. Domowitz and B. Steil (1999, op. cit.).

65. P. Handa, R. Schwartz, and A. Tiwari (2004, op. cit.)

66. Wagner and Edwards ["Best Execution," *Financial Analysts Journal*, vol. 49, no. 1, 1993, pp. 65–71] estimate trade delay costs at 0.20 percent of value for so-called liquidity-neutral markets (i.e., those exhibiting no momentum). They also find that 24 percent of orders go uncompleted and that the nonexecution costs on the unfilled component average 1.80 percent. As their finding on the proportion of uncompleted orders substantially exceeds the 4 to 5 percent unearthed by Keim and Madhavan ["The Cost of Institutional Equity Trades," *Financial Analysts Journal*, 1998, pp. 50–69] and Perold and Sirri ["The Cost of International Equity Trading," working paper, Harvard University, 1993], this may simply be an artifact of their proprietary database.

67. See Fant and O'Neal, "Temporal Changes in the Determinants of Mutual Fund Flows," *Journal of Financial Research*, vol. 23, no. 3, 2000, pp. 353–371; Sirri and Tufano, "Costly Search and Mutual Fund Flows," *Journal of Finance* 53, 1998, pp. 1589–1622; and Goetzman and Peles, "Cognitive Dissonance and Mutual Fund Investing," *Journal of Financial Research* 20, 1997, pp. 145–158.

68. See the SEC's web site: www.sec.gov/news/studies/softdolr.htm.

69. See the U.K. Treasury web site: www.treasury.gov.uk/docs/2001/myners_report0602.html.

70. Concerns expressed by the U.K. National Association of Pension Funds that this might merely encourage broker-dealers to widen spreads actually serve to highlight the benefits of disintermediating the trading process, such that spreads are determined by the direct interaction of investor buy and sell orders.

71. See Neuberger [Schwartz, Byrne, and Colaninno (2004a, op. cit.)] for discussion and further references.

CHAPTER 6

Order-Driven Markets

A pure order-driven market is a trading environment where all of the participants are investors seeking to buy or to sell shares for their own portfolio purposes. Trades occur in the order-driven market because the participants differ from each other in two fundamental ways. The first way is obvious—some investors are seeking to buy shares and others are looking to sell shares. The second way is more subtle—some investors choose to place limit orders and others decide to trade by market order. The environment is called *order-driven* because the limit orders that are placed by some of the participants set the prices at which others can trade by market order.

Participants in a *pure* order-driven market are referred to as *naturals* (the natural buyers and sellers). No intermediary participates as a trader in a pure order-driven market. Rather, the investors supply liquidity to themselves: The natural buyers are the source of liquidity for the natural sellers, and vice versa. The naturals fall into four groups: market and limit order buyers and market and limit order sellers. For trading to be possible, the buyers need the sellers (and vice versa), and for trades to be realized the limit order placers need the market order placers (and vice versa). Because of this interdependency between the groups, we view the order-driven market as an ecology and consider how the market achieves an ecological balance.

Order-driven markets can be structured in two fundamentally different ways. First, with a *continuous* market, a trade can be made at any moment in continuous time that a buy order and a sell order meet in price. In the continuous market, trading is generally a sequence of bilateral matches. In contrast, in a *call auction*, orders are batched together for a simultaneous execution, in a multilateral trade, at a specific point in time. At the time of a call, a market-clearing price is determined and buy orders at this price and higher execute, as do sell orders at this price and lower.

The continuous and call auction environments can be combined. Call auctions are typically used at the beginning of each trading session to open the market. Calls can also be used to close and to restart the market (the major U.S. and European equity markets do this) periodically during a trading session (Deutsche Börse runs one intraday call).

CONTINUOUS TRADING

As we have noted, to operate effectively, an order-driven market requires that some public participants place limit orders and that other public participants place market orders.[1] To understand how this works, we consider the cost of placing a limit order, the compensation for placing a limit order, and why some but not all investors will choose to place limit orders. We also explain why, in an order-driven market, a limit order to buy will never be placed too close to a limit order to sell, and vice versa. In other words, we explain why a bid-ask spread exists in an order-driven market. We start by presenting the analytic framework.

Analytic Framework

Consider a group of investors who have already decided the specific number of shares that each wishes to buy or to sell. Assume that each participant knows the maximum price that he or she would be willing to pay to buy shares or the minimum price that he or she would be willing to receive to sell shares. These maximum and minimum values are referred to as *reservation prices*. The concept of a reservation price is useful. If, for instance, a buyer with a reservation price of $55 a share succeeds in purchasing 100 shares at $52, we can assess the gains from trading as $3 a share ($55 − $52), or as $300 in total ($3 × 100 shares). Different investors generally have different reservation prices. Each investor's reservation price depends on his or her own risk tolerance and assessment of share value. Investors' reservation prices change with the advent of new information (news), reassessments of information, and changes in risk tolerance and cash positions.

We simplify the discussion by allowing for just two types of orders—limit orders and market orders.[2] Limit orders are sometimes referred to as *priced orders*. For a buy limit order, the price specified is a *maximum* value. That is, a limit buy priced at $30 is to be executed at any price up to $30, but no more. For a sell limit order, the price specified is a *minimum* value. That is, a limit sell priced at $25 is to be executed at any price down to $25, but no less. Limit buy orders that are priced below limit sell orders (and limit sell orders that are priced above limit buys) are entered on a limit order book.[3] As we discuss in Chapter 1, "The Role of an Equity Market," in a pure order-driven system, there are either market or limit orders, and no other types of orders.

A market order is an unpriced order. It is an order to buy or to sell shares at the best price available on the market. In the continuous order-driven environment, limit orders that have been placed on the book establish the prices at which the market orders will execute. This can be seen with reference to the limit order book that is depicted in Exhibit 6.1. The exhibit shows limit orders to buy (bids), placed at prices from $10.65 up to $10.95, and limit orders to sell (offers), placed at prices from $11.30 down to $11.10. The numbers shown under the columns labeled "Bids" and "Offers" are the total numbers of shares placed at each price. For instance, the number 35 shown in the Bids column at $10.95 indicates that 3,500 shares are sought for purchase at a limit price of $10.95. These shares might be represented by one order for 3,500 shares, by two orders (perhaps one for 1,500 shares and a second for 2,000 shares), or by three orders or more.

Notice that, for the book displayed in Exhibit 6.1, no orders have been placed at four of the prices—$11.25, $11.05, $11.00, and $10.85. The absence of orders at $11.25 and $10.85 are gaps in the book that can occur by chance. These gaps are sometimes referred to as *air pockets*. On the other hand, the absence of orders at $11.05 and at $11.00 is not simply a matter of chance. These values are within the bid-ask spread. Specifically, the spread is the lowest offer ($11.10) minus the highest bid ($10.95). Given this particular book, a market order to buy will execute at $11.10 (the best, most aggressive offer), and a market order to sell will execute at $10.95 (the best, most aggressive bid). We explain shortly why the spread is not simply the product of chance.

The limit order book depicted in Exhibit 6.1 is a snapshot of the orders that exist at a moment in time. As time passes, new limit orders may arrive, and existing orders may be canceled or turned into trades by the arrival of market orders. We classify the kinds of events that can trigger order arrival or cancellation in two categories—*liquidity events* and *information events*.

The liquidity events are unique to each individual. Someone receives money to invest, somebody else incurs an expense that requires the sale of shares, and/or a third person simply reassesses information and changes his or her mind about a stock's value. The order flow triggered by liquidity

	Bids (00)	Price	Offers (00)	
		11.30	91	
		11.25	0	Air pocket
		11.20	52	
		11.15	24	
		11.10	7	
Bid-ask spread		11.05		
(10.95–11.10)		11.00		
	35	10.95		
	70	10.90		
Air pocket	0	10.85		
	20	10.80		
	67	10.75		
	39	10.70		
	46	10.65		

EXHIBIT 6.1   Limit order book.

events is uncorrelated across individual participants. In contrast, an information event (the arrival of news) affects all participants. An information event generates a wave of orders as price searches for its new equilibrium.

Cost of Placing a Limit Order

Two risks underlie the cost of placing a limit order: (1) the risk that the limit order will not execute at all or immediately and (2) the risk that an information event will cause the limit order to execute. Assume that a limit order to buy 500 shares at the best bid of $10.95 has just been placed on the book and that the 3,500 shares shown at $10.95 in Exhibit 6.1 are in front of it. Let the order be a *day order* (i.e., if it does not execute, it is automatically canceled at the close of the trading day). For the new order to execute in full, one or more market orders to sell a total of 4,000 shares must be sent to the market before the end of the trading day. The investor who placed the order for 500 shares at $10.95 faces nonexecution risk simply because this might not happen. In the meantime, if the price of the stock rises, the investor will have to pay a higher price on the following trading day if he or she still wishes to buy.

Regarding the second risk, if the limit order does execute, the investor who placed it will bear a cost if the execution was triggered by the market order of an "informed trader." This can happen because an information event may occur and the investor may not receive the news in time to cancel his or her order. How will that investor feel if he or she buys 500 shares at $10.95 as the quotes are dropping to $10.50 bid, $10.60 offered?

When an information event happens, placing a limit order is a "heads you win, tails I lose" situation. If the news is bullish, prices rise and the order does not execute (too bad, it's heads, the other guy wins). If the news is bearish, prices fall, the limit order executes, and the quotes fall further (oops, it's tails, I lose). When an adverse information event triggers the execution, the limit order placer suffers, to put it mildly, "ex post regret." So, you might ask, why would anyone ever submit a limit order in the first place?

Compensation for Placing a Limit Order

The compensation for placing a limit order and therefore providing liquidity to others is attributable to the pricing dynamics of the continuous order-driven market. After being driven in one direction, there must, be a tendency for price to reverse direction and revert back toward its previous level. This pricing dynamic is referred to as *mean reversion*. Any variable is said to mean-revert if, after being pushed away from its average, it tends to revert back toward its average.

To understand what is involved, return to Exhibit 6.1 and consider a limit order that has been placed at $10.90 at a time when the market spread is given by the quotes $10.95 bid and $11.10 offer. Assume sell orders come in that trigger transactions down to a price of $10.85. Our customer's limit order executes at the price at which it was placed ($10.90), and price drops another nickel. But then the market strengthens and the quotes revert back toward their previous values, $10.95 bid, $11.10 offer. Rather than having bought immediately at the $11.10 offer, our customer has acquired shares at $10.90, and the stock has resumed trading at its previous level. This leaves the customer better off by 20 cents a share. Profit possibilities like this can compensate for the two risks: the nonexecution risk and the risk of trading with a better-informed customer.

When prices mean-revert, price volatility is accentuated. Mean reversion generally occurs in relatively brief intervals of time (typically intraday), and consequently price volatility is accentuated for relatively brief intervals of time. Think of it this way. Price is driven down and then it bounces back up, or price is driven up and then drops back down. These zigs and zags that occur during the day can largely offset each other, and in the absence of any major news event, price at the close of the day can wind up fairly near to where it was at the open.

What causes the mean-reverting process and accentuation of intraday volatility? Alternatively stated, which of the two types of events we have focused on can trigger the mean-reverting price changes: liquidity events or information events? The liquidity events. News implies that prices should change to a new level; liquidity events need not. When the sell or buy orders do not reflect a marketwide reassessment of share value, the price changes they produce tend to attract new, contra-side orders that push values back toward their previous level.

In summary, we have the following. A liquidity event that results in a price decline could cause a limit buy order to execute (or one that would result in a price increase could cause a limit sell order to execute). After being driven down (or up), price tends to revert back up (or down). The limit order customer profits as price mean reverts after his or her order has executed.

There is one more thing to note. Mean reversion and accentuated short-period price volatility are essentially the same thing.

A Market in Balance

As previously noted, for an order-driven market to function, some participants must choose to place limit orders and others must decide to place market orders. After all, without limit orders, there would be nothing for the market orders to execute against, and without market orders, the limit orders would never execute. How does a population of participants naturally separate into one group that goes the limit order route and another that elects to trade by market order?

Consider two investors, one with a relatively well-balanced portfolio and the other with a relatively unbalanced portfolio, and recall that one of the costs of placing a limit order is the risk that the limit order will not execute. Which of these two investors will be less concerned about nonexecution risk? Clearly, the one with the relatively well-balanced portfolio will be less concerned and, being less concerned, will be more patient. Consequently, for a spectrum of participants, the more patient traders (those holding better-balanced portfolios) will place limit orders so they can profit from the accentuated volatility, and the more eager traders (those holding more unbalanced portfolios) will place market orders so they can avoid running the risk of not executing.

How does the market reach a balance between limit order traders and market order traders? Recall that the compensation for placing a limit order is the accentuation of short-period volatility and that, with thinner books, liquidity events trigger bigger price swings. In other words, there is an inverse relationship between the depth of the book and short-period volatility accentuation. Thus, as the book fills with more limit orders, the compensation for placing a limit order decreases. When volatility reaches a level that is just sufficient to compensate the marginal limit order placer, the depth of the book and the accentuated short-period volatility are optimal. At this point, the limit order traders and the market order traders are supporting each other appropriately, and the market is in ecological balance.

The Bid-Ask Spread

The bid-ask spread is a cost of trading for market order customers and a return for limit order customers.[4] For this reason, we care about both its existence and its size. Thus, we ask, why do bid-ask spreads exist in order-driven markets?

There is a simple answer to the question. If a buy and sell order meet in price, a trade occurs immediately, and as the orders are executed they disappear from the book. Therefore, for buy and sell orders to be sitting on the book, they must be at different prices. With decimal pricing and a one-cent minimum allowable price change, if the bid is $22.10, the lowest offer that can sit unexecuted on the book is $22.11.[5] Consequently, a spread of at least one cent must exist.

There is a more challenging question. What, other than chance, might account for a spread larger than the minimum allowable price change? The answer involves understanding the strategy behind when and where to place a limit order. Picture an investor who is pondering (1) whether to attempt to trade by limit order, or to trade with certainty by market order, and (2) the price at which to place the limit order if the limit order route is taken. The investor's strategic decision will take two factors into account—(1) the relative benefit of trading by limit order rather than by market order and (2) the probability that the limit order will execute. We deal with the benefit first.

To illustrate, let's consider the placement of a buy order. We have previously noted that the per-share monetary gains from trading may be assessed as the difference between an investor's reservation price and the price at which he or she transacts. Four points follow:

1. The monetary benefit of buying by market order equals the investor's reservation price less the offer price (remember, a market order to buy executes at the ask).

2. The monetary benefit of buying by limit order equals the investor's reservation price less his or her own limit price (in a continuous market, limit orders execute at their own limit price).[6]

3. The *differential* monetary benefit of buying by limit order rather than market order is therefore the offer price minus the limit price.

4. The differential monetary benefit of buying by limit order rather than market order decreases as the investor's limit order is placed ever closer to the offer, and the benefit is infinitesimal if the limit order is placed infinitesimally close to the established offer.

Regarding the probabilities of order execution that face our investor, we have the following:

- A market order would execute with certainty at the offer price. Thus, if the limit bid is equal to (or greater than) the offer, the probability is 1 that the buy order will execute at the offer.[7]
- In the range of prices less than the offer, the probability that the limit order will execute increases as its price is raised toward that of the offer.
- If the limit order is placed infinitesimally close to the established offer, the probability that it will execute is discretely (not infinitesimally) less than 1.

Continuing with the last bullet point, the probability of order execution remains discretely below unity, because a posted offer that is not accepted may cease to be available (it could be canceled or hit by someone else's buy order), and the opportunity to trade at that price may not arise again.[8] Simply stated, the difference between being extremely close to making a transaction and actually consummating the trade is not infinitesimal.

The existence of a spread that is wider than the minimum allowable tick size depends critically on the last bullet point. To see this, assume a tick size that is far less than a penny—assume that the tick size is infinitesimal. Should any investor ever place a buy limit infinitesimally close to an already posted offer or a sell limit infinitesimally close to an already posted bid? The answer is unambiguously *no*. It never makes sense to accept a finite risk of not executing in an attempt to realize an infinitesimal gain.

We are now able to say why spreads exist in order-driven markets. The reason is that a new limit order will never be placed "too close" to an already posted counterpart order. This is because the attractiveness of trading with certainty by market order at a previously posted sell (or buy) exerts a *gravitational pull* on any incoming buy (or sell) order. The new buy (sell) is attracted to the offer (bid); it is submitted as a market order; a trade is triggered; and the previously posted sell (buy) order is eliminated from the book. Accordingly, for any new limit order to be placed on the book, its price must be far enough away from the counterpart quote to lie outside the gravitational pull of the counterpart quote. Thus a new limit buy will not be placed "too close" to an already posted offer, and a new limit sell will not be placed "too close" to an already posted bid. Consequently, there will always be a spread between the best bid and offer.

Spreads that are wider than the minimum tick size are common, especially with penny pricing. For any individual stock, the size of the spread depends on the strength of the gravitational pull. The gravitational pull is stronger for stocks that are higher-priced, that trade less frequently, and that are more price-volatile. Stocks that fall into these categories are expected to have wider spreads. Because order execution rates are less, spreads are also generally higher for less liquid stocks. Moreover, the gravitational pull is also stronger for larger orders because they arrive at the market with relative infrequency. Consequently, the spread between larger buy and sell orders tends to be wider.

CALL AUCTION TRADING

Two realities of the continuous order-driven market are apparent from our previous discussion: (1) Short-period (e.g., intraday) volatility must be accentuated because it is mean reversion that provides the compensation for limit order traders, and (2) a spread must exist between the highest-bid and the lowest-ask quotes in the market. Neither of these realities applies to a periodic call auction. Calls are a very different trading environment. In terms of matching, a call is like a still picture whereas the continuous market resembles a movie.[9]

What Is a Call Auction?

We have noted that an order-driven market can be structured in two fundamentally different ways: With a *continuous* market, a trade can be made at any moment in continuous time that a buy order and a sell order meet in price, whereas in a *call auction*, orders are batched together for a simultaneous execution. At the time of a call, a market-clearing price is determined, and buy orders at this price and higher execute, as do sell orders at this price and lower.[10]

The order book for an electronic call is usually open, which means that participants can see orders on the bid and the ask side on an anonymous basis. In the electronic call auctions typically in use in Europe, public participants receive, with a few seconds delay, the five cumulated best bid and ask prices by size (i.e., number of shares), so they have a good, although slightly delayed, inside view of the order book.

Toward the end of an auction, the book is closed, which means that participants can see the spread or the hypothetical price only at a specific moment in the book. This is to avoid manipulation of the price discovery procedure. There are two rules of thumb for an order-driven market with an open order book:

1. "You get what you see."
2. Price-time priority: "First come, first served."

The call auction form of trading died out in the precomputer age but has made its reentrance today as an electronic marketplace. An electronic call auction has been incorporated in recent years in a number of market centers around the world, most notably Deutsche Börse, Euronext (the

Paris, Amsterdam, Brussels, and Lisbon exchanges), and the London Stock Exchange. These electronic calls are not being used as stand-alone systems, but have been combined with continuous trading to create hybrid markets. When it comes to trading, one size does not fit all. With a hybrid system, an investor can select among alternative trading venues depending on the size of his or her order, the liquidity of the stock being traded, and the investor's own motive for trading.

Call auctions and continuous trading both have their advantages and their shortcomings. In most exchanges, both methods are combined—as are order-driven and quote-driven facilities[11]—to form an optimum structure for all kinds of users. In principle, an auction appears to be the ideal way of determining the equilibrium market price at a specific point in time. Continuous trading, on the other hand, is more apt to resemble an ongoing crawl around a dynamically evolving equilibrium price.

Many retail customers are accustomed to trading with immediacy. Nevertheless, if there were retail orders only, periodic calls would probably be the better way to provide fair and equitable treatment to every investor. However, markets must also cope with the problem of handling big block orders, as discussed in Chapter 5, "Institutional Order Flow." A lot of interaction with the market is needed to trade large orders. That is where some see the advantage of continuous trading. It offers a special kind of interaction between the market participants—opportunities to test the market and to get information from the market. For big orders, periodic calls may not provide the kind of flexibility that some participants want.

In Europe, in particular, this has led to combinations of both call and continuous systems. Call auctions are typically used at the beginning of each trading session to open the order-driven markets. The opening price has special importance because orders that have come in during the overnight trading halt are normally considered to have an equal right to be filled, at least partly, at the opening price. Setting the opening price should therefore be done carefully—be it by a well-structured auction or through a less formalized process. Calls are also used to close the market. The major U.S. and European equity markets do this, for example, to sharpen the determination of cash prices for use in the derivative markets. Some exchanges also run periodic calls during a trading session (Deutsche Börse's market model includes one intraday call). An intraday call is particularly important for securities with low trading volume.

Order Handling

Orders are handled differently in call auctions than in continuous trading, and the time clock is used differently. With a call auction, trades are made at specific points in time rather than whenever, in continuous time, a buy and a sell order cross. To accomplish this, orders submitted to a call auction that could otherwise have been matched and executed are batched together for a multilateral clearing. The clearings are generally held at predetermined points in time (at the open, at the close, and/or at set times during the trading day).

As noted, at the time of a call, the batched orders are matched, and a single clearing price is established. The single clearing price reflects the full set of orders submitted to the call. Buy orders at this value and higher execute, as do sell orders at this value and lower. Because all executed orders clear at the same price, there is no bid-ask spread in call auction trading. Further, with single-price clearing, buy orders priced above the single clearing value and sell orders priced below it receive price improvement.

Alternative Call Auction Designs

Many variations in auction design exist. Calls can be held "on request" instead of at predetermined, regular intervals. Multiple (discriminatory) pricing in a call is possible. The amount of precall pricing information to reveal is a decision variable. Traders may be free to change their orders/quotes until the last moment, or there may be restrictions of various kinds. And so forth.

Taking an aerial view, we identify four basic types of call auctions (with several variations in between):

1. *Price scan auctions.* In a price scan auction, a sequence of prices is "called out" until a value is found that best balances the buy and sell orders. The NYSE call auction opening best fits into this category. The exchange specialists periodically announce indicated opening price ranges, traders respond with their orders, and, as they do, the specialists adjust their indicated opening prices.[12]

2. *Sealed bid auctions.* In a sealed bid auction, participants submit their orders in sealed envelopes that are not opened until the time of the auction. These are totally closed-book (nontransparent) auctions during the preopen phase and, consequently, no participant knows what orders the others are submitting. The term may also be applied more broadly when orders are submitted electronically or by other means if pretrade orders and indicated clearing prices are not revealed to participants. The U.S. Treasury's new issues market is a good example of the sealed bid auction.

In an electronic trading environment, the auction can be set up with various degrees of preauction transparency that allows traders to react to an indicated clearing price that is continuously displayed as the market forms. This functionality characterizes the third category of call auctions:

3. *Open limit order book.* With an open limit order book, posted orders are displayed to the public in the precall order entry period. As the time of the call approaches, the procedure also identifies and updates an indicated clearing price that, at each instant, is the value that would be set in the call if the call were to be held at that instant. At the time of the call, the book is frozen and the indicated clearing price becomes the actual clearing price. The open limit order book call is used in most electronic order-driven trading platforms around the world.

The fourth category is not, strictly speaking, a call because it does not undertake price discovery. However, because it is based on the principle of order batching, we include it here:

4. *Crossing networks.* A crossing network does not discover price. Rather, buy and sell orders are matched in a multilateral trade at a price that is set elsewhere. Generally, the value used at a cross is either the last transaction price or the midpoint of the bid-ask spread set in a major market center. In the United States, ITG's intraday Posit crosses, Burlington Capital Markets' BLOX, and Instinet's after-hours cross are good examples of this facility.

Order Batching and Price Determination

Exhibits 6.2 to 6.5 describe order batching and price determination in a call. In each of these figures, share price is shown on the vertical axis, and the number of orders is shown on the horizontal axis.[13] The number of shares sought for purchase or offered for sale is conventionally displayed on the horizontal axis, but the exposition is simplified by assuming that all orders are for the same number of shares (e.g., one round lot).

Exhibit 6.2 displays the individual buy and sell orders. The horizontal axis gives the total number of orders (buys plus sells) that have been placed at each price. At each price, the orders are arrayed according to the sequence in which they have arrived. At the price of 52, just one sell order has been placed. At 51, a sell order arrived first, then a buy order. At 50, two buy orders arrived followed by one sell order. And so on.

Exhibits 6.3 and 6.4 show how the individual buy and sell orders are aggregated. Only the buy orders (both individual and aggregated) are shown in Exhibit 6.3. Because the price limit on a buy order is the highest price at which the order is to be executed, the buy orders are cumulated from the highest price (in this case 51) down to the lowest (47). At 51, there is just one order to buy. Two additional buy orders have been entered at 50; thus, at 50, there are three buy orders. At yet lower prices, one order has been placed at each of the prices, 49, 48, and 47. Thus, the

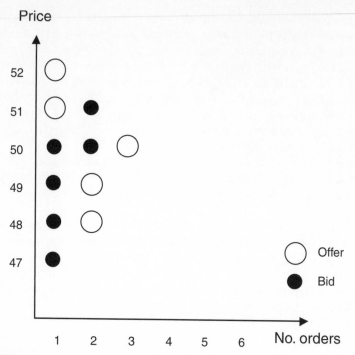

EXHIBIT 6.2　Batching of customer orders.

cumulative number of orders at these prices is four, five, and six, respectively.

Only the sell orders (both individual and aggregated) are shown in Exhibit 6.4, and they are also cumulated. Because the price limit on a sell order is the lowest price at which the order is to be executed, the sell orders are cumulated from the lowest price (48) up to the highest price (52). There is only one sell order at each of the prices, and the cumulative number of sell orders increases by one order as we move from the single order at 48 to the five orders at 52.

The cumulative buy and sell orders are matched together in Exhibit 6.5 to determine the clearing price at which they execute and the specific orders that execute. At the intersection of the two curves, price is 50 and the number of orders is three. Thus, three buy orders execute (the one placed at 51 and the two at 50) and three sell orders execute (the one placed at 48, the one at 49, and the one at 50). Note that three is the maximum number of orders that can execute: At the higher price of 51 there is only one buy order, and at the lower price of 49 there are only two sell orders. For this reason, the clearing price in a call auction is typically iden-

Price

EXHIBIT 6.3 Cumulation of the buy orders.

tified as the value that maximizes the number of shares that execute (and, in the special case presented here, the number of orders that execute).

Note that the most aggressive buy orders are matched with the most aggressive sell orders. This is because orders receive price priority. Namely, the most aggressive orders (on either side) are executed first. If several orders have the same price limits, the order that was input first is executed first (time priority). In the example depicted in Exhibit 6.5, three of the executed orders receive price improvement (the buy at 51, the sell at 49, and the sell at 48). The less aggressive orders (the buys at 49, 48, and 47 and the sells at 51 and 52) remain unexecuted. These orders may be rolled into the continuous market, held for the next call, or canceled, depending on the wishes of the investor.

In Exhibit 6.5, at the market-clearing price of 50, the cumulated sell orders match the cumulated buy orders exactly. What if no price exists that gives an exact match? For instance, what would happen if, everything else being constant, three buy orders rather than two were entered at 50? The decision rule would still pick 50 to be the price (this value would still maximize the number of orders that execute), but with a cumulative of

EXHIBIT 6.4 Cumulation of the sell orders.

only three sell orders at 50, only three of the four buy orders can be executed.

A further decision rule is needed to specify which three of the four orders to pick. The rule commonly used is the *time priority rule:* Orders execute according to the sequence in which they were placed, with the first to arrive being the first to execute. Time priority is valuable in call auction trading—it gives participants an incentive to place their orders earlier in the precall order entry period.[14]

Price Setting Algorithm in Auctions

Consistent with standard microeconomic analysis, prices and transaction volumes are set by the intersection of cumulated bid and offer curves. If these curves are continuous, apart from extremely unlikely situations, they always lead to a clearly defined price and to an associated trading volume (the maximum executable volume, given participants' expressed desires to buy and to sell shares). In electronic auctions, the criterion used to select

EXHIBIT 6.5 Matching of the cumulated buy and sell orders.

the market-clearing price is typically stated as "the maximization of trading volume (or turnover)."

In actual markets, however, cumulative bid and offer curves are not smooth, but are step functions. This is because price and quantity are both discrete variables (there is a minimum price variation, and shares are normally traded in board lots).[15] Additionally, orders tend to cluster at round integers (e.g., there are more orders with a limit of euro 27 than of euro 26.95 or euro 27.05).

With step functions, additional criteria are needed for setting prices at the auctions. In the previous subsection, we noted one rule, the time priority rule, to determine exactly which order executes if the cumulated buys and sells are not equal at the selected price. But step functions can lead to another problem—two or more prices can be tied according to the primary criterion, the maximization of trading volume. We next consider the price-setting algorithms that can be used in this situation.

Exhibits 6.6 to 6.9 illustrate the most common criteria for setting prices. They present a systematic picture of an order book, which includes all orders, cumulating orders from market orders, and then the most aggressively priced limit orders to the least aggressively priced limit orders. This means that buy orders are cumulated in a descending order and sell orders are cumulated in an ascending order. In Exhibit 6.6, maximization of turnover leads to an unambiguous transaction point: 3,000 shares to buy and 3,000 shares to sell execute at $99. At 98.75, only 2,500 shares could be traded because of the available sell orders; at 99.25, the buy orders would be the limiting factor and only 2,100 shares would trade. Additional criteria are needed if two or more prices satisfy the maximization of turnover criterion.

The second criterion (after the maximization of turnover) is the minimization of the number of unexecuted orders. This is known as the *criterion of smallest surplus* (see Exhibit 6.7). Both prices, 99.00 and 98.75, lead to a trading volume of 3,000 shares. By setting a price of 99.00, only a surplus of 500 (on the sell side) remains; with a price of 98.75, a surplus of 1,000 shares on the buy side would remain.

Buy orders, no. of shares				Sell orders, no. of shares		
	Cumulated				Cumulated	
Individual	At the price	From highest price	Price (limit)	From lowest price	At the price	Individual
400 + 300	700	700	Market			
. . . .	. . . .	. . . .	>100			
200	200	900	100			
300	300	1,200	99.75			
400	400	1,600	99.50	4,200	500	200 + 300
200 + 300	500	2,100	99.25	3,700	700	700
800 + 100	900	3,000	99.00	3,000	500	500
1,000	1,000	4,000	98.75	2,500	300	100 + 200
700 + 200	900	4,900	98.50	2,200	300	300
			98.25	1,900	300	100 + 200
			98.00	1,600	100	100
			< 98	. . . .	. . . .	. . . .
			Market	1,500	1,500	700 + 800

EXHIBIT 6.6 Setting the price: The maximization of turnover criterion.

Buy orders, no. of shares				Sell orders, no. of shares		
	Cumulated			Cumulated		
Separate	Per price	From highest price	Price (limit)	From lowest price	Per price	Separate
400 + 300	700	700	Market			
....	....	....	>100			
200	200	900	100			
300	300	1,200	99.75			
400	400	1,600	99.50	4,700	500	200 + 300
200 + 300	500	2,100	99.25	4,200	700	700
800 + 100	900	3,000	99.00	3,500	500	500
1,000	1,000	4,000	98.75	3,000	800	100 + 700
700 + 200	900	4,900	98.50	2,200	300	300
			98.25	1,900	300	100 + 200
			98.00	1,600	100	100
			<98	....	....	....
			Market	1,500	1,500	700 + 800

EXHIBIT 6.7 Setting the price: The smallest surplus criterion.

If there are two or more prices that satisfy the first and second criterion, the *criterion of market pressure* is applied. As can be seen from Exhibit 6.8 there are two prices, 98.75 and 99.00, which produce both a maximum trading volume of 3,000 shares and a minimum surplus of 1,000 shares. For both prices the surplus is on the buy side, which drives prices up; the highest price in the set of alternative solutions, 99.00 in the example, is chosen to be the market price. If the surplus would be on the sell side, the lowest in the set would be chosen.

Finally, it is possible (albeit highly unlikely) for two prices to yield the same maximum turnover, with equal surpluses, with one being on the buy side and the other on the sell side (see Exhibit 6.9). In this case, the price that is closest to the most recent price (typically referred to as the *reference price*) is selected, 99.00 (and not 98.75) in the example (because 99.00 is closer to the previous price of 99.50). In very special situations, these four criteria may be insufficient. Additional rules are needed if too much time has passed since the last reference price was set and if, in the meantime, prices in the broad market have moved to a different level.

Buy orders, no. of shares				Sell orders, no. of shares		
	Cumulated			Cumulated		
Separate	Per price	From highest price	Price (limit)	From lowest price	Per price	Separate
400 + 300	700	700	Market			
....	....	....	>100			
200	200	900	100			
300	300	1,200	99.75			
400	400	1,600	99.50	4,200	500	200 + 300
200 + 300	500	2,100	99.25	3,700	700	700
800 + 1,100	1,900	4,000	99.00	3,000	0	0
0	0	4,000	98.75	3,000	300	100 + 200
700 + 200	900	4,900	98.50	2,700	800	800
			98.25	1,900	300	100 + 200
			98.00	1,600	100	100
			<98	....	....	....
			Market	1,500	1,500	700 + 800

EXHIBIT 6.8   Setting the price: The market pressure criterion.

Relationship between Limit and Market Orders

Limit orders and market orders are very different order types in continuous trading, but are virtually the same in call auction trading. The properties of market orders and limit orders for the call and continuous market are shown in Exhibit 6.10. For the continuous market, limit orders set the prices at which market orders execute, and limit orders sitting on the book provide immediacy to the market orders (i.e., the market orders execute on arrival). Limit order traders are willing to wait patiently for an execution, and they are the liquidity providers. In a continuous market, market order traders demand immediate liquidity.

In contrast, market orders in the call environment are nothing more than extremely aggressively priced limit orders. Specifically, a market order to buy has an effective price limit of infinity, and a market order to sell has an effective price limit of zero. Participants in a call auction all wait until the next call for their orders to execute, and thus market orders in a call auction do not receive immediacy as they do in continuous trading.

Buy orders, no. of shares				Sell orders, no. of shares		
	Cumulated				Cumulated	
Separate	Per price	From highest price	Price (limit)	From lowest price	Per price	Separate
400 + 300	700	700	Market			
. . . .	. . . .	. . . .	>100			
200	200	900	100			
300	300	1,200	99.75			
400	400	1,600	99.50*	4,700	500	200 + 300
200 + 300	500	2,100	99.25	4,200	700	700
800 + 100	900	3,000	99.00	3,500	500	500
500	500	3,500	98.75	3,000	800	100 + 700
700 + 200	900	4,400	98.50	2,200	300	300
			98.25	1,900	300	100 + 200
			98.00	1,600	100	100
			<98	. . . .	. . . .	. . . .
			Market	1,500	1,500	700 + 800

*Previous price.

EXHIBIT 6.9 Setting the price: The most recent price criterion.

The distinction in continuous trading that limit order placers supply liquidity while market order placers demand liquidity does not apply to call auction trading. In a call auction, all participants supply liquidity to each other. However, with an open book call, those participants who placed their orders early in the precall order entry period are key to the book-building

	Market orders	Limit orders
Continuous order-driven market	• Execute at the best counterpart • Execute immediately • Immediacy demanding	• Execute at price of the order • Delayed or no execution • Immediacy supplying
Call auction	• Execute at the clearing price • No immediate execution • Not immediacy demanding	• Execute at the clearing price • No immediate or no execution • Not immediacy supplying

EXHIBIT 6.10 Order handling in a call versus a continuous market.

process. As we discuss subsequently, early order placers are the catalysts for liquidity supply.

The Electronic Call Auction

More than 100 years ago, the New York Stock Exchange was a call market (nonelectronic, of course). In some respects, the nonelectronic call was a fine system for participants on the exchange floor, but it had deficiencies for anybody away from the floor. Investors not physically present had little knowledge of what was happening (the calls offered no transparency), and access to trading was limited because shares of a stock could be exchanged only periodically (when the market for the stock was called). On May 8, 1869, the call procedure was abandoned when the NYSE merged with a competing exchange, the Open Board of Brokers, and became a continuous trading environment.

The Tel Aviv Stock Exchange through the 1970s and the Paris Bourse before the 1986 introduction of its electronic market, Cotation Assistée en Continu (CAC), were also nonelectronic call auctions that did not survive. Call auction trading had been very popular with continental European exchanges in the earlier days when they still had floor trading. But with growing competition among exchanges, continuous trading became increasingly popular. This went hand in hand with extended trading hours. Both developments meant that the volume at the opening call got thinner and its importance was reduced. The widespread trend to fully automated trading on most European exchanges, however, has allowed for new solutions and combinations.

In recent years, tremendous advances in information technology and a slew of other developments in the industry have paved the way for the call's reentry. With an electronic open limit order book, participants everywhere around the globe are able to see the auction as it forms and can enter their own orders with electronic speed. Compared to traditional floor trading, electronic trading offers new flexibilities for fine-tuning market architecture. Automated order book trading usually starts with an opening call and uses a call to resume trading after any halt. As noted, the major European and U.S. exchanges have also introduced closing calls, primarily to provide "better" closing prices for the derivative markets. For securities with little liquidity and less frequent trading, one or two calls per day may suffice.

While information technology (IT) can be used advantageously in continuous trading, it is essential for efficient call auction trading. Moreover, the call auction is an extremely good environment for the application of IT. In a continuous market, IT speeds up the rate at which orders can be submitted, displayed, and turned into trades, and in so doing it accentuates the importance of nanoseconds. In an electronic call auction environment, on the other hand, IT is used to sort and cumulate orders and to find the clearing prices. In a call auction, the computer is used to do one thing in particular that it was created to do—namely, to compute.

The electronic call auction is appealing for small-cap and mid-cap stocks because order batching augments the efficiency of liquidity provision by focusing liquidity at specific points in time. The procedure also has particular appeal for large-cap stocks because it caters to the needs of institutional participants whose portfolios are mostly made up of these issues. Market impact is reduced for the institutional investor, because the call is a point-in-time meeting place and, as noted, batching orders in a multilateral trade focuses liquidity. For all stocks, commissions may be lower due to the greater ease of handling orders and clearing trades in the call auction environment.

For the broad market, electronic call auctions can reduce price volatility, unreliable pricing, unequal access to the market, and various forms of manipulation and abuse.[16] Further, the electronic call auction is an explicit price discovery facility. That is, batching many orders together for simultaneous execution at a single price produces a consensus value that may better reflect the broad market's desire to hold shares. Consequently, the electronic call auction is a good opening facility for the continuous order-driven market.[17] Moreover, because it is an explicit price discovery facility, call auction trading can be used to dampen short-period (e.g., intraday) price volatility.

One feature of call auction trading that has been thought by some to be a drawback is that it does not provide transactional immediacy (participants have to wait for a call). With call and continuous trading combined in a hybrid market structure, this limitation ceases to be a deficiency. In any event, immediacy involves a cost (bid-ask spreads and market impact costs) that not all investors wish to pay. Retail and institutional customers who place limit orders are not looking for immediate executions, and many institutional customers are more concerned with anonymity and keeping trading costs low than with obtaining immediate executions.

To deliver its promise of being a highly efficient trading environment, a call auction must attract sufficient volume. To accomplish this, some order placers must be incented to enter their orders early in the precall order entry period. The early stages of book building cannot be taken for granted, however, especially for an auction that opens the market at the start of a trading day. Some participants, particularly big institutional customers, are reluctant to post orders that could reveal their trading intentions, particularly when the book is thin.[18] Nevertheless, early order placers, the catalysts for liquidity supply, are needed. Two incentives for early order placement are (1) the use of time priorities and (2) reduced commission rates for early order entry. The inclusion of retail customers who are less concerned that their small orders will have any meaningful impact on the clearing price also helps. Finally, a market maker could play an important role in animating book building during the precall order entry period.

OPTION PROPERTIES OF LIMIT ORDERS

It is widely recognized in the academic literature and by many practitioners that an investor who places a limit order extends a free option to others who might then execute against it by submitting a market order.[19] The option characteristics of a posted quote were first identified and analyzed by Copeland and Galai.[20] These authors showed that, by posting a bid, a dealer effectively writes a free put option to public sellers. Similarly, by posting an offer, he or she effectively writes a free call option to public buyers. In this section of the chapter, we focus on limit orders (not on dealers' quotes). More important, we do not consider the option extended, but the option an investor implicitly receives when placing a limit order.

Analytical Framework

Consistent with the traditional microstructure literature and our own discussion, we consider two kinds of events that can explain the change of security prices: liquidity events and information events. *Liquidity events* are defined as the execution of orders placed by investors seeking to trade only for individually motivated reasons (e.g., their own reassessments of share value and personal cash inflows and outflows). *Information events* are defined as the execution of orders placed by investors seeking to trade because of news that affects expectations about the future prices of shares. News is known by all participants, but not simultaneously. We assume that some investors receive the news instantaneously and that the rest receive it just after an information event has occurred. We allow for investors' to have divergent expectations based on their interpretation of news.

We simplify the analysis by considering that an investor's trading window extends through the next event (i.e., transaction), which corresponds to the arrival of the next market order in a continuous market or to the next auction in a call market. Our purpose is to show that the payoff the investor obtains from a limit order depends on (1) whether a liquidity event or an informational event occurs and (2) whether the order is placed in a continuous market or a call auction.

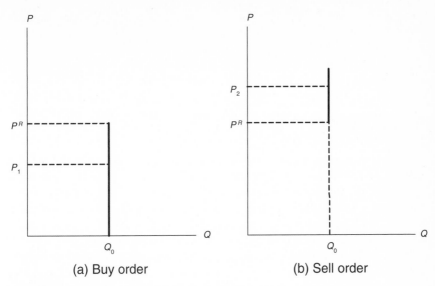

(a) Buy order   (b) Sell order

EXHIBIT 6.11 An investor's buy and sell orders.

For simplicity, we consider an investor who has already chosen the number of shares (Q) of a security that he or she wishes to trade. That is, we take quantity to be an exogenous variable in the analysis.[21] Exhibit 6.11 illustrates the buy order function of an investor who wants to buy Q_0 shares of a security, and the sell order function of an investor who wants to sell Q_0 shares of a security. In the exhibit, P^R denotes the investor's reservation price for the quantity Q_0 shares. As we have previously noted, a reservation price for a buy order is the maximum price the investor is willing to pay for the Q_0 shares, and, for a sell order, P^R is the minimum price that he or she is willing to receive for the Q_0 shares.[22] We let the investor's reservation price depend on his or her expectations about the future value shares might have.[23]

Identifying the reservation price for Q_0 shares enables us to specify the monetary value to the investor of buying Q_0 shares at some price P_1 lower than P^R, or of selling Q_0 shares at some price P_2 higher than P^R. Economists typically refer to the monetary value of trading as consumer or producer surplus. For simplicity, we simply write *surplus*, which is the difference between the investor's reservation price and the transaction price, times the number of shares traded.[24]

Clearly, an investor will trade a given number of shares of the security only if he or she expects to obtain a surplus from the trade, and the objective of the investor when placing an order is to maximize the expected value of the surplus received. Optimal order placement, therefore, considers both the surplus received from an order if that order executes and the probability of order execution. We do not determine the optimal placement of an order, but focus primarily on the surplus, which is described by a payoff diagram.

Investor's Surplus in the Continuous Environment

We first analyze the surplus an investor can obtain from placing a limit order in a continuous environment. Consider the case of an investor willing to buy, for his or her own cash flow reasons, one share of a security with a reservation price of \$50.[25] Because limit orders execute at their price limits in a continuous market, the investor will set a price limit strictly below his or her reservation price. Assume that the investor sets a price limit of \$47. Exhibit 6.12 shows the surplus that he or she can obtain from this limit buy order when the next transaction results from the execution of 2 contra-side order placed by an investor seeking to trade for a cash flow reason only.

In Exhibit 6.12, P_{lim} is the price limit of the order, and P_T is the value to which a liquidity event drives the transaction price. Because of the price priority rule used for limit order execution, the limit buy order placed by

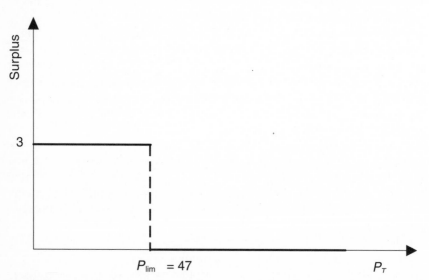

EXHIBIT 6.12   Surplus from a one-share limit buy order with a liquidity event.

the investor at \$47 does not execute if P_T is above \$47. This will be the case if the next market order is (1) a buy order or (2) a sell order that is not large enough to execute all limit buy orders with priority placed at \$47 and above. Alternatively, the limit buy order does execute if the next market order drives the transaction price to \$47 or below.[26] In this case, the investor receives a \$3 surplus even if P_T is less than \$47. That is, by placing a limit buy order in a continuous market, the investor cannot benefit from a further fall in the transaction price.

The payoff diagram in Exhibit 6.12 corresponds to that of a binary put option that pays a fixed amount of \$3 if the stock price is equal to or below its strike price of \$47, and that pays nothing if the stock price is above its strike price. This is the financial asset that the investor receives from placing a limit buy order at \$47 in a continuous market when only a liquidity event can occur during his or her trading window.

But a news event can also trigger an execution of the order before the limit order trader receives the information and withdraws the order. Exhibit 6.13 shows the payout for a limit buy order at \$47 when an information event occurs during the investor's trading window. In the exhibit, P_1^R is the investor's revised reservation price after he or she receives the news (i.e., just after the information event occurs), and P_T is the value to which an information event drives the transaction price. If an information event occurs without driving P_T to \$47 or below, the payout to the investor is zero. This is the case when the information event is (1) the advent of bullish news or (2) the advent of bearish news but the next market sell order is not large enough to execute the limit buy order at \$47. If an information event drives P_T below the price limit, the order executes. The limit order trader will profit if the information event follows the advent of bearish news that does not drive his or her own reservation price, P_1^R, below P_{lim}. On the other hand, the limit order trader will lose if the information event follows the advent of bearish news that does drive his or her own reservation price below P_{lim}.

We have shown that the payoff the investor obtains from a limit order in a continuous market depends on whether a liquidity event or an information

	$P_T < 47$	$P_T = 47$	$P_T > 47$
$P_1^R > 47$	$P_1^R - 47 > 0$	$P_1^R - 47 > 0$	0
$P_1^R = 47$	0	0	0
$P_1^R < 47$	$P_1^R - 47 < 0$	$P_1^R - 47 < 0$	0

EXHIBIT 6.13 Surplus from a one-share limit buy order with an informational event.

event occurs during his or her trading window. This result suggests that, vis-à-vis a participant who trades immediately by market order in a continuous market, a participant who trades by limit order obtains a claim on the next liquidity or information event that occurs, and that this claim can affect the investor's final wealth position.

Investor's Surplus in the Call Environment

We next analyze the surplus an investor can obtain from placing a limit order in an electronic call auction that operates as follows. At time t_0, the exchange opens the limit order book and, until the time of the call (time T), investors can place limit and market orders in the book without their orders being executed. At time T, the exchange freezes the limit order book and determines the clearing price of the security, which is the price at which all trades take place.

Again, we first consider an investor seeking to buy, for his or her own cash flow reasons, one share of a security with a reservation price of $50. Because limit orders execute at the common clearing price in a call auction, the investor will set a price limit equal to his or her reservation price (unless the investor is large enough to expect that the order will have market impact). Exhibit 6.14 shows the surplus that this investor can obtain from a one-share limit buy order with a price limit of $50 if a liquidity event occurs.[27]

The value to which a liquidity event drives the clearing price in the call auction is defined as P^C. The limit buy order placed by the investor at $50 does not execute if P^C is not equal to or lower than $50. This will be the case if the cumulated quantity to buy at $50 or above is greater than the cumulated quantity to sell at $50 or below. Alternatively, the order does execute if P^C is $50 or below. In this case, because the order executes at the common clearing price, the investor receives a surplus that is contingent on P^C. The lower is P^C, the higher is the surplus that the investor obtains.

The payoff diagram, shown in Exhibit 6.14, corresponds to that of a standard put option with a strike price of $50 and an expiration date corresponding to the time of the call auction. This is the financial asset that the investor receives from the placement of a limit buy order set at $50 in a call auction when only a liquidity event can occur during his or her trading window.

The payoffs that the investor receives from a limit order in the call and continuous environments when a liquidity event occurs are both shown in Exhibit 6.15. Contrasting the payoff diagram alone without considering the probability distributions of P^C and P_T, suggests that the payoff to a limit order in the call is superior to that in a continuous market. We see in Exhibit 6.15 that, because it is written at a price of $50 (which is the

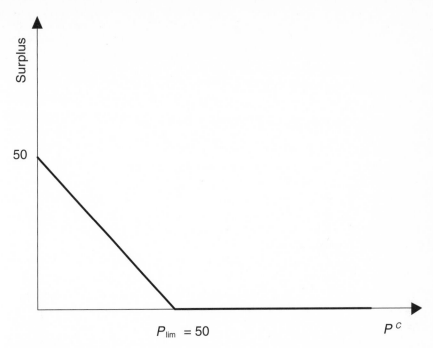

EXHIBIT 6.14 Surplus from a one-share limit buy order with a liquidity event.

investor's reservation price) rather than at a price of \$47, the limit order in the call has a positive payoff in the price range from \$47 to \$50, and in the continuous market the limit order does not. Moreover, because it executes at the common clearing price rather than at the price limit of the order, the limit order in the call has a payoff greater than \$3 in the price range below \$47, and in the continuous market the limit order does not. However, when the execution probability is also taken into account, we are not able to conclude that the trading claim the investor receives from the placement of a limit order in a call auction is unambiguously superior when a liquidity event occurs. The reason is that the probability of P_T reaching any given value in the continuous market does not, in general, equal the probability of P^C reaching that value in the call auction.

As in the continuous market, the placement of a limit order in a call auction can result in an undesirable outcome if news occurs before the call and triggers an execution of the order at a clearing price above the investor's revised reservation price.[28] Exhibit 6.16 shows the payout for a

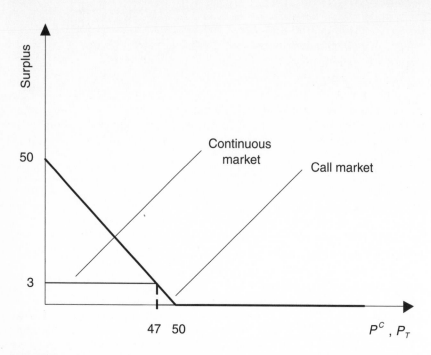

EXHIBIT 6.15 Surplus from a liquidity event in the call and continuous markets.

limit buy order at \$50 in a call auction when some investors place orders because of the advent of news.

Note that P_1^R is the investor's revised reservation price after he or she receives the news. If an information event occurs without P^C being driven to \$50 or below, the payout to the investor is zero. If an information event drives P^C below the price limit, the order executes. The limit order trader profits if the information event drives P^C below his or her revised reserva-

	$P^C < 50$	$P^C = 50$	$P^C > 50$
$P_1^R > P^C$	$P_1^R - P_C > 0$	$P_1^R - P_C > 0$	0
$P_1^R = P^C$	0	NA*	NA
$P_1^R < P^C$	$P_1^R - P_C < 0$	$P_1^R - P_C < 0$	0

*NA = not applicable.

EXHIBIT 6.16 Surplus from a limit buy order with an informational event.

tion price. This can be the case if the information event follows (1) the advent of bullish news known only by some market participants, (2) the advent of bearish news that has been overestimated by market participants, or (3) in general, if the reservation price of our investor does not fall as much as that of others. On the other hand, the limit order trader loses if the information event results in P^C being above his or her revised reservation price. This will be the case if the information event follows the advent of bearish news that is not known or is underestimated by other market participants.

Contrasting Exhibits 6.13 and 6.16 shows that the limit order trader does not obtain the same payoff following the advent of bearish (bullish) news in the call and the continuous environments. First, because the investor places his or her reservation price in the call auction, his or her limit order will execute if P^C is in the range from $47 to $50, whereas the limit order submitted in the continuous market at $47 will execute only at $47 and below. In this case the investor will profit if the information event follows (1) the advent of bullish news that does not drive P^C above his or her reservation price or (2) the advent of bearish news that does not drive his or her reservation price below the clearing price. Second, because the investor trades at a common clearing price and not at the price limit of his or her order, the advent of bearish news that changes the investor's reservation price as well as P^C does not guarantee a loss to the limit order trader in a call auction. Only if the information event drives P^C below the investor's revised reservation price, P_1^R, will the investor lose, and his or her loss will be less if the clearing price is below $47.

Discussion

By placing a limit buy (sell) order, the investor gives the right to other market participants to sell (buy) the security at the price of the limit order in the continuous market and at the clearing price in the call auction.[29] Consequently, the investor can lose if news occurs and triggers an execution of the limit buy (sell) order at a price above (below) his or her revised reservation price, and the investor can profit if the order executes due to a liquidity event.[30] By considering together the option implicitly extended and the option implicitly received, we see that the loss the investor would sustain from a news event (the option extended to others is exercised) is the price the investor must pay to benefit from a liquidity event (the option implicitly received by the investor is exercised). Alternatively stated, the payoff the investor receives from a liquidity event is the compensation he or she obtains from writing a "free" option to other participants.

Further, we have shown that the compensation obtained from the implicit option held has the payoff of a *binary option* in the continuous market and the payoff of a *standard option* in the call auction. This difference highlights an important distinction between the call and continuous environments and suggests that introducing a call auction implicitly introduces a new financial asset for investors. Our analysis highlights three attributes of these new options:

1. The options are nontradable assets.

2. Unlike traded standard and binary options, the options that investors receive from limit orders when a liquidity event occurs are free.

3. While these options have the same payoff as traded options, they are not redundant assets. The reason is twofold. (1) The claims have very short maturity, and (2) they have a strike price fixed only by the investor with respect to very short term price changes, which are usually not available for traded options.

Our analysis of the options embedded in limit orders when a liquidity event occurs could be extended in a number of ways. One important consideration involves the placement of a large, institutional order in a call auction. As we have shown, a small uninformed retail customer will place a limit order at his or her reservation price in a call auction. An institutional investor will not do this because the clearing price can be adversely impacted by his or her order. Instead, the institutional investor will place an order at a price less aggressive than his or her reservation price, depending on his or her expectations about the market impact of the order. Because orders on the book are valuable information from which institutional investors form their expectations about market impact, an open limit order book call auction will reduce the cost implied by this trading consideration.[31]

Our analysis also has important implications for information release.[32] The analysis of the payouts for information events in both the continuous and the call environments underscores the fact that, on expectation, information release that affects price behavior after a participant has placed his or her order is undesirable. It is, of course, the adverse effect of information events that explains why investors require liquidity events to compensate them for placing limit orders. It follows that, if the information events are less likely to occur, more liquidity providing limit orders will be submitted to the market. In light of this, we see a further benefit of holding multiple call auctions during a trading day: The calls establish predetermined points in time that controllable information release can be pegged to. One would expect that the more complex the information, the earlier it would be released before the start of a call, and that relatively simple news announcements can be made up to the time the limit order book is opened to receive orders. From the opening of the book until the auction, no controllable information release should occur.

NEED FOR ADDITIONAL MARKET STRUCTURE

Our discussion in the preceding section of the option properties of limit orders underscores the fact that call and continuous auctions are very different trading environments. We have suggested that the introduction of a call along with continuous trading effectively creates a new financial asset: the option obtained by a limit order trader when the limit order is submitted to a call auction rather than to a continuous trading venue.

Uniting call auction and continuous trading in a hybrid structure considerably strengthens an order-driven market. Nevertheless, a variety of factors can stress the order-driven environment, and further market structure is needed. Order-driven markets require considerable transactional frequency to attract adequate liquidity provision from limit orders placers, and this may not be achievable with low-cap and mid-cap stocks. Large institutional customers place major liquidity demands on the markets for all stocks, and their orders, if not properly handled, can disrupt price formation and trading. The difficulty of price discovery is accentuated after the advent of major news. Under conditions of accentuated uncertainty, sellers may suddenly rush forward, buyers may step aside, and prices may go into free fall.

In light of all of these sources of stress, further market structure is needed. For the most part, intermediaries provide this additional structure, which is the topic we turn to in the next chapter.

NOTES

1. For the analytical foundation of the analysis pertaining to the placement of limit orders in a continuous order-driven market, see Puneet Handa and Robert Schwartz, "Limit Order Trading," *Journal of Finance*, 1996, pp. 1835–1861. We use that foundation in this chapter.

2. Order-driven markets typically allow for more complex types of orders. Stop-loss orders, for instance, are instructions to buy if price *rises above* a given value or to sell if price *falls below* a given value. Hidden orders (sometimes

referred to as *iceberg orders*) allow for all or part of a large order to be entered into the computer of an electronic trading system without being disclosed to the market (this order type is common in the European markets). The limit price of an order for one stock may also be linked to and automatically change with some other value, such as the price of another stock or the value of a market index. And so forth. Special instructions can also be placed on orders: "all or none" (execute the order in full or not at all), "fill or kill" (execute the order immediately or not at all), and so forth.

3. A limit order priced more aggressively than a counterpart quote (i.e., a limit buy order with a price higher than the best offer, or a limit sell order with a price lower than the best bid) is referred to as a *marketable limit order*. Marketable limit orders are handled like market orders up to the price at which the investor has capped the order.

4. For the analytical foundation of the analysis pertaining to the existence of the bid-ask spread, see Kalman Cohen, Steven Maier, Robert Schwartz, and David Whitcomb, "Transaction Costs, Order Placement Strategy, and Existence of the Bid-Ask Spread," *Journal of Political Economy*, April 1981, pp. 287–305.

5. Look again at Exhibit 6.1 and observe that the price column is in 5-cent increments. The minimum allowable price change is commonly referred to as the *tick size*, or *minimum price variation*.

6. There are exceptions to limit orders executing at their own price. If a large trade is negotiated at a price above the best offer or below the best bid, the lower-priced offers or higher-priced bids on the book may be included in the block trade and executed at the block trade's price. This procedure results in limit orders in the continuous market occasionally being price-improved. Another exception is when limit orders execute in a single price call auction. As we discuss in the next section of this chapter, limit orders are routinely price-improved in call auction trading.

7. The buy order will not execute fully, however, if it is for more shares than are posted at the offer. To simplify the discussion, we ignore this possibility.

8. See Cohen, Maier, Schwartz, and Whitcomb, op. cit., for a mathematical proof that the execution probability remains below unity by a discrete amount.

9. Richard Maier, SWX Swiss Exchange, made important contributions to this section, for which we are grateful.

10. Part of this section has been adapted from Robert A. Schwartz, "The Call Auction Alternative," in *Call Auction Trading: New Answers to Old Questions*, Robert A. Schwartz, John Aidan Byrne and Antoinette Colaninno, eds., Kluwer Academic Publishers, 2003. Some of the material is also in Nicholas Economides and Robert A. Schwartz, "Electronic Call Market Trading," *Journal of Portfolio Management*, spring 1995, pp. 10–18.

11. In a quote-driven market, the quotes of a dealer or market maker establish the prices at which others can trade by market order.

12. The Paris Bourse's market, before the exchange introduced electronic trading in 1986, was a classic price scan call auction. When the market for a stock was

called, an auctioneer would cry out one price after another, scanning the range of possibilities, until an acceptable balance was found between the buy and sell orders.

13. This section is adapted from Robet A. Schwartz, "The Call Auction Alternative," in Robert A. Schwartz, ed., *The Electronic Call Auction: Market Mechanism and Trading, Building a Better Stock Market*, Kluwer Academic Publishers, 2001.

14. Further situations can be described that require more complex rules of order execution. As is typically the case, the set of decision rules required for an actual operating system is far more complicated than those we need consider to achieve a basic understanding of a system. We consider further decision rules in the subsection that follows.

15. Even if board lots are reduced to one share, or if fractions of board lots are acceptable for trading, it is still not normally possible to deliver fractions of a share.

16. For further discussion of the properties of call auction trading, see Kalman J. Cohen and Robert A. Schwartz, "An Electronic Call Market: Its Design and Desirability," in *The Challenge of Information Technology for the Securities Markets: Liquidity, Volatility, and Global Trading*, Henry Lucas and Robert Schwartz, eds., 1989, pp. 15–58, and Nicholas Economides and Robert A. Schwartz, (1995, op.cit.).

17. The call auction is also a good opening facility for the quote-driven (dealer) market.

18. For further discussion, see Archishman Chakraborty, Michael S. Pagano, and Robert A. Schwartz, "Bookbuilding," Baruch College working paper, 2004.

19. This section is adapted from Nicole Beiner and Robert A. Schwartz, "The Option Properties of Limit Orders in Call and Continuous Environments," in Robert A. Schwartz, ed., *The Electronic Call Auction: Market Mechanism and Trading, Building a Better Stock Market*, Kluwer Academic Publishers, 2001.

20. T. E. Copeland and D. Galai, "Information Effects on the Bid-Ask Spreads," *Journal of Finance* 38, 1983, pp. 1457–1469.

21. This assumption may not correspond to investors' behavior in real markets, since the number of shares placed may depend on the depth and width of the market at the times investors implement their trading decisions.

22. More specifically, the reservation price is the maximum (minimum) price the investor is willing to pay (receive) when the alternative to Q_0 shares is to not trade at all. This is the price that makes the investor indifferent between trading Q_0 shares and not trading at all. Note that if an order for Q_0 shares does not execute, the investor in fact does not trade.

23. For simplicity, we assume that after a limit order has been placed, the investor's reservation price changes only with the receipt of news. Because we do not assume homogeneous responses to news, we allow investors to revise their reservation prices differently based on a news event.

24. For $Q_0 = 100$, $P^R = \$50$, and $P_1 = 47$, the investor's surplus from a purchase is $(P^R - P_1)Q_0 = (50 - 47)100 = 300$. The investor's surplus from a sale is similarly defined as $(P_2 - P^R)Q_0$, except that the (lower) reservation price is subtracted from the (higher) price realized from the sale.

25. The analysis can be easily extended for an investor willing to buy more shares or willing to sell more shares.

26. For simplicity, we ignore the possibility of the limit order not executing at $P_T = 47$ because other orders have been placed in the book before it at this price.

27. When no news occurs during the call, all orders that are placed and executed are from investors seeking to trade for their own cash flow reasons.

28. Note that the limit order trader can change or withdraw his or her order if he or she receives the news before the call auction.

29. That is, if the clearing price is lower (higher) than the price limit of the order.

30. As shown previously, in some cases the investor can also benefit if his or her limit order executes because of an information event.

31. A buy order in a call with a price limit below the investor's reservation price has the payoff of a knock-in option with a strike price equal to the reservation price and a barrier equal to the price limit. It is easy to show that the cost institutional investors incur when placing a price limit lower than their reservation price corresponds to the value of a short position in a knock-out option.

32. The timing of much information release is controllable (e.g., micro news, such as quarterly earnings and dividend announcements, and macro news, such as unemployment and inflation statistics). The timing of news releases concerning acts of nature (e.g., fires and storms), of course, is not controllable.

CHAPTER 7

Intermediated Markets

In the previous chapter, we showed how public investors (the naturals) can meet in a pure, nonintermediated market, provide liquidity to one another, set prices, and trade. We now turn to intermediated markets. *Intermediation* means the participation of a third party in trading. Intermediaries include brokers, dealers, market makers, and specialists.

A broker handles a customer order as the customer's agent. In contrast, a dealer is a principal who commits capital to a trade, buying from public sellers and selling to public buyers. A market maker is a dealer with special obligations to make a good, orderly market by running his or her own book and taking the corresponding risk. Currently, dealers in the equity markets are widely referred to as *market makers*. In this chapter, we use the two terms interchangeably. A specialist is an intermediary on the U.S. exchanges who operates as both a broker (agent) and dealer (market maker). Each stock listed on the New York Stock Exchange (NYSE) is assigned to one specialist firm that has an affirmative obligation to make a fair and orderly market for that stock.[1]

A market maker realizes revenue from the spread between his or her bid and offer quotes. With a larger spread, more revenue can be realized from a given volume (turnover). On the other hand, for a given spread, revenues are higher the greater is the trading volume (turnover) in a stock. With a highly liquid stock, a market maker profits mainly from volume, not from his or her spread being large.[2]

Exhibit 7.1 shows a book that is characteristic of a quote-driven market. There are five market makers: Cat, Cod, Dog, Plum, and Tuna. Each of the five is making a *two-sided market* (posting both a bid and an ask). The

Dealer	Bid	Dealer	Ask
Cat	26.00	Tuna	26.20
Cod	26.00	Plum	26.20
Dog	25.90	Cat	26.30
Plum	25.90	Cod	26.30
Tuna	24.80	Dog	26.30

EXHIBIT 7.1   Market-maker quotes.

bids establish the prices at which the public can sell. They are on the left, arrayed from the most aggressive (highest) to the least aggressive (lowest). The asks establish the prices at which the public can buy. They are on the right, arrayed from the most aggressive (lowest) to the least aggressive (highest). The *inside market* (bid-ask spread) is the most aggressive ask (26.20) minus the most aggressive bid (26.00), or 20 cents.[3] On both the bid and the offer side, some of the market makers have posted identical quotes. There are no secondary rules of order execution (such as time priority) in pure quote-driven markets. Each customer selects the market maker to whom he or she wishes to direct an order. Directing an order to a specific dealer firm is referred to as *preferencing.*

Brokers, dealers, market makers, and specialists, along with exchanges and other trading systems, supply services to investors who are seeking to buy or to sell shares for their own investment reasons. The suppliers of trading services are referred to as the *sell side.* Customers who require trading services (the investors) are referred to as the *buy side* (they buy trading services). Large institutional investors (e.g., mutual and pension funds) have their own buy side trading desks that interact with the sell side desks.

Buy side traders are commonly faced with the challenge of handling orders up to 100,000 shares, 500,000 shares, 1 million shares, or more. Wayne Wagner, chairman of the Plexus Group, recently stated, "Our data show that over half of institutional decisions to trade exceed 20 percent of [a stock's] average daily trading volume."[4] As we discuss in Chapter 5, "Institutional Order Flow," big orders may be broken into smaller pieces and fed to the market carefully over an extended period of time (up to a day or more). Alternatively, a search for a buy side counterparty may be undertaken to bring a large buyer and large seller together to execute a block trade (10,000 shares or more). Or a larger trade may be executed, in part or in whole, against dealer capital.

For all customers, trading in mid-cap and small-cap stocks typically requires sell side assistance, as does trading big-cap stocks in blocks. With fewer shares outstanding, fewer investors, and, consequently, relatively sparse order flow, the ecology of the limit order book can break down for thinner issues. When this happens, market-maker services are needed.[5]

Intermediation takes two forms: (1) the provision of market-maker capital and (2) special order handling. We consider both in this chapter.

MARKET-MAKER-PROVIDED CAPITAL

A dealer intermediated market is referred to as *quote-driven*. The quotes of the intermediary establish the prices at which the naturals (investors) can trade by market order.[6] In a pure quote-driven environment, market makers are the only source of the quotes. We first consider market-maker operations in a pure quote-driven environment.

Overview of Market-Maker Operations

A market-maker firm trades from its own inventory as a *principal*. When public investors want to buy, a market-maker firm sells *from its own portfolio*, reducing a long position or going short. When public investors want to sell, a market-maker firm buys *for its own portfolio*, reducing a short position or going long. Market makers indicate their willingness to buy or to sell by their quotes. A market maker's quotes consist of two parts: a bid to buy and an offer to sell, along with the share sizes that the two quotes are good for. A market maker will commonly trade in larger size than he or she is quoting and/or will replenish the quotes after a trade. Public investors sell at the market maker's bid and buy at the market maker's ask.

Market makers with long positions hope that share values will move upward so that they can sell from inventory at higher prices. Market makers with short positions hope that share values will move downward so that they can profit by covering their short positions (buying back shares) at lower prices. In general, market making is most profitable when prices mean-revert, as we saw to be the case with limit order traders. But market makers can never know for sure. Future price changes are uncertain, and accumulating inventory (either long or short) is risky.

Dealers try to avoid accumulating excessively long or short positions. The location of their quotes is their basic inventory control mechanism. The procedure is somewhat akin to steering a boat. With a boat, the pilot adjusts the tiller and the boat responds. But the response is sloppy, depending on wind, tide, and the vessel's own momentum.

Picture a market maker who wants to reliquify after having acquired a long position of 150,000 shares. He or she will adjust the quotes downward. By improving on the offer (posting a lower ask), the market maker is indicating a more aggressive willingness to sell shares. By posting a lower bid, the market maker is discouraging further public selling. Alternatively, a market maker with a large short position will raise the offer to discourage public purchases and will raise the bid to encourage public sales. But after having adjusted the tiller, the market maker has to wait for the public's response to bring his or her inventory back to a reasonable target level.

There is an alternative inventory control mechanism. A market maker can also trade with another market maker. This procedure is more akin to steering a car. With a car on a dry road surface, the driver turns the wheel and the car responds immediately and exactly. It is common for one market maker who is long to sell shares (that were bought from customers) to another market maker who is short and wants to buy shares (that were sold to customers), or vice versa. The transaction is referred to as *interdealer trading*.

Transparency   An important attribute of an equity market is its *transparency*. In a transparent market, public participants can easily obtain good information about current market conditions. Transparency has two major components: *Pretrade transparency* refers to quotes and quote sizes, and *posttrade transparency* refers to transaction prices and trade sizes. Pretrade transparency is important because the quotes describe trading possibilities that currently exist (although there can be bluffing in the setting of quotes). Posttrade transparency is important because an actual transaction means that both a buyer and a seller have agreed on a price. However, a completed transaction has occurred in the past, and the market information that it has generated can rapidly become stale.

Transparency is a big issue in market structure. Many constituents typically call for more transparency. Trading requires investors to make tactical decisions: How do you time your orders? How do you size your orders? At what prices would you be willing to trade? In which market do you want to trade? Observing market-maker quotes and seeing recent trades facilitates the timing, sizing, and pricing of customer orders. There is another factor: Knowing the quotes, trade sizes, and transaction prices better enables public buyers and sellers to monitor and to assess the quality of the executions they have received.

Greater transparency is commonly thought to translate into better market quality in terms of liquidity, stability, fairness, and price discovery. However, it is not clear that a more transparent quote-driven market will be more liquid. As we subsequently discuss, too much transparency hurts the market makers, and this can result in their providing less capital to market making. It is also not clear that transparency adds to price stability in a dealer market. If, in a pure quote-driven market, greater transparency results in market makers committing less capital to market making, there will be less liquidity, and with less liquidity, prices will be more volatile.[7]

Transparency's impact on fairness is less ambiguous. A marketplace is perceived as being fairer if participants know the array of prices at which trades are being made and can better assess the quality of their own executions. Transparency is also desirable for price discovery. However, we have to be cautious with this one. If there is less liquidity in the market and prices are more volatile because market makers are committing less capital to market making, price discovery will be less accurate as well. In conclusion, we certainly care about transparency, but greater transparency does not necessarily lead to better market quality.

To see this more clearly, let's put ourselves in the position of a market maker. Assume that we have just acquired a sizable inventory while buying from a large mutual fund. Our customer's desire to sell has been shifted to us, and we are now in the position that the mutual fund had been in. We need to work off that position. There is a phrase in the industry that captures this: "Shares sold to a market maker are still for sale." This is because the market maker is not the final customer, despite the fact that the order is in his or her book (and neither is the market maker the ultimate source of liquidity, as noted in Chapter 3, "Liquidity").

How does this relate to transparency? The point is, having just bought from a public seller, we now want to pass the parcel on to a public buyer. Just as the mutual fund does not want others to know that it has entered the market as a seller until after the shares have been sold, neither do we want other dealers or the public to know that we are now looking to sell the shares. The success of any market-maker firm depends on its ability to hide large positions, and we do not want our inventory revealed by a trade publication. While the public does not see our inventory directly, market participants can be very good at inferring it from our trades. This is why less transparency in the form of delayed trade publication may be desirable in the dealer market.[8]

In reality, few markets are totally transparent, including order-driven markets. Whether to reveal an order is a choice typically given to a public investor, even when the investor has already conveyed the order to the market. Institutional investors in particular need this choice.[9] Choice is provided to them in a number of ways by floor-based markets such as the New York Stock Exchange and by electronic trading platforms such as that run by the Paris Bourse (Euronext Paris). For instance, a floor trader on the NYSE typically reveals only parts of a large order, which he or she *slices and dices* and trades over an extended period of time. In Paris, large investors can enter *iceberg orders*, where only a part is revealed to the market and the remainder is hidden (i.e., not revealed) on the book.

In the Nasdaq environment, a public trader may give a large order to a market maker. The dealer may execute part or all of the order against his or her own inventory or seek counterparties for all or part of the order. The dealer will "work" any unexecuted portion of the order over time. Regardless of the specific route taken, it is not in the interest of the client and/or the market maker for the trade to be publicly revealed until the client's order has been executed in full and the dealer has reliquified. Consequently, it is not optimal for a dealer market to be highly transparent.

Competition   The most obvious way that market makers compete with each other is by how aggressively they set their bids and offers. If the spread is constant and the bid and offer are raised, the quotes are more aggressive on the bid side. If the bid and offer are lowered, the quotes are more aggressive on the offer side. The only way to become more aggressive on both the bid and the offer simultaneously is to narrow the spread.

Competing by aggressive quote setting is not so simple, however, because of preferencing. *Preferencing,* as we have noted, refers to a customer choosing to send an order to a particular market maker regardless of what the dealer might be quoting at the time. This can be done because there is no time priority rule in a quote-driven market. Public customers are free to pick randomly the market-maker firm to whom they send an order, or they can select the market maker based on previously established relationships. Orders are typically preferenced to a market maker who has developed a special relationship with a particular customer.

What if the market-maker firm with whom the customer chooses to trade is not posting the most aggressive quotes? Because his or her quote was less aggressive than the best quote on the market, the market maker is not obliged to take the order, but generally will accept it to maintain a good relationship with the customer. When the market maker does accept an order, he or she will typically fill it at a price equal to the most aggressive bid or offer existing at the time the order is received. For instance, if the best bid on the market is 50, a sell order preferenced to a dealer quoting a $49.90 bid will be filled at 50. This practice is referred to as *quote matching.*

Preferencing diminishes a market maker's incentive to compete via the aggressiveness of his or her quotes. While a market-maker firm that is quoting at the best bid or offer has a somewhat higher probability of receiving the next incoming order (especially if it is alone at the quote), the next order could still be preferenced to a market maker who is not on the inside market. This being the case, what does a market-maker firm accomplish by raising the best bid or lowering the best offer? It will have raised the bid or lowered the offer that the other market makers will have to match, and it may not itself receive the next order. The incentive to do this is not high unless the market maker has good reason to believe that the best posted bid and offer are clearly out of line with the broad underlying desire of participants to buy and sell shares.

If market makers have only a weak incentive to quote aggressively, how do they compete? By developing good customer relationships. An institutional investor will call a specific dealer house because it has received good service from that firm in the past. If a dealer either turns down a customer or executes the customer's order at an inferior price, the customer will think twice before preferencing an order to that dealer firm again.

A dealer may also give price improvement. Price improvement refers to the practice of executing a market buy order at a price lower than the best posted offer, or executing a market sell order at a price higher than the best posted bid. Market makers get to know their customers. Consequently, they can differentiate between customers who are apt to be trading for liquidity reasons and customers who are likely to have come to the market because they are in possession of new information. Liquidity-motivated customers include, for example, an indexer who is trading to rebalance its portfolio to track an index, or a mutual fund experiencing cash inflows or outflows from its investors. On the other hand, a value investor with the reputation of being a good stock picker may be trading because of better information. Dealers are more apt to give price improvement to customers whom they believe are trading for their own individual reasons rather than because they are in possession of private information that will soon become common knowledge.

Market makers also offer an array of ancillary services that enable them to attract order flow. For instance, they may provide customers with research reports on companies and/or computer software and/or data for investment analysis. They may offer direct computer links that result in faster executions than customers could achieve elsewhere. And so forth.

Because of the way in which dealers compete, their spreads tend to be wider than in an order-driven environment. In a pure order-driven market, an incoming order executes against a contra-side order that has been selected according to two strict criteria: price and time. The most aggressively priced order executes first, and if two or more orders are tied at the most aggressive price, the order that has been placed first executes first. If there is a lengthy queue of orders at the best bid or offer, a newly arriving buy (or sell) order can get priority simply by being priced one tick above the best bid (or one tick below the best offer). Aggressive pricing to get ahead of the queue results in a narrowing of the spread. Because this does not occur in the quote-driven market, spreads tend to be wider than in the order-driven environment.

What effect does preferencing have on market makers' profitability? More orders will be preferenced to a market-maker firm that has good customer relationships. This is highly desirable for the firm. For one thing, a firm's net revenue is related to its trading volume. Additionally, a firm that sees a larger percentage of the order flow has an advantage with regard to price discovery and thus can set its quotes more knowledgeably.

Preferencing, however, is not an unmitigated good. It is excellent for a dealer firm to receive preferenced orders, but, as we have seen, inventory control is then more difficult. With preferenced order flow, posting the *most* aggressive quote on the market does not ensure that a market maker will receive the next incoming order, and posting *less* aggressively than the best bid or offer does not ensure that the market maker will not receive the next incoming order. This further suggests why controlling inventory through quote changes more closely resembles steering a boat than a car. The greater difficulty of controlling inventory can negatively impact a firm's profitability.

Under what regime do market makers prefer to operate—one with preferencing or one with strict time and price priorities? Preferencing is an industry practice, and presumably dealers are comfortable with it or they would not have continued the practice. Nevertheless, preferencing is a two-edged sword.

Market-Maker Services

A market-maker firm is characterized by the nature of the transactional services that it provides to the buy side. We next consider the supply of immediacy and liquidity to individual customers and the provision of price discovery for the broad market.

Immediacy   The classic dealer role is the provision of immediacy. Buyers and sellers arrive sporadically in a continuous trading environment and need a way to meet. Chapter 6 shows how the limit orders entered by some participants establish the prices at which other participants can trade immediately by market order. In the quote-driven environment, market-maker quotes play this role. The market maker is continuously present, buying when a public seller arrives and selling when a public buyer arrives. The market maker is the medium through which public buyers and sellers meet each other. With market-maker intervention, public participants can trade with immediacy even though they arrive at the market at different moments in time.

Liquidity   Liquidity provision is a service that is commonly attributed to market makers. As we discuss in Chapter 3, "Liquidity," this attribution is not, strictly speaking, correct. As with the order-driven market, the ultimate source of liquidity for public buyers is natural sellers, and the ultimate source of liquidity for public sellers is natural buyers. The market maker simply helps the public buy and sell orders come together.

A market maker cannot be the ultimate source of liquidity. After buying shares from a public seller, the market maker hopes to sell those shares to a public buyer, and vice versa. If the quotes are set properly, and if the public buy and sell orders are reasonably balanced, the market maker's inventory will stay reasonably flat (close to zero). But if the public buy and sell orders do not offset each other sufficiently, an inventory imbalance will develop. When it does, the market maker is forced to reliquify by adjusting the quotes or by interdealer trading.

Price Discovery Price discovery is the process of finding share values that best reflect the broad market's desire to buy and to sell shares. In the order-driven environment that we focused on in the previous chapter, price discovery occurs as public participants place their limit and market orders with regard to their own assessments of share value and their own beliefs about where prices might currently be heading. No single participant has individual responsibility for price discovery in a pure order-driven market.

One set of participants does play a key role with regard to price discovery in the quote-driven environment—the market makers. They do so because the substantial portions of the aggregate order flow that they each see give them a feel for the relative balance between public buy and sell pressures. Furthermore, misjudging the order flow can be very costly for a market maker.

What is the price that the broad market is looking to discover? This question can be answered with reference to Exhibit 7.2. To simplify the discussion, let there be just one market maker, and assume that all orders are the same size so that we can plot orders rather than shares on the horizontal axis. The downward-sloping step function in Exhibit 7.2 describes the cumulated public buy orders. The upward-sloping step function describes the cumulated public sell orders. These two curves are constructed in the same way that we constructed the buy and sell curves shown in Exhibits 6.3 to 6.5 (in Chapter 6) with regard to the call auction. Namely, the buy curve is obtained by cumulating orders from the highest-priced buy to the lowest, and the sell curve is obtained by cumulating orders from the lowest-priced sell to the highest. Steps exist in the buy and sell curves because quantities arrive in discrete amounts at discrete prices.

In one critically important way, the buy and sell curves in Exhibit 7.2 differ from those shown for the call auction in Exhibits 6.3 to 6.5. For the call, we cumulate orders that have *actually been submitted* to the market. For the market-maker environment, we cumulate orders that are *expected to arrive* at each price.[10] Specifically, the *expected arrival rate* is the number of orders that are expected to arrive in some next brief period of time (e.g., the next hour), depending on the market maker's bid and offer. But nobody can be certain about future order flow. The best a market maker can do is to post the quotes, wait, and find out. For this reason, the arrow pointing to the equilibrium price in Exhibit 7.2 is labeled "stochastic equilibrium."

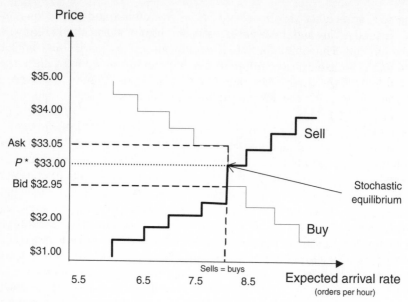

EXHIBIT 7.2 Price discovery in a quote-driven market.

Assume that the buy and sell curves depicted in Exhibit 7.2 accurately describe the propensities of public participants to buy and to sell shares. The intersection of these two curves identifies the price that would equate the number of buy orders that are expected with the number of sell orders that are expected to arrive.[11] We have labeled the price that balances the expected arrival rates P^*, which is an equilibrium value. It is a value that participants collectively are trying to discover and that everyone individually would like to know. It is the value that, ideally, the market maker's quotes should bracket. In Exhibit 7.2, P^* is 33.00, and the market maker is shown to be quoting 32.95 bid, 33.05 offer.

Market-Maker Revenues

How are market makers compensated for the services they provide to the buy side? From three sources: the bid-ask spread,[12] appropriately trading the order flow, and commissions.

Bid-Ask Spread The classic source of dealer profits is the dealer's bid-ask spread. Sometimes the spread is referred to as the *jobber's turn* (*jobber* is the older British term for market maker). If the bid and the offer are reasonably stable over time, and if the dealer repetitively buys at a lower bid and sells at a higher ask, he or she profits from the round-trips. A *round-trip* is first buying and then selling (or, for a short position, first selling and then buying). The spread is the return for one round-trip. The return for just one purchase or just one sale is conventionally taken to be half of the spread. From the customer's perspective, half of the spread is commonly viewed as the price per share of immediacy. In a pure quote-driven environment, a public customer has no choice but to buy immediacy and to pay its cost.

All else being equal, wider spreads lead to greater profits for market makers. Three factors in particular determine the size of the inside market spread (the gap between the best bid and offer): share price, trading volume, and the cost of market making. Share price is important because *percentage spreads* tend to be fairly constant across different price levels, all else constant. Accordingly, the *dollar size* of the spread will be higher for a higher-priced stock. For instance, a $100 stock will have a spread that, all else equal, is roughly 10 times the spread for a $10 stock.

Larger average trading volume results in tighter spreads, all else being equal. More frequent trading makes it easier for market makers to reliquify (i.e., to get out of accumulated positions, either long or short), and being able to trade down faster to a comfortable position contains a market maker's risk exposure to information change.

Higher market-making costs lead to wider spreads for the same reason that higher production costs generally lead to higher sales prices in any competitive industry. We subsequently focus on the costs of market making.

Trading the Order Flow   The second revenue source for a dealer is the short-term trading profits realized from successfully trading the order flow. A dealer is not a long-term investor in the stocks that he or she is making a market in, and is not interested, per se, in trading the stocks. Rather, having a good sense of the dynamics of the order flow and how to interact with it, the dealer, in effect, is "trading the order flow." Trading the order flow would not be profitable if share prices, except for bouncing between bid and offer quotes, followed a random walk.[13] But as we saw in Chapter 6, for the order-driven market the dynamics of order arrival can result in prices trending in one direction and then mean-reverting back toward a previous level.[14]

A successful dealer has a sense of when, on net, to buy (i.e., to accumulate a long position) and when, on net, to sell (i.e., to accumulate a short position). That is, a successful dealer may anticipate when a preponderance of sell orders has depressed prices for noninformational reasons, or when a preponderance of buy orders has raised prices for noninformational reasons. The short-term price swings give market makers an opportunity to buy shares at temporarily depressed prices and to sell them at temporarily inflated prices. The market maker profits by reversing out of his or her position as prices mean-revert.

The short-term mean reversion coexists with accentuated short-period volatility, and the volatility accentuation is a profit opportunity for market makers just as it is for limit order traders. However, when trading the order flow, a market maker will incur substantial inventory swings. The venture is risky.

Commissions A market-maker firm's third revenue source is commissions charged to customers. While any sell side participant who operates in the dual capacity of both broker (agent) and dealer (market maker) routinely charges brokerage commissions, dealers, historically, have not. Dealers customarily make *net trades*. That is, a customer buys at the dealer's offer or sells at the dealer's bid and incurs no additional charge. The dealer simply earns profits from the round-trips that he or she makes. However, following the transition to a one-cent tick in the United States that was completed in 2001, dealer spreads have narrowed and revenue has shrunk to the point where some market makers are starting to charge commissions.

Market-Maker Costs

Two distinctive costs characterize market-maker operations: the cost of carrying an unbalanced inventory and the cost of trading with a better-informed contra party (the cost of ignorance).

Cost of an Unbalanced Inventory We know from portfolio theory that an investor can manage risk by proper portfolio diversification and that a properly diversified portfolio provides the investor with a risk-appropriate expected return. A market maker, however, is not a typical investor. A market maker is buying or selling, not for his or her own investment purposes, but to supply shares to others or to absorb them from others. In so doing, the market maker commonly acquires a poorly diversified portfolio and accepts risk that could have been diversified away.

The expected return on a stock compensates for nondiversifiable risk (which is measured by beta). What compensates the market maker for accepting diversifiable risk? The classic answer is the bid-ask spread. Whatever makes inventory control more difficult—be it preferencing, price volatility attributable to news releases, relatively infrequent order flow in a small-cap stock, or the stochastic nature of the order flow—translates into more costly market making and hence wider spreads.

Cost of Ignorance The cost of ignorance is the cost of receiving an order from a better-informed trader. Assume a market maker has posted a bid at 50, an offer at 50.10, and that the equilibrium price for a stock jumps to 53. An informed trader comes in and buys at the 50.10 offer. The market maker loses from that trade because the bid and the offer will both rise and the market maker will have sold at a lower value (50.10). After the market maker sees where prices are going, he or she will regret having traded with the better-informed counterparty. The principle is as follows: Whenever a trade is triggered by a better-informed order hitting a market maker's quote, the market maker will have *ex post regret*.

Stated more broadly, inaccurate price discovery is costly to a market maker. We can see this by returning to the monopoly dealer model and Exhibit 7.2. We have used P^* to identify the price that best balances the expected rate of buy and sell orders and have shown that, in equilibrium, the market maker will set the offer above P^* and the bid below P^*. We also noted that P^* is not observable in the continuous market because the buy and sell curves are built, not on actual orders, but on the number of orders that are *expected to arrive* in a relatively brief, future interval of time (e.g., the next hour). If the quotes do straddle P^*, the arrival of buys is expected to balance the arrival of sells, and the dealer's inventory should stay in reasonable balance. However, ex post, the actual arrivals of buys and sells will likely not balance exactly because actual rates generally differ from expected rates by some random amount.

More important, a serious inventory imbalance can develop if the market maker misjudges the location of P^* or if, unbeknownst to the dealer, a news event causes P^* to jump (either up or down). Consider Exhibit 7.3. We see a situation where the demand for the stock is higher than the market maker has anticipated, either because of mistaken judgment or the occurrence of a bullish news event that the dealer has not yet learned about. We see that P^* is 34 and that the dealer's quotes are 32.95 bid, 33.05 offered. As informed buyers jump on the 33.05 offer, the rate of sales to the public rises and the rate of purchases from the public falls. With the order flow to the market maker out of balance, the dealer quickly acquires a short inventory position. As a control mechanism, the dealer will raise the quotes, hoping once again to straddle P^* and to return to a flat inventory position. In the process of adjusting the quotes, however, the market maker will be buying shares at a price that is higher than the price at which he or she had previously sold them.

Exhibit 7.4 depicts the opposite situation: The demand for the stock is lower than the market maker has anticipated, either because of mistaken judgment or the sudden occurrence of bearish news that the dealer does not yet know about. We see that P^* is 32 and that the dealer's quotes are 32.95 bid, 33.05 offered. As informed sellers jump on the 32.95 bid, sales to the dealer increase and purchases from the dealer fall. Now the market maker quickly acquires a long position. The dealer will lower the quotes,

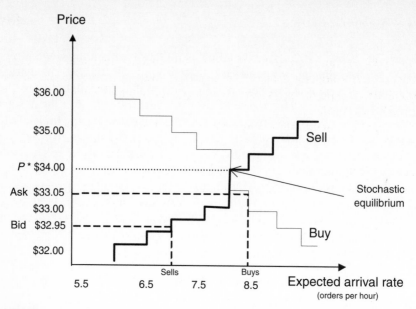

EXHIBIT 7.3 Price discovery in a quote-driven market: Market-maker quotes are too low.

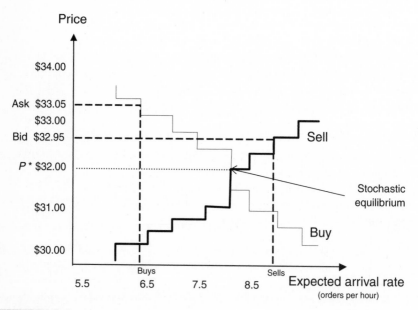

EXHIBIT 7.4 Price discovery in a quote-driven market: Market-maker quotes are too high.

trying once again to straddle P^* and to return to a flat inventory position. In the process of adjusting the quotes, however, the market maker will be selling shares at a price that is lower than the price at which he or she had previously bought them.

Achieving accurate price discovery is not easy, and inaccurate price discovery is costly for the dealer. What compensates the market maker for the cost of ignorance? The revenue that the dealer receives from transacting with liquidity traders (who are sometimes referred to as *uninformed traders*) must be large enough to offset the costs of dealing with better-informed traders. Could dealers exist without liquidity traders? They could not. No dealer can stay in business by trading only with better-informed participants. Without liquidity traders, the market makers would close down their operations and the market would collapse.

SPECIAL ORDER HANDLING

Intermediaries, in addition to providing capital for trading, facilitate order handling. They do this in two primary ways: (1) They facilitate the price improvement of customer orders, and (2) they facilitate the market timing of customer orders.

Price Improvement

Price improvement means that an order is executed within the spread. Namely, a buy order is executed at a price lower than the best posted offer, or a sell order is executed at a price higher than the best posted bid. Why might this happen?

In a competitive market-maker environment, a dealer might give price improvement to a customer who has negotiated a better price. The dealer might want to give better treatment to a frequent customer, to one with whom he or she is attempting to develop a better relationship, or to one who is more apt to be trading for non-information-related reasons (e.g., an index fund).

We have previously discussed the difficulty of price discovery and the risky dealer inventory positions that can develop when the quotes do not bracket the unobservable equilibrium price, P^*. A straightforward defense against not knowing the location of P^* is for a market maker to raise the offer and lower the bid (widening the spread increases the likelihood that the quotes bracket P^*). Then, with a wider spread, the market maker might price-improve an incoming order that he or she has reason to believe is not from a more knowledgeable participant (i.e., one who might have superior knowledge of the current value of $P*$ or of how $P*$ might jump once new information that he or she possesses becomes common knowledge).

Price improvement may be linked to price discovery in a more proactive way. A dealer might be more apt to give price improvement selectively if, at the moment that an order arrives, he or she observes more pressure on one side of the market than on the other. For instance, if buyers appear to be more prevalent then sellers, sell orders are more apt to be price-improved than buy orders, and vice versa. This is also true for an order-driven market such as the New York Stock Exchange, which includes intermediaries in its market structure.

On the NYSE, each stock is allocated to one specialist firm, and specialists play a key role with respect to price discovery for the stocks assigned to them. The process of discovering a new price level is manifest in the adjustment of the quotes and, given the quotes, to price improvement being offered predominantly to one side of the market or the other.

A link between price improvement and price discovery is indicated by a relationship that has been observed by Handa, Schwartz, and Tiwari between price improvement and two variables: market balance and market direction.[15] Market balance is measured as bid size (the number of shares posted at the bid) relative to ask size (the number of shares posted at the offer). Market direction is measured as the change of the midpoint of the best bid and offer on the market over the 15-minute interval within which a trade has been made. Handa et al. observed that, when the bid size is larger than the ask size (all else being constant) and/or when the market is rising (all else being constant), buyers receive less price improvement (buy prices are closer to the offer) and sellers receive more price improvement (sell prices are further above the bid). They also found that the opposite result holds when sell orders are larger than buy orders and/or when the market is falling. In this case, buyers receive more price improvement and sellers receive less. These relationships indicate that price improvement is not simply a matter of good fortune and/or bargaining ability, but that it is part of the price discovery process.

Price improvement serves another useful purpose for a market center that is the primary venue for price discovery. In the United States, for instance, prices for NYSE-listed stocks are predominantly set on the NYSE even though the stocks also trade in satellite markets (e.g., the regional exchanges and various alternative trading systems). The satellite markets are said to *free-ride* on NYSE price discovery. This does not please the Big Board. An interesting way for the exchange to defend itself against free riding is to be less transparent about the prices that it sets. NYSE specialists have some ability to do this by letting spreads be wider and then price improving orders after they have arrived at the exchange. The exchange stresses that customer orders sent to another market may, as a consequence, miss an opportunity to be price-improved.

Price improvement on the NYSE may be given either by a stock exchange specialist or by a floor broker who steps forward and takes the contra side of the trade. The process of exposing an order to floor traders takes some amount of time. Interestingly, this procedure cannot be simply replicated by a fully electronic trading system. With an electronic platform, nanoseconds can matter and the time clock is relentless—customers must be able to hit posted limit orders and achieve immediate executions with certainty. An execution cannot be delayed, even for a split second, while a better price is being sought, because, in the interim, another order might arrive and the electronic system would not be able to handle it instantaneously. Nevertheless, instantaneous price improvement can be given in one way—by allowing hidden orders to be placed within the posted spread. Designated market makers do this at Deutsche Börse, the primary German stock exchange. With a hidden order between the best posted bid and offer, a market order can execute instantly at a price that has been improved vis-à-vis the posted quotes.

Market Timing

Price discovery is a dynamic process that involves (1) investors revealing their orders and (2) the orders being translated into trades and transaction prices.[16] The process takes time and is far from trivial. Because price discovery is not instantaneous, individual participants have an incentive to *market-time* the placement of their orders. Intermediaries who are uniquely positioned to see and to understand the order flow can help their customers do this. The intermediary may be an actual person or an electronic system.

In the United States, floor traders facilitate the market timing of customer orders. Consider an NYSE floor trader who has just been instructed to buy 100,000 shares of XYZ Corporation for a mutual fund. A price limit would typically be stipulated, but the order is not a typical limit order and it is not placed on a limit order book. Rather, it is an *NH order.*

NH stands for *not held* to time or to price. Holding a broker "to a time" means that a market order must be executed as quickly as possible after it has been received. Holding a broker "to a price" means that he or she must execute the order at a price that is at least as good as the one that was available when the order was first received. For instance, if a floor broker receives an order to buy 500 shares at market and can lift an offer at 25, that broker is held to executing the market order at 25 or better. This requirement does not apply to an NH order. With an NH order, the floor trader works the order patiently, attempting to obtain a better execution for the customer. Consequently, the floor trader and the customer both accept the risk of eventually receiving an inferior execution or no execution at all. NH orders are sometimes referred to as *discretionary orders*. With a discretionary order, the broker is not held to a time or a price.

The floor trader with the 100,000-share NH buy order will typically proceed as follows. The broker will keep the order hidden in his or her pocket, will work it over an extended period of time, and will turn it into trades one piece at a time according to the broker's judgment and sense of market timing. The special handling enables the floor broker to execute each tranche of the order in response to market events as they occur. By hiding the unexecuted portion of the NH order and working it carefully, the floor trader is striving to contain any market impact cost attributable to others knowing about the order and front-running it. He or she is also attempting to balance market impact (the cost of being too aggressive) with the opportunity cost of missing the market (the cost of being too patient). The balancing act calls for knowledge of current market conditions, and it requires finesse.

With limit order book trading, a limit order is first placed on the book where it sits for some period of time and is then turned into a trade if and when a contra-side market order arrives. Note the following about the procedure.

- The limit order book environment offers each participant a choice between two strategies: (1) place a limit order, be a liquidity supplier, and wait, or (2) place a market order and demand immediate liquidity.
- An order on the book reflects conditions that existed when it was placed, and a stale limit order results in a transaction price that does not properly reflect current market conditions.

Neither of these conditions applies to an NH order. Working an NH order with finesse is a mixed strategy. Floor traders attempt to be liquidity suppliers, hoping that the market will come to them. However, if current conditions indicate that the market is likely to move away, a floor trader will step forward with all or part of the order and trigger a trade. In other words, the floor trader will switch between being a liquidity supplier and being a liquidity demander. Successful switching behavior requires a good knowledge of current market conditions.

Given today's technology, large buy side traders can obtain extensive knowledge of current conditions at their trading desks, and many are able to control their own orders without the services of an intermediary. Whether the physical presence of intermediaries on a trading floor conveys a further informational advantage remains a subject of debate in the United States, although most of the European markets have by now closed their floors. Nevertheless, evidence suggests that working NH orders on a trading floor does help contain trading costs.

As orders on the book and in the crowd of traders on the floor change, a floor trader monitors the configuration of the market and decides whether to step ahead of the limit order book by offering a better price, whether to trade with another contra-side floor trader, or whether to wait patiently for a more advantageous opportunity. In making this decision, the floor trader assesses the market in a number of ways, including the order imbalance for the stock, the current price behavior of related stocks and stock market indices, the mood of traders on the floor, and the amount of time remaining in the trading day.

Let's return to the floor trader who is working the NH order to buy 100,000 shares of XYZ Corporation. Assume a situation where the day is young, the market is fairly flat or drifting down, and sell orders on the XYZ book outweigh the buys. Under these conditions, the floor trader will wait patiently for the price of XYZ to fall. Perhaps it does. Perhaps part of the 100,000-share order does get executed. But then let the broad market turn bullish. As it does, new limit orders to buy XYZ are placed on the book, and a surge of market buy orders thins out the sell side of the book. As the buy-sell imbalance reverses, traders in front of the XYZ post get excited, and by now the 4:00 P.M. close is approaching. Under these conditions, our floor trader who is working the 100,000-share buy order steps forth more aggressively and initiates a trade.

By operating in this fashion, a successful floor broker can better control trading costs for the customer. A smoother integration of a large order into the market also conveys benefits to the broader market in the form of less erratic price discovery and an attending reduction of intraday price volatility. Nevertheless, the services of a floor broker are not costless, and around the world exchange floors are being replaced by fully electronic trading platforms. We anticipate that, increasingly, market timing will be facilitated by an electronic intermediary.

Most recent on the scene has been the use of computer technology to generate trading decisions based on contemporaneous market data in a procedure referred to as *algorithmic trading*. To a considerable extent, algorithmic trading mirrors the actions of floor brokers working not-held orders. What is the best context within which to make real-time trading decisions, direct person-to-person interaction, or computerized information and decisions rules? In pondering this question, one is reminded of the chess games played between Kasparov and the IBM computer. The grand master has been very hard to beat, but one is tempted to think that time is on the side of Big Blue. At some point in the future, we might even see two or more algorithms trading with each other.

HYBRID MARKETS

If intermediation is not required, investors should have the option to trade in a nonintermediated environment and not pay for services that they do not need. The order-driven market discussed in Chapter 6 has excellent properties, particularly for liquid stocks, retail order flow, and markets that are not under stress. But illiquidity is a serious problem, particularly for the mid- and small-cap issues; many orders are too big to be easily digested in the market (primarily those generated by institutional customers); and stress characterizes all markets on a daily basis. Accordingly, intermediaries have important roles to play. These involve, first and foremost, providing dealer capital, participating in price discovery, facilitating market timing, and animating trading.

In the past, the London Stock Exchange and Nasdaq were, for the most part, pure dealer markets. On the other end of the spectrum, the Paris Bourse, Deutsche Börse, and other continental exchanges ran call auctions. The Tokyo and other Far East exchanges have been and currently are continuous order-driven environments that include call auctions at market openings and closings. Yet historically in many exchanges, one sees features of a hybrid market. A striking example is an order-driven market like the New York Stock Exchange. The Big Board includes specialists (who participate in trading as market makers) and other floor traders (who work orders on a not-held basis). Also included in the broader NYSE marketplace are upstairs trading rooms that include dealers who provide proprietary capital to facilitate block transactions.

In recent years, major markets around the globe have been explicitly designed as hybrids. Limit order books have been introduced in the Nasdaq market (SuperMontage) and the London market (SETS). Market makers are included in order-driven platforms throughout Europe. Virtually all markets globally now include call auctions. This advance toward hybrids has been driven by the fact that different participants have different trading needs depending on their size, motive for trading, and the characteristics of the stock (or list of stocks) being traded. For the broad market, a hybrid structure can sharpen price discovery, provide enhanced liquidity, and help to stabilize a market under stress.

Market makers have a vital role to play in the hybrid structure. We will see this in further detail in the next two chapters, which turn to the current scene in, respectively, the United States and Europe.

NOTES

1. NYSE, Constitution and Rules, Rule 104, Functions of Specialists. See Chapter 8, "The Evolving Scene in the United States," for a further discussion of specialist operations.

2. The European blue chips are a good example. Handling these issues, which are traded in order-driven open order books, is a pure-volume, small-margin business.

3. Until recently, Nasdaq market-maker bids and offers had to be for a minimum of 1,000 shares. Currently, they are free to size their quotes as they wish.

4. Remark made at the Securities and Exchange Commission's Market Structure Hearings, New York City, October 29, 2002. Plexus is a firm that gathers and analyzes trading-related data from more than 115 money management firms that, collectively, represent approximately 20 to 25 percent of exchange volume worldwide.

5. For less liquid stocks, the market maker plays a key role in supplying liquidity through quoting. With more liquid stocks, on the other hand, "liquidity attracts liquidity" from investors who post their own orders in the market. A market maker is less needed for the frequently traded big-cap issues where the spread is narrow and there is breadth and depth in the order book. A good example is the Kursmakler (dealer) System versus the Xetra trading platform in Germany. The most liquid stocks basically trade 100 percent on Xetra, while the less liquid stocks still need the market-making support of a Kursmakler.

6. Material in various parts of this chapter have been adapted with permission from Robert A. Schwartz and Bruce W. Weber, "Economics of Market Making," Nasdaq's HeadTrader web site www.academic.nasdaq.com/headtrader, © 2004, The Nasdaq Stock Market, Inc. Produced for the Nasdaq Educational Foundation. Adapted with permission.

7. In a hybrid quote-driven, order-driven system, if transparency attracts limit orders, it is difficult to measure the trade-off between (1) having more orders in the order book and (2) less market-maker capital.

8. It is important to distinguish between two terms *trade publication* and *trade reporting*. Trade publication is the public dissemination of a trade price. Trade reporting more narrowly means reporting a trade to a regulatory authority: the NYSE, the National Association of Securities Dealers (NASD), and/or the SEC in the United States. Reporting does not expose the inventory positions of the dealer that traded to other dealers. It is the publication of large trades (putting them on the ticker tape) that market makers wish to delay. By rule, both large and small trades on Nasdaq must be reported within 90 seconds of execution. These trade reports are then instantaneously disseminated to the public.

9. That is why anonymity is of utmost importance. Posttrade anonymity is delivered in European markets by a central counterparty (CCP).

10. The formulation is in Mark Garman, "Market Microstructure," *Journal of Financial Economics*, June 1976.

11. Note that, because the market maker sells to the buyers and buys from the sellers, the expected number of trades equals the expected arrival rate of buy orders plus the expected arrival rate of sell orders.

12. This is also true for multiple market making (e.g., in Eurex), where they have to share the spread.

13. If a stock's returns are not correlated over time, the stock's price is said to be following a *random walk*.

14. Mean-reverting and trending behavior are attributable to liquidity events, momentum trading, and the dynamic process of price discovery.

15. Puneet Handa, Robert Schwartz, and Ashish Tiwari, "Price Improvement and Price Discovery on a Primary Market: Evidence from the American Stock Exchange," *Journal of Portfolio Management*, fall 1998.

16. This section draws on Puneet Handa, Robert Schwartz, and Ashish Tiwari, "The Economic Value of a Trading Floor: Evidence from the American Stock Exchange," *Journal of Business* 77, no. 2, pt. 1, April 2004, pp. 331–355. © 2004 by The University of Chicago. All rights reserved.

CHAPTER 8

The Evolving Scene in the United States

The major U.S. equity markets include two national stock exchanges, the New York Stock Exchange (NYSE) and American Stock Exchange (Amex); Nasdaq; five regional stock exchanges;[1] and several exchangelike organizations that have come to be known as alternative trading systems (ATSs) and electronic communications networks (ECNs). The two powerhouse markets are the NYSE and Nasdaq. The NYSE had its origins in the "Buttonwood agreement" of 1792 and the adoption of a constitution and a name, New York Stock & Exchange Board, in 1817.[2] The Buttonwood agreement was so called in honor of a tree on Wall Street under which 24 brokers signed an agreement to impose off-board trading restrictions on each other and to establish minimum fixed commissions.

Nasdaq started operations in 1971. A product of the over-the-counter (OTC) dealer market, Nasdaq was run under the regulatory umbrella of the National Association of Securities Dealers (NASD).[3] Initially, Nasdaq was not a market, but the NASD's Automated Quotations (AQ) system. Its striking success as a system resulted in its name being applied to the market that it helped to create.

Prior to the success of Nasdaq, the natural progression for a U.S. company as it grew from a small start-up to a major firm with national prominence was first to trade OTC, then to list on the Amex, and finally to transfer its listing to the NYSE. This changed as Nasdaq first eclipsed the Amex and then challenged the NYSE by retaining many of its premier listings such as Microsoft and Intel. Until the latter part of the 1990s, the NYSE and Nasdaq gave companies a well-defined choice between listing on a primarily order-driven agency/auction market or on a competitive dealer market. The two market structures have remained different, but Nasdaq is no longer a predominantly quote-driven environment.

The NYSE always had a dealer component (its specialists and the upstairs market-maker firms). Nasdaq evolved into a hybrid quote-driven and order-driven market following the introduction in 1997 of new order handling rules that were set forth by the U.S. Securities and Exchange Commission. The SEC's new rules required that limit orders from public traders, for the first time, be properly represented in the Nasdaq quote montage. Nasdaq's transformation into a hybrid has been reinforced by the growth of the ECNs and by a widening acceptance of the fact that these order-driven trading platforms are indeed part of the broader Nasdaq marketplace.

In recent years, in response to the combined forces of technology, competition, and regulation, change in U.S. market structure has accelerated and will undoubtedly continue apace for the foreseeable future. Nasdaq and the NYSE are both heading toward new and uncertain futures. In this chapter, we first describe the classic NYSE, Nasdaq, and ECN/ATS markets. We then discuss a succession of critical events that have brought the U.S. equity markets to where they are today.

THE NEW YORK STOCK EXCHANGE

The NYSE is a hybrid market where orders for the purchase and sale of listed securities are consolidated on a trading floor and interact in a predominantly auction environment. Orders are routed to exchange specialists who operate in the dual capacity of broker and dealer. As brokers, specialists match public orders that they have received with other public orders and with the orders of other professional traders. As dealers, they take the other side of the trades themselves, thereby providing immediate liquidity. They also act as auctioneers with respect to the execution of orders held by floor traders.

A specialist oversees the competition between floor traders and the limit order book (which he or she represents) and steps in as a dealer when necessary. NYSE-listed securities are also traded on other U.S. exchanges, in the upstairs broker-dealer market, and overseas. Price discovery generally occurs at the NYSE, and many traders prefer to have their orders routed to the Big Board. Of all trades in NYSE-listed issues that were reported on the Consolidated Tape in 2002, 82 percent of share volume took place on the NYSE.

Organizational Structure of the NYSE

The NYSE is a not-for-profit corporation governed by a board of directors that sets NYSE policy and supervises its operations. Members of the NYSE are either individuals who own or lease a membership (called a *seat*) or nominees (partners or employees) of member firms that own or lease seats. The number of seats has been fixed at 1,366 since 1953. Seats can be bought, sold, or leased, and their price, as set by buyers and sellers, reflects the demand to hold a seat.[4] Because NYSE member firms are also members of the NASD, many broker-dealer firms are simultaneously members of the NYSE, customers of the NYSE, and competitors of the NYSE.

The major players who operate on the NYSE's trading floor are specialists, house brokers (sometimes referred to as *commission house brokers*), and direct access brokers.

Specialists Specialists supply immediate liquidity to the market by providing two-way quotes in the absence of other trading interest. As dealers, specialists buy for and sell from their inventory. As agents, specialists handle limit orders for the stocks assigned to their trading posts. Currently, there are seven specialist units, with the two largest accounting for 44 percent of all trades that are handled by specialists. We consider the specialists in further detail subsequently.

House Brokers Employed by the brokerage houses, these floor brokers are a link between the brokerage houses and the specialist posts. The house brokers receive orders from their firms' clients and either execute them with the specialist, with each other, or cross the trades. A cross trade occurs when the broker has both a buy and a sell order for the same stock. All floor trades must be reported to and approved by the specialist.

Direct Access Brokers These brokers perform the same functions as the house brokers, but they are not employed by a brokerage house. Rather, the direct access brokers are independent firms that execute orders for their own customers (predominantly institutional customers). Minimal intermediation is involved when a buy side customer electronically sends his or her order directly to a direct access broker.

Listed Companies

As of year-end 2003, the Big Board listed 2,574 common stocks with an aggregate market value of $12.1 trillion. To be listed, a company must satisfy minimum standards of quality and size, must be willing to release adequate information about its operations, and must attract sufficient public interest. Interested specialist firms apply for the allocation of newly listed securities. The NYSE's Stock Allocation Committee allocates the securities to a specialist unit that then becomes responsible for making a market in that stock.[5]

SuperDot

In 1976, the NYSE instituted its Designated Order Turnaround (DOT) system that brokers use to route orders directly to specialists' posts on the trading floor. Since then, DOT has been upgraded significantly, and the improved electronic order routing system is currently known as SuperDot. The system can be used for orders up to 100,000 shares, and it has the capacity to handle in excess of 2 billion shares daily. Currently, 75 percent of the orders that execute at the NYSE are delivered by SuperDot. Orders that come in through SuperDot are referred to as *system orders*. Floor brokers provide the alternative delivery method. We analyze the difference between the delivery systems (system orders and floor orders) in Chapter 7, "Intermediated Markets."

Specialists

Trading at the NYSE is centered on the specialists—market professionals who, as we have noted, function as both principal (market maker) and agent (broker's broker).[6] Each NYSE-listed stock is assigned to one specialist firm. A specialist is bound by certain responsibilities and restrictions with regard to a listed corporation and his or her own trades.[7]

All orders for a stock that are sent to the NYSE converge at the specialist post to which that stock is assigned. When trading is heavy, floor traders pack in about the post and the specialist conducts an auction. As auctioneer, the specialist is responsible for (1) ensuring that orders are handled in conformity with acceptable auction practice and (2) determining the orders that have priority (i.e., who gets a trade). A specialist may *stop a stock* (i.e., guarantee an execution at a *stop price*). The request to stop a stock may be initiated at a floor broker's request for a public trader.[8]

Specialist operations are particularly critical at the start of the trading day. The NYSE opening bell rings at 9:30 A.M., but the market for an individual stock does not open until the specialist finds a price that balances the buy and sell orders that have entered the book in this stock. Specialists do this by matching market orders that have come in through the electronic order entry system, public limit orders and eligible market orders that come into their electronic display books, and orders from the trading crowd. This special opening is a form of call auction trading (a procedure discussed in Chapter 6,

"Order-Driven Markets"). At the opening call, a specialist establishes a price that he or she believes best balances the accumulated buy and sell pressures (i.e., that best reflects the market's aggregate desire to hold shares of the stock). In setting the opening price, the specialist will commit his or her own capital by buying for or selling from his or her own account to balance the orders.[9]

Throughout the trading day, specialists have an affirmative obligation to make a *fair and orderly market* for the stocks assigned to them. Fair and orderly is viewed as the absence of excessively large and erratic price changes in brief trading intervals. This means that a specialist must intervene in trading to keep price changes *acceptably* small by buying for and selling from his or her own account against a prevailing market trend. What is acceptable has been defined by the NYSE with reference to the price level at which the stock is trading, the stock's trading volume, and so forth. Accordingly, specialists dampen the intraday volatility of prices, but they do not peg prices. If the underlying pressure exists for a price to increase or decrease to a new level, the price does go to the new level. Specialist intervention is intended only to dampen swings that occur either because of thinness on one side of the market or as a result of the difficulties of price discovery. Fair and orderly prices are valued because they give participants more assurance that prices will not jump erratically as orders are being received and turned into trades.

At times, the specialist is not expected to keep price changes within normal limits. When sizable price movements occur because of major stock-specific news, the market may not be able to find a new price and handle trades efficiently at the same time. Under this condition, the specialist may, with the permission of a floor official, *halt trading*. During a stock-specific trading halt, the specialist has time to assess market conditions, and traders have time to digest the news and revise their orders.

The extreme volatility during October 1987, and especially the precipitous decline on October 19, 1987, showed that the liquidity specialists are able to provide to a market under stress is limited[10] and that trading halts for specific issues may not arrest a broad decline. During the 1987 crash, specialist capital proved inadequate relative to the enormous selling pressure from institutional and retail traders. The NYSE's criteria for a fair and orderly market were unsupportable when the market dropped over 500 points in a single day. Following the crash, the NYSE introduced marketwide trading halts called *circuit breakers* in the hope of containing excessive volatility.

NASDAQ

Nasdaq is a decentralized, electronically linked market that comprises thousands of geographically dispersed, competitive dealer and member firms connected together by telephones, electronic systems, and computer screens. The philosophy behind the Nasdaq market is very different from the one that characterizes the NYSE. Rules of order handling and trade execution are simpler, and competitive forces are relied on more than explicit regulation to promote liquid, fair, and orderly markets.

To understand the operations of the Nasdaq market, one must appreciate the services provided by dealers, the costs the market makers incur, and the dynamic pricing and inventory policies that they employ. These are discussed in Chapter 7, "Intermediated Markets." A dealer market, by its very nature is a multi-market-making market that is physically fragmented across the various competitive market-maker firms. Any firm can make a market for any given issue with only minimal entry barriers.

In 2002, nearly 300 firms were actively committing capital to making markets in Nasdaq stocks. A minimum of two market makers is required for each stock, and the number of market makers per stock averaged 14. Between 3 and 50 dealers typically make a market in any one stock, with the more actively traded issues attracting a larger number of dealers. On December 18, 2003, for example, 100 dealer firms were making a market for Cisco. The more market makers there are for an issue, the stronger is the competition to get a quote executed, the larger the amount of capital that can be committed to providing liquidity, and, all else being constant, the tighter is the stock's bid-ask spread.

The Nasdaq Stock Market

The 1938 Maloney Act amendments to the Securities and Exchange Act of 1934 created the NASD as a self-regulatory organization (SRO). The NASD, headquartered in Washington, D.C., has primary responsibility for regulating brokers and dealers and, in this capacity, has imposed a uniform set of rules for its members.[11] It also develops and operates the technological infrastructure that facilitates the operations of its members. The NASD's first major electronic system, Nasdaq, began operations in 1971. Nasdaq was not an order execution system, but a nationwide electronic network that, for the first time, displayed market-maker quotes for Nasdaq issues on terminals in brokerage offices across the country. Prior to Nasdaq (the system), the OTC market was linked by telephone lines among market-making and other member firms.

The real-time, electronic Nasdaq system has had a tremendous impact on the efficiency of the market. It has integrated the dealer market, caused spreads to tighten, and improved the quality of price discovery and trade execution. With this success in hand, in 1982, the NASD introduced the Nasdaq National Market, or Nasdaq/NM, as its premier market. By the end of 2001, Nasdaq listed 3,663 companies (the largest and most actively traded) with a market cap of roughly $2.9 trillion.

Issues on the Nasdaq/NM list are the largest and most actively traded stocks. Along with the publication of bid and ask quotations, stocks traded in the Nasdaq/NM are subject to last sale price and volume reporting. Nasdaq/NM market makers are required to report transaction prices and sizes to the NASD within 90 seconds of a transaction's occurrence.

Before its start in 1971, dealer firms feared the competition that the Nasdaq system would introduce, and they were most reluctant to display their quotes on the screen. However, to do business, a dealer firm must receive orders from brokers, and Nasdaq has enabled those firms that make the best markets to receive more of the order flow. A dealer firm can now successfully get order flow and make a market in a stock it has not previously traded simply by registering its intention a day in advance and then posting quotes on the screen.

Nasdaq market makers do not have a franchise in the stocks they handle. Issues are not assigned to, but are selected by, the market maker firms. When a dealer firm is registered as a market maker for an issue, it must make a two-sided market by continuously posting both bid and offer quotations for the issue. Unlike NYSE specialists, Nasdaq market makers do not have a regulatory obligation to maintain a fair and orderly market. A dealer firm is also free to stop making a market for an issue whenever it so chooses, although if it does so it is not allowed to resume market making in that issue for 20 business days.

Contrast of Nasdaq and the NYSE

Nasdaq and the NYSE are very different marketplaces. Historically, Nasdaq has pointed to the advantages of its competitive multiple-market-maker system. The NYSE, employing a model that is based on competition between public orders, stresses its advantages as an agency/auction market, and emphasizes the importance of its specialist system. The differences between the two markets discussed here are summarized in Exhibit 8.1.

Trade Initiation Nasdaq has traditionally been quote-driven, in contrast to the NYSE's order-driven, agency/auction market. Market makers are allowed to take the initiative in finding buyers and sellers. NYSE

	Nasdaq	NYSE
Trade initiation	Dealer market Quote-driven Active interaction with the order flow	Agency/auction market Order-driven Passive interaction with the order flow
Competition	Multiple dealers	Single dealer and public order flow
Flexibility	Freedom to select stocks Primary and secondary market operations	Stocks are assigned Secondary market operations only
Information flows	Deal directly with customers Close contact with firms	Consolidated order flow and floor information
Price discovery	No formal procedure Competitive quotations centrally displayed	Market opening procedure Consolidation of the order flow
Regulation	SRO for member firms Obligation to continuously quote firm two-sided market Rely on competition to limit abuses	SRO for member firms Affirmative obligation Specialist trading restrictions

EXHIBIT 8.1 Traditional Nasdaq market versus NYSE.

specialists must assume a more passive position; they post their quotes and wait for other traders to respond.

Competition   Nasdaq market makers compete with each other, and they have been reluctant to accept additional competition from the public order flow. Traditionally, this market has depended on interdealer competition to keep markets fair, orderly, and liquid. The NYSE, with just one market maker per issue (the specialist), depends on competition from public limit orders, floor traders, specialists on other exchanges, and its own surveillance system to keep markets fair, orderly, and liquid.

Flexibility   Nasdaq market makers are free to select the stocks in which they make markets. They face no significant regulatory impediments to becoming, or ceasing to be, market makers for an issue. A specialist firm, on the other hand, must apply for the right to be the market maker for a newly listed issue. Once assigned by the exchange's stock allocation committee, an issue is rarely given up by a specialist firm and is almost never taken away. Broker-dealer firms are free to participate in the new-issues market, although a firm that does so must temporarily give up market making for an issue in the secondary market when it acts as underwriter for the same company in the primary market. NYSE specialists operate in the secondary market only.

Information Flows Specialists are prohibited from dealing directly with institutions. Nasdaq market makers, on the other hand, can receive orders directly from customers, including institutional traders. This direct contact gives OTC dealers an information advantage that NYSE specialists do not enjoy. A market maker can better sense the motive behind an order—namely, whether it is informationally motivated or instead is an "informationless" order (e.g., from an index fund). Some market makers maintain close contact with the firms whose securities they trade, and brokerage houses with Nasdaq trading operations commonly act in an advisory capacity for these firms. NYSE specialist firms have no such relationship with their listed companies. Specialists, on the other hand, have an information advantage that is not shared by the Nasdaq market makers—they see a larger fraction of the order flow because order flow is more consolidated in exchange trading.

Price Discovery Market makers sense the public's buy-sell propensities by posting quotes and observing the market's response, as discussed in Chapter 7, "Intermediated Markets." Consolidation of the public order flow on the trading floor of the NYSE gives exchange specialists a more comprehensive knowledge of buy-sell propensities in the broader market for an issue. The NYSE opens each trading session with a call auction, which is a price discovery mechanism. Nasdaq recently introduced a closing call and anticipates instituting an opening call in the near future.

Regulation Competing Nasdaq market makers face fewer rules and regulatory restrictions than NYSE specialists, and the dealer market relies more on the pressures of a competitive environment to discipline the dealer firms. Because specialist firms also execute public orders on an agency basis, they have a fiduciary responsibility to give executions that are consistent with exchange auction rules. Furthermore, competing market makers do not have the affirmative obligation to maintain a fair and orderly market as do the exchange specialists.[12] Consequently, the rules, regulations, and surveillance of specialist operations are of necessity more elaborate on the exchanges than in the Nasdaq market.

SuperMontage

Trading started on SuperMontage, Nasdaq's electronic order display and execution system, in October 2002.[13] The system allows market participants

to enter quotes and orders at multiple prices and displays aggregated interest at five different prices on both sides of the market (ranging down from
the bid quote and up from the ask quote). The system offers full anonymity
and price and time priority, allows market makers to internalize orders,
includes preferred orders, and allows market makers and ECNs to specify a *reserve size* (i.e., market participants have an option not to display
their full order).

The advent of SuperMontage has gone a long way toward completing
Nasdaq's transformation from a quote-driven market to a hybrid market
that contains both quote- and order-driven features. As noted, Nasdaq is
currently adding a third component to the hybrid—a call auction that will
be run to both open and close the market. The hybrid has not been easy
to achieve. SuperMontage is a complex system that took the better part of
five years to design and to go through the regulatory approval process.
Currently, it competes with an Alternative Display Facility (ADF) that
is operated by the NASD. It is too early to judge the ultimate success
of SuperMontage, but without question the system is key to Nasdaq's
prospects going forward.

ECNs AND ATSs

Instinet, which started operations in 1969, was the first electronic communications network (although it was not referred to as an ECN until the latter part of the 1990s, when the SEC introduced the term as part of its
investigations that led to the 1997 order handling rules). As its name (an
acronym for "Institutional Network") suggests, Instinet was designed to be
a trading system for institutional investors. The system enables customers
to meet and trade electronically in an anonymous, disintermediated environment. For many years, Instinet was viewed by many as an alternative to
(and competitor of) the traditional Nasdaq dealer market. However, its
presence has turned the broader Nasdaq marketplace into a hybrid environment. This has been a benefit to its large buy side customers (the institutional traders) and thus to the issuers that Nasdaq wishes to retain.

Dealers were always free to use Instinet for their own trades, but initially were revealed as dealers in the system. In 1987, Instinet was acquired
by Reuters and, in June 1989, dealer anonymity was introduced. With this
change, order flow to Instinet increased sharply. Instinet, in effect, became
an interdealer broker (IDB) for the Nasdaq market makers.[14] Instinet went
public on May 18, 2001, and its IPO was a big success. The shares, priced at
$14.59 at the IPO, rose 22 percent that day to close at $17.67.

With its order-driven electronic platform and limit order display for customers, Instinet looks very much like an exchange. However, the company registered with the SEC, not as an exchange, but initially as a broker-dealer firm and currently as an ECN. Instinet has long taken the position that it is nothing more than a broker-dealer and that it operates in the upstairs market much as does any other broker-dealer firm that puts trades together for large customers. The only real difference, according to Instinet, is that it does the job electronically. This view underscores the difficulty of differentiating an exchange from a broker-dealer firm in a technologically advanced environment. The SEC reflected the ambiguities involved by coining a new term to refer to Instinet—*electronic communications network*. A number of new competitors to Instinet have now taken up this organization form.

Other alternative trading systems (ATSs) also emerged, starting with Investment Technology Group's (ITG) Posit, which started operations in the turbulent month of October 1987. Posit is a crossing network that, much like Intinet's after-hours cross, matches customer buy and sell orders that meet or cross each other in price at a price established in the NYSE or Nasdaq market. A more recent entrant in the field is Burlington Capital Markets' Burlington Large Order Cross (BLOX). The crossing networks have offered an attractive alternative to institutions that are willing to trade at a market price without their orders having any effect on what that price turns out to be. The two major drawbacks of the crossing networks are (1) that their execution rates tend to be low and (2) that if they draw too much order flow away from the main market, they can, to their own detriment, undermine the quality of the very prices on which they are basing their trades. These limitations can be overcome in a call auction environment that includes price discovery.

Two ATSs based on call auction principles were the Arizona Stock Exchange (which started operations in 1991 and has been inactive since 2001) and OptiMark (which started operations in 1999 and has been inactive since 2000).[15] Neither of these systems succeeded in attracting critical-mass order flow. Their experiences point up the difficulty of implementing an innovative new trading system that has to compete with an established market center, especially when the new system provides independent price discovery.

A more recent arrival, LiquidNet, started operations in 2001.[16] LiquidNet is an alternative trading system that enables institutional customers to meet anonymously, negotiate a price, and trade in large sizes (average trade size is nearly 50,000 shares). Part of LiquidNet's ability to attract order flow is attributable to its customers being able to negotiate their trades with reference to quotes prevailing in the major market centers. In other words, LiquidNet's customers do not have to participate in significant price discovery (more than 90 percent of all LiquidNet's executions are within the spread). Further, LiquidNet customers' anonymity and knowledge that counterparties in the system also wish to trade in size offers them some assurance that their orders will not have undue market impact. A key feature of the LiquidNet system is that customer matches are found electronically, and negotiations are also conducted electronically by the natural buyer and seller.

Harborside+, which started operations in 2002, is another venue that, like LiquidNet, enables institutional customers to find each other and negotiate their trades. Customers first send Harborside+ indications of interest (IOIs), and Harborside+ technology is used to find potential matches among the counterparties. When a potential match is found, Harborside+ personnel take over, contact the counterparties, and facilitate a negotiation while keeping the buyer's and the seller's identities confidential. As stated on its web page, "It is Harborside+'s contention that the many nuances in block trading require flexibility beyond that found in electronic trading systems."[17]

The systems thus far described in this section have all been designed for institutional customers. This is not surprising, given that efficient handling of institutional order flow is by far the biggest challenge facing our markets (see Chapter 5, "Institutional Order Flow"). This exclusive focus on the institutions changed, however, in 1997 with the arrival of several new ECNs. Archipelago, which started operations in January 1997, handles both institutional and retail order flow. The customer base of another new ECN, Island, has been retail. In September 2002, Island was acquired by Instinet, and the two companies are currently consolidating their operations in a single electronic marketplace called INET.

The ECNs and ATSs, for the most part, share several characteristics. They are for-profit, order-driven operations that can include intermediaries but are not irrevocably based on intermediaries. They honor strict price and time priorities. They offer speed, low commissions, anonymity, and transparency. Their customers retain more control over their own orders than they do in the classic NYSE and Nasdaq markets. This new environment, however, is not without its drawbacks. The multiplicity of systems has fragmented the order flow, and competition between the different markets has reduced sell side revenue, eroded profits, and impaired the provision of market-maker capital.

Order flow fragmentation has led to the emergence of some new technology firms that provide order management, handling, and routing services. The routing services in particular address the fragmentation problem (which currently pertains primarily to Nasdaq stocks). One of the more popular order routers is Lava, a service that is used by many of the major brokerage firms. A market order routed through Lava uses proprietary

Lava technology to select a marketplace, primarily on the basis of a stock's recent trading activity. Firms such as Lava are commonly referred to as *smart order routers*, or *consolidators*. In essence, they consolidate information from various markets so that the customer can get the most favorable execution across markets. For users, the fragmentation problem is diminished.

WINDS OF CHANGE

From the Buttonwood agreement in 1792 until the mid-1970s, the U.S. markets basically evolved naturally, without guidance from government regulators or the "scientific" advice of industry consultants or academicians. Major regulations were introduced in the 1930s, but these primarily addressed issues of manipulative and other abusive behavior rather than market structure per se. It was the 1975 amendments (called Section 11-A, or National Market System Amendments) to the Securities Exchange Act of 1934 that marked the first major government foray into market structure regulation.

The 1975 Amendments

The 1975 amendments to the Exchange Act had a profound impact on the industry. First, they precluded the securities exchanges from imposing fixed commission rates. Second, they mandated the development of a National Market System (NMS) and charged the SEC with the responsibility for facilitating its establishment.

The objective of the National Market regulation was to strengthen the forces of competition in a free market environment. Governmental deregulation was subsequently extended in the United States to other industries—banking, airlines, trucking, telecommunications, and electricity. The congressional amendments set forth four broad goals that the NMS was to achieve:

1. Enhance the economic efficiency of transactions (i.e., reasonable transaction costs).
2. Ensure fair competition among brokers, dealers, and markets.
3. Ensure the broad availability of information on quotations and transactions.
4. Provide the opportunity, consistent with efficiency and best execution, for investors' orders to be executed without the participation of a dealer.

A few years after the passage of the amendments, Donald Stone, a leading NYSE specialist and soon to be vice-chairman of the NYSE stated, "The momentum that Congress and the SEC have set in motion has created a tidal wave of change and activity that will leave the equity markets of the United States as unrecognizable as the original thirteen colonies."[18] Stone's prediction was fulfilled within a decade. The industry was transformed by the new legislation. Initially, the elimination of fixed commissions had the greatest impact. But that was only the beginning.

Various pieces of a National Market System (NMS) have been instituted as follows:[19]

- *Consolidated Tape.* A consolidated reporting system was first proposed by the SEC in 1972. The Consolidated Tape with its unified reporting rules was put into place in 1974.
- *Clearance and Settlement System.* The National Clearance and Settlement System was developed in 1976. The system combined the clearing corporations of the NYSE, Amex, and the NASD to form the National Securities Clearing Corporation (NSCC).
- *Consolidated Quotation System.* The Consolidated Quotation System (CQS) became operational in 1978. CQS sends floor information to data vendors.
- *Intermarket Trading System.* The Intermarket Trading System (ITS) was established in April 1978. At first, ITS linked only two exchanges (NYSE and Philadelphia) and was limited to 11 stocks. ITS now connects each of the two national exchanges with the five regional exchanges and the Nasdaq market. However, at the current time, ITS is based on an antiquated technology, and (as of this writing) its days appear to be numbered.

While the institution of these four pieces appeared to have satisfied the congressional mandate, Congress had not specified in the 1975 amendments exactly what the national market system was to be. Rather, a National Market Advisory Board (NMAB) was established to work out the design for the SEC. The NMAB, however, reflected all too well the deeply divided industry that it represented. It failed to achieve its objectives in the two years it was given and met for the last time on December 12, 1977. However, the approach implemented in ITS did have its origins in the discussions of the NMAB.

At the time, the SEC had been involved historically with setting rules and with supervising the markets, primarily to prevent undesirable conduct and to ensure the adequate capitalization of member firms. The commission, therefore, was not prepared to undertake, by itself, the difficult task of satisfying the congressional mandate to design a new system. Consequently, the industry witnessed much debate and suffered through much uncertainty during the first years after the 1975 amendments.

The debate centered on two issues in particular: (1) removal of the exchange prohibition on off-board trading that dated back to the 1792 Buttonwood agreement and (2) consolidation of customer orders for a security in a single limit order book known as a consolidated limit order book (CLOB). A CLOB was never instituted, but the off-board trading restrictions have been removed. As we discuss in Chapter 11, "Regulation," the debate over off-board trading was protracted and intense. Many in the industry felt that if wrong decisions were made with respect to either this issue or the CLOB, the exchange structure as it was known would be destroyed, much to the detriment of all.

Essentially, the four NMS goals boil down to two: (1) integrate customer orders in the marketplace and (2) consolidate market information. The integration of orders produces the quotes and prices, and this is the information that is to be consolidated and broadly distributed. If public buy and sell orders do not meet in an orderly fashion, noisy information results, short-run price volatility is accentuated, and the NMS goals are not met. Consequently, much attention has been given by the U.S. regulatory authorities to the *consolidation and dissemination* of information. Less thought has been given to the *production* of information. The quality of the trading information produced depends on the efficiency with which orders are handled and translated into trades.

Regarding the efficiency of order handling and trade execution, the U.S. regulatory authorities have been torn between two objectives. On the one hand, they recognize the advantages of strengthening competition between order placers by consolidating order flow. On the other hand, they see the benefits of strengthening competition between alternative trading venues. How can they achieve both? To restate the problem, having alternative trading venues fragments the order flow (which is not good), but consolidated order flow leads to monopolistic power (which is also not good). The SEC has attempted to achieve a reasonable balance by regulating the markets much as one regulates water temperature before taking a shower—a little more cold versus a little more hot, a little more consolidation of the order flow versus a little more infusion of competition.

Connectivity has been turned to as a way of tying alternative venues together to achieve competition between the various market centers and between customer orders. But connectivity between systems is not the same as consolidating all orders in a single book (a CLOB). With connectivity:

- All markets are not necessarily accessible to all participants.
- Strict time priorities across all orders cannot be achieved.

- Free riding on the public goods–type services of a central market is facilitated (as discussed in Chapter 4, "What We Want from our Markets," and in Chapter 11, "Regulation").

Congress's involvement with market architecture issues actually started in the 1960s when it ordered the SEC to sponsor the *Institutional Investor Study*. The report, filed with the SEC in 1971, focused largely on the competitive structure of the securities markets, the profitability of specialist operations, and the behavior of institutional investors (a group that, while far larger now, was at the time big enough to prompt the study). Then Congress passed the Exchange Act amendments of 1975 calling for a "national market system." The two motivations for the NMS mandate were: "the maintenance of stable and orderly markets" and "the centralization of all buying and selling interest so that each investor will have the opportunity for the best possible execution of his order, regardless of where in the system it originates."[20]

But best execution cannot be achieved without information, and this led the SEC to believe that the development of a central market system requires that all price, volume, and quote information be available to all investors, for all securities, in all markets.[21] In its December 1999 *Market Data Concept Release*, the SEC stated:[22]

> One of the most important functions that the Commission can perform for retail investors is to ensure that they have access to the information they need to protect and further their own interests. . . .
>
> Although it intended to rely on competitive forces to the greatest extent possible to shape the national market system, Congress also recognized that the Commission would need ample authority to achieve the goal of providing investors and broker-dealers with a central source of consolidated market information. . . .
>
> The consolidated, real-time stream of market information has been an essential element in the success of the U.S. securities markets. It is the principal tool for enhancing the transparency of the buying and selling interest in a security, for addressing the fragmentation of buying and selling interest among different market centers, and for facilitating the best execution of customers' orders by their broker-dealers. Broad public access to consolidated market information was not the fortuitous result of private market forces, but of planning and concerted effort by Congress, the Commission, the SROs, and the securities industry as a whole. . . .

A regulatory authority cannot become intimately involved with the production, distribution, and pricing of market information without at the same time interfering with the natural formation of a marketplace. For this reason, despite repeated SEC statements that market structure should be determined by competition and not by the regulators, the commission has, over the years, become ever more deeply involved in the design of the U.S. markets.

Implicit Collusion

In 1994, two professors, William Christie and Paul Schultz, published a paper in the *Journal of Finance* that has had far-reaching consequences for the U.S. equity markets in general and for broker-dealer firms and the Nasdaq market in particular.[23] Christie and Schultz found that Nasdaq dealers were commonly avoiding odd-eighth quotes (e.g., 60⅝).[24] Further, the authors suggested that dealers were "implicitly colluding" to keep spreads artificially wide. Following an investigation of Nasdaq and its dealers by the Department of Justice and the SEC, a class action lawsuit was filed. On November 9, 1998, approval of the court was issued for a settlement in the aggregate amount of $1.027 billion.[25]

Further, communications between broker-dealers about market conditions were discouraged by a Department of Justice requirement that their conversations be taped. This has made price discovery more difficult in the Nasdaq market, particularly at market openings. We will return shortly to the impact all of this has had on the Nasdaq market.

The Order Handling Rules

Continuing to press for greater transparency of price and quote information, the SEC in 1997 instituted new order handling rules: (1) Any market maker holding a customer limit order must display that order in his or her quote. (2) If a market maker has placed a more aggressively priced quote in an electronic communications network, that market maker is okay if the ECN displays the top of its book in the Nasdaq quote montage. (3) However, if that ECN's own best quotes are not in the quote montage, then the market maker must update his or her own quote in Nasdaq to match the ECN quote.

The proverbial cat was out of the bag. The new requirements set the stage for the electronic communications networks to enter the field. Before the rules were instituted, Instinet was the one and only ECN. By September 1999 there were nine. To capture order flow, all a new ECN needed was to be a gateway that attracted some customers to place limit orders on its electronic book. Connectivity with other markets (either directly or through one of Nasdaq's own systems) would then enable market orders from the customers of other firms to reach its book and trigger trades.[26] One of the new

ECNs, Archipelago, states on it web site, "In January 1997, the U.S. Securities and Exchange Commission (SEC) implemented new Order Handling Rules that revolutionized trading in NASDAQ® securities. The new rules created the opportunity for Electronic Communications Networks (ECNs), such as the Archipelago ECN, to interact directly with the NASDAQ National Market® System. The Archipelago ECN was formed in December 1996 in response to these rules."

The SEC-enforced consolidation, transparency, and accessibility of price information quickly caused the flow of limit orders to fragment onto multiple books, and the ECNs' cheap, fast, and anonymous trading has forced Nasdaq to alter its trading systems and organizational structure. Then, with the passage of time, consolidation started taking place among the ECNs: Instinet has acquired Island; Archipelago has acquired the Pacific Stock Exchange (Instinet/Island along with Archipelago currently account for the lion's share of ECN volume), and on May 25, 2004, Nasdaq announced that it will acquire one of the other new electronic Markets, Brut ECN, currently owned by Sun-Gard Data Systems. As the dust settles, Nasdaq no longer resembles the market it was when the decade of the 1990s was coming to an end.

Decimalization

In its efforts to further strengthen competition and to reduce bid-ask spreads, the SEC has pushed for a reduction in the tick size (minimum price variation). In the United States, the tick size had historically been set at one-eighth of a point. Under pressure from the SEC, the NYSE and Nasdaq reduced the tick size from an eighth to a sixteenth in 1997, and then completed the transition from sixteenths to pennies in 2001.[27]

The minimum price variation sets a floor on the size of bid-ask spreads, and a relatively large tick size can keep spreads wider than they otherwise would be, especially for lower-priced stocks. The wider spreads, of course, translate into higher returns per round-trip for market makers and into higher transaction costs per round-trip for customers. Does this justify changing the tick size? The answer depends on whether the change has other consequences.

Spreads have narrowed, but there have been other consequences as well. When one-eighth pricing was the norm, there were eight price points per dollar. With pennies, there are 100. Consequently, less liquidity is concentrated at each price point and depth at the inside market (the best bid and offer) has dropped off.[28] As it has, the speed with which quotes change has accelerated. In the new regime, quote screens for active stocks commonly flicker faster than the eye can follow.

A small minimum price variation also affects participant trading strategies. By raising a bid or lowering an offer by just one penny, a participant can step ahead of a limit order on the book. The practice, referred to as *pennying*, undermines the importance of time priorities and discourages participants from submitting limit orders in the first place. Picture a situation where a 5,000-share limit order to buy has set the market bid at $50, and a 1,000-share market order to sell arrives and is shown to the crowd on the NYSE trading floor. A specialist or floor trader can step ahead of the book and buy the shares at $50.01. If price goes up, the specialist or floor trader can flip out of the position and realize a profit that increases, penny for penny, with the price of the stock. If it appears that price is about to fall, he or she can sell the shares at a loss of just one cent per share by hitting the limit order at $50 (assuming that the 50 bid has not executed or been canceled). This asymmetry reflects the free option value that a limit order extends to other participants (the cost is capped at one cent while the profit potential is unbounded).

Currently, there is talk about going to subpennies, and not all of it is positive. Andrew Brooks of T. Rowe Price had this to say: "Sub-pennies are illegitimate, except for a 5-cent stock. Maybe a 20-cent stock. But certainly not a thirty-dollar stock. Sub-pennies are confusing, they are distracting, and they bring no value to anybody. It is ridiculous for order flow to be directed to somebody because their bid or offer is better by a sub-penny."[29] With respect to penny pricing, William Christie (who, with his coauthor Paul Schultz had called attention to the odd-eighths issue) stated, "In retrospect, however, we were naive in expecting pennies to balance the interests of the many trading constituencies, since a penny tick size has destroyed the critical roles played by price priority and limit orders. Any investor, including market specialists, can offer meaningless price improvement, step in front of existing limit orders, and render such orders virtually worthless."[30]

Fracturing the order flow over multiple price points and discouraging limit orders is harmful to market quality. The smaller tick size can result in higher intraday volatility and a less transparent market. The NYSE has responded to the transparency effect by introducing "Liquidity Quotes," an innovation that Paul Bennett of the NYSE described as follows: "The idea is to create a mechanism whereby people can actually find liquidity on the book. They are not going to find it at the inside quotes because the inside quotes are so narrow now. The inside quotes are flickering around like crazy. But if people are willing to go a few cents outside of them, I believe that they will be able to find the depth."[31]

With Liquidity Quote, the specialist for a stock, based on his or her own judgment, states a lower bid and a higher offer at which a more substantial number of shares are sought for purchase or offered for sale. Essentially, Liquidity Quote is an attempt to repackage the information that had been provided at the best bid and offer when the minimum price variation was an eighth of a point. Thus far, however, Liquidity Quote has not been heavily used.

The Trade-Through Rule

When a transaction occurs at a price that is higher than the best posted offer or lower than the best posted bid, and orders at these better prices are not included in the transaction, a *trade-through* is said to occur. Namely, the better-priced orders have been "traded through."[32] Trade-throughs are not allowed in the listed (exchange) market. That is, strict price priority is enforced across all publicly displayed orders and markets. The argument in favor of this rule is that it is fair to limit order traders, and that it thus encourages the placement of limit orders.

However, there are drawbacks as well. For one thing, the trade-through rule prevents a new alternative market or trading system designed to provide independent price discovery from competing on the quality of the price discovery that it delivers. A second problem is that executing at the "best price" is not simply accomplished when some markets are "fast" (the electronic markets) and others are "slow" (the floor-based markets). As reported in *Traders Magazine*, Sanjiv Gupta of Bloomberg has explained it this way: "As it stands, the faster electronic markets must wait for the slower responding NYSE to make sure traders get the best price. That's because of the listed market's infamous trade through rule." He provides an example: "IBM is listed at 93.40. If an institution could buy 20,000 shares in milliseconds at 93.41, it would usually accept it, given a choice. It does not want to wait 45 seconds. That's because the institution could end up buying only 200 shares at 93.40."[33]

Currently, the SEC is considering allowing at least a *de minimus* exception to the rule (two or three cents a share for orders of up to 500 shares). SEC commissioner Cynthia Glassman stated, "In their current incarnation, trade-through rules permit slow markets to halt fast markets for an order for a very small number of shares, which prevents competition in fast markets. . . . So for me, the questions are: Do they [the no-trade-through rules] in fact protect limit orders in the penny environment? Or are we entrenching slow markets?"[34]

The no-trade-through issue underscores the extent to which computer technology has altered the markets since the 1975 amendments were passed. Perhaps our thoughts about what makes a good national market system ought to be changed as well.

A Tale of Two Markets

The NYSE and Nasdaq have each faced major competitive, technological, and regulatory challenges in the past decades. In the not-too-distant future, either or both of these markets could cease to exist, at least as we currently know them. Nevertheless, the NYSE and Nasdaq have followed very different paths in recent years.

The NYSE has invested heavily in technology. The Big Board has introduced new systems such as OpenBook, Institutional Express, Direct+, and eBroker in order to support its trading floor. But its basic market model has not changed over the years. The NYSE has retained its brand as an intermediated, floor-based market. On the floor, brokers still handle customer orders and specialists are still responsible for making fair and orderly markets for the stocks that have been assigned to them. And the exchange has not demutualized.

Orders at the NYSE may be received and information disseminated with electronic speed. Nevertheless, the clock still moves at the pace at which it has ticked for the past 200-plus years at the most critical point in the transaction process—when orders meet orders and are translated into trades. That is, a computer may fire an institutional-sized order to a direct access floor broker in less than a second from anywhere in the world, but once received, that floor broker still has to walk to the appropriate specialist's post and, once there, work that order carefully over an extended period of time. The NYSE's continuing domination of its market is no doubt explained, in part at least, by the fact that floor brokers and specialists, in direct face-to-face contact, continue to add value (see Chapter 7, "Intermediated Markets"). And so, despite all the pressures to change, the NYSE has not thus far veered away from its basic game plan.

The same cannot be said for Nasdaq. Over the past decade, this market center has reengineered itself from a competitive dealer market into a partially quote-driven, partially order-driven hybrid composed of competing dealer houses and electronic trading platforms, including SuperMontage and those of the ECNs. Its key function is no longer that of a membership organization that supplies trading infrastructure and regulatory oversight to the broker-dealer community. Nasdaq is separating from the NASD, demutualizing, and has applied to the SEC to be registered as an exchange.

Today, Nasdaq's chief facility is its electronic trading platform, Super-Montage. Nasdaq is increasingly coming to resemble an ECN. In the process, it has encountered major problems, including the loss of substantial market share. In an August 2003 *Business Week* cover story, Dwyer and Borrus wrote,[35]

> *The question now is: Will Nasdaq survive as a thriving market for tech stocks? It is under assault on all sides. While it pursued a business model that faced tortuous regulatory delays, super fast electronic communications networks (ECNs) such as Reuters Group LLC's Instinet, stole its lunch. As a result, ECNs have snatched*

*almost half the trading volume in Nasdaq-listed stocks, or 2½ times
as much as Nasdaq's own trading system.*

To what may this change in Nasdaq's fortunes be attributed? The *Business
Week* article stated that the market's problems are ". . . largely self-inflicted.
Its recent history resembles a Greek tragedy of epic proportions, complete
with management miscues, fierce infighting among constituents, costly
regulatory misunderstandings, and a big dose of hubris."[36]

More is involved. The market, which grew rapidly in size and in luster,
came to be named after the information system upon which it was based.
In 1982, the Nasdaq/NM (National Market) was established for the most
prominent Nasdaq issues. The success of this new market can be attributed
in good part to clever marketing and to a most important fact: Its prominent issues were dominated by high-growth technology companies.

As Nasdaq emerged as a major market and as a clear, viable alternative
to the NYSE, it remained a dealer-intermediated market. As discussed in
Chapter 7, "Intermediated Markets," a dealer market is characterized by
the absence of time priorities, by preferencing and quote matching, and by
interdealer communications that are transmitted by interdealer trading and
telephone conversations. But Christie and Schultz discovered (as we have
discussed) that Nasdaq dealers were avoiding posting odd-eighths quotes.
With the odd-eighths eliminated, the minimum price variation (and hence
the minimum bid-ask spread) was effectively a quarter of a point. Of
course, quarter-point spreads were more profitable than one-eighth
spreads for the dealers. Could the dealers' avoidance of odd-eighth quotes
be attributed to implicit collusion? As we have noted, the Department of
Justice and the SEC investigated this possibility, a class action lawsuit was
filed, a $1.027 billion settlement resulted, and the Nasdaq market has not
been the same since.

Technology played a role in the reengineering of Nasdaq. In both the
London and Nasdaq dealer markets, the computer has made the order-
driven market increasingly attractive, especially for large-cap, liquid
stocks. Competitive pressures played a role. These have included the
strength of the NYSE; the emergence of technologically advanced, electronic order-driven platforms in Europe along with the ECNs and ATSs in
the United States; and the increasing sophistication of buy side traders. In
the years following the historic price-fixing lawsuit, the SEC has also
played a major role in shaping Nasdaq's market model: to wit, the new
order handling rules and decimalization. Moreover, Nasdaq (like other market centers) has been required to get regulatory approval for every major
change in its trading system and organizational structure.

The approvals were slow in coming. With regard to Nasdaq's application for exchange status, Kramer wrote,[37] "Nasdaq isn't even a registered

exchange. The NASD retains voting control over Nasdaq unless the SEC approves it as a national securities exchange. So to achieve self-regulatory status—separate from that of the NASD—Nasdaq has been pressing the SEC to obtain an exchange registration. The result? The SEC has dragged its feet for two years."

Nasdaq's exchange registration is a complex issue. With its dealer market heritage, Nasdaq allows orders to be internalized in a way that could set a strong precedent for other U.S. exchanges—it could challenge the requirement that orders on an exchange be publicly exposed.[38] SEC inaction with regard to Nasdaq's exchange status might also be attributed, in part at least, to turnover in the chairman's office at the SEC.[39] After Arthur Levitt resigned as SEC chairman, an August 2003 *Newsday* article stated it this way: "Many months elapsed before the nomination of Harvey Pitt, who then quit under fire. The third in a succession of SEC chairman faced with the application for Nasdaq exchange status, William Donaldson, is studying it."

There have been further ramifications. As it fought to retain its aura of excellence and to regain momentum, Nasdaq attempted to expand by acquiring the American Stock Exchange, by developing overseas ventures in Europe and Japan, and by investing more than $100 million in its new trading platform, SuperMontage. No benefits were realized from the Amex purchase, and Nasdaq's European and Japanese markets have been shut down. The bottom line is, Nasdaq was thrown off its original game plan and since then has had to fight hard to regain its stride and to maintain its network.

It is critical for any market that its network not be impaired. Wunsch described the thinking as follows:[40]

> *The reform-induced breakup of the stock market network . . . is undermining more than liquidity and price discovery. It is also dissolving the potential to exploit network effects on which the business models of most exchanges, brokers and dealers depend. As the membership structures that held the network in place disintegrate, continuous markets are losing their capacity to support brandable services related to their operation. While the rapid rise of ECNs and e-brokers appears to herald a durable business opportunity for the winners, in fact these shifting shares are just the beginning of what will become a relentless process of commoditization from which none are safe. Powerful old continuous trading brands—NYSE, Nasdaq, Merrill Lynch, Instinet—may indeed disperse to the winds under the onslaught of their new competitors. But the newcomers will not celebrate long, for they will soon realize that the same regulatory policy that created their apparent opportunity will permanently prevent profits.*

Wunsch's statement is applicable to both the Nasdaq and NYSE markets. The ATSs and ECNs, which have made major inroads in the Nasdaq marketplace, have thus far had little success in the NYSE marketplace. But this could change. Increasingly, the institutions are expressing discontent with NYSE executions. Many believe that executing their large orders at the Big Board simply costs more than it should. From their experience with trading Nasdaq stocks electronically, the institutions are increasingly demanding the speed, control, anonymity, and consistency that electronic trading offers.

The core of the situation at the NYSE is that its market structure has become more suitable to small retail customers. Penny spreads are thought to serve the retail customer well. Unfortunately for large traders, penny prices have scattered liquidity over many more price points, and depth has dropped at the inside market (the highest bid and the lowest offer). Institutional trading is far lumpier than the nibble-sized pieces that routinely trade on the exchange. A recent study of institutional trading by the Plexus Group showed that more than 52 percent of the dollars traded on the exchange are in trades of fewer than 10,000 shares. Portfolio managers commonly want to adjust their holdings in amounts that range up to and well above 100,000 shares.

As discussed in Chapter 5, "Institutional Order Flow," institutional customers are slicing their big orders into much smaller pieces. Their "large pegs" are being whittled down to match the tiny holes (the opportunities to trade) that they are supposed to fit into, and the problem is growing. The NYSE's *Fact Book* reports that the highest annual average trade size peaked back in 1988 at 2,303 shares and has declined steadily ever since. In August 2003, the figure stood at 503 shares, according to www.nyse.com. This low level of shares per trade has not been seen since 1975.

As the orders are broken into digestible-sized pieces, their executions necessarily stretch out in time. The larger the order, the less likely it is to be completed within a day. The Plexus study showed that 77 percent of smaller trades (those averaging 2,000 shares each) traded on the same day that they were placed; the one-day completion rate fell rapidly to just 7 percent as order size increased to half a day's trading volume. What happens to cost as order executions are stretched out in time?

In the imagery of Wayne Wagner of the Plexus group, the "prying eyes" of others can detect a sequence of small but persistently one-sided order flow. Perhaps a large fund is entering a sequence of buy orders. Market insiders such as hedge funds, proprietary trading desks, and day traders can pick up a pattern. They buy up the supply of stock and, in so doing, drive up the stock's price up, then sell to the frustrated institution at the higher price. The result is a bulking up of costs. Plexus found that costs for the smallest orders average 0.06 percent per trade, and the number soars to 1.27 percent for large institutional sell orders. These statistics reflect the difficulty the NYSE (and other markets) face in handling institutional-sized orders.

Another storm cloud is hanging over the Big Board. Specialist operations, as we have noted, are at the center of the NYSE's agency/auction market, and their participation rates have increased following the introduction of penny pricing. On April 22, 2003, the NYSE announced a probe into specialist operations. The market makers were accused of front-running customers' orders and illegally interpositioning themselves between public customers (i.e., selling to public buyers at relatively high prices and, at roughly the same time, buying from public sellers at relatively low prices). On October 16 of that year, the NYSE announced that it will bring disciplinary action against, and seek to impose fines on, the five largest specialist firms. On October 17, the SEC issued a formal order of investigation. And on December 16, Calpers, the giant California pension fund, announced a civil lawsuit against the NYSE and its seven specialist firms. The charges have renewed questions about the efficiency of the NYSE's floor-based, specialist-oriented system vis-à-vis the electronic trading platforms that now characterize most other markets around the globe. On March 30, 2004, the SEC announced that the actions against the specialist firms had been settled; without admitting or denying the allegations, the five firms agreed to pay a total of $241.8 million in penalties and the return of excess profits to investors.

A further blow hit the Big Board in 2003. In September of that year, Richard Grasso stepped down as its chairman and CEO amid a huge outcry following the disclosure that his multiyear compensation package exceeded $139 million. Grasso had been an enormously important person for the NYSE. He was a strong leader and figurehead. He got the listings. He maintained the structural integrity of the exchange and its floor-based model. With today's powerful winds of change (technology, competition, and regulation), there is something to say about keeping the Big Board on an even keel. But Grasso met up with a nasty formula: $139 million (his claim) plus his being a regulator (in line with the NYSE's SRO obligations) plus corporate ethics in the spotlight (in the post-Enron and Tyco era) equals trouble.

The combination of institutional discontent, specialist improprieties, and the issues surrounding Grasso's resignation have opened the window wide for regulatory intervention in the organizational structure and market architecture of the exchange. On the competitive front, pressures have remained intense. On January 12, 2004, Nasdaq announced a dual-listing initiative and the decision of six NYSE firms (including Hewlett-Packard, Charles Schwab, and Walgreens) to list on Nasdaq as well as on the NYSE. In Nasdaq's press release, its president and CEO Robert Greifeld stated that, with dual listing, "we can provide a unique opportunity for public companies to trade on Nasdaq and to experience the benefits of an electronic model with multiple, competitive participants."[41] The longer-run effects of this initiative should be interesting, especially if the SEC modifies the trade-through rule previously discussed in this chapter.

Currently, two interconnected factors are giving the NYSE its distinct branding: (1) its self-regulation of its members (including those on its trading floor) and (2) its trading floor. If responsibility for surveillance of the exchange's floor operations is passed to a separate regulatory entity, what will happen to its floor? Should the floor be replaced by an electronic platform, as many are now advocating? Should the floor be combined in a hybrid structure with an electronic platform so that the exchange may claim to be a "fast market" and so retain the protection it believes it receives from the trade-through rule?[42] These are indeed thorny issues. They go to the very core of what the exchange is and does. However they are resolved, history might show that the events of 2003 have set in motion a reengineering of the NYSE market, much as the accusations of price collusion in 1994 sparked the reengineering of Nasdaq.

The exchange is still receiving roughly 80 percent of the order flow for its listed stocks. It is still the place where liquidity is focused and prices are discovered. Both the NYSE and Nasdaq have been vital for the capital-raising ability of their listed companies, and the contribution of both of these markets to the vibrancy of the U.S. economy has been enormous. Care must be taken to ensure that their networks are not impaired. But problems do exist with U.S. equity market structure. Recognizing them, the SEC, under the leadership of its current chairman, William Donaldson, is moving toward formulating new market regulation referred to as "Reg NMS." Events in the coming years will show how all this plays out.

NOTES

1. These are ArcaEx (formed following Archipelago's acquisition of the Pacific Stock Exchange), Chicago Stock Exchange, Pacific Stock Exchange, Philadelphia Stock Exchange, and the National Stock Exchange (formally the Cincinnati Stock Exchange). In addition, the International Securities Exchange is currently trading options, but at some time in the future this exchange might expand its product base.

2. The NYSE, as of 2004, claims to be 212 years old. Harking back to its previous name, the NYSE is often referred to as the "Big Board." It took its current name—New York Stock Exchange—on January 29, 1863. For further history, see James E. Buck, ed., *The New York Stock Exchange: The First 200 Years*, New York 1992.

3. The *over-the-counter* market originated in an era when stocks were bought and sold in banks and the physical certificates were passed "over the counter."

4. In addition to the regular NYSE members, 60 individuals have obtained either physical or electronic access to the trading floor by paying an annual member-

ship fee. Unlike regular members, electronic or physical access members have no rights to the assets of the NYSE, if distributed.

5. The committee's allocation procedure takes into account the specialist firm's prior performance record, the firm's score on the Specialist Performance Evaluation Questionnaire, which is filled out quarterly by floor brokers, and the characteristics (such as industry type) of the issues currently assigned to the specialist firm. Requests made by the newly listed companies are also considered by the allocation committee.

   Delisting of a stock is possible, but occurs very infrequently and only with difficulty as long as a stock continues to satisfy the listing criteria. The NYSE will grant a delisting request if, pursuant to NYSE Rule 500 the following three conditions are all met: (1) at least two-thirds of the holders of outstanding shares vote in favor of delisting; (2) no more than 10 percent of the shareholders object; and (3) delisting is approved by a majority of the company's board of directors.

6. NYSE Rule 104 says that the duty of a specialist is ". . . to maintain a fair and orderly market, or to act as an odd-lot dealer in such security." Rule 104.10 states that the function of a specialist, in addition to the effective execution of commission orders entrusted to him or her, is "the maintenance . . . of a fair and orderly market . . . which . . . implies the maintenance of price continuity with reasonable depth, and the minimizing of the effects of temporary disparity between supply and demand."

7. With regard to a listed company, a specialist:
   - Must make at least one annual contact with an official of the corporation.
   - May not be an officer or a director of the corporation.
   - May not accept orders directly from officers, directors, principal stockholders of the corporation or from the corporation itself.
   - Neither the specialist nor anyone associated with the specialist (e.g., a partner or clerk) may participate in a proxy contest or in a contest for a change of management of the corporation.

   With regard to his or her own trades as a market maker, a specialist:
   - Cannot buy for his or her own account while holding unexecuted market orders to buy, cannot sell for his or her own account while holding unexecuted market orders to sell, and must always give priority to equally priced limit orders. This is known as the specialist's *negative obligation* (i.e., the specialist is not allowed to trade ahead of a public order at the same price at which the public order would execute).
   - May not charge a brokerage commission and be a dealer in the same trade.
   - Cannot trade with an order that he or she is holding on the order book without the permission of a floor official.
   - May not solicit orders in stock in which he or she specializes.
   - May not accept orders from an institution or deal directly with an institutional investor.
   - Is restricted in his or her freedom to buy shares at a price higher than the last transaction price (on an uptick) or to sell shares at a price lower than

the last transaction price (on a downtick). This "tick-test rule" prevents the specialist from accentuating a market imbalance.

8. If the specialist succeeds in finding a better price, the stop is off. Once an order is executed in the crowd at the guaranteed price, the specialist must execute the stopped order and inform the floor broker that the stop has been *elected*.

9. When an opening price is not determined within 15 minutes due to major informational change, opening is *delayed* and the specialist sends out price indications. When an acceptable price is found, the market for the stock is opened and trading begins.

10. It is of the utmost importance for a specialist to be able to distinguish a technical price change from a price change generated by news. If it is technical, he or she should intervene. If it is fundamental, other measurements must be taken into consideration. A specialist firm does not have an obligation to put itself out of business.

11. The NASD has established the *Rules of Fair Practice*. These apply to the financial integrity of member firms, sales practices (including a maximum 5 percent markup policy, which prevents NASD members from profiting unreasonably at the expense of their customers), market making, and underwriting activities.

12. Nasdaq market makers cannot be subjected to price continuity or stabilization tests because they do not have exclusive franchises.

13. All Nasdaq stocks were on the system by December 2, 2002, following nine implementation phases.

14. The company has also run an after-hours crossing referred to as Instinet's crossing network. Their main system, however, has always been their continuous electronic market.

15. The Arizona Stock Exchange, owned and operated by AZX, was regulated by the SEC as an exchange with a limited-volume exemption. OptiMark was operated as a facility of the Pacific Exchange for NYSE-listed equities and as a facility of the Nasdaq Stock Market for Nasdaq equities.

16. LiquidNet also started operations in Europe in November 2002.

17. Negotiations start at 25,000 shares (except for thinner issues), and the midpoint of the national best bid and offer (NBBO) is used as a reference point.

18. Donald Stone, "Future Shock Is Here," in E. Bloch and R. Schwartz, eds., *Impending Changes for Securities Markets: What Role for the Exchange?* JAI Press, 1979.

19. For further detail, see Steve Williams, "The Evolving National Market System," in Y. Amihud, T. Ho, and R. Schwartz, eds., *Market Making and the Changing Structure of the Securities Industry*, D.C. Heath and Company, 1985.

20. See S. Rep. No. 94-75, 94th Cong., 1st sess. 7 (1975) ("Senate Report"). For further discussion, see *SEC Market Data Concept Release*, Release No. 34-42208, December 9, 1999.

21. See, for instance, Statement of the Securities and Exchange Commission on the Future Structure of the Securities Markets (February 2, 1972), 37 FR 5286. Also See *SEC Market Data Concept Release*, op. cit., pp. 5, 7, 33.

22. *SEC Market Data Concept Release*, op. cit.

23. W. Christie and P. Schultz, "Why Do Nasdaq Market Makers Avoid Odd-eighth Quotes?" *Journal of Finance* 49, 1994, pp. 1813–1840.

24. At the time of the Christie-Schultz study, the minimum price variation (tick size) was still one-eighth of a point.

25. Opinion by the Honorable Robert W. Sweet, 94 Civ. 3996, U.S.D.C., Southern District of New York.

26. A market maker could use a Nasdaq system (SelectNet) to send an order it has received to another market maker or to broadcast the order to all market makers. As quote providers, an ECN could also connect directly into SelectNet. SelectNet included a negotiation feature that allows a participant (market maker or ECN) to accept, reject, or counter a received order. SelectNet has now been superseded by SuperMontage.

27. Specifically, the SEC pushed the markets to convert from fractional pricing to decimal pricing, but not to pennies per se. The markets, however, went immediately to pennies. They properly anticipated that any market that set a higher price variation (e.g., a nickel or four cents) would immediately be undercut by a competitor going to a smaller amount (e.g., four cents or three cents). Essentially, the penny tick was the result of a race to what, at the time, appeared the bottom. Not long·after, however, talk started about going to subpennies.

28. Robert McSweeney of the New York Stock Exchange has stated, "The depth of the inside quote has diminished 67% due to the expansion of the number of price points." See *Coping with Institutional Order Flow*, Robert A. Schwartz, John A. Byrne, and Antoinette Colaninno, eds., Kluwer Academic Publishers, 2004 forthcoming.

29. See *Coping with Institutional Order Flow*, Robert A. Schwartz, John A. Byrne, and Antoinette Colaninno, eds., Kluwer Academic Publishers, 2004, forthcoming.

30. William G. Christie, "A Minimum Increment Solution," *Traders Magazine*, November 2003, p. 40.

31. See *Coping with Institutional Order Flow*, Robert A. Schwartz, John A. Byrne, and Antoinette Colaninno, eds., Kluwer Academic Publishers, 2004 forthcoming.

32. For example, if a sell limit order on the book at 50.10 remains unexecuted after a trade takes place at 50.12, the 50.10 sell order has been traded through.

33. Steve Watkins, "Is the Specialist System Doomed?" *Traders Magazine*, November 2003, p. 35.

34. Steve Watkins, op. cit., p. 38.

35. "The Crisis at Nasdaq," Paula Dwyer and Amy Borrus, *Business Week*, August 11, 2003, pp. 65–71.

36. Paula Dwyer and Amy Borrus, op. cit., p. 65.

37. Hilary Kramer, "Free the Nasdaq!" WSJ.com, *Wall Street Journal Online*, August 14, 2003.

38. See Isabelle Clary, "Why Hasn't the SEC Turned Down Nasdaq?" *Securities Industry News*, August 18, 2003, p. 4.

39. See Susan Harrigan, *Newsday*, August 18, 2003.

40. R. Steven Wunsch, "What's Driving Market Structure? Technology or Regulation?" in Robert A. Schwarz, ed., *The Electronic Call Auction: Market Mechanism and Trading*, Kluwer Academic Publishers, 2001.

41. Nasdaq press release, "Nasdaq Announces Dual Listing Program with Six Participating Companies," January 12, 2004.

42. As of this writing, the SEC is considering its position regarding the trade-through rule. A likely resolution will include the right of a fast market to trade through a slow market but not another fast market. Thus, to retain its protection under the trade-through rule, the NYSE is attempting to be classified as a fast market by beefing up its electronic system, Direct+.

CHAPTER 9

The Evolving Scene in Europe

W
e now turn to the other side of the Atlantic and consider the current scene in the European equity markets. The European markets have their own special features that, based on culture and tradition, mirror European fragmentation.

History is an important part of the picture. Markets began developing in many European centers in the Middle Ages.[1] The Paris "Pont-au-Change" (Exchange Bridge) was mentioned as early as 1141. In the city of Brugge, today's Belgium, trading took place in front of the house of the noble family Van der Boerse. That is where, around 1360, the terms *bourse*, *Börse*, *borsa*, *bolsa*, *börs*, and so on were coined. The first exchange was founded in Antwerp, Belgium, about 1530, mainly for trading commodities and bills of exchange. In the following decades, a number of impressive exchange buildings were constructed in Amsterdam, London, Copenhagen, and elsewhere.[2]

A landmark change occurred in 1602. Equity shares were issued for the first time by the Dutch East India Company, which needed more capital to finance its prospering trading activity.[3] The company's shares started trading on the world's oldest stock exchange, Amsterdam. The new capital-raising technique found followers, and trading in securities and commodities started to develop side by side. So, too, did the regulatory decrees.

The founding of real stock exchanges started about 1800, at more or less the same time on both sides of the Atlantic. As noted in Chapter 8, "The

---

Richard Meier, SWX Swiss Exchange, has participated as a coauthor of this chapter.

Evolving Scene in the United States," the history of the New York Stock Exchange goes back to the Buttonwood agreement of 1792 and to the formation of the New York Stock & Exchange Board in 1817.[4] The London Stock Exchange's founding document was signed on 1802. In France, Napoleon defined the "monopolistic" rights of the French *agents de change* (brokers) in 1807. The exchanges of Brussels (1801), Rome (1802), and Milan (1808) are all based on the decrees of Napoleon.

Paris played a particularly influential role in the nineteenth century as the financial center of the European continent. In this role, the Paris Bourse had a decisive influence on the market architecture of other exchanges. The Swiss exchanges, created between 1850 and 1900, used a form of *à la criée* (open outcry) system that was patterned after the French method of exchange trading. Following their formation, the trading systems of the European bourses remained much the same until the late 1980s.

Today, all of the European exchanges combined are smaller than the U.S. exchanges, but their share of the global market has been growing, and their development in the past 10 to 15 years has been seismic. Their transformation from old, sleepy bourses into modern electronic marketplaces started in 1986 with an alteration of the London Stock Exchange that was so extensive it has been dubbed "Big Bang." Among other things, Big Bang replaced the exchange's old-style *jobbers*. The jobbers (dealers operating from booths on London's trading floor) had been displaying only minimal quotation and price information. They were replaced with modern-day *market makers* who posted their quotes on a screen-based system, Stock Exchange Automated Quotations (SEAQ), that was patterned after Nasdaq. With SEAQ, two things happened. First, within days, trading moved upstairs into the broker-dealer houses and London closed its floor. Second, the exchange started attracting major order flow for continental European listings away from the continental exchanges.

Not surprisingly, London's competitive success shook up the continental exchanges and led them to overhaul their trading systems. From Stockholm to Madrid and from Paris to Switzerland and Frankfurt, old floors were replaced by modern, electronic, order-driven trading platforms. As the transformation was completed, the order flow for domestic securities came back to the continental markets. By the early 1990s, SEAQ's international market, SEAQ-I, started to collapse.

At about the same time, Central and Eastern Europe were opening up, and reforms that were instituted in this area have created new potential. Many new exchanges have started operations in Central and Eastern Europe. More broadly, European exchanges continue to be a work in progress. Parts of our text will undoubtedly be outdated before this book reaches its publication date. It is therefore useful not only to take a snapshot of the present moment, but also to look back to recent developments and to the dynamic forces that are behind them. These will remain critically important for the foreseeable future.

Statistics of the World Federation of Exchanges (WFE) for 1982 show a market capitalization for shares of $1.3 trillion (U.S. dollars) for its U.S. member exchanges.[5] This contrasts with $0.4 trillion for its European members for the same period, or 28 percent of the U.S. figure. By the end of 2002, the dollar value grew to $11.1 trillion for the United States and $6.2 trillion for Europe, raising the value of European shares from 28 percent to 56 percent versus the United States.

The number of exchanges and the degree of concentration paints another picture for Europe. By the end of 2002, the WFE had four members in the United States. About 75 percent of North American market capitalization was concentrated on the NYSE, and the Big Board accounted for 40 percent of the world capitalization (in terms of WFE membership). The WFE has 19 member exchanges in Europe. London, the largest exchange in both turnover and market capitalization, has a domestic market cap of U.S. $1,808 billion, which is less than 30 percent of the market cap of the combined continental European markets. There are more than 50 European stock exchanges if we include regional exchanges (mainly in Germany) and the sizable number of exchanges in Central and Eastern Europe that are not members of WFE. Many European exchanges—and all that claim a certain importance—are members of the Federation of European Securities Exchanges (FESE). (See Exhibit 9.1)

THE EUROPEAN MARKET MODEL

Twenty years ago, a variety of market models were in use in Europe. London had a quote-driven, floor-based system that was centered on its jobbers. Various kinds of predominantly order-driven, floor-based systems prevailed on the continent, where intermediaries basically served as trade facilitators. Many of the continental practices followed the French "open outcry" call auction (*à la criée*), which centered on traders gathered around trading rings. It is not surprising that, with this range of alternatives, debates started about how best to structure trading in a modern environment.

Debates about Trading Systems

The past two decades have seen stormy debates, at times almost religious wars, about (1) floor-based versus fully automated off-floor trading, (2) order-driven versus quote-driven trading, and (3) continuous versus call

Exchange	No. of Listed Companies			Mkt. Cap. Domestic Equity	Turnover in Equities, Funds, etc.			Bonds		Warrants	
	Domestic	Foreign	Total		Domestic	Foreign	Total	No. of Listings	Turnover	No. of Listings	Turnover
Athens	339	1	340	84,547.1	33,197.3	2.3	33,199.6	n/a	40.6		
Bratislava	366	0	366	2,203.7	588.2		588.2	70	25,831.5		
Budapest	50	1	51	13,227.9	7,230.8		7,230.8	65	1,211.8		
Copenhagen	188	7	195	93,700.6	60,054.3	46.8	60,101.1	2,320	925,542.4		
Cyprus	152	0	152	3,807.3	264.1		264.1	n/a	4.1		
Deutsche Börse	684	182	866	855,452.0	1,195,957.4	6,272.0	1,202,229.4	7,215	400,591.6	21,431*	40,371.6*
Euronext	1,047	n/a	n/a	1,646,178.0	1,690,777.0	717.0	1,691,494.0	n/a	23,462.0	3,770	4,733.0
Helsinki	142	3	145	135,000.7	145,710.9	205.6	145,916.5	266	41.9	231	477.4
Iceland	48	0	48	7,360.6	6,318.7		6,318.7	325	12,288.6		
Irish	55	11	66	67,443.8	38,821.8	59.1	38,880.9	3,716	37,233.7	5	2.1
Italian	271	8	279	487,446.4	730,838.0	6,631.3	737,469.3	509	148,873.5	2,594	11,447.8
Lithuanian SE	45	0	45	2,782.5	161.0		161.0	n/a	401.3		
Ljubljana	134	n/a	n/a	5,660.1	857.3		857.3	n/a	477.5		
London	2,311	381	2,692	1,923,168.0	3,450,790.7	136,569.6	3,587,360.3	9,763	1,913,677.0	545	323.1
Luxemburg SE	44	198	242	29,597.8	363.7	0.1	363.8	21,285	379.6	1,795	48.8
Malta SE	14	0	14	1,467.1	30.8		30.8	n/a	118.5		
Oslo	160	20	180	75,779.1	67,571.5	860.3	68,431.8	826	119,111.6	68	33.2
Prague SE	37	1	38	12,287.9	7,446.7	24.1	7,470.8	47	33,560.4		
Spanish Ex. (BME)	3,191	32	3,223	575,765.8	839,387.9	168.7	839,556.6	2,653	2,763,426.0	1,056	1,602.6
Stockholm	262	20	282	229,354.8	268,093.7	4,260.3	272,354.0	1,412	1,097,077.5	1,101	615.0
SWX, incl. Virt-x	289	130	419	576,462.0	516,320.9	41,126.5	557,447.4	1,259	157,732.8	2,662	13,499.8
Warsaw	188	1	189	29,349.8	12,066.3		12,066.3	70	1,327.6	35	1.6
Wiener Börse	104	21	125	44,811.0	9,788.9	15.0	9,803.9	2,571	507.5	590	17.6
Total	10,121	1,611		6,902,854.0	9,266,771.4		54,302		7,663,009.0	35,883	73,173.6

*Including figures of Stuttgart Stock Exchange (which is the European market leader and covers about 80 percent of the German figures).

EXHIBIT 9.1 Statistics on FESE member exchanges (December 2003).

auction trading. These debates have been settled for all markets except the major U.S. exchanges. Today, practically all of the exchange systems in Europe are hybrid structures. The hybrids encompass (1) order-driven systems that include some market making and (2) continuous trading that includes call auctions at openings, at closings, and in some cases intraday as well. Even the few remaining floor exchanges in Europe offer alternative possibilities for electronic access. Markets have become hybrids because, as we note in the conclusion to Chapter 7, "Intermediated Markets," markets must meet a range of customer needs. (See Exhibit 9.2.)

Why did some exchanges switch to electronic trading sooner than others, and why do a few still avoid taking that step, which seems so obvious for most exchanges? The reasons have been consistent within countries, across Europe, and worldwide. They pertain to the size and importance of an exchange and to the franchise value of its floor. The bigger an exchange, the more important is the franchise value of its floor. Alternatively stated, the smaller an exchange, the more readily will its members give up the floor franchise to realize the benefits of full automation. Many new exchanges in Central Europe did not even bother introducing a floor, but installed an electronic system at their inception.

Automation is a prerequisite for centralizing exchanges. For instance, Switzerland centralized three stock exchanges (Basel, Geneva, and Zurich) with its first electronic trading platform. Automation is also important for internationalization. That is, only with an electronic platform can an exchange build upon an international network by placing its trading stations or front ends with members outside the country (for example, the Zurich Stock Exchange has done this in London). In so doing, an exchange can get its product services to its customers and attract more order flow.

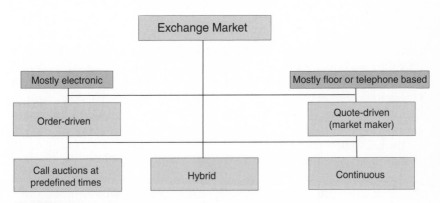

EXHIBIT 9.2 Different market models: A systematic overview.

The large U.S. exchanges will be the last to give up their floor franchises. Floor-based exchanges spend large amounts on information technology (IT) to support their floors. The Swiss exchanges had computer operations that were of similar size both before and after full automation. The difference is the use to which the automation is put. In some respects, preserving the floor makes the use of IT more complicated because it requires a great deal of human-machine interaction.

The debate about call auctions versus continuous trading is linked to the debate about order-driven versus quote-driven trading. As discussed in Chapter 6, "Order-Driven Markets," call auctions are typically used to open trading in an order book environment. Depending on the rules of a market, calls are also used at the end of the trading day to close a market and during the day. There are good arguments in favor of call auctions. They are technically desirable for opening and reopening a market, execution cost can be lower with them, price discovery is sharper, and the system is inherently more fair. Nevertheless, a lot of trading is still done in the continuous mode. As discussed in Chapter 5, "Institutional Order Flow," very large orders require special treatment to avoid excessive market impact. The big orders are commonly sliced and diced and carefully worked over an extended period of time. Program trading, pairs trading (e.g., the coordinated buying of shares in one company and selling of shares in another company), and coordinated trading in cash and derivatives markets may also be more effectively carried out in a continuous trading environment.

Consequently, calls and continuous markets both have their virtues. The two must be combined in a hybrid model to give participants the options they need to meet their portfolio objectives.

Elements of the European Market Model

The European exchanges automated their trading in the 1980s and 1990s. In spite of their diverse look and feel, most exchange practices are now quite similar. In 1999, eight leading exchanges of Europe (those of Amsterdam, Brussels, Germany, London, Madrid, Milan, Paris, and Switzerland) met and discussed forming a big alliance. A European market model emerged that describes the major regulatory principles and technical devices for bringing bids to buy and offers to sell together to create prices and trades.[6] The key parts of the European market model are as follows:

- Trading is predominantly electronic.
- It is primarily order-driven, but is also combined with various ways of market making (quote-driven).
- There are combinations of continuous trading with call auctions (opening, closing, and in some cases intraday auctions).

- There is a separate central order book for each trading instrument (each stock, bond, warrant, fund certificate, etc.).
- There's a similar price-setting algorithm.
- The model follows price-time priority. The most aggressively priced limits (the highest bids and the lowest offers) get first priority in matching. Among orders with the same price limit, those that were placed first get the highest priority.
- Trading encompasses both round lots and odd lots.
- Trading halts for the entire market and per stock are parametized and are triggered in clearly defined market conditions.
- There's a similar array of order types (market, limit, stop, iceberg, basket orders, orders for the opening auction only, etc.).

EXCHANGE SERVICES

During the 1990s, European exchange officials anticipated that consolidation would lead to a substantial reduction in the number of exchanges in Europe. This competitive pressure spurred the exchanges to strengthen their systems and to improve their services to protect their markets. When European exchanges began their automation projects, the new systems tended to mimic trading practices that characterized the earlier floor-based trading systems. It was initially expected that traders would input their orders or quotes one by one as they arrived, or as each trader decided to quote. But new dynamics of order management soon eclipsed these simplistic practices, and automation went beyond simply "paving the old cow paths."

Trading Capacity

Computerized trading allowed for new trading strategies. An in-depth, intraday analysis of trading, transaction by transaction and price by price, can reveal certain recurring patterns. Attempts to exploit these patterns have led to the development of *rule-based trading*. The profitability of this kind of trading does not lie in picking the right stocks in relation to fundamental determinants of share value, but in finding patterns that can be exploited in relatively brief moments in time. With the tools provided by automated, rule-based trading, many small pricing distortions can be quickly exploited to realize tiny short-term profits per trade from a very large number of trades. Of late, hedge funds have blossomed using this kind of strategy.[7]

As a consequence, one sees a trader buy shares and then sell them, sometimes only a second or so later. Derivatives and a lot of interesting new instruments and techniques have come to play an important role in the process. These strategies depend on computerized trading. Program trading is now common, and the specter of the 1980s has seemingly come true: Computers are trading with computers, although the programs and triggers are still under the control of human traders.

The new strategies have led to a drastic multiplication of the number of transactions and, in so doing, have required that exchanges rapidly increase their capacities. In part, developments in the IT industry have enabled the provision of the additional capacity. Also, some exchanges (e.g., SWX Swiss Exchange) now charge extra fees for excessively high quote-transaction rates to enhance the quality of the quotes and to avoid having thousands of quotes choke up the system without resulting in a transaction. Nevertheless, these fundamental changes in customers' needs and trading strategies require additional systems capacity and new system architecture to handle efficiently the far larger amount of data. Structural changes will undoubtedly continue for some time into the future, and, as they do, the industry will continue to experience major transformations.

Market Segmentation

As an important means of strengthening the economies in Europe, the European Union (EU) has sought to foster easier financing for start-up companies. Part of this activity involved supporting and promoting a new exchange, Easdaq. Easdaq was intended to be a pan-European exchange for junior companies; its mission was to facilitate earlier exit possibilities for venture capitalists.

Easdaq and the new-economy bubble triggered a good deal of thinking on the part of traditional exchanges about how best to provide customers with more appropriate services. With its advent, the "New Market" segments were born. Most popular in this arena were markets geared mainly to IPOs. The German *Neuer Markt* and the French *Nouveau Marché* in particular were tremendous successes. In Germany, for the first time, the broad public started to take notice of the stock market. This lasted, however, only until the equity bubble of the 1990s burst, after which markets for young companies that had been so bustling became much quieter places. These new markets have since been closed down.

But already much earlier, many exchanges had introduced special segments for companies that choose not to be on the main market. Listing requirements for these parallel markets (also called *second sections*, *Nebenbörsen*, *Freihandel*, etc.) were typically less demanding. The successful London version of this market (the Alternative Investments Market, or AIM) even enjoyed a few important tax advantages for its companies.

Some exchanges traded many foreign securities. Listing, trading, and also settlement rules were all adapted to specific situations. In Switzerland, U.S. shares and German shares had some very different legal characteristics (they were settled differently, for example, the use of depository receipts instead of original shares). Exchanges also applied different trading systems for different liquidity segments of their markets. Paris was the typical example with its three different trading systems: *Cotation à la criée, cotation par opposition*, and *cotation par casier.*[8] These examples show that exchanges have been responsive to market needs and have worked hard to optimize rules and mechanics.

The shift in financial research and in asset allocation from a country approach to a sector approach has led to new definitions of liquidity pools for all European blue chips (e.g., pharmaceutical companies, automotive companies, and other clusters). Exchanges have created new segments based on strategic goals, such as providing new services, improving service levels, and getting new customers. When index options and index futures were introduced in the derivatives markets, new segments were created with a view to satisfying the specific needs of the derivatives markets. And many more new segments have emerged. Deutsche Börse created Xetra European Stars and Xetra U.S. Stars to attract more trading in foreign blue chips.[9] The SWX created a segment for pure holding companies with special listing requirements. The Copenhagen Stock Exchange created new "quality segments" for companies that follow more stringent disclosure rules than are required by law. The Madrid Stock Exchange launched Latibex, a platform for trading Latin American stocks in euros. Several exchanges developed new market segments for exchange traded funds (ETFs), for repos, for eurobonds, and so forth.

Diversification of Services

Apart from developing new market segments, exchanges have also ventured into new business areas. Many have gained a great deal of IT know-how that can be used for other lines of business. Euronext has large stakes in its own listed IT company, ATOS, and in GL, a company that provides systems for accessing a multitude of electronic markets through one portal.[10] The SWX uses its IT and securities know-how to provide various services to the investment funds industry. The Copenhagen Stock Exchange has specialized in providing investor relations services for their listed companies. Copenhagen does so by offering listing packages that go beyond just regulatory listing (e.g., they provide extra exposure to companies that provide more disclosure). The Luxemburg Stock Exchange has traditionally specialized in listing services, while its trading activity has been quite limited. Even the small Ljubljana Stock Exchange in Slovenia has sold its trading system to several exchanges in the region.

While Europe has suffered from fragmentation and vast diversity, the silver lining is that an impressively broad spectrum of services for market users has resulted. This is one reason why electronic communications networks (ECNs) never got a strong foothold in Europe even though, in the past decade, they have been very successful in the United States.

Governance of Exchanges:
The Demutualization Debate

Historically, most exchanges were not-for-profit organizations owned by their members. However, many exchanges have now considered transforming from a traditional mutual or cooperative organization into a for-profit, shareholder-owned company. The change is referred to as *demutualization*.

Demutualization is linked to the earlier phenomenon of deregulation. Deregulation did not have to do with reducing regulation per se, but was about dismantling fixed commissions and similar monopolistic structures of exchange members.[11] Demutualization, a blow to both the trading firms and the exchanges, massively impacted exchange franchise values because it reduced the interest of the trading firms in being exchange members. For some exchanges, demutualization was a way to gain more freedom to undertake strategic moves in their broader market fields. As the traditional ties loosened, the trading firms and exchanges both considered new types of services, and as they did, they became potential competitors of one another.

The Stockholm Exchange triggered the new developments by going public in 1993. Briefly afterward, it was taken over by OM. At the time, OM was both the Swedish options and futures exchange and also an active supplier of trading systems for other exchanges. OM is now the mother company of Stockholmsbörsen, and it is listed on its daughter company's exchange.

A demutualized exchange may adopt several forms, each of which raises its own issues and concerns. Some exchanges have demutualized and become public companies listed on their own markets (e.g., Deutsche Börse, Euronext, the London Stock Exchange, and Stockholm). Others have demutualized but remained private corporations with their previous members as owners. Quite a number of exchanges (e.g., SWX) have retained the legal form of an association.

Should an exchange be a mutual, utility organization or a demutualized, profit-seeking, corporation? At the current time, there are a lot of different views but no compelling reason for one solution over the other. Nevertheless, looking to the future, we expect that a competitive market in trading services will likely give the least-biased judgment about the best trading system, the best organization, the best market segments, the best order handling procedures, and so on. In the meantime, the demutualization debate has launched quite a few discussions about the self-regulatory powers of exchanges. We turn to this debate in the next section of the chapter. The issue has a good deal of relevance to the current scene in Europe.

EUROPEAN EXCHANGES AND THE PROCESS OF EUROPEAN INTEGRATION

Capital markets and the financial services industry have received a lot of attention in the European integration process. A unified capital market was intended to be a major driving force for bolstering the economic power of Europe. A considerable impetus for consolidation came in the early 1990s, in the form of the Investment Services Directive (ISD). Immediately after, the finance industry was busy preparing for the euro as a common currency. About this same time, most of the European exchanges had completed the automation of their trading systems.

In the 1990s, a united capital market for Europe appeared to be just around the corner, and, even though there were still eight exchanges in Germany, seven in Switzerland, four in Spain, and so on, it seemed clear to the insiders of the European exchange industry that exchange consolidation was unavoidable. It was generally expected that within 10 years the number of exchanges in Europe would shrink to just three or four major institutions. This development was consistent with a general trend toward more consolidation in many other business sectors. However, integrating 25 national capital markets into one is not a simple matter.[12] It is one thing for people to do business around the globe; it is a totally different matter to harmonize business rules and conditions on a political level.

Legislation for a Pan-European Capital Market

Legislation and regulation are the main tools politicians and administrations use to drive an integration process, and a wide variety of legislative initiatives ensued. The European Commission developed the Financial Services Action Plan (FSAP) aimed at establishing a uniform capital market in Europe.[13] With it, the EU leaders cultivated far-reaching hopes that this regulatory program and the resulting reform would make the EU the most competitive economic area in the world. This reform went hand in hand with reforms of the political and legislative processes. The European Parliament and its commissions got a far more significant role in the EU lawmaking process. The Lamfalussy Report led to the introduction of a system of second-, third-, and fourth-level legislation.[14] Ordinances and implementing provisions should be able to be adopted more swiftly and simply. It was proposed that a European Securities Commission (ESC) at the finance ministry level and the Committee of European Securities Regulators (CESR) should be appointed to oversee these second- and third-level processes in securities legislation. To make this presumably expedited process politically acceptable, a highly transparent but cumbersome consultative procedure was put in place.

Numerous laws and directives pertain to the EU stock exchanges. The Investment Services Directive (ISD) is the legal basis of securities trading in the EU. When it first became effective in 1993, the ISD brought about the single European "passport" mechanism. *Passporting* defines a system of mutual acceptance of other EU countries' rules without truly harmonizing all of the details of the various rules. Only basic elements have to be identical or closely similar. The Prospectus Directive is another major piece of legislation.[15] At the time, the Market Abuse Directive (covering insider dealing and price manipulation) was seen as a key development in the war against terrorism. Many other legal documents in fields such as corporate governance, clearing and settlement, takeovers, accounting, auditing, analysts' activities, rating agencies, conglomerates, taxation, and transparency are also being instituted. A further part of the big picture is the capital adequacy directive, which is based on the rules of the Basel Accord.[16]

In this context, the Federation of European Securities Exchanges (FESE) has a particular role to play. The federation, with its secretariat in Brussels, ensures an ongoing communication between EU officials (commission, parliament, and administration) and exchange practitioners.[17]

Government Regulation versus Self-Regulation

Regulation in many ways defines an exchange and its business outlook. It can enhance competitiveness or it can undermine it. Interestingly, when the Financial Services Authority (FSA) was created in the United Kingdom, an objective enshrined in the regulatory authority's statute was to further the competitiveness of London as a financial center. Harmonization in the field of legislation and regulation requires that many decisions be made either for or against a broad spectrum of concepts and systems. One of the most fundamental issues concerns the balance between government regulation and self-regulation.

Self-regulation is the wrong word for a good thing. Self-regulation seems to imply that market participants regulate themselves. If this were the case, it would lead to an impossible situation replete with conflicts of interest. Self-regulation actually means regulation by a private (nongovernmental) organization, typically the market operator (e.g., an exchange organization). The market operator (e.g., the NYSE) is not regulating itself, but rather its members (the seat holders and broker-dealer member firms). The responsibility has been delegated to the market operator by a government regulator.

Market operators always have some regulatory power, and participants must follow the rules that the market operator has imposed. It therefore is not simply government regulation versus self-regulation, but cooperative regulation between the government and the market operator. Regulatory efficiency is highest when there is a good balance between the two so that the benefits of self-regulation (closeness to the market, adaptiveness, flexibility) are taken advantage of, while the public regulator ensures orderliness, equal treatment, and investor confidence. There is no universal optimum; rather, a balance must be found pragmatically for every situation in every field of regulation. The regulatory activities of an exchange primarily cover traders, trading firms, and issuers (disclosure), but they may also cover investors' behavior in the market. Finally, it is important to note that setting the rules is one thing, and enforcing them is something else.

Optimum regulation was not as big an issue in Europe when markets operated largely within national boundaries. But with global competition intensifying between financial centers, having a good regulatory structure in place has become critically important. One aspect of the issue is the balance between government regulation and self-regulation. Another is that alternative government regulatory systems compete with each other, especially when investors, with the click of a mouse, can take their business to a different jurisdiction. In many cases, regulators try to prevent investors from evading their protection. In so doing, they risk becoming an instrument of protectionism. Even more, they risk getting into a collusive situation with the very firms that they oversee. Self-regulation has historically been more prominent in some European countries than in others, and the regulatory situation is particularly complex from a European perspective. (See Exhibit 9.3.)

Fragmentation versus Consolidation

As we have noted, consolidation was generally expected in the early 1990s. Ten years later, we are far from meeting those predictions. A number of alliances and even mergers have been tried. Exhibit 9.4, provided by FESE, shows this better than words. But while many have failed, a few have more or less succeeded. Euronext is a remarkable success—the company is

- Council of the EU: http://ue.eu.int/
- European Commission: http://europa.eu.int/comm/index_en.htm
- European Parliament: www.europarl.eu.int/home/default_en.htm (Committee on Economic and Monetary Affairs)
- European Central Bank (ECB): www.ecb.int
- Committee of European Securities Regulators (CESR): www.europefesco.org
- More information, names, and addresses can be found on the FESE web page: www.fese.org (European Directory)

EXHIBIT 9.3   European institutions (political, administrative, regulatory).

under a single management that includes the exchanges of Paris, Amsterdam, Brussels, Lisbon, and Liffe (the London International Financial Futures Exchange), as well as some clearing and settlement organizations.

In the Norex alliance, the exchanges of Stockholm, Copenhagen, Oslo, and Iceland joined forces to use the same electronic trading system with, by and large, the same trading rules. Apart from that, they have remained independent, national exchanges. Recently HEX, the Helsinki Stock Exchange, was bought by OM to form OMHex. Along with the Stockholm and Helsinki exchanges, this includes the two Baltic stock exchanges from Talinn and Riga, which were taken over by Helsinki some time ago. Deutsche Börse acquired the second-largest international European settlement organization, the Luxembourg Clearstream (Cedel at that time), by merging Clearstream with its own clearing and settlement organization, the Deutscher Kassenverein. Deutsche Börse also created a service organization, Deutsche Börse Systems, which has considerable potential, and in the derivative business, the Deutsche Terminbörse merged with SOFFEX (the Swiss derivative exchange) to create Eurex, a leading worldwide international derivatives exchange.

In Switzerland, seven local exchanges were closed to pave the way for the launch of the fully automated SWX Swiss Exchange. This has been the largest exercise of its kind in Europe in terms of truly reducing the number of exchange organizations. SWX also owns and runs virt-x in London. While virt-x is legally an exchange of its own under U.K. regulations, businesswise it is a London branch of the SWX.[18]

The experience of the past decade has shown that substantively merging exchanges is an extremely difficult undertaking. Each exchange is deeply rooted in its own organizational, technical, legal, and regulatory framework, and a dense network of traditions, culture, and vested interests is involved. This will not be easily changed. Simply concentrating on IT may make consolidation appear to be easier, but this is far from the truth.

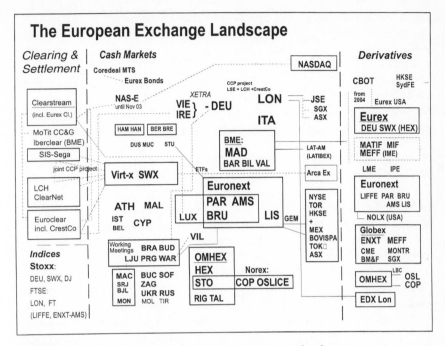

EXHIBIT 9.4   The heterogeneous European exchange landscape.
Source: Federation of European Securities Exchanges www.fese.org.

In essence, the acquiring exchange wants, through the takeover, to buy the acquired exchange's order flow and the participation of its customers. It is not looking to buy the IT system (trading platform), because to realize economies of scale, all of the transaction flows must be run on one platform (presumably that of the buyer). In the end, one of the two IT systems, including hardware, software, and people's know-how, must be written off.

The business case for a merger must have significant advantages for both of the merging exchanges and their members/customers, and this can be extremely difficult to achieve. (1) The out-of-pocket costs are high for one party to the merger to switch from one system to the other. This is true for an exchange, and it is even truer for its members. (2) The same applies to investment protection. One side of a merger has to give up its systems and completely write off its previous investments. The write-off and switching are costly in and of themselves, but the contrast is stark compared to the other side of the merger that is able to keep its systems and build on its previous investments, its existing know-how, and its experience. Consequently, after an exchange has invested heavily in its own trading systems, even the IT side is a tough, tough win. (3) The transaction is not about money only,[19] but also power—the power to set the rules, to set prices, and to set listing criteria. It is extremely difficult to build up a tailor-made merger agreement that achieves an optimum combination of money and power.

A paper by Harold Hau points out another interesting perspective on consolidation.[20] The paper's title could have been "Language Matters." Hau considered information asymmetries and proprietary trading profits on Germany's Xetra system. His main finding, based on 756 professional traders in eight different countries, is that non-German-speaking market makers significantly underperform their German-speaking counterparts in both statistical and economic terms. Geographic proximity has much less relevance. For traders in Austria and in German-speaking Switzerland, there was no appreciable difference compared to their German colleagues. If language matters as much as Hau's paper suggests, Europe is indeed a long way from true pan-European consolidation. Rather, consolidation will occur in its own way on a federalist level, and a lot of local flavor will be retained.

The arguments in favor of consolidation that were enumerated 10 years ago have not lost their validity. Investors still prefer more uniform trading and regulatory systems. Cross-border transactions are still far too costly, mainly on the clearing and settlement side. Costly IT infrastructures could still be used more effectively. Traders would still like to trade European blue chips on a single platform. These drivers for European consolidation will not go away. Pan-European blue chips are led by customer needs:

- Pan-European and global corporations should have the opportunity to raise capital on one European platform.
- Investors should have one pool of liquidity, one market with a single set of rules and regulations, and one technology for trading European blue chips.
- Exchange members have the same need for uniformity as the investors and, additionally, should be able to benefit from centralized portfolio-management, risk-management, and back-office operations.

Local stocks, on the other hand, must be traded locally. For them, there is no trade-off between a pan-European exchange and a local market. Consequently, the equity markets must be segmented: European blue chips should be traded on a European trading platform, and other stocks should be traded on a local market (preferably on the same technical system).

For a number of major reasons, cross-border consolidation may take a good deal longer to accomplish, and it might occur in very different ways than was initially expected. With this in mind, we note the following four issues.

1. Although English has become the corporate language in many European companies and business circles, Hau's study shows that poor English cannot effectively replace a mother tongue. To make money in market making, one must understand management statements fully, including not just what they say, but also what they actually mean and what they are alluding to between the lines. The difficulty of achieving this understanding no doubt explains, in part at least, why liquidity is so "sticky," why it is so extraordinarily difficult to lure liquidity away from a home market.

2. Securities markets are normally regarded as "one market." However, every trading instrument (or group of trading instruments) actually has a market of its own. A trading venue is a conglomerate of distinct markets for a number of distinctly different instruments. A market's infrastructure may provide an excellent liquidity pool for, say, Nestlé, but there is no guarantee that it will also be a good venue for Deutsche Telecom. The U.S. markets have been quite successful in luring trading away from South American markets, but the European exchanges by and large have managed to retain most of the trading in their domestic stocks. Surprising in this regard is the former Helsinki Stock Exchange. (Helsinki and Stockholm have merged to form what is now known as OMHex.) It has sometimes been referred to as the "Nokia Stock Exchange" because Nokia accounted for more than 50 percent of its trading volume. Helsinki, a rather small exchange, has successfully defended its huge flagship stock in spite of numerous attacks by several other exchanges.

    Every federal market in Europe is world champion in trading and settling its own stocks (i.e., has the narrowest spread and lowest settlement costs). A good example that illustrates the strength of a home market is the double listing of DaimlerChrysler in Germany and at the NYSE. Overall volume went up due to this second listing at the NYSE, but the execution of most of this novelty-created volume still took place in Frankfurt in Xetra, the home market for DaimlerChrysler.

3. The market for securities services is special and highly complex. Securities services are often referred to as a *value chain*. The main functions of the chain, as discussed in Chapter 1, are order gathering, order matching (with price setting), clearing, and settlement. This value chain has become extremely complex, especially when portfolio and risk management and cross-border activities are included. The basis for providing services is a vast network, a *value web*. Of course, many customers simply want straightforward execution services, but highly sophisticated customers may be more interested in the whole value web, including the availability of many service providers that are

needed only occasionally. In this context, the prices for securities services are difficult to relate to specific costs. Moreover, a slightly cheaper and/or more efficient trading system will not necessarily attract a lot of trading. Before changing its business model, a provider of securities services has to assess the influence of any change on its overall business network (or value web), many parts of which involve trust that can be developed only over a long period of time. A "better" system that replaces just a small part of a value chain but that puts the entire chain in danger is of little interest to the trader who has developed his or her own network over the years.

4. Technology for multiaccess systems now enables easy access to a large number of exchanges throughout the world without traders having to deal with the trouble and the cost of establishing direct access to each exchange system. Several of these exchange portals are available today, and more are in development for the future.

In short, it is far from clear how the fragmentation-versus-consolidation debate will evolve. Resolution of the issue has taken far longer than expected, and there are good reasons to believe that it will continue for some time to come. In the meantime, new developments will evolve, and exchange organizations will likely expand into a variety of new types of companies. The various drivers for change will interact and, in so doing, will lead to unexpected and unintended consequences. The outcome might be the emergence of new kinds of highly networked service companies that specialize in various market segments and combinations of services. The end result will undoubtedly involve what Schumpeter termed "constructive destruction," along with a lot of reconstruction. Whatever the outcome, consolidation of the European exchanges has proved to be a challenging task. There will be no easy wins.

CLEARING AND SETTLEMENT

Attention in the European arena has also turned to clearing and settlement.[21] The wake-up call came from several studies that showed the cost of clearing and settlement in Europe to be approximately 10 times higher than in the United States. Subsequently, more detailed investigations clarified that costs for many of the national clearing and settlement systems in Europe were quite similar to costs in the United States, but that they jumped to a totally different level when cross-border services were involved. To some extent, this may be related to the lack of competition, but for the most part, it is another consequence of fragmentation. In the EU alone, there are 19 Central European Depositories (CSDs) and 2 International CSDs (ICSDs), Euroclear and Clearstream. The first Giovannini report showed that as many as 11 different intermediaries and 14 two-party instructions may be needed for a single cross-border equity transaction to be cleared and settled. The report lists 15 barriers to efficient cross-border clearing and settlement in the European Union.

Why is it that a highly efficient national system does not work so well when linked across borders? The answer lies in a combination of reasons:

- A broad array of barriers to efficient cross-border clearing and settlement exist in the EU. They relate to technical requirements, market practices, taxation, and legal certainty (such as the finality of settlement).
- Various national legal requirements make it impossible to introduce truly riskless delivery against payment on cross-border levels.
- Multiple services are needed to move out of one national system and into another. A telling analogy is the difficulty of transferring from one national railway system to another when there are national differences in gauge, electricity systems, signaling and warning systems, ticketing systems, and so on.
- Overcoming all of the obstacles is far more than a technical problem. Besides law and accounting, location, language, and culture all matter.
- Some service providers have the requisite systems and know-how to deal with all of the inefficiencies and complexities. For them, there is no benefit to changing the status quo.

This is not to say that the obstacles will not be overcome in the foreseeable future. Deutsche Börse's acquisition of Clearstream, for the purpose of merging the ICSD with the German CSD, offers considerable potential for improving the situation in the medium to long term. Benefits could be amplified by bringing Clearstream and Eurex Clearing closer together. Benefits can also be attributed to Euronext's cooperation with the other ICSD (Euroclear) and its participation on the London Clearing House (LCH). This certainly will make not only trading but also cross-border clearing and settlement easier, at least within the Euronext world. The SWX group is thus far the only exchange to offer choice with regard to clearing and settlement. SWX operates highly efficient clearing and settlement links that are almost identical to the national systems. After a trade of Swiss blue chips through virt-x, clearing can be done through the Swiss x-clear of SegaIntersettle (SIS) or through the London Clearing House (LCH). SWX offers three options for settlement: SIS, the London Crest, and Euroclear. The Swiss Exchange also has a link to Clearstream.

The situation is evolving in clearing and settlement, just as it is in trading, but new solutions will not be easily available. This is because virtually every change that is made, although only technical at first sight, has strategic implications for the formidable array of market players who are involved.

NOTES

1. See Siegfried Bley, *Börsen der Welt*, Frankfurt, 1977.

2. When the exchange in Frankfurt was founded on September 9, 1585, it did not follow the tradition of erecting an impressive building. See *Börsen-Zeiten*, Bernd Baering, Frankfurt 1985, p. 47.

3. See Femme S. Gaastra, *The Dutch East India Company, Expansion and Decline*, Leiden, 2003.

4. See *The New York Stock Exchange: The First 200 Years*, James E. Buck, ed., New York, 1992.

5. At the time, the WFE was named Federation International de Bourse de Valeur (FIBV). Further information can be found at www.world-exchanges.org.

6. For further discussion, see Reto Francioni, *Marktformen zum Handel von Unternehmensanteilen*, in Wertorientiertes Start-Up-Management, Ulrich Hommel and Thomas C. Knecht, eds., Verlag Franz Vahlen, München, 2002, pp. 541–562. Also see *Deutsche Börse Group, Market Model Stock Trading*, Deutsche Börse's web site, http://deutsche-boerse.com.

7. We note this in Chapter 8, "The Evolving Scene in the United States," with respect to the higher trading costs that institutions perceive when slicing and dicing their orders and working them over time. It is a far different situation than that described by the efficient market hypothesis (see Chapter 2, "From Information to Prices").

8. Before automating, the Paris Bourse had three types of trading on its floor: The *cotation à la criée* was an opening auction combined with subsequent continuous trading. The *à la criée* at the rings (*la corbeille*) was the main trading system for all major stocks. It was all forward trading. *Cotation par opposition* was used for the spot market of major stocks which had their main market at the rings. Bourse officials collected the orders and set the price at a certain time using the maximum turnover criterion. The *cotation par casier* was the system for the bulk of the listed companies with little trading volume. The system was much the same as the *cotation par opposition*, but with no official regularly involved.

9. Under Xetra European Stars and Xetra U.S. Stars, Deutsche Börse trades a number of major non-German blue chips that are part of important blue-chip indices, like DJEuro Stoxx 50 and the U.S. Dow Jones Industrial Average.

10. For many banks and brokers, GL provides an easy solution for accessing a large number of exchanges, like DJEuro Stoxx 50 and the Dow Jones Industrial Average.

11. We discuss these issues further in Chapter 11, "Regulation."

12. There are 25 exchanges after the accession of many Central and Eastern European countries.

13. See Yannis V. Avgerinos, *Regulating and Supervising Investment Services in the European Union*, Palgrave MacMillan, 2003.

14. Until recently, all forms of EU legislation had to go through the same approval process. It is now recognized that there is a hierarchy of legislation (e.g., laws, then acts, then bylaws, then ordinances). Legislation at the low end of the hierarchy usually deals with less important, often technical, issues, and it is easier to change legislation at this level because the approval process is less cumbersome.

15. Under the Prospectus Directive, any prospectus issued and approved in one of the EU countries "gets passported" for all other EU countries; it does not need any further approval to be used in a different EU country.

16. The Basel Capital Accord is an agreement of the Basel Committee on Banking Supervision, which operates within the Bank of International Settlements in Basel, Switzerland. The accord defines minimum standards for banks' capital, which obviously plays a major role for the safety of the banking infrastructure of economies (see www.bis.org).

17. FESE provides useful documentation about ongoing legislative and regulatory processes. Its web site is www.fese.be.

18. There is a regulatory split: The issuers are regulated under Swiss law, and all trading activities are regulated by the FSA.

19. Regarding the monetary side of the equation, the acquiring stock exchange will have made a good investment only if, because of the acquistion, it is able to charge sufficiently high commissions in the future (which means that its future customers will bear part of the up-front cost).

20. Harald Hau, "Location Matters: An Examination of Trading Profits," *Journal of Finance*, vol. 56, no. 5, 2001, pp. 1959–1983.

21. We discuss clearing and settlement in greater detail in Chapter 10, "Clearing and Settlement."

Clearing and Settlement

A fter a trade has been executed it falls into the clearing and settlement process. Clearing involves risk mitigation and matching shares that have been bought with those that have been sold to determine the obligations between parties with the prime purpose being risk reduction. The process involves netting a set of trades to obtain one settlement figure and offsetting all gross transactions to obtain one trade to be settled. Settlement involves the actual transfer of money and shares between the trading parties. The clearing and settlement process contains inherent costs and risks (e.g., the risk of default or failure). Inefficient posttrade operations, at minimum, unduly inflate the explicit costs of trading, and this has an underlying impact on commission rates.

Under normal conditions, for the most part, posttrade processes are taken for granted, and it is the pretrade market structure issues that generally attract the lion's share of the public attention. We see and are very aware of economic problems involved in pretrade order handling, price discovery, competition, technological inertia, and so forth. The problems involved in posttrade clearance and settlement, on the other hand, are primarily technological and legal in nature and, if the systems work adequately, they do not attract much attention. But clearing and settlement are vitally important to the overall viability and efficiency of an equity market, and they cannot be taken for granted. If the highly visible pretrade market structure issues are likened to the part of an iceberg that is above the water, posttrade clearing and settlement issues are the part of the iceberg

Michael Jaeggi, SWX Swiss Exchange, has participated as a coauthor of this chapter.

that is below the water. Although not in the focus of many participants, these issues are absolutely critical. If they run aground, they can lead to systemic risks that have the power to bring down a market and/or its participants.

Our discussion of clearing and settlement is developed primarily in the European context. On a generic level, our remarks apply to the United States as well, but, for two reasons, some of the fundamental issues we deal with are accentuated in the European arena. First, the array of different legal and tax regimes in Europe accentuate the complexity of cross-border clearing and settlement within Europe. Second, the electronic trading platforms that characterize European markets facilitate straight-through processing (STP) and the use of central counterparties (CCPs)—institutional structures that we pay particular attention to in this chapter.[1]

The first step to understanding clearing and settlement is to become familiar with the basic institutions that participate in the process. We identify the institutions here, and we define and discuss them as the chapter progresses:[2]

CCP = central counterparty

CSD = central securities depository

ICSD = international securities depository

ICM = individual clearing member

GCM = general clearing member

NCM = nonclearing member

BACKGROUND

The history of clearing starts with money and gold in eighteenth-century Europe. In 1773, a clearinghouse was opened in London close to the London money market. On the other side of the Atlantic, the clearing of gold and checks was introduced in New York on October 4, 1853, on the initiative of the cashiers of local banks.[3] By the end of the nineteenth century, various countries had introduced payment systems that were based on either national postal services or their banking communities. These services allowed the reasonably efficient transfer of money without necessarily requiring physical delivery for each individual transaction.

In Germany, by 1883, the central bank (Reichsbank) was running classic paper-based net settlement systems (*Abrechnungstellen*) organized around the exchange of vouchers to offset claims and obligations between credit institutions. Only net positions were settled in the accounts of the central bank. Participants were usually credit institutions located at the site of a subsidiary of the central bank. Sometimes several different banking locations were connected by an interregional netting system. This paper-based process was used until March 2000.

Today, clearing is widely used in several "communities" where participants have claims against each other. The process is well known by an organization like the International Air Transport Association (IATA), which uses a complex clearing system to ensure that ticket revenues go to the airlines that have transported the passengers. Practically every national payment system uses a clearing mechanism to transfer money. Postal services and telephone companies have clearing systems. Standardized futures and options markets have had clearing arrangements since their inception. European equity markets, however, have implemented appropriate clearing infrastructures only recently. A nationwide infrastructure may cover several exchanges (as does DTCC in the United States), or it may cover only a single domestic exchange. Commodity markets, the worldwide postal organization, and practically all telephone operators have clearance systems. Today, every equity market organization, such as an exchange or an operator of a market platform, is responsible to its local regulators for ensuring that trading parties meet the obligations they incur by the trades they undertake.

Clearing and settlement covers all processes that occur after a trade has been executed to finalize the transaction. The actions involve the post-trade transfer of money and securities. Currently, the settlement period for equity trades is usually two $(T + 2)$ or three $(T + 3)$ days after the trade date. Clearing, including *netting* and *offsetting*, is performed at the close of trading.[4] Clearing organizations are part of the chain of organizations involved in the settlement process that take responsibility for fulfilling the obligations attributed to them.[5] Today, national payment traffic is handled by centralized clearing between banks. It is largely done by netting and by offsetting payments. All checks, money orders, and payments are cleared in a procedure that, universally, is highly automated. The activity is generally viewed as a commoditized process that, in most cases, is under the control of a central bank.

Risk management is very important in money clearing. The risk that a party cannot fulfill its obligation is a threat to the entire system. When it comes to delivery, each participant in a clearing system must be able to fulfill its obligations that result from the clearing process. Failure to meet these obligations can have a severe impact on the financial stability of a system. The failure of one participant can create systemic risk across an entire market infrastructure. To minimize the systemic risks, the entry criteria to become a member of a clearing organization, and the obligations of a member, are significant.

The risk structure of a clearing organization reflects the potential failure in delivering shares or transferring funds at the end of a trading day. A clearing organization centralizes the risk of open positions and guarantees that obligations will be fulfilled. A clearinghouse reduces (if it does not entirely remove) all bilateral risks that pertain to members of a particular market in which it operates. That is, a major part of the risk is covered by each member, while large catastrophic events are covered by the mutual ownership structure of a clearinghouse.[6]

Clearing is a widely used expression for offsetting or netting obligations across a community. Clearing in an equity market also concentrates the risks to all participants within a single organization.

Central securities depositories have either the status of a specialized bank, a recognized investment exchange, or are completely regulated by specific law. The mission of a clearinghouse is to settle trades as securely and efficiently as possible. The clearing element aims to reduce the number of settlements and to concentrate the counterparty risks in a central place where they can be managed. Reducing the number of settlement events can reduce trading participants' needs for liquidity, and it significantly decreases operational risks. Having standardized products and operating terms enables transactions to be cleared more efficiently.

The future of clearing in the financial markets will include other instruments such as warrants, bonds (which are already cleared in some markets), structured products, and funds. A potential further development of the clearing process will be to de-link the cash and the equity processes. That is, central counterparty (CCP) would enable the netting of cash into one amount and the netting of equity into another. The settlement of the equity would then be free of payment but guaranteed by the clearing organization. Clearing will also further concentrate on linking the risks of cash, equity, and the relevant derivatives against one collateral pool.

CLEARING IN EQUITY MARKETS

Equities traded on international markets are almost without exception dematerialized (although OTC and retail business still typically uses materialized paper transactions).[7] Dematerialized securities are held within a Central Security Depository (CSD), and the settlement of a transaction and subsequent change of beneficial ownership is usually through book entry.[8] The classic clearinghouse in an equity market acts as a central counterparty (CCP).[9] In so doing, a clearinghouse becomes a seller for each buyer and a buyer for each seller. The CCP assumes responsibility for the failure of any market member to fulfill his or her obligations. In principle, the liability of a clearinghouse is shared by each and every participant. All participants are obligated to fulfill all trades that they have executed. To mitigate the risk of a member failing, the clearinghouse holds margin (mostly covered by collateral) against open positions from its members.[10]

Marketplaces with CCP arrangements require that their members have clearinghouse agreements to prevent any damage that would result from the failure of any participant. Centralized risk management ensures that each actor has its fulfilment risk covered by the CCP.[11] The quality of the collateral to cover margin is of paramount importance to the risk mitigation process. For example, a member could not collateralize its clearing positions with stock or bonds issued by itself, as this would double the risks accepted by the CCP.[12] The collateral must be sufficiently liquid to ensure that, in the case of need, the CCP can liquidate it. A CCP's counterparty risk management includes default management.[13] Having become the buyer to each seller and the seller to each buyer, the CCP can also provide posttrade anonymity (participants see the clearinghouse only as their counterparty).[14] This further enables bilateral settlement netting in the clearinghouse to, in effect, become multilateral netting.[15] Settlement in the form of delivery versus payment (DVP), or receive against payment, is the standard method used to fulfill the obligations arising from net trades.[16] This procedure can be tightly monitored by a clearinghouse. Due to netting and strict monitoring, performance in terms of settling on intended settlement dates has increased significantly.[17]

The implementation of central counterparty clearing has become more important in today's environment with international electronic markets and automated matching processes that give access to members residing outside of their countries—or even on different continents. In this setting, a participant cannot avoid counterparty risk by choosing his or her counterparty prior to a trade. But players, both large and small, need to secure virtually risk-free counterparty positions.[18] Most seriously, in tightly linked markets, even smaller participants may create systematic risk if they fail.[19]

The choice of settlement location is an important element in cross-border trading.[20] Clearing members may settle all of their net positions at a clearinghouse in their preferred settlement locations. If necessary, the CCP will realign the cash and equity between different settlement locations.

Exhibit 10.1 depicts the classic structure of a market that is built around a CCP. After a trade is executed on an exchange, the details of the trade are passed to the clearinghouse. Having received all of the details for a trade, the clearinghouse is in a position to become the legal counterparty of the trading parties. In understanding the operations of a clearinghouse, the first relationship to consider is the one between an investor and his or her intermediary.[21] The relationship may be split between the investor's broker-dealer, banker, asset manager, and custodian. The intermediary must be a member of the exchange.[22] Membership in the clearinghouse is a precondition for doing business on the exchange. An arrangement may be

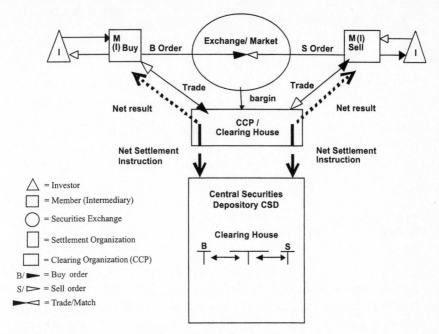

EXHIBIT 10.1 Classic structure of a market that has a CCP.

a direct membership in the clearinghouse (GCM or ICM) or an indirect connection (NCM) through another party who is a general clearing member (GCM).[23] Each exchange appoints at least one clearinghouse to clear its business. The clearinghouse and the exchange may be independent, or they may be operations within the same organization. The term *vertical silo* indicates that the exchange, the clearinghouse, and the settlement organization are all entities totally or substantially owned by the same company or group.[24]

In contrast, a *horizontal model* separates the business into three layers: trading, clearing, and settlement.[25] Technically, all clearinghouses are highly integrated within the local market infrastructure of both trading and settlement. With the horizontal model, clearing organizations and central securities depositories may serve several exchanges or even markets.

A central counterparty usually serves one market in one country, but it is possible for a CCP to serve multiple markets in multiple countries. The central counterparty may also be built by more than one organization. In the case of cross-border clearing through two jurisdictions, a second clearinghouse may act as a sub-CCP, being a completely separated legal entity governed by an agreement.[26] If the market is truly cross-border, the

CCP and the sub-CCP must agree on a standard set of rules, regulations, and contractual agreements that cover behavior and that harmonize issues such as corporate actions.[27] The basic principle is that, for cross-CCP trades, the sub-CCP acts as a GCM of the main (umbrella) CCP.[28] Therefore, the sub-CCP will usually deliver the margin for its open positions to the umbrella CCP. In Europe, both Euronext and virt-x have arrangements that enable cross-border clearing. Most other markets have decided to implement one CCP that offers clearing in one legal jurisdiction and to have cross-border clearing transacted under the supervision of one regulator within one country's legislation.[29] Two organizations, the Group of CCP12 and the European Association of Clearing Houses (EACH), are investigating solutions to manage risks across CCPs.[30]

Eligibility of Equity for Clearing

To be cleared, equity shares must be fully fungible and traded on an organized and recognized investment exchange (RIE) that issues transparent and fair settlement prices.[31] The shares must also be sufficiently liquid to give confidence that the clearinghouse will not be left in a situation where it cannot fulfill its obligations. Currently, for operational reasons, only equity that is fully dematerialized and that can be transferred through book entry at the CSDs is eligible for the clearing process.[32] The settlement of paper-based, nondematerialized equity trades is not currently eligible for the clearing process.

Clearing Member Accounts with a Clearinghouse

Clearing accounts are held by clearing members at a clearinghouse. All traded activity is booked through these accounts. It is standard practice for margin accounts to be segregated to ensure that the separate positions of nonclearing members (NCMs) and principal businesses are clearly visible.[33] The clearing accounting includes both equity and cash. The movements resulting from trading, netting of trades, and settlements are all booked.

- *Cash account.* All cash movements for a member go through the cash account. The cash account must be fully funded and, in normal circumstances, must always have a positive balance. The cash account may be with a third-party bank rather than with the clearinghouse directly.
- *Margin account.* Margin requirements and collateral given to the clearinghouse to cover the requirements are booked in *margin accounts* that are segregated between the GCM's principal and client

business.[34] Any shortfall in margin will create a *margin call.*[35] A member who fails to keep a positive balance in his or her margin account is subject to technical default.[36]

- *Open net position account.* Entries in this account are the trades that are awaiting settlement in the CSD.
- *Gross trades account.* Gross trades are important for the clearing-house and the clearing member, as they build the basis to reconcile the net for settlement in equity and cash.
- *Settlement accounts.* These accounts are usually held by the clearing member in the necessary CSD to deliver, or receive against payment, the relevant amount of stock.

Netting and Offsetting

Netting is the process of reducing the sum of all trades/contracts to one settlement figure that fulfills the obligation and reflects the open risk. The trades remain open until settlement has taken place. *Offsetting* is the process of replacing all gross transactions by one trade that then has to be settled. *Bilateral netting* has historically been used, but compared to multilateral netting, it is less efficient. By introducing a central counterparty, the efficiency of multilateral netting can be realized, as each counterparty sees only the CCP as his or her own trading counterparty. Netting and the offsetting of the shares traded, and of the cash for payment, has an old tradition among traders. Netting is used to reduce the number of separate settlement movements, the risk of settlement failure, and both the direct and indirect costs of transferring the same equity several times (i.e., the capital costs and handling fees charged by the CSDs).

With equities, netting must be done simultaneously on two levels—the cash level and the security level. Consequently, the process is rather complex. We illustrate the flow of shares for a particular security between clearing members in Exhibits 10.2 to 10.7. Exhibit 10.2 shows how the gross trades that have occurred are settled with no clearing. Four members are shown in Exhibit 10.2 (members A, B, C, and D). Each arrow in the exhibit represents a trade between two members and indicates the direction in which the equity is moving between them (each arrow points to the buyer and away from the seller). When it comes to delivery (settlement), the money subsequently will flow in the opposite direction.

Exhibit 10.2 shows 11 trades that will require 11 settlements in the form of delivery versus payment. For instance, the two horizontal arrows at the top of the exhibit show that member A has bought three shares from member C, and that C has bought two shares from A. All of the other pairwise combinations of the members show two trades (one each in each

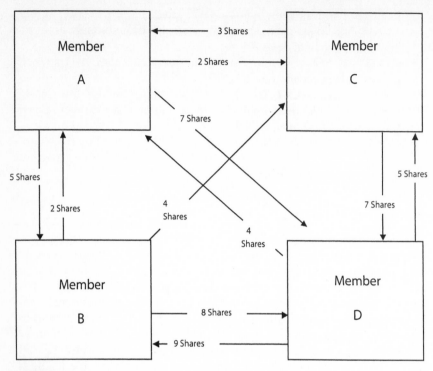

EXHIBIT 10.2 Gross trades to settle gross (no clearing).

direction), except for the B-C combination, where only one trade occurred (B sold four shares to C). Exhibit 10.3 presents the same information in table form. The structure illustrated by Exhibit 10.2 and Exhibit 10.3 requires only settlement (no clearing infrastructure is needed).

Using the same set of 11 gross trades, Exhibits 10.4 and 10.5 show how clearing and settlement change with the introduction of bilateral netting. The thin arrows in Exhibit 10.4 are identical to those shown in Exhibit 10.2, but the fat arrows introduced in Exhibit 10.4 show the direction of the net bilateral settlements. For instance, the horizontal fat arrow at the top of the exhibit shows that settlement between member A and member C involves C delivering one share to A (the difference between A's purchase of three shares from C and C's purchase of two shares from A). Note that, with bilateral netting, only 6 settlements are needed to settle the 11 gross trades. Bilateral netting does not require any special common infrastructure—the processing can be handled by the trading counterparties themselves.

Continuing to work with the same set of 11 gross trades, Exhibits 10.6 and 10.7 show the effect that multilateral netting through a CCP has on

What Trade	Impact on A	Result B	Result C	Result D	Settlement Y/N
A sell to B	−5	+5			Yes
B sell to A	+2	−2			Yes
A sell to C	−2		+2		Yes
C sell to A	+3		−3		Yes
B sell to D		−8		+8	Yes
D sell to B		+9		−9	Yes
C sell to D			−7	+7	Yes
D sell to C			+5	−5	Yes
A sell to D	−7			+7	Yes
D sell to A	+4			−4	Yes
B sell to C		−4	+4		Yes

EXHIBIT 10.3 Overview of trades and settlements with gross trades to settle gross (no clearing).

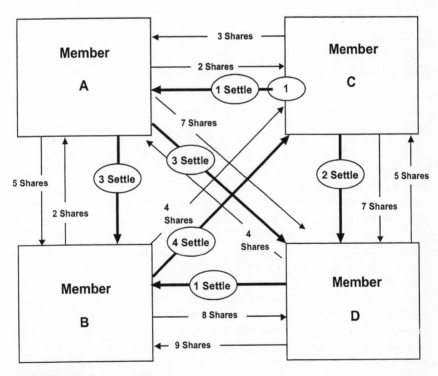

EXHIBIT 10.4 Bilateral netting.

What Trade	Impact on A	Result B	Result C	Result D	Settlement Y/N
A sell to B	−5	+5			No
B sell to A	+2	−2			No
A deliver to B	−3	+3			Yes
A sell to C	−2		+2		No
C sell to A	+3		−3		No
C deliver to A	+1		−1		Yes
B sell to D		−8		+8	No
D sell to B		+9		−9	No
D deliver to B		+1		−1	Yes
C sell to D			−7	+7	No
D sell to C			+5	−5	No
C deliver to D			−2	+2	Yes
A sell to D	−7			+7	No
D sell to A	+4			−4	No
A deliver to D	−3			+3	Yes
B sell to C		−4	+4		No
B deliver to C		−4	+4		Yes

EXHIBIT 10.5 Overview of trades and settlements with bilateral netting.

clearing and settlement. Note that all of the fat arrows in Exhibit 10.6 go, not from member to member, but from each member to the CCP. The number of gross trades made are actually doubled (for instance, the three shares that A bought from C are replaced by three shares bought by the CCP from C and three shares that the CCP sells to A). The bilateral netting between each member and the CCP is, in effect, multilateral netting between the members. The multilateral netting reduces the number of separate settlements from the six shown for bilateral netting to four (each of the four members need settle only with the CCP).

Netting on a multilateral basis involves bringing together all possible combinations of members. Aggregating all of the cash and share positions minimizes the number of possible settlement movements. Multilateral netting has a complexity that can be managed centrally only where all relevant information is consolidated (i.e., in the CCP). Markets with many clearing participants can significantly reduce the number of separate settlements by the introduction of a CCP clearinghouse. The relative

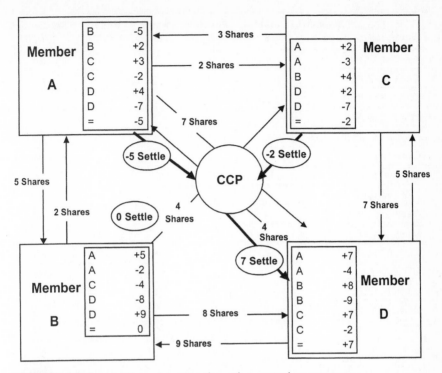

EXHIBIT 10.6 Multilateral netting through a central counterparty.

efficiency of multilateral netting increases as the number of clearing participants and their trading volume increase.

Settlement Finality: Change of Ownership

Settlement finality is important and must be in line with liquidation procedures in case of the financial failure of a member. A trade executed on an exchange is legally binding, but in instances of default, fulfilling, or settling, the trade may be challenged by a liquidator. Matching a trade on an exchange transfers the beneficial and legal ownership between the parties involved. The generation of a net transaction still represents multiple changes of ownership, although netting does replace the gross transactions. As netting takes place only for the same value date (the intended settlement date, or ISD), all corporate events are possible on the net value.[37] With respect to gross trades, finality after netting the transactions is fulfilled by the net creation and the subsequent settlement of the net

What Trade	Impact on A	Result B	Result C	Result D	Result CCP	Settlement Y/N/0*
A sell to CCP	−5				+5	No
B sell to CCP		−2			+2	No
CCP sell to B		+5			−5	No
CCP sell to A	+2				−2	No
A sell to CCP	−2				+2	No
C sell to CCP			−3		+3	No
CCP sell to C			+2		−2	No
CCP sell to A	+3				−3	No
B sell to CCP		−8			+8	No
D sell to CCP				−9	+9	No
CCP sell to D				+8	−8	No
CCP sell to B		+9			−9	No
C sell to CCP			−7	+7		No
D sell to CCP			+5	−5		No
CCP sell to D			−7	+7		No
CCP sell to C			+5	−5		No
A sell to CCP	−7				+7	No
D sell to CCP				−4	+4	No
CCP sell to D				+7	−7	No
CCP sell to A	+4				−4	No
B sell to CCP		−4			+4	No
CCP sell to C			+4		−4	No
Net A to CCP	−5				+5	Yes
Net B to CCP		0			0	0
Net C to CCP			−2		+2	Yes
Net D to CCP					−7	Yes

*Zero shares have to settle if there is a balance in the cash side of the transaction.

EXHIBIT 10.7 Overview of trades and settlements with multilateral netting through a central counterparty.

transaction on an ISD.[38] Settlement has to be final,[39] because the clearing-house relinquishes its margin requirement at the point of settlement.

Functional Elements

As we have noted, a CCP becomes a buyer to each seller and a seller for each buyer. This special kind of intermediating is a key part of the entire value chain. In terms of turnover and transactions, the CCP is the biggest member of a market. In its central position, the clearinghouse transfers all fulfillment-related risk from its members to itself.

Depending on the rule book of an exchange, an *open offer concept* means that the CCP or clearinghouse member has agreed to accept all trades executed on the market.[40] The CCP will accept the trade by registration, but it is also able to reject it under very specific circumstances.[41] The basic principle is that, for executions on an exchange that are supported by a CCP regime, there is at no time a direct bilateral contract between a buyer and a seller. Legally, if the open offer is rejected,[42] no trade ever existed, or else the existing contract between the two participants must be *novated* (i.e., replaced by a bilateral trade).

Risk Management

Our discussion of risk management starts with three kinds of risk that are borne by each member in the bilateral settlement model:

1. *Operational and transfer risk.* Both technical and human failure may cause transfers of either money and/or title to fail. These risks are covered by the CCP with respect to a guarantee of settlement that, in the worst case, may be made in cash. A clearinghouse does not guarantee delivery on settlement day, but given its strict regimes, it generally manages to achieve very high settlement rates for the due dates.

2. *Counterparty risk.* Counterparty risk is the risk that the trading counterparty will not fulfill his or her obligation either to deliver securities or to pay cash. This could be the result of cash or solvency problems.[43]

3. *Market risk.* Market risk can contribute to counterparty risk because changing share prices affect the amount required to replenish an open position (i.e., the margin requirement). Market risk is an important parameter for margin calculation.[44]

Each of these risks can be expressed with reference to replacement value. If a member fails, the clearinghouse will close out the defaulting member's positions to fulfill that member's obligations toward the other members. Counterparty risk is managed at different levels through the requirements to become a member of a clearinghouse. Currently, most clearinghouses differentiate between types of clearing members (direct clearing members, individual clearing members, or private or nonclearing members).[45] The differentiation is based on the type of business being cleared.

For Europe, the Federation of European Security Exchanges (FESE) recommends that a clearing member fulfill certain general requirements. The member must have:

- Adequate capitalization.
- Regulatory status as a financial service provider.[46]
- Arrangements to fulfill the settlement of transactions, including its own adequate infrastructure.
- Arrangements to provide collateral that guarantees the clearinghouse has full rights of title. In practice, using cash as collateral is the simplest but not necessarily the cheapest method. Government bonds can be given as collateral and can be held in a CSD outside the local legal regime of the clearinghouse. These arrangements must be robust to ensure the integrity of the CCP and its ability to access the bonds in the event of default.
- Procedures, systems, backup plans, and sites to ensure the physical, operational, and technical security for continuity of the various linkages with the clearinghouse.
- Adequate trained and educated staff to reduce the operational risks involved.[47]
- A contribution to the clearinghouse's risk fund in case of a default. This creates a second line of defense after the use of the defaulting member's collateral and margin.[48]

A clearinghouse, on a regular basis, must continually check to ensure that these requirements are fulfilled by its members on an ongoing basis.

Member positions are revalued while a transaction remains open or unsettled. To mitigate the maximum possible damage a member could inflict, the margin is calculated for each member on the basis of a worst-case scenario: the maximum amount of net damage that a member can inflict on the clearinghouse if its position has to be closed out. The *initial margin*, required at the moment a trade is accepted by the CCP, may be calculated using either a pure risk approach or a more static approach (i.e., a flat amount to be multiplied by the number of shares involved in a trade).[49] With each trade, positions are changed, and, in principle, the margin has to be recalculated. The initial margin is usually only calculated overnight and called on the morning of T + 1. This position covers a 24-hour period in the replacement value of a security.[50]

A *variation margin* (also called a *maintenance margin*) is the margin requirement based on a recalculation of risk using actual market prices after a position has been established. A shortfall in the variation margin leads to an intraday *margin call.*[51] The variation margin takes into consideration all new trades and settlements that have been completed, and fails to complete accurate positions that remain open.[52]

What is the biggest risk that must be contained in a market? The risk that the default of one member will cause systemic risk that in turn can lead to other members defaulting. One default leading to others is called a *knock-on.* A clearinghouse must be able to prevent knock-ons from occurring. In practice, the remaining risk to a market probably will be the knock-on effect in OTC business or in any other noncleared business.[53] The potential damage from a default can be estimated.[54] To show how, let us make the unrealistic but simplifying assumption that a normal distribution, over a relatively contained range of values, describes the distribution of share prices. With this assumption, the standard deviation of the equity prices as of a relevant point in the future can be used to represent risk. The standard deviation describes the nonsystemic risk for the relatively short period that a position is open. However, systemic risk also exists. While the standard deviation describes a fairly stable environment, it does not capture systemic risk. When markets close after an event such as September 11, 2001, it quickly becomes apparent that the risk is systemic.[55] At these times, the clearinghouse cannot know where to set the settlement price for the margin calculation.

Calculation Methods of Evaluation for Variation Margin

There is a large variety of submethods, all based on either the *premium/price plus* or the *portfolio* approach.

- *Premium/price plus.* This method, adapted for the cash markets from the traded options area, is the simplest method to use. The net position is first calculated and the net result matched against the closing price of the market. Then, using the statistical normal distribution of the closing price, a percentage is calculated that is used to determine the dollar amount required to close out a position against the average price of the open net position.[56] Premium plus is still used today in many markets. There is a variety of ways in which the clearinghouses determine the percentage price fluctuation. The following provides an example.

Trade price (U.S.$):　　　　　100
End of day price (U.S.$):　　　110
Price change　　　　　　　　　　10

Seller margin:
Price change (10) + 1 standard deviation X closing price (110) = margin required

Buyer margin:
Price change (−10) + 1 standard deviation X closing price (110) = margin required

---

- *Portfolio approach.* This approach, largely in use in recent years, considers not just a single stock net, but the behavior of a portfolio, taking into consideration a worst-case scenario that encompasses all of the positions that a market participant is holding (cash, equity, forward agreements, bonds, derivatives, etc.). The portfolio approach takes into account the fact that, if a member defaults, the whole portfolio that it is holding will be affected. The portfolio approach enables the clearinghouse to require less margin without compromising its risk management.

All calculation methods are based on the gross trades for each equity being consolidated into a net position. Margining on gross transactions would lead to unnecessarily high margins and would make a market noncompetitive.

A clearinghouse requires that those margin liabilities be covered until all open trades are settled through the settlement process. The liabilities are covered by the corresponding members through the collateral that they pledge and maintain. Margin requirements may be satisfied by the delivery of cash or collateral that is under the full control of the clearinghouse.[57] The arrangements must be very clear in order that the collateral may not be challenged by other creditors in the case of insolvency. In some regulatory regimes, the clearinghouses have extra protection.[58] Within the European Union, each clearinghouse should receive enough protection with the EU Settlement Finality Directive (issued by the EU Commission). Cash settlement is the ultimate result in case of the failure of a member, and it represents the last option if a stock ceases to be deliverable.

The next issue we consider involves the handling of default. Default does not necessarily mean insolvency.[59] On equity markets, default is normally defined by a participant not fulfilling his or her obligations pertaining to a trade in a timely and materially correct manner. The handling of default depends on the legislation in place in the jurisdiction where a trade has been made. Almost all marketplaces have strict rules on defaulting. Usually an exchange, together with its clearing organization, has rules in place to protect all participants to a particular trade and to deal with the systemic consequences of a member not fulfilling his or her obligations.

Default rules are synchronized with insolvency legislation.[60] In some countries, clearing organizations are given special regulatory protection.[61] The process of defaulting takes the following principal steps.

- Declaration of default by the exchange, the clearinghouse, or the regulator.
- All open transactions that involve the failing member are frozen (i.e., the settlement process is stopped).[62]
- Nonclearing member positions are transferred to another general clearing member (if the failing member is a general clearing member).[63]
- All open positions are closed out.
- A buy-in or sell-out takes place to reduce title positions to zero.[64]
- The remaining debt, if any, resulting from the buy-in or sell-out is then fulfilled according to the following eight-step formula:[65]
  1. Margin given in cash by the defaulting member. If insufficient,
  2. Margin given as collateral is sold to transfer into cash. If insufficient,
  3. The contribution by the failing member to the risk fund is deducted. If insufficient,
  4. The mutual risk fund provided by all clearing members is drawn down. If insufficient, then
  5. Deduct from the accumulated profit of the clearing house,
  6. Draw from an insurance policy (some clearinghouses do this),
  7. Draw additional funds from clearing members to restore the mutual risk fund, and
  8. Draw from the capital of the clearinghouse.

For most of the defaults in equity markets, the first two barriers have been sufficient, and thus far no case has gone beyond step 3.

Post-Trade Anonymity

Participants in a trade can have posttrade anonymity because the CCP is the legal counterparty in each trade.[66] The anonymity granted depends on the arrangements of the particular securities exchange. The primary motive for granting anonymity is the important need of participants to hide their investment and trading strategies from each other. Anonymity is natural in an order-driven market where specific trading counterparties cannot be chosen at the point of trade.

SETTLEMENT

We next turn to the settlement of trades. First we consider settlement in terms of delivery versus payment.

Delivery versus Payment: Finality

Delivery versus payment is, in principle, a process that significantly reduces most of the risks of settlement fulfillment by ensuring the simultaneous movement of cash and securities in opposite directions. The delivery process and the payment process must not be split. In most environments, finality of settlement in a CSD is defined with exactitude by directives on settlement finality or by national regulation. In the area of insolvency, settled trades cannot be unwound by an administrator.[67] But there is a problem—a trade that has been executed may not be valid if the buyer or the seller, at the time of the trade, was already insolvent. In this instance, the execution of a trade would be fraudulent and could be unwound by the exchange, provided that it has not been accepted by the CCP. Once a trade has been accepted by the CCP, it must stand.

Settlement Cycle

The worldwide standard settlement cycle used in equity markets is T + 3 (or in some cases T + 2). Several initiatives to shorten the process to T + 0 (immediate) or T + 1 have been taken without success, largely because the shorter cycles would require the harmonization of other financial markets (such as foreign exchange markets and money markets).[68] Theoretically, a reduction to T + 0 or even T + 1 would make the entire risk management part of clearing largely obsolete. It would also reduce clearing to netting and to supplying posttrade anonymity. It would practically require that all securities and funds be in one real-time system. Reality shows that this may not be possible:

- Intermediaries may buy or receive stock from a place different than where they have to deliver it. The need for a longer period (two to three days) is very important when securities have to be transferred between countries.

- Foreign exchange transactions may be involved, and transferring the correct currency takes two working days. This would usually be handled by the agent that settles within the CSD.
- Settlement systems would be required that are fully real time, including the currency, and this would require participants to carry far larger cash positions.

Cross-Border Settlement

Cross-border delivery versus payment (DVP) is based on the fact that national CSDs are the effective depositories where equities are held. Outside holdings in, for example, international central securities depositories (ICSDs) are linked either through direct connectivity or through a correspondent bank. If the CSDs are linked together, they can operate on the basis of an *omnibus account* that holds cash against collateral. Or they can make linked settlement.[69]

Cross-border settlement in securities was originally done via correspondent, agent banking, or custody arrangements. International investment banks and brokers would hold a safe custody account with a bank in the other country. A trade would result in a DVP movement to fulfill the trade against their correspondent through the respective central securities depository. This principle is called the *home CSD* principle.[70] Some CSDs today are directly linked, but the process is the same.

Custody

A custody service handles all administrative issues involving holding shares, collecting dividends, withholding taxes, accounting of stock dividends and splits, and so on. Custodial services are provided by the home CSD and, internationally, through agents, custodians, and correspondent banks that offer the service to their clients.

LINKS

Trading, clearing, and settlement organizations are integrated or linked together in various ways that we consider in this section.

Exchanges to Clearing Organization

The straight-through processing (STP) of trades enables vertical integration to become a reality on a technical level. Consolidating clearing organizations and linking them cross-border requires infrastructures that are based on high-performance technology.

Exchange with Integrated Clearinghouse: The Vertical Model

The vertical model is not only a technical but also a legal integration of the trading, clearing, and settlement organizations. The vertical silos are relatively closed to outside members (an ISD with T + 2 settlement prevents closure to outsiders who have a T + 3 role).[71] The vertical silos are usually highly efficient and cost-effective within their own domestic arenas, but can give very limited choice to their members. These environments have been attributable to national market legislation and to many years of supplying their services to domestic members. They offer single regulation and infrastructure, but do not provide the flexibility required by many international trading entities.

Exchange with Link to Clearinghouse: The Horizontal Model

Some exchanges have managed to integrate more than one clearinghouse into a structure as described previously in the umbrella, sub-CCP model.[72] In most cases, a clearinghouse handles clearing for more than one market. In the United States, in particular, the DTCC handles virtually all equity clearing throughout the nation. The idea of the one CCP for Europe being the natural monopoly proved to be theoretically efficient, but, given all the legal, practical, and tax barriers involved, this model has been slow to develop.[73]

Exchanges to Settlement Organizations Smaller national markets that deal primarily with small caps, warrants, bonds or structured products, have strong, direct links to settlement organizations. Participants know their counterparties and there is no clearing, netting, or risk management.

Integration to Settlement Integration with the settlement organization is usually quite good. Exchange operators pass the settlement instructions on in their capacity as agents, under a power of attorney given by the account owners. All risk involved in the settlement is taken on by the members of the exchange. As a standard, these national exchanges use a single CSD.

Links to the Bilateral Settlement Model Bilateral settlement models are supported by some exchanges that bypass clearing. In this structure, an exchange takes control of the necessary repositioning in order to supply cross-CSD settlement and to give members the choice of settlement location or allow only one CSD per security for settlement.

A FINAL WORD

Our discussion of clearing and settlement suggests just how complex the operations of an entire market actually are. Modern clearing systems have removed significant risk from the equity business. Nevertheless, some systemic risks remain. An ongoing integration of European and transatlantic markets, and an attending reduction of systemic risk, will be a challenge for the next decade.

NOTES

1. In the United States, the Depository Trust & Clearing Corporation (DTCC), the holding organization for several clearinghouses, combines some of the attributes of a CCP and a central securities depository (CSD).

2. The reader who wishes further detail on clearing and settlement may find it in the following references: David M. Weiss, *After the Trade Is Made: Processing Securities Transactions*, 3rd edition, Prentice Hall, 2004; Merviyn J. King, *Bank and Brokerage Back Office Procedures & Settlements: A Guide for Managers and their Advisors*, and David Loader, *Clearing, Settlement and Custody, Securities Institute Global Capital Markets*, Butterworth-Heinemann, September 2002.

3. The clearinghouse would give participants certificates that enabled them to collect cash or shares at a bank. See *Historical Perspective*, published by the New York Clearinghouse, 2003.

4. *Netting* is the process of collapsing all trades and contracts into one net settlement figure that fulfills the obligation. Usually the underlying gross trades are fully closed at the point the net trade is created. *Offsetting* is the process of replacing all transactions with one trade that then has to be settled. Offsetting reduces the number of trades that have to be separately settled.

   Insofar as risk is any variation in an outcome, it includes qualitative and quantitative elements as well as undesirable and desirable outcomes. See Lawrence Galitz, *Financial Engineering*, revised edition, Pittman Publishing, London, 1995, p. 5.

5. With a large offsetting and netting capability among the direct participants of a market, a significant number of trades are settled before delivery.

6. The majority of clearinghouses have mutual risk funds that are sponsored by all of their clearing members.

7. *Dematerialization* means that the owner's beneficial rights are still with the equity, but that there is no physical certificate in existence. There are many examples of how this certification of ownership may be achieved. A simple one is for the issuer to promise to print a certificate in the future if one is requested.

8. A *CSD* is usually a facility provided per country. In most cases it is mutually owned by its users. Some international central securities depositories (ICSDs), such as Euroclear and Clearstream International, have taken over the mutual ownership, but still operate these facilities on the same principles.

   The change of ownership is done on the market. The settlement involves delivering money or equity to the correct accounts, in terms of making the transaction final and giving the new owner full control of his or her possessions. *Book entry* means a transfer without physical delivery, credit or debit cash, or safe custody account.

9. All important equity, options, and futures markets have central counterparty clearing.

10. The margin must cover the potential loss in case the clearinghouse has to step in in place of the failing actor on the market. A collateralization of positions is also possible in a bilateral trading place.

11. If a member is involved in all transactions that a market makes, risk management is automatically centralized. Under the clearinghouse risk management, we must also include the process of dealing with failure and damage waiving.

12. If a participant turns government bonds of an AA country, the risk that the clearinghouse in the end is exposed to would be the failure at the same time of the particular member and particular body that issued the collateral.

13. Default management is an important part of the clearinghouse function. In some regulatory regimes the clearinghouse has priority before other interests are taken. Collateral and risk fund contributions normally may be called by a liquidator only after the fulfillment.

14. Posttrade anonymity is required to protect liquidity providers or other participants from being visible in terms of volume and also behavior.

15. Bilateral settlement netting involves building the net between two parties, and the savings that are realized are restricted to the two participants. Netting of all against all (multilateral netting) is far more efficient.

16. A standard process is applied by the central securities depository to reduce the technical transfer risk. The process always leaves the participant with either the equity or the money in case of a failure.

17. Timely settlement could become well over 99.8 percent, as seen at virt-x, for example.

18. A CCP clearinghouse position is considered to be risk free and, therefore, may be large. In most countries it does not need to follow a capital adequacy rule or capital adequacy rules are respectively adjusted.

19. The failure of a small member can block large parts of settlements with a relative small amount of equity or cash, and therefore can be dangerous for other members. A famous example of settlement risk is the failure of the German Herstatt bank. On June 26, 1974, Herstatt had taken in all its foreign currency receipts in Europe, but had not made any of its U.S. dollar payments, when German banking regulators closed down the bank at the end of the German business day. This put severe pressure on several other banks.

20. In the European market, participants have two relations, one to the national CSD, the other to a different location for nondomestic equity. When it comes to settling foreign securities, an international CSD (ICSD) and agent banks are important solutions for most players.

21. Relationships may be more complex when nonclearing members and agents are involved, but the principle remains the same.

22. Exchanges require that clearing arrangements be confirmed before they confirm the membership. In practice, a membership is specified as "clearing member" or as "nonclearing member."

23. A *direct clearing membership* is able to clear the business that the exchange member has done in its capacity as a principal. A *general clearing member* (GCM) is able to clear trades that were done by a third-party exchange member. The GCM is completely liable for all these transactions toward the clearinghouse. All the processes between a national CSD, the clearinghouse, and the national exchange(s) are highly efficient.

24. Whether to be a *vertical silo* is a governance issue. Technically, all major clearinghouses are highly integrated with the relevant markets.

25. Participants in the *horizontal model* are, governancewise, independent as suppliers to a market.

26. There are different standards in different countries. Currently there is no firm European standard established, which means there are different functionalities for different markets.

    A *cross-border* trade involves participants from two independent countries, each with its own legislation and regulations. The sub-CCP is a fully functional clearinghouse, taking all functions as long as both legs of a transaction are cleared though itself. When a cross-CCP transaction arises, the umbrella or main CCP will act as the CCP, and the sub-CCP will act in its capacity as a general clearing member.

27. Besides the payment of dividends with all the tax implications, the election rights have to be processed through the construction, which is quite difficult, as CSDs offer very different kinds of support on these events.

28. The minimum relationship has to be a legal and procedural agreement about how to deal with cross-CCP transactions.

29. The perfect sample is Eurex Clearing, which offers remote clearing out of European countries, but it is all regulated by the German Bundesaufsichtsamt für den Werpapierhandel (BaFin).

30. All major equity clearinghouses are represented in this Group of CCP12. They are discussing (among other issues) how to link CCPs in relation to consolidation.

31. Settlement prices are required to calculate the margins the relevant members must have. The settlement price determination may be different for OTC-traded instruments.

32. The settlement is done after netting and offsetting through a book entry at the CSD. The clearing members have either direct or indirect access through an agent's access to the relevant settlement location.

33. Segregation is important in the case of default. The clearinghouse will transfer the segregated positions. Segregation protects the NCM from a default of its GCM.

34. There are different methods of handling. Broadly viewed, one concept is to register all collateral, assess its value, and then compare it with the need of the registered trades.

35. If the clearinghouse issues a margin call, the clearing member must satisfy the request within hours. Most of the clearinghouse's members have direct access to the payment account in the central bank of the relevant clearing member.

36. *Default* means failing to fulfill the obligations of an open trade position. The clearinghouses have the power to declare default. When they do, they proceed to balance the relevant members' open positions, buy in or sell out the balances, and cover any possible loss by the margin put up by the defaulting member.

37. The *value date* is the date of payment and delivery. It is also called the *intended settlement day*. The value date is used for all interest calculations.
    Corporate actions such as dividend payment, buyer election, and the separation of rights have to be processed through the net that is created by the clearinghouse. Only trades that are to be settled on the same date may be netted.

38. In some areas, the intended settlement date is also called the *value date*.

39. *Finality* means that it cannot be unwound by anyone.

40. The sender of the offer commits to take any trade agreement and to become a part of the trade unless the receiver of the offer has rejected the offer.

41. The London Clearinghouse Equity Clear® service is based on the open offer.

42. Rejection is very rare, but in an independent environment the clearinghouse must be able to protect itself from receiving any additional trades that were made when arrangements were not in place with a particular member or the traded instrument is not eligible for clearing anymore.

43. For smaller members, the failure of a large counterparty may force them out of business.

44. The margin calculation should ensure that the clearinghouse has enough collateral to cover the replacement cost of the position over the nonsettled period. The margin requirement is calculated on the basis of the net open positions.

45. Names of these clearing members depend on the clearinghouse. It may also be the "clearing participant."

46. Brokers, banks, and securities dealers have a similar status in all different legislations.

47. Eurex Clearing Derivatives introduced a clearing and settlement exam in 1999. Members must have people on their staff who have passed this exam.

48. The *risk fund* of a clearinghouse usually is a mutual fund managed by the clearinghouse that should prevent large damage to a market. The funds are provided by the clearing members. In the *default procedures*, clearinghouses have several layers that are referred to as lines of defense against failure.

49. The initial margin may be changed later during the day when netting is performed if it is charged at the moment of trade.

50. If the respective member were to default, the clearinghouse would probably sell out or buy in the open trades. Depending on price moves on the market, this may be at quite different prices. The replacement value is the cost to replace the delivery by something that will not be settled anymore.

51. *Margin calls* can be satisfied in cash or collateral, depending on the rules of the clearinghouse. Failing to cover a margin call is severe and usually triggers the default process.

52. A variety of CCPs make a cut for settlement before the opening of the market. Settlements must be completed or margin put up for the next 24 hours.

53. This noncleared business in the financial community is covered by normal risk management and subsequently by capital adequacy.

54. The clearing will calculate the maximum damage the member can create if all movements of the price are against his or her current position.

55. Several stock exchanges were closed after the September 11, 2001, attack. This had two effects. First, the actual price of the equity could not be determined, and second, no participant was able to trade to a flat position. Sharp price movements at such a time would have to be considered systemic risk.

56. The gross trades may have different prices. When they do, the weighted average price of the net position is often taken for the margin calculation.

57. Some clearinghouses require part to be cash, or they may accept only collateral that can quickly be turned into cash.

58. English law, U.K. Company Act, Section 7.

59. *Default* is used in the sense that an actor does not fulfill the obligations he or she has with respect to delivery or payment and, vis-à-vis the clearinghouse, does not deliver the margin required to cover its positions.

60. Insolvency legislation is national. There is no binding international insolvency regulation.

61. U.K. Company Act, Section 7, gives priority and protection to preferred parties; among them are the clearinghouses.

62. At least, all settlements in which the defaulting member is involved are stopped.

63. This is dependant on the arrangements the NCM and GCM have, and it may vary.

64. This involves buying or selling so that the equity balance is net (i.e., the consequences of all positions is transferred into a cash position that then may be used against the margin collateralized). Usually, the buy-in and sell-out is done by an agent on behalf of the clearinghouse.

65. Some clearinghouses request a cash account for each clearing member, and the buy-in and sell-out is done against this account. The balance is then brought to zero using the same mechanisms shown.

66. Electronic markets also have pretrade anonymity.

67. This is very basic for the operations of a clearinghouse. In case this protection is not granted, a clearinghouse would have to ask for significantly more contributions to the risk fund and would probably have to hold the funds for longer periods of time.

68. Some closed national infrastructures would be capable, but on the international platform it has so far proved to be infeasible.

69. Under linked settlement, two settlements are linked, and the DVP takes four steps that cannot be interrupted.

70. The home CSD is the one that maintains all book entries for the dematerialized equity.

71. For example, the German Xetra uses T + 2, whereas, for the same stock, virt-x uses T + 3. Consequently, arbitraging by, for example, buying on virt-x and selling on Xetra does not work unless a member would lend the security for one day.

72. The horizontal models separate trading, clearing, and settlement into three levels. The three organizations are independent and therefore act in terms of business also on the horizontal level.

73. It would create a single CCP for Europe clearing all markets.

CHAPTER 11

Regulation

E quity markets in the United States and around the world are being reshaped by the simultaneous convergence of three powerful forces: technology developments, intensified competition (both domestic and global), and regulation. Each of the three may be viewed as desirable or well intentioned, but their joint impact is producing results that are difficult to predict, hard to control, and not easy to understand. What we are witnessing is not a revolution. It is an earthquake. In this chapter, we focus on the role that regulation has played in policing and shaping the equity markets.

The U.S. regulatory structure is three-tiered. Closest to the operating level are the exchanges and the National Association of Securities Dealers (NASD). These market centers are known as self-regulatory organizations (SROs). The SROs monitor trading and have oversight responsibility for

This chapter has been written by Robert A. Schwartz and does not necessarily reflect the views and opinions of Reto Francioni.

Material in this chapter was drawn with permission from *The Electronic Call Auction: Market Mechanism and Trading*, Robert A. Schwartz, ed., Kluwer Academic Publishers, 2001 (two chapters by Schwartz, "The Call Auction Alternative" and "Technology's Impact on the Equity Markets"); *Regulation of the U.S. Equity Markets*, Robert A. Schwartz, ed., Kluwer Academic Publishers, 2001; "Controlling Institutional Trading Costs: We Have Met the Enemy, and It Is Us," Robert A. Schwartz and Benn Steil, *Journal of Portfolio Management*, vol. 28, no. 3, spring 2002, pp. 39–49; and "Best Execution: A Candid Analysis," Robert A. Schwartz and Robert A. Wood, *Journal of Portfolio Management*, vol. 29, no. 4, summer 2003, pp. 37–48.

their member firms. Two major government agencies comprise the second regulatory level: the Securities and Exchange Commission (SEC) and the Commodities Futures Trading Commission (CFTC). These agencies monitor trading, police listed companies and market centers with regard to securities law, and set policy for a wide spectrum of issues. The third regulatory level is the U.S. Congress. Both the SEC and the CFTC are responsible to Congress, the source of the legislation governing the securities markets.

The goals of regulation are threefold:

1. Assure an honest market.
2. Enhance market efficiency with regard to the provision and pricing of broker-dealer services.
3. Enhance market efficiency with regard to the pricing of shares traded.

As discussed by Schreiber and Schwartz, these three goals are not compatible in all respects: (1) Interdealer competition (which, ceteris paribus, reduces spreads and commissions) fragments the order flow (which can impede the efficiency of price discovery).[1] (2) The imposition of trading halts (to enhance the stability and fairness of the market) delays access to the market (which for some traders represents an inefficiency). (3) Prohibitions on insider trading (to safeguard honesty and fairness) limit access to the market for some traders and can delay the impact of new information on stock prices. And so forth. Resolving the conflicts between the regulatory goals is a major problem for the regulators.

There is a deeper issue: attaining the proper balance between the restrictions explicitly imposed by a formal regulatory body and those implicitly imposed by the competitive forces of a free market. This chapter considers the conceptual issues involved. We begin by focusing on the sources of market failure for the equity markets.

SOURCES OF MARKET FAILURE

The private market gives socially desirable results under some conditions when traders compete freely with one another while adhering only to certain basic legal requirements as defined by contract law. However, for various reasons, a market may fail to reach a socially desired equilibrium with respect to the price established and the number of shares traded even though the broader legal context is well defined. Regulators face a difficult challenge when addressing the manifestations of market failure.

Specification of the Rules of a Market

A membership exchange like the NYSE can be viewed as a book of rules. The Big Board does not participate in trading. Its members—most important, specialists, other floor traders, and broker-dealers—do the trading. The NYSE provides the infrastructure (e.g., order handling and reporting systems), oversight and surveillance, and the rule book.

To a considerable extent, demutualized exchanges, electronic communications networks (ECNs), and other alternative trading systems (ATSs) do the same. Consequently, the various markets all compete, in part at least, via the rules that they establish. But all markets operate under a broader set of government-established rules and regulations. Specification of the governmental rules is not part of the market process. The flow of traffic on our roads and highways provides an analogy.

Drivers are free to select their points of origin, the destinations of their travels, and the routes that they follow. If multiple routes exist between two frequently selected points, drivers may compete with one another in their route selection. They also compete in terms of lane selection and other aspects of positioning. Such competition between drivers tends to even out the flow of traffic. If the competition is efficient, we have a result equivalent to that given by the random walk of stock prices: When traffic is heavy, expected transit times are similar for various alternatives, and any one driver can select his or her route by random process (it is not possible in a fully arbitraged equilibrium to predict what the better alternative will be).

The desirability of this result in no way implies that traffic should not be governed by a regulatory authority. Indeed, speed limits should be set, traffic lights should be installed at busy intersections, certain types of vehicles should not be allowed on certain roads, and so on. The competitive environment cannot determine these rules. Traffic regulations must be set by the body politic. So, too, must the laws that govern equity trading. For instance, if spatial consolidation of the order flow is desired, one of the rules should be that all orders for a security must be routed to the same market center.

The regulators cannot avoid making certain decisions. It is tempting in a complex situation to let the market decide. However, there are some things that the market cannot decide. To avoid setting certain rules by legislative authority could be as disastrous as turning off the traffic lights in the financial district of lower Manhattan or downtown Zurich. In this section of the chapter, we consider various causes of market failure that justify regulatory intervention. In part, the intervention may be on the government level, and, in part, it may be on the market center level.

Market Power

Market power in economic analysis typically refers to the ability of a selling firm, because of its size in relation to the aggregate of all other sellers in an industry, to realize excess profits by increasing price above the value that would prevail under competitive conditions. Equivalently, a buyer who is large in relation to other buyers in aggregate realizes excess profits by depressing price below the competitive equilibrium. All traders benefit from having this power. All players wish to be large in relation to their own side of the market. In the securities industry, the economic units thought to have this power are the suppliers of marketability services.

In the 1970s, the premier securities markets in the United States were the two national exchanges (NYSE and Amex), and the key participants in these markets were the specialists. Each stock listed on an exchange was then, as it is today, assigned to one specialty firm. Until May 1, 1975, the commission structure was fixed. Members of the NYSE were required to take their orders for listed securities to an exchange for execution. Institutional traders, along with other public traders, were not (and still are not) permitted to enter their orders directly.[2] Twenty-five-plus years ago, the NYSE and the Amex were considered clubs that only the privileged few could join. Since then, the Nasdaq market has also developed into a premier trading arena, and, more recently, a slew of ECNs and ATSs have emerged.[3]

Twenty-five-plus years ago, control over price, order flow, and membership in the club gave the exchanges an enviable position of power. For some in government, this power implied monopoly control of marketability services. Accordingly, the price of marketability services (commissions and spreads) was deemed too high, and market-maker profits were thought to be excessive. More recently, competition has intensified among exchanges, ECNs, and ATSs. Nevertheless, concern about market centers wielding market power persists in the United States. In a June 2003 article in *Traders Magazine*, Bresiger wrote, ". . . regulators and others want multiple market models. This is a way to promote competition, which should mean better execution standards for individual investors, who will pay lower transaction costs."[4]

Market power affects the outcome of trading in the equity markets in another way as well. Some traders are large vis-à-vis the other side of the market (some buyers are large in relation to sellers, and some sellers are large in relation to buyers). Size in this context results in market impact effects. No trader wants this kind of power. All would rather be price takers than have their orders push price in the wrong direction. We discuss the problem of handling institution order flow in greater detail in Chapter 5, "Institutional Order Flow."

Externalities

Externalities, along with market power, are another widely recognized cause of market failure. A classic example of a *negative* externality is the soot generated by a production process. For instance, if a power company that produces electricity is not responsible for the particles of dirt that exit its smokestacks, the social cost of this air pollution is not taken into account in the output and pricing of electricity. If *all costs* associated with the production of electricity are not taken into account by suppliers, electricity is overproduced in the free market.

As discussed in Chapter 4, "What We Want from Our Markets," positive externalities exist in trading. Investors who post orders on the market convey a benefit to the market in aggregate. Limit orders stabilize market prices, facilitate price discovery, and act as catalysts that attract other orders to the market. Limit order traders are not, however, separately compensated for providing this service. Because *all benefits* associated with the placement of orders are not taken into account by the decision makers, an undersupply of limit orders can be expected in the free market.

The market failure implied by the externalities of market making provides economic justification for the affirmative obligation of the NYSE specialist. This market maker is responsible for supplementing the order flow to provide orderliness to the price formation process.

Public Goods

Public goods are similar to externalities in that their production is not governed by the market forces that attend the standard exchange of goods and services. (See Chapter 4 for further discussion of public goods.) Classic examples of public goods are a lighthouse in a harbor and military defense. The characteristics shared by these goods are the following: (1) One person's consumption does not reduce the amount available for others; (2) people who do not pay for the good cannot be excluded from consuming it; and (3) whatever quantity is made available for the public good is available for all consumers. These attributes of public goods lead consumers to understate their demand for them in the marketplace, which prevents the private market from supplying these goods in socially optimal amounts. Consequently, the decision concerning the output of a public good must be made collectively by the body politic.

The public goods–type services of a securities market are those that provide a fair and orderly market: (1) market surveillance to protect against exploitation, fraud, manipulation, and other violations of the rules; (2) price discovery; and (3) price stabilization.

A broad range of investors benefit from a fair and orderly market. The prices established in the premier asset markets signal information to investors. Assets are evaluated for various legal purposes in relation to prices established in the major market centers. Price basing is used for the redemption of equity mutual fund shares and for the evaluation of estate-held shares. Prices set in the futures markets are used to establish prices in associated cash markets. A fairer, more efficient secondary asset market reduces the cost to corporations of raising fresh capital in the new-issues market. And so on.

The benefit any individual trader realizes from the public goods aspects of market making does not reduce the amount available for others. A single quantity of each of the public goods–type marketability services is provided to the market, and individual investors benefit from these marketability services even though they may not have paid for them. Accordingly, these services would be undersupplied in the free market. This provides further justification for dealer, specialist, and regulator interference in the operations of the equity markets.

Principal-Agent Relationships

A principal-agent relationship exists when a principal engages an agent to act on his or her behalf. The agent is responsible for exercising maximum effort and skill on behalf of the principal, and the contractual agreement between the two should give the agent the proper incentives to do so. Additionally, the principal will monitor the agent as best as he or she can. But contracts are never perfect and neither is performance monitoring, especially when critical information pertaining to the agent's decisions is not available. Consequently, a principal-agent problem exists: Agents may make decisions that are not in the best interests of the principals. Principal-agent relationships exists when intermediaries are involved in the trading process. We refer to this problem in particular in our discussion of commission bundling (see the section, "Soft Dollars").

Asymmetric Information

As we have previously discussed (see Chapter 3, "Liquidity," in particular), trading in securities markets is motivated by informational change and by changing liquidity needs. Information change generates informational asymmetries. Insiders (particularly corporate management) have more information than public traders. Some public participants (*informed traders*) have more information than other public participants (*liquidity traders*). Informed public traders may also be better informed than professional market makers (dealers and specialists).

Information asymmetries are a particularly vexing and costly problem. Because dealers and specialists widen their bid-ask spreads to protect against the advantage that better-informed traders may have (see Chapter 7, "Intermediated Markets"), information asymmetries increase the cost of transacting for liquidity traders. Further, if the dissemination of information consistently favors some investors over others, those at an informational disadvantage may reduce their participation in the market. This reduction causes markets to be thinner, resulting in a further deterioration of the quality of the marketplace.

It is not possible to eliminate informational asymmetries totally. There are, however, various approaches to dealing with the problem: (1) Impose trading restrictions on those who can be identified as having superior information (the so-called insiders); (2) improve the systems used to disseminate information; and (3) halt trading to allow news to be disseminated and assessed before trades are made. Each of these approaches is not a costless solution, however.

Transaction Price Uncertainty

Transaction price uncertainty, which is endemic to the equity markets, affects the flow of orders to the market. In continuous trading, in particular, the order flow itself establishes the transaction prices that are realized ex post. Because of this two-way causality (expectations of price affect order flow and order flow affects price) and given that, with continuous trading, price discovery is an extended, dynamic process that occurs while trades are being made, realized transaction prices generally differ from equilibrium values. Consequently, a community of traders does not achieve an equilibrium distribution of share holdings after any round of trading.

Inertia

Inertia in a dynamic environment retards technological change. Inertia need not imply the laziness of economic agents, but may be due to the cost of adopting a new technology. Consider, for instance, the introduction of a keyboard with an improved configuration. The standard keyboard is known as the *qwerty* keyboard because of the six keys on its upper left-hand side. An alternative keyboard known as *Dvorak* has been scientifically designed and is reputedly more efficient, but has not succeeded in the marketplace. The reason may lie in the following observations:[5]

- Countless people know and use the touch system with the current arrangement of the keys. People acquainted with the qwerty keyboard would profit from learning the Dvorak keyboard only if the new system has a sufficient *differential advantage* for them over the old arrangement, discounted over the remaining years they expect to be using a keyboard.
- People just learning to type will realize a return on their investment from the *total benefit* of knowing the new system.[6]
- There are advantages to all typists knowing and using similar equipment. The benefit to any individual of knowing the new system may therefore be large if the market in aggregate converts to the new system, but small if the market in aggregate does not.

Consequently, the failure of existing typists to convert to the new system reduces the benefits of the superior technology to new typists, new typists therefore learn the older system, and the new and better typewriters are not produced even though the social benefits may in aggregate outweigh the costs.

Technological inertia is most likely to occur when change is comprehensive rather than incremental. Comprehensive change affects an entire system (for instance, the full array of keys on a keyboard); partial change involves the components of a system (for instance, the location of the function keys). It may be possible in certain situations to achieve a comprehensive change by a series of partial changes, but such a switch in technology is often not possible.

Since 1975, technological development in the equity markets industry has been substantial. Starting in the latter half of the 1970s in the United States, electronic equipment was introduced to route orders and to disseminate information. The Toronto Stock Exchange instituted the first exchange-based electronic trading platform (the Computer Assisted Trading System, CATS) in 1977. The Tokyo Stock Exchange introduced its electronic platform (Computerized Order Routing and Execution System, CORES) in 1982, and Paris followed with its CAC market (Cotation Assistée en Continu) in 1986. Other European bourses have done the same, and today all of the major markets in Europe have incorporated fully electronic trading systems.

In the United States, Instinet was founded in 1969 as an electronic block-trading system for institutional investors, and the Cincinnati Stock Exchange, the first electronic exchange in the United States, started operations in 1978. Additional electronic facilities opened in the United States soon after the SEC's new order handling rules were introduced in 1997. Most prominent are Archipelago (formed in December 1996 and granted exchange status by the SEC in October 2001) and Island (included in the

Nasdaq quote montage in January 1997 and acquired by Instinet in September 2002).

But turning the clock back a quarter of a century, we see that computerized trading did not have an easy beginning. The responses to the first proposals were emotional and pessimistic. For example, in the late 1970s, Paul Kolton, then chairman of the board of the Amex, commented that the introduction of an electronic system based on a consolidated limit order book (CLOB) "seems not an orderly step but a drastic departure; it is less a measured progression than a giant leap, with the landing place obscure."[7] Allen and Zarembo discussed the initial hesitancy on the part of NYSE specialist units to accept the exchange's new automated display book (which is not an execution system).[8]

An electronic display book was first introduced on the NYSE in June 1983 for one stock, Pan Am. On its first day, a news release concerning the company resulted in the stock trading at three times the normal volume, making it the most active issue on the NYSE (more than 1 million shares changed hands that day). Because of the system's success with the heavy volume, it was called upon on November 21, 1983, to handle the anticipated order flow of nearly 2 billion newly listed shares when the seven Baby Bell companies simultaneously started trading following the AT&T divestiture. The ease with which this extraordinary challenge was met resulted in widespread acceptance of the electronic display book by the NYSE specialists.

London's experience following the introduction of SEAQ, an electronic billboard, was also dramatic. The London Stock Exchange (LSE) had invested several million pounds to upgrade its floor in preparation for its Big Bang in October 1986. By January 1987, equities trading had left the floor entirely, and it did so at a speed that was astonishing. Clemons and Weber[9] quote a trader as saying, "Within five minutes of Big Bang, on Monday morning, it was clear to me that the floor was dead."

Computerized trading represents a comprehensive change from nonelectronic trading.[10] The change has required professional traders to adapt to an entirely new way of operating, and those involved with systems design have met enormous resistance. Technological inertia has dulled the incentive to develop new trading systems in the first place and has slowed their adoption by major market centers.

Europe has seen the conversion to electronic trading platforms in its major market centers. Initially, the competitive success of the London Stock Exchange's international quotations system (SEAQ-I) pressured the continental European bourses to enter the electronic age. Then the success of these computerized order-driven facilities pressured the London Stock Exchange to introduce its own electronic order-driven facility (Stock Exchange Electronic Trading Service, SETS) on October 20, 1997.

THE REGULATORY PROCESS

In the presence of market failure, one typically considers turning to government regulation to achieve the socially optimal production, distribution, and pricing of resources. Unfortunately, the political process is itself flawed, and government interference may not enhance the efficiency of a marketplace.

The political process involves a different incentive structure than the private market: the maximization of votes rather than the maximization of financial wealth. And political power (the ability to win votes) differs from economic power (the command of financial resources over all resources, both real and financial). Consequently, the political process operates very differently than the private market.

Government Failure

Our discussion of the regulatory process begins by noting several causes of government failure.

The Distribution of Political Power   The distribution of power across participants in the political process differs from the distribution of power in the market process. Some who are large in the private market are small in the political arena, and vice versa. The political process typically admits outsiders whose main concerns are not the fortunes of a particular industry or the pros and cons of a particular issue. As a consequence, considerations that are not germane to the operations of a specific industry may enter political decisions, and the solutions attained by political consensus may be distorted.[11]

Inadequate Procedural Safeguards   Procedural safeguards in the governmental process differ from those implicit in the market process. The private market itself is a strict regulator—those who do not operate profitably typically do not survive. Unfortunately, government officials who do not regulate well may nevertheless survive as regulators. Instituting effective procedural safeguards is at best costly; at worst, it may be impossible.

Jurisdictional Disputes   The governmental process may involve competition between rival government authorities for regulatory turf. For instance, the growth of futures and options trading in the early 1980s caused confusion in the United States about which agency, the Securities and Exchange Commission (SEC) or the Commodities Futures Trading Commission (CFTC), should have jurisdiction over these new products.[12]

Regulated firms typically have some freedom to choose their regulators, and regulators typically compete for their constituency.[13] This competition affects the decisions made by regulators, may prejudice the outcomes of the political processes, and further diminishes one's confidence that government intervention will enhance the economic efficiency of the regulated industry.

The Cost of Regulating Regulation is costly, and government funds are limited. The fact that government funds are allocated by a budgetary process embedded in a political environment further suggests that funds may not be distributed efficiently across competing government projects.

Imperfect Knowledge More than some may realize, regulators often do not fully understand the problems encountered by an industry and do not know how best to develop and to institute reasonable solutions. In the United States, both the SEC and the CFTC have solicited opinions, held hearings, and deliberated long and hard about various critical decisions. However, much remains that is not known about the nature of competition in the equity markets. For example, the problems outlined in the preceding section of this chapter are not easily perceived and, when perceived, are thorny to resolve. All told, the boundaries of knowledge are among the toughest limitations faced by those who seek to govern the market process.

THE EVOLVING REGULATORY FOCUS

Despite imperfections in the political process, regulation of the securities markets is needed and has grown substantially since the Securities Acts of 1933 and 1934. As noted at the beginning of this chapter, the regulatory goals for the securities markets are threefold: (1) to ensure an honest market, (2) to enhance efficiency with regard to the provision and pricing of broker-dealer services, and (3) to enhance efficiency with regard to the pricing of shares traded.

Honesty

To operate efficiently, a market must first and foremost be honest. The honesty of a market entails guarding against manipulation of information, prices, and trading volume and preventing abuses of power and position by insiders and professionals.

Federal regulation of the securities markets began with the Securities Act of 1933 and the Securities Exchange Act of 1934. The primary motivation for this legislation was to ensure reasonable information disclosure and to prevent dishonesty and market manipulation. The acts were designed to protect the ignorant from being exploited by those who might distort reality and entice the gullible into undesirable transactions.

The SEC has been particularly concerned with the fairness of the information flow, and the agency has devoted major resources to preventing the abuse of power by insiders. For those involved with the activities of a corporation (with positions ranging from top management to the proofreader in a print shop), information is a freely generated by-product of some other activity. A primary objective of insider trading regulations is to prevent those for whom information is a free by-product from making excess trading profits at the expense of others who do not have a fortuitous position vis-à-vis the information flow. We consider insider trading in greater detail in the next section of this chapter.

On August 15, 2000, in a further attempt to promote full and fair disclosure of new information, the U.S. Securities and Exchange Commission adopted Regulation FD. As we state in Chapter 2, "From Information to Prices," Regulation FD requires that any information provided to some stock analysts and/or to any other securities market professionals who may themselves seek to trade on the basis of that information must be publicly, not selectively, disclosed.

Efficiency of the Market for Broker-Dealer Services

The second regulatory objective is to enhance market efficiency with regard to the provision and pricing of broker-dealer services. This aspect of efficiency entails keeping commissions and spreads competitive and ensuring the financial responsibility of broker-dealer firms.

Concern about the competitive efficiency of the markets developed with the back-office crisis of the 1960s. The unexpected increase of the order flow in the 1960s led to a substantial increase in brokerage firm failures, as the houses could not keep up with the paperwork, and the number of failures to deliver mounted.

The growing number of failures and the inadequacy of the trust funds established by the SROs led Congress to pass the Securities Investor Protection Act of 1970. This act established government insurance of customer accounts. With the insurance came enhanced government interest in controlling the industry to prevent the continuing failure of broker-dealer firms. Congressional involvement in operational issues and the competitive structure of the markets was thereby established.

In the 1970s, commissions charged for handling large institutional orders had become exorbitant, and institutional traders were fragmenting the markets in their efforts to avoid these rates. Related issues concerning the competitive efficiency of the markets included the absence of spatial integration among various parts of the industry, the quasi-monopoly position of various market makers (primarily the stock exchange specialists), and restrictions on entry into certain market centers (primarily the two national exchanges).

Congressional concern about the competitive efficiency of the market for broker-dealer services resulted in the enactment of the Securities Acts amendments of 1975. The legislation had two provisions of particular import: (1) as the first governmental step in deregulation, it precluded the securities exchanges from imposing fixed commissions, and (2) it mandated the development of a national market system.

Efficiency with Regard to the Pricing of Shares Traded

The third regulatory objective is to enhance market efficiency with regard to the pricing of shares. This aspect of efficiency entails improving the market's architecture to facilitate price discovery.

The CFTC has recognized price discovery as a major function of a securities market, because prices discovered in the futures markets are commonly used for price determination in associated cash markets. Indeed, a major economic rationale for the futures markets is their price-basing function. For instance, the price of cocoa is believed to be more accurately determined by the aggregation of many buyers and sellers in the market for cocoa futures than by the aggregation of a far smaller number of firms that buy and sell the cocoa itself. Therefore, cocoa traders look to the futures markets to set their spot prices.

Price discovery has not as yet been adequately recognized as a function of the major equity markets. Nevertheless, as has been emphasized in a number of places in this book, price discovery is a major issue. Clearly, a 25-cent discrepancy in the price of a stock far exceeds the brokerage commission on a transaction. In addition, there are further costs of inaccurate price discovery. As noted, prices established in the major market centers signal information to traders, are used for price basing in related markets, and are used in the evaluation of estate-held shares, equity mutual fund shares, and so on.

Efficient price discovery is the most difficult of the three regulatory goals to comprehend and to implement. However, it is the objective that pertains most closely to the attributes of the equity markets that make these markets unique. Given the importance of accurate price discovery, it would be desirable for regulators to pay appreciably more attention to the objective.

INSIDER TRADING

The primary objective of regulation is to ensure an honest market.[14] To this end, restrictions on insider trading have been instituted to prevent abuses of position. The pertinent legislation in the United States is Section 10(b) of the Securities and Exchange Act of 1934 and SEC Rule 10b-5.

Corporate insiders have a fiduciary responsibility vis-à-vis public shareholders. However, the ability to produce information presents a corporate insider with an opportunity to profit at shareholders' expense. For instance, the management of a profitable corporation could, if unrestricted, realize personal gain by selling shares short while jeopardizing the profitability of the firm. Insiders, being better informed than public investors, are also in a position to profit from the advantages offered by an asymmetric distribution of information.

Studies have shown that corporate insiders indeed realize abnormal profits when they trade the equity shares of their own firms.[15] Evidence presented by Givoly and Palmon (1985) suggests, however, that excess returns are usually attributable to superior general knowledge, not to insiders keying their transactions to particular announcements or events. Such returns are perfectly legal. What is not allowed is for insiders to trade on information that has not yet been made public.

Gross abuses of positions of power should be disallowed, from the viewpoint of both fairness and efficiency. In extreme cases, the harm done to uninformed traders has no justification. As stated by John Shad, former chairman of the SEC, insider trading "is the few taking advantage of the many. If people get the impression that they're playing against a marked deck, they're simply not going to be willing to invest."[16] If disgruntled traders cease to participate in a market, prices are depressed and trading becomes thinner, to the detriment of all.

In the United States, *insiders* are defined as the officers and directors of a corporation and as any investor who owns more than 10 percent of a corporation's outstanding shares. Such individuals are required by the 1934 Securities Act to report any transaction in the stock of their host corporation within 10 days after the month of the transaction. This information is contained in the *Official Summary of Securities Transactions and Holdings*, which is published monthly by the SEC. Corporate insiders are also prohibited from selling shares short and must return all short-run (six months or less) profits realized from trading their host company's stock.

Further, it is illegal for anyone to participate in a transaction that takes advantage of inside information that is unavailable to others involved in the trade. This restriction, imposed by SEC Rule 10b-5, has provided the foundation for most federal enforcement concerning fraudulent conduct.

The wording of Section 10(b) of the 1934 act encompasses a wide spectrum of securities fraud that the Securities and Exchange Commission may proscribe by the rule-making authority granted to it. Rule 10b-5, known as the *disclose or abstain rule*, was set forth by the SEC in 1942. A key provision of 10b-5 is that it applies to any transaction by anybody, not just to a corporate insider.

The specific criteria for determining fraud under Rule 10b-5 have subsequently been established by the federal courts. Most important, to be in violation of the rule, the information used by a trader must be found to be material. That is, if revealed, the information would have to affect a contra party's trading decision. The trader must also know that the information is unavailable to the public. An individual in possession of such nonpublic information has an obligation to disclose it before participating in a trade based on it. A failure to disclose such information thus constitutes fraud, and it is fraud that Section 10(b) of the 1934 Act was intended to prevent.

An example is provided by the Texas Gulf Sulphur case.[17] Texas Gulf Sulphur had kept secret a major ore discovery, made in November 1963, while it tried to purchase the remainder of a section of land surrounding the find. The corporation issued pessimistic news releases that denied the discovery and depressed the value of the company's stock. Meanwhile, certain corporate insiders and some outsiders who had been given the information purchased shares of the corporation. At the time of the initial discovery, Texas Gulf Sulphur stock was trading at the $17 level. On April 16, after information on the find was publicly released, the stock traded at 36⅜. By May 15, the share price had risen to 58¼. The Second Circuit Court of Appeals found that the information was material, that it was secret, and thus that trades based on it were in violation of the 1934 act.[18]

Another case involving insider trading under the 1934 act involved a stockbroker (Gintel) who was not an insider of the corporation to which the information pertained.[19] From November 6 through 23, 1959, Gintel bought approximately 11,000 shares of Curtiss-Wright stock for discretionary accounts under his control. On November 24 and 25, he started selling some of these shares. On the morning of November 25, the directors of Curtiss-Wright—including a member (Cowdin) from Gintel's firm—approved a reduction in the quarterly dividend from $.625 per share to $.375 per share. During a recess in the directors' meeting, Cowdin telephoned a message to

Gintel about the dividend cut. Gintel, on receiving the news, transmitted two orders to the exchange—one to sell 2,000 shares for 10 accounts and one to sell short 5,000 shares for 11 accounts. The orders were executed at 11:15 A.M. and at 11:18 A.M., at prices of 40¼ and 40⅜, respectively. News of the dividend cut appeared on the Dow Jones ticker at 11:48 A.M. Shortly thereafter, trading was halted on the exchange because of the large number of sell orders received. The price was 36½ when trading resumed; Curtiss-Wright closed on November 25 at 34⅞.

Cowdin's relationship with Curtiss-Wright prohibited him from selling the shares without disclosing the news. The SEC held that, by extension, it was in contravention of insider trading restrictions for Gintel, a stock-broker in Cowdin's firm, to have acted on the information supplied directly by Cowdin. Gintel had clearly accelerated his selling activity before the news was publicly announced, and the damage was material. The SEC held that Gintel's clients should not have expected him to pass on the benefits of the inside information to them at the expense of the public. Consequently, the commission ruled that Gintel's actions were in violation of Section 10(b) and Rule 10b-5.

The extent of liability for noncorporate members acting on nonpublic information has subsequently been the object of much debate. The SEC has taken the position that no one who possesses nonpublic information may trade on the basis of the information until it has been made public. This position has been modified in the courts, however. In *Vincent F. Chiarella v. United States*, the U.S. Supreme Court limited the applicability of Rule 10b-5 by confining the definition of an insider to one who has a "relation-ship of trust and confidence with shareholders."[20]

Chiarella, as a printer for Pandick Press in 1975 and 1976, handled various documents that contained announcements of corporate takeover bids. Although the names of the companies involved were concealed until final printing, Chiarella was able to deduce corporate identities from other information in the documents. He realized more than $30,000 in profits from trades based on his deductions.

Chiarella was convicted for violating Section 10(b) of the 1934 act and SEC Rule 10b-5. The court of appeals affirmed his conviction. The Supreme Court, however, reversed the decision in 1980. The reason for the reversal was that Chiarella was not a fiduciary or agent for any of the corporations involved, hence was under no obligation to disclose information before trading on it, and therefore his use of the information was not fraudulent. The decision established that "a duty to disclose under Section 10(b) does not arise from the mere possession of nonpublic market information." In the opinion of the court, financial unfairness per se does not constitute fraud. Although Section 10(b) is a catchall provision, "what it catches must be fraud."[21]

The Supreme Court further restricted the class of outsiders who could be in violation of the 1934 act in another landmark case, *Dirks v. Securities and Exchange Commission.*[22] Dirks, an officer of a broker-dealer firm specializing in investment analyses of insurance company securities, was informed by a former officer of Equity Funding of America that the fund's assets were greatly overvalued. Dirks investigated the allegations, found them to be correct, and openly discussed the information with various investors and clients. Over a two-week period, while Dirks pursued his investigation, the price of Equity Funding shares decreased from $26 to $15. Shortly thereafter, Equity Funding's records were impounded by the California insurance authorities, and fraud was established.

The SEC held that Dirks was in violation of the 1934 act because of his repeated allegations of fraud to investors who subsequently sold their stock in Equity Funding. On being censured by the SEC, Dirks sought review in the court of appeals, which then also entered judgment against him. In 1983 the decision was reversed by the U.S. Supreme Court

The Supreme Court based its decision on the following. No monetary or personal benefit was received by an Equity Funding employee for revealing information to Dirks. Rather, their motive was to expose a fraud. Therefore, no employee of Equity Funding had violated his or her duty to the corporation by passing information to Dirks. Hence there could be no derivative breach of duty by Dirks, who himself had no fiduciary obligation to Equity Funding's shareholders.

The Dirks case established that disclosure constitutes a breach of an insider's fiduciary duty only if it is motivated by personal gain.[23] Further, if there is no breach of duty by an insider, there is no derivative breach by an outsider (e.g., the security analyst). The Supreme Court's determination in the Dirks case therefore allows an analyst to dig out information about a corporation and to trade on that information without its being publicly revealed.

A distinction is now made between *private* information and *inside* information, and trading on the basis of private information is now allowed. This is essential to the informational efficiency of the marketplace. The trading profits a stock analyst can generate are an incentive for information to be brought to light and analyzed in the first place. Without this incentive, an insufficient amount of information may indeed be supplied in the marketplace.

The SEC has pressed forward in recent years in its efforts to control insider trading. In the spring of 1986, the commission exposed an enormous insider trading scandal: On May 12, Dennis B. Levine was charged with making $12.6 million from trading illegally on inside information concerning corporate takeovers. Six months later, on November 14, Ivan F. Boesky agreed to pay a penalty of $100 million to settle charges of trading on information illegally obtained. In February and early March of 1987, additional major charges were made by the SEC. Then, on March 19, 1987, Boyd L. Jefferies agreed to plead guilty to two charges that involved securities law violations.

The dollar sums involved in these cases were huge, and the people and firms involved were prominent. Levine was a managing director at Drexel Burnham Lambert. Boesky and Jefferies were both founders and chief executive officers of well-known firms (the firm that Jefferies started still carries his name). Others caught were associated with respected brokerage houses, including Kidder Peabody, Merrill Lynch, and Goldman Sachs.

The wave of insider trading at the time was largely related to the takeover action of the 1980s. Much of the trading activity centers on risk arbitrageurs such as Boesky and on people in frequent contact with them, such as Levine and Jefferies. Corporate restructuring is typically arranged with extensive participation from investment bankers. The investment banking firms, however, are also involved in arbitrage and other trading activities for their own accounts and for the accounts of institutional investors. Sophisticated communication systems had been developed to bring clients together and to trade large blocks of stock.

The arrangement of a single takeover in the 1980s was far more complex than it had previously been. In 1986, Sterngold wrote,[24] "Ten years ago, those involved in the secret planning for a takeover, even a big one, would have barely filled a table for eight at the Four Seasons. But the simple days are gone. The complexities and aggressiveness of Wall Street's takeover activity today require battalions of specialists who, in the normal routine of their jobs, arrange the deals and must resist the temptation to buy and sell the stocks before the takeover is announced. These deal makers are Wall Street's new 'insiders.' "[25]

By the 1980s extensive efforts were being made by securities firms to disguise the names of merger candidates, to protect or to shred sensitive documents, and to control the flow of people and of information into and out of offices. But it is not an easy matter in an environment of communications networks and complex financial operations to control the flow of information and to police those who might use information for their personal gain. In 1986, Berg wrote in a *New York Times* article, "Wall Street is a warren of information 'networks'—cliques that exchange information regularly to win out over investors who are not part of any clique."[26]

The financial community was shocked by the scandals. The feeling of the Street was reflected in a statement by Max Chapman Jr., who at the time was president of Kidder, Peabody & Co.: "I'm saddened [by the revelations of insider trading on Wall Street]. But I'm not ready to condemn the industry. This business is still based on a person's word and reputation; we do billions of dollars of business every day, on the telephone. This industry is based on good faith and honesty of the players. I still believe in that."[27]

The SEC and Congress responded to the insider trading scandals by considering further legislation. The key legislative rule under which many prosecutions have been made, Rule 10b-5, was set forth by the commission in 1942, with relatively little discussion and only a limited realization of the extensive array of abuses to which it would subsequently be applied. The government's chief reliance has been on case law that has evolved from court decisions such as those we have considered. The foundation for many of the SEC's cases has been the concept of misappropriation of information. The commission, however, has in the past resisted offering a precise definition of insider trading because of a belief that doing so would restrict its flexibility in prosecuting violators.

Then, in August 1987, the SEC changed its position and for the first time advanced a definition of insider trading to be used in proposed legislation, new Section 16A of the Insider Trading Act of 1987. The SEC's proposal would forbid trading by those in possession of nonpublic information that is material and that has been wrongfully obtained by, among other things, bribery, theft, or the breach of confidentiality arising from any contractual, fiduciary, personal, employment, or other relationship with the issuer, current or potential investors, various government officials, and others. The following excerpt from the proposed Insider Trading Act of 1987 was reported in the *New York Times* on August 8, 1987 (p. 34):

> *It shall be unlawful for any person, directly or indirectly, to purchase, sell, or cause the purchase or sale of, any security while in possession of material nonpublic information concerning the issuer or its securities, if such person knows or recklessly disregards that such information has been obtained wrongfully or that such purchase or sale would constitute a wrongful use of such information.*

The SEC's proposed definition of *wrongful* is intended to cover situations currently encompassed by the concept of misappropriation. The proposal would also lighten the burden of proof for prosecutors by replacing a "use standard" with a "possession standard." That is, the commission would have to prove only that an individual *possessed* inside information, not that the person actually *used* the information, when participating in a questionable trade. The legislation would further remove any personal benefits test (the demonstration of "benefits," which may be intangible, has often proved extremely difficult). In addition, the new definition would eliminate the condition that someone who has passed information in question to others must have done so in anticipation of realizing a personal benefit. Thus a tipper would be liable for the trades of tippees, even if the latter are not themselves liable.

The passing years have seen more insider trading cases. One of the most dramatic events involved a strikingly small trade. On December 27, 2001, on the advice of her broker, the well-known expert in tasteful living, Martha Stewart, sold all of her 3,928 shares of ImClone. The advice was based on information that had not yet been publicly released: that the Federal Drug Administration was about to reject the company's application for a new cancer drug, Erbitux. On December 27, ImClone opened at $63.49 and closed at $58.30. Brooke A. Master of the *Washington Post* wrote that the trade gave Stewart "at least $45,000 more than she would have had if she had sold on Dec. 31, 2001, after the FDA news became public, the indictment said."[28]

Stewart and her former broker were not indicted for trading on insider information, however. Their wrongdoing was, as stated by Master, that "they conspired to obstruct a probe into her personal stock sales by lying to investigators, making up conversations and—in the broker's case—altering a key document to support their story." Stewart was found guilty of obstruction of justice on March 5, 2004.

Insider Trading and Market Efficiency

A fundamental economic question remains unanswered: Do the insider trading restrictions increase or impair the efficiency of the marketplace?[29] Manne was one of the first to argue against the trading restrictions.[30] According to Manne, the profits realized through insider trading should be allowable as a reward for entrepreneurship. Manne and others have argued further that insider trading, although admittedly causing losses for those who are contra parties to the insider trades, benefits the broader community of investors by keeping prices more closely aligned with the underlying determinants of share value.

The unavoidable vagueness of any legal definition of insider trading, conflicts of interest caused by the law, and the formidable problem of enforcing the restrictions have also been advanced as reasons for changing the law. Consider the problem of vagueness, for instance. Assume that an outsider deduces that merger talks are taking place between two companies because some employees have let slip that at each company top management had participated in weekend meetings. It would not be allowable for the outsider to pay for this information. But what constitutes payment? A kind word? Flowers? Football tickets?

What constitutes information? Knowledge, for instance, that an important line of credit is being requested from a commercial bank is not inside information. But what if the bank indicates that the request is likely to be honored? What if the bank indicates that the request will be honored in three business days?

Insider trading restrictions have resulted in conflicts of interest. One department of an investment bank may, for instance, be in possession of information concerning a client firm that is relevant for customers of another department of the bank. The bank's fiduciary responsibility to the client firm dictates that the information be kept secret, but the bank's fiduciary responsibility to customers calls for disclosure. Securities firms have attempted to avoid such conflicts of interest by separating various departments by an information barrier known as a *Chinese Wall*. Nevertheless, investment banks at times find themselves in a no-win situation with regard to information that a client is unwilling to make public.

Bloch reports an example:[31] *Slade v. Shearson, Hammill & Co., Inc.* [CCH Fed. Sec. L. Rep. 94,329 (1974)]. The registered representatives of Shearson, Hammill & Co. promoted the stock of Tidal Marine at a time when the investment banking department of the securities firm knew that a large part of Tidal's fleet was damaged. Tidal was unwilling to allow Shearson to divulge the information; a Chinese Wall at Shearson prevented the investment bankers from passing the information on to the registered reps. And Shearson was not allowed to solicit customers without revealing all of the information that the firm had. Shearson, of course, could have stopped trading in the client's stock. However, the very act of not trading would itself have signaled the existence of new information to the market. It appeared that whichever way Shearson could have turned, it would not have fully satisfied the dictates of the law.

Trading based on inside information is difficult to control. In a global environment, trades can be made in countries where restrictions do not exist, and funds can be transferred into and out of foreign banking accounts.[32] The six-month trading restriction can be circumvented by negating a long position in equity shares with an offsetting position in an option written on the stock. These actions are difficult to detect. In addition, an insider can, without restriction, exploit information relating to his or her own firm by trading the equity shares of a competitor, supplier, or customer firm that is also affected by the information.

The arguments both for and against insider trading restrictions are substantial. At the heart of the issue is a market failure—the failure of the free market to achieve an efficient and equitable distribution of resources when the distribution of information among market participants is asymmetric. Longer-term goals are overlooked when undue attention is paid to realizing the quick profits of a trader, and the social cost of insider trading is high, both in terms of fairness and because resources are diverted from more fundamental activities relating to production and investment. On the other hand, the power of the informed traders does keep share prices more closely aligned with the fundamental determinants of corporate value. Furthermore, the complexity of the question is compounded by the fact that government failure is also involved—the problems attributable to informational asymmetries are not well understood, and controlling insider trading is costly.

One way to control insider trading would be to create an environment where the act of trading is diminished in importance. This calls for simplifying the process. Continuous trading systems are dynamically inefficient in the very short run. News is neither instantaneously disseminated nor immediately understood. Consequently, traders respond asynchronously to informational change. Because they do, continuous trading accentuates the importance of minutes and even seconds. This is not always desirable.

THE END OF FIXED COMMISSIONS

The first major government-mandated structural change in the securities industry in the United States was the elimination of the fixed commission structure on May 1, 1975. At the time there was much concern about the effect the change might have. Some people thought it would be disastrous. Today, the deregulation is generally accepted as a success.

Commission income accounted for roughly half of the gross income of member firms of the NYSE in the period 1971 to 1974.[33] As one might expect, broker-dealer firms competed fiercely for this income. Brokerage firms offer a package of services—order handling, record keeping, custodial services, advisory services, dividend collection, and research. In the era of fixed commissions, commission dollars alone typically paid for the entire package. The components other than order handling were in essence a rebate to customers in the form of services rather than in hard dollars.

Therefore, a brokerage firm was able to lower the price it charged for order handling by bundling services (we also refer to the procedure as *commission bundling*). A major ancillary service included in the brokerage package was, and still is, research. The array of research reports may not have been nearly as valuable as direct dollar rebates, but as part of the package the reports were a free good, and as a free good they were accepted.

The Securities Exchange Act of 1934 had exempted the NYSE from certain statutes in the U.S. antitrust legislation, and until the 1975 amendments the exchange had been free, subject to permission from the SEC, to set minimum commission rates on stock transactions.[34] In 1968, the NYSE appealed to the commission for a rate increase. To the exchange's surprise, the U.S. Department of Justice intervened by presenting to the SEC a brief that not only questioned the need for the requested rate increase, but that challenged the very existence of fixed minimum rates.[35] This brief set into motion the events that led to the total elimination of fixed commissions on May 1, 1975.

Three undesirable consequences of the fixed commission structure had become increasingly apparent with the growth of institutional trading:

1. The level of the minimum rates was excessively high (purportedly, the excess portion of commissions in relation to the cost of order handling ranged as high as 90 percent for large orders).[36]

2. The market was being fragmented by large traders turning to regional exchanges and to the third market to escape the fixed commission structure.

3. Ancillary services (research, etc.) were being oversupplied.

After the SEC had opened its investigation of the issue, the burden of proof lay with those who sought to retain the fixed commission structure. The NYSE, as leader of the defense, advanced four main arguments:[37]

1. *Destructive competition in the brokerage industry.* The exchange argued that because of economies of scale in brokerage, more efficient brokerage houses would drive less efficient houses out of business in a fully competitive environment. The elimination of fixed (high) rates would therefore lead to increased concentration in the brokerage industry. According to the exchange, the price of brokerage services would then actually be higher for customers because of the enhanced market power of the large firms.

2. *Price discrimination.* The exchange argued that competitive rate setting would cause the price of brokerage services to be lower for large traders than for small traders because of the greater bargaining power of the institutional traders. Therefore, prices would not be proportionate to costs for traders of different size, and the price discrimination would unfairly disadvantage small investors.

3. *Ancillary brokerage services.* The exchange argued that fixed minimum commissions were required to ensure that certain essential services other than order handling be provided by the brokerage houses. The primary concern expressed by the exchange was that the quantity and quality of research would be impaired if competition were allowed to drive commissions to a level that just covered the cost of order handling.

4. *Market fragmentation.* The exchange argued that fixed minimum commissions were needed to keep the market from fragmenting. Under the fixed commission structure, member firms were given a rate

discount for orders brought to the exchange floor. The NYSE believed that this pricing advantage provided the incentive needed to retain its membership, that without fixed commissions it would lose membership and the order flow would fragment, and that with fragmentation various exchange services such as market surveillance could not be adequately provided.

How valid are these arguments in light of economic theory, the realities of the marketplace, and history? With regard to the first argument, might commission rates ultimately be higher if big firms were allowed to drive weaker firms out of business and then impose noncompetitive prices? This could indeed occur if average costs for a securities firm are negatively related to volume because of economies of scale in brokerage. It was not inappropriate, therefore, for the NYSE to attempt to establish empirically that average costs do fall with firm size in the brokerage industry.

However, what would the advisable economic policy be if economies of scale exist in brokerage? The efficient regulatory solution in such a case would be to allow only a few firms (the biggest and the best) to be the providers of the service and then to regulate those firms. That is, rather than establishing a minimum commission at a high price to ensure the existence of inefficient firms, a maximum commission should be stipulated at a low value to keep the price of brokerage in line with the cost of providing the service. The economies-of-scale argument, therefore, did not support the exchange's case.

Furthermore, the exchange's empirical findings with regard to economies of scale have been challenged by a number of subsequent studies,[38] and, in fact, an alarming increase of concentration did not occur in the brokerage industry in the years after the deregulation in 1975. Firms of varying sizes have coexisted, and specialty firms have found their niche in the industry. According to Tinic and West (1980), there is no evidence that the elimination of fixed rates has enabled larger brokerage firms to improve their relative position in the industry. Let us turn, therefore, to the exchange's second line of defense: the price discrimination argument.

Because the fixed commission structure itself clearly implied price discrimination (against the large traders), price discrimination was a tenuous argument for the exchange to advance. Furthermore, with negotiated rates the price discrimination argument does not hold on theoretical grounds if sufficient competition exists between the brokerage firms. The reason is that, with competitive pricing, prices are set in relation to costs irrespective of demand elasticities in different market segments.

Exhibit 11.1 shows commission rates for selected months from April 1975 through December 1978. Rates did fall appreciably over the period for institutional orders of all sizes and for the larger orders of individual

	0–199		200–999		1,000–9,999		10,000+	
	Cents per share	% of principal	Cents per share	% of principal	Cents per share	% of principal	Cents per share	% of principal
Rates for institutions by order size								
Apr-75	59.60	1.50	45.70	1.28	27.60	0.83	15.00	0.57
June	54.50	1.30	36.80	1.06	21.30	0.63	12.10	0.46
Sept	51.70	1.30	34.50	1.03	20.40	0.59	11.50	0.42
Dec	48.90	1.19	31.90	0.99	18.90	0.57	10.40	0.38
Mar-76	50.30	1.15	33.80	0.94	19.00	0.54	10.80	0.36
June	50.00	1.13	33.40	0.93	19.50	0.53	10.90	0.35
Sept	46.70	1.11	31.10	0.87	18.40	0.50	10.20	0.33
Dec	47.00	1.11	31.20	0.91	17.60	0.51	10.00	0.33
Mar-77	44.30	1.01	28.80	0.83	16.00	0.46	9.80	0.33
June	43.70	1.07	28.10	0.85	15.50	0.47	9.70	0.33
Sept	40.40	1.05	26.10	0.83	14.50	0.46	9.10	0.32
Dec	40.40	1.07	25.40	0.83	14.00	0.45	8.90	0.33
Mar-78	40.20	1.09	25.00	0.84	13.90	0.47	8.10	0.33
June	43.10	1.10	27.00	0.83	14.40	0.44	8.50	0.30
Sept	42.50	1.03	26.90	0.79	14.40	0.43	8.70	0.30
Dec	40.70	1.03	24.50	0.78	13.70	0.44	7.80	0.31
Rates for individuals by order size								
Apr-75	50.10	2.03	32.60	1.86	19.50	1.38	8.80	0.76
June	51.00	2.06	32.30	1.85	19.00	1.33	7.70	0.60
Sept	51.10	2.07	31.30	1.81	17.90	1.24	8.20	0.51
Dec	47.20	2.17	29.10	1.87	16.30	1.26	5.90	0.25
Mar-76	50.70	2.07	32.10	1.85	18.40	1.34	5.90	0.57
June	53.20	1.97	33.20	1.74	18.80	1.22	7.30	0.45
Sept	51.70	2.01	32.70	1.73	18.30	1.18	7.30	0.49
Dec	49.50	2.05	31.60	1.76	17.40	1.19	5.30	0.43
Mar-77	51.40	2.02	32.50	1.76	17.40	1.18	5.60	0.23
June	51.60	2.05	32.70	1.78	17.80	1.15	4.60	0.35
Sept	51.30	2.07	32.40	1.74	17.10	1.06	6.10	0.32
Dec	48.70	2.11	30.80	1.77	16.10	1.09	5.70	0.35

EXHIBIT 11.1 Commission rates, April 1975 through December 1978.

	0–199		200–999		1,000–9,999		10,000+	
	Cents per share	% of prin- cipal	Cents per share	% of prin- cipal	Cents per share	% of prin- cipal	Cents per share	% of prin- cipal
Mar-78	52.50	2.23	33.10	1.86	17.70	1.16	5.40	0.35
June	54.80	2.15	35.00	1.78	19.10	1.15	7.80	0.49
Sept	56.00	2.01	35.10	1.72	19.00	1.12	6.50	0.35
Dec	52.80	2.10	32.70	1.76	17.90	1.10	5.90	0.48

Table from S. Tinic and R. West, "The Securities Industry under Negotiated Broker-age Commissions: Changes in the Structure and Performance of New York Stock Exchange Member Firms," *Bell Journal of Economics and Management Science,* spring 1980.

Original source: *Survey of Commission Charges on Brokerage Transactions,* Office of Securities Industry and Self-Regulatory Economics, Directorate of Economic and Policy Research, Securities and Exchange Commission (July 26, 1979), Tables A-12, A-13, and A-14.

EXHIBIT 11.1   *(Continued)*

traders. Rates for individual orders in the 200- to 999-share range remained essentially stable, however, and rates actually increased for individual orders in the 0- to 199-share range. Is this realignment of the rate structure the con-sequence of differential demand elasticities and price discrimination against small traders? Given the evidence that the brokerage industry is reasonably competitive and that there are economies of scale in order handling,[39] these adjustments are more likely to have been attributable to cost relationships and to the elimination of price discrimination against large traders.

The NYSE's third line of defense focused on the provision of ancillary services. Whether bundled or not, the ancillary services would in theory be provided in optimal amounts in a competitive environment as long as no cause of market failure were operative. A market failure argument is possi-ble, however, because the production and use of one of the services, research, may involve externalities. The reason is that market prices depend on the information set. But the prices in turn signal information to traders and to the firms whose securities are traded, and they may be used for price basing in related markets. Therefore, a decline in the quantity and quality of information production may distort security prices and so be unacceptable to the community in aggregate.

Would a sufficient amount of information be produced as a private good in a free market? Was information being overproduced when commission rates were fixed? These are difficult questions to answer because the empirical evidence is fragmentary and conjectural. All told, however, there is little indication that either the quantity or the quality of research has diminished appreciably with the introduction of negotiated rates. Furthermore, individual investors now have the freedom not to obtain, and not to pay for, research that is not desired. As Tinic and West indicate,[40] "Under fixed rates and the bundling of services, many investors 'consumed' research for which they would not have paid hard cash. If they were now unwilling to buy these services outright, who would want to say that this was bad?" In any event, following the elimination of fixed commissions, something happened that has surprised many observers of the market—as we discuss subsequently, the practice of commission bundling has not ceased.

The exchange's fourth argument, that the elimination of fixed commissions would cause the market to fragment as the exchange lost members, is totally unsupportable. The market fragmentation that gave impetus to the deregulation was in fact attributable to the fixed commissions. That is, rather than holding the exchange's membership together, the umbrella of fixed commissions created unjustifiably high rates that drove institutional orders away from the national exchange markets.

The exchange never did need fixed commissions to hold its membership together. As seen in numerous places throughout this book, order flow attracts order flow and, ceteris paribus, bigger market centers operate more effectively because they are bigger. The NYSE had failed to appreciate this. The exchange lacked confidence that its attractiveness as a market center was due to the orderliness of the markets that it provided. The reality is, the NYSE never needed a fixed commission structure to survive. The Big Board lost neither members nor order flow in the years following the introduction of negotiated commissions.

We now have had more than a quarter of a century of experience with negotiated commissions. As seen in Exhibit 11.1, the deregulation, for the most part, did cause rates to fall appreciably. The changing rate structure has benefited the larger investors and, with the advent of discount brokerage houses, the retail customers as well. By and large, the brokerage industry appears to be competitive, the exchange has not lost membership, and the NYSE's market, over a quarter of a century later, has not fragmented. There is no evidence that the quantity or quality of research has declined, and individual investors are now free to select the package of brokerage services they prefer. The change from fixed to negotiated rates, on many counts, must be deemed successful.[41]

In the early months of 1975, the advent of negotiated rates had caused great concern in the industry. But reasons were not then, and have not since, been advanced that would justify this concern on the basis of the market failure arguments considered earlier in this chapter. Nevertheless, in recent years, competition between various ECNs and ATSs, primarily with regard to trading Nasdaq stocks, have driven commissions to appreciably reduced levels. To a large extent, trading services have been commoditized.

The bad news is that a commoditized environment is not very profitable for the suppliers of trading services. In the face of shrinking profits, one might expect a continuing move to consolidation. Just possibly, after the dust has settled, commissions will start to rise again. Interestingly, this chain of events has overtones of the NYSE's first argument—namely, that unfixing commissions would lead to destructive competition in the brokerage industry. Additionally, a lower commission income induces specialists to intensify their efforts to profit from proprietary trading, a development that puts them in a more adversarial role (rather than facilitator role) vis-à-vis their customers. Thus the regulation, while generally accepted as desirable, is not without its negative, unintended consequences.

ELIMINATION OF OFF-BOARD TRADING RESTRICTIONS

The fixed commission structure was not the only arrangement that caused the exchange markets to appear noncompetitive—there were also off-board trading restrictions.[42] These restrictions, of which the best known was NYSE Rule 390, required member firms to take their orders for listed securities to the floor of an exchange for execution. The exchange regulation forced consolidation of the order flow and limited competition between dealers and market centers.

The debate over off-board trading was far more heated, prolonged, and complex than the deliberations over the elimination of fixed commissions. As of 1975, NYSE Rule 394 prohibited both agency and principal executions away from the exchange floor. After the Securities Acts amendments of 1975, the rule was modified (and its number changed to 390) to allow agency transactions away from the exchange floor. Member firms, however, were still prohibited from participating as principals in off-board trading. This prohibition prevented these brokerage houses from assuming a dealership function and thereby kept them from making their own markets in listed stocks. In 1980, member firms were allowed on an experimental basis to make off-board markets for all issues listed after April 26, 1979. Still, the SEC continued to press for the total elimination of the off-board trading restriction. Finally, the NYSE decided to rescind the rule. On May 5, 2000, the commission approved the exchange's request for a rule change and 390 was gone.

The exchange's off-board trading rule first came under scrutiny in a 1965 SEC confidential staff report. The SEC did not call for repeal of the rule, however, until the commission was charged, by passage of the 1975 amendments, "with an explicit and pervasive obligation to eliminate all . . . competitive restraints that could not be justified by the purposes of the Exchange Act."[43] At the time, the NYSE was considered by many an exclusive club that only the privileged could join, and the exchange's fixed commission structure had recently been found anticompetitive and unjustified. In this context, the off-board trading restrictions appeared to be another anticompetitive barrier that the exchange had erected to protect its narrow self-interest. Consequently, in June 1977, the SEC announced that it would mandate the removal of Rule 390 by the end of the year.

In response, a cry of alarm was sounded by many market participants, certain academicians, and some members of Congress. The expressed fears over removal of the off-board trading restrictions carried far more conviction than the concerns voiced about the end of fixed commissions. It quickly became apparent that the off-board trading issue was not as straightforward as the elimination of fixed commissions. In early December 1977, the SEC postponed the elimination of the rule.

In July 1980, the SEC instituted Rule 19c.3, which freed exchange members to make off-board markets for issues listed on the exchange after April 26, 1979. The day before this rule became effective, the *Wall Street Journal* (July 17, 1980, p. 3) reported that Morgan Stanley and Merrill Lynch had both announced plans to trade in-house what have come to be known as "19c.3 stocks." The article stated that "Most major broker-dealers say they will begin trading listed stocks if competitive pressures make such a move advisable." At the time, it appeared that substantial order flow might be diverted from the exchange markets.

By mid-1983, however, Merrill Lynch, Morgan Stanley, Paine Webber, Goldman Sachs, and virtually all of the other large firms had stopped making markets in 19c.3 stocks. In-house market making is an inherently costly operation because of the considerable amount of financial capital that market making requires. The design of the 19c.3 experiment biased the results because in-house market making in the newly listed 19c.3 stocks was not as profitable as market making in the established volume leaders such as IBM and Exxon might have been. And, in part, the stock exchange specialists simply had more firepower and so won the war: Brokerage houses that competed with the specialists by making in-house markets for 19c.3 stocks might have received unfavorable treatment by the specialists when they turned to the exchange markets to rebalance their inventory positions. Whatever the reason, the experiment did not succeed. The debate concerning the total removal of off-board trading restrictions continued, however.

Although the SEC's 19c.3 experiment failed to increase competition between market makers and did not resolve the consolidation/fragmentation debate, the commission's involvement with the issue was successful in certain respects. To understand this, the following four facts must be recognized:

1. The Securities Acts amendments of 1975 mandated the development of a national market system, but did not say precisely what such a system would be. Rather, the act set forth certain broad goals to be achieved. One of the goals was fair competition among brokers, dealers, and markets. Another was the opportunity for investors' orders to meet without the participation of a dealer.[44] These goals are vague and inconsistent in certain respects. Understandably, the SEC had difficulty achieving them.

2. Furthermore, the SEC had not been involved with the design of the market's architecture before the 1975 amendments. Rather, the commission had historically been responsible for setting rules and procedures to prevent conduct contrary to the public interest and for overseeing and policing the markets. Accordingly, the new design responsibilities assigned to the SEC were not easily carried out by the commission.

3. The design and implementation of a national market system was impeded by the myriad conflicts of interest that prevailed among dealers, specialists, traders, exchange officials, issuing corporations, brokerage houses, self-regulatory groups, and the SEC itself. Thus the SEC was responsible for achieving a vaguely formulated goal in the face of extensive opposition.[45]

4. The legal power to mandate the removal of NYSE Rule 390 gave the commission considerable control over the NYSE and various other groups in the industry. Whether by intention or by luck, the commission's most successful move following the 1975 amendments was to threaten, but not to put into effect, the total removal of the off-board trading restrictions.

Thus the commission used its authority to remove Rule 390 to get the industry to move itself forward. The threat, made credible by the recent elimination of fixed commissions, worked. The exchanges opened their doors to new members, the clublike atmosphere of the NYSE has largely disappeared, and an intermarket linkage system (ITS) was put in place. But NYSE Rule 390, though diminished, continued to stand.

The experience with off-board trading has been very different from the experience with fixed commissions. Rate fixing was widely viewed as anticompetitive and undesirable, but off-board trading restrictions appear to have some justification. Wherein lies the difference?

As noted, there are externalities in trading, and there are public goods aspects to market making. Traders benefit from a market in which orders are consolidated, trading priority rules are enforced, prices are set with reasonable accuracy, price movements are kept orderly, and trading is closely monitored. The superiority of such a market may not, however, guarantee its existence. The reason is that traders individually may have an incentive to turn to off-board markets.

An off-board market can compete with a national exchange by guaranteeing timely executions at competitive prices. Furthermore, because it does not assume the affirmative obligation to make a fair and orderly market, and because it does not provide the stock watch, market surveillance, and other services of an exchange, an off-board market may charge lower commissions than the exchange market. Assume this to be the case and that, consequently, an appreciable part of the order flow is diverted from a major market center. What might then ensue?

Price discovery on the exchange could become less accurate, and the investor protection provided by the exchange's stock watch and surveillance systems could deteriorate. In addition, spreads might increase and prices could become more volatile because of the reduced order flow. These changes would in turn cause the exchange to be a less desirable trading arena; accordingly, the order flow to the exchange could decrease further, and the output of exchange services could be further impaired. In such an event, the quality of the in-house markets would also suffer. Consequently, the detrimental effects would be widely felt. Nevertheless, the prospect of this occurring would not be taken into account by investors when making their individual trading decisions. This is because of the externalities and the public goods aspects of market making that are involved.

To date, however, the NYSE's market has not fragmented. In 1999, the year before Rule 390 was removed, 82.47 percent of the share volume for NYSE-listed securities and 72.74 percent of the trades were on the exchange. In 2001, the first full year without the order consolidation rule, trading was even more concentrated on the Big Board: The NYSE captured 84.01 of the share volume and 84.61 percent of the trades.[46]

But the jury is still out on this one. In June 2003, Nasdaq reported that its market share of volume and of trades were 67.5 percent and 54.4 percent, respectively.[47] Two ECNs, Instinet and Archipelago, are now accounting for roughly 40 percent of the volume for Nasdaq shares, and Nasdaq's SuperMontage is doing 17 percent.[48] The electronic markets could also start to make inroads into the NYSE market.

TRADE–THROUGH RULE

In the United States, a trade-through rule that applies to the listed market but not the Nasdaq market requires that trades be made at the best posted bids or offers. Actually, it should be called the "no trade-through rule." If, for example, a bid of $45.10 has been entered, a sell order should not circumvent that bid and execute at $45.09 or less, because doing so would "trade through" the $45.10 bid. If a trade-through occurs and the injured customer complains, he or she must be compensated for the monetary loss.

The SEC, in what is shaping up to be a major market structure initiative, is currently reconsidering its trade-through rule for the listed market, a move that is commonly perceived to threaten the Big Board's dominance. The change proposed by the SEC is that fast, computerized marketplaces would not be allowed to trade through each others' orders, but that prices set by slower, floor-based markets could be traded through. This pressures the NYSE to become a fast market quickly in order to save trade-through, and the exchange is responding by beefing up its Direct+ facility (an ECN-like service).

A beefed up Direct+ would effectively make the exchange both a fast and a slow market. The NYSE argues for the benefits of such a hybrid structure, and—if the gambit works—may thereby be able to preserve trade-through protection for its market. In addition to these initiatives on the listed side, the commission might also impose a trade-through rule for the Nasdaq market to avoid appearing inconsistent. What is good public policy regarding the issue?

Essentially, disallowing trade-throughs is equivalent to imposing price priorities across all markets that a stock trades in. In the abstract, price priority is desirable. If a market order to sell can execute at $45.09 at a time when a buy limit order has established the best bid at $45.10, the participant who placed the limit order at $45.10 faces a greater risk of not executing. Thus trade-throughs discourage the placement of limit orders. They also disadvantage any retail customer who, while more than likely not knowing it, has received an inferior execution. Recognizing this, order-driven trading venues typically impose a price priority rule for their own market (and often a time priority rule as well).

The thorny issue about the trade-through rule involves its application across markets in a fragmented environment. The immediate problem is that price is not the only dimension of a trade, and an investor (particularly a large institutional customer) might have a good reason other than price for preferring one market over another. As we discuss in Chapter 5, "Institutional Order Flow," the big players commonly slice and dice their orders, and submit the pieces to the market over a protracted period of time. Ultimately, the price paid or received for the entire package matters most; the price for each individual tranche does not. A large trader may be willing to "pay up" to execute a large order quickly before others see his or her footprints in the market and front-run the remaining parts of the order. If the individual pieces cannot be executed quickly, with certainty, under the institutional trader's control, and with anonymity, a worse price might be realized for the entire order.

Currently, much attention is being paid to the distinction between floor-based markets such as the NYSE, which offer order handling by human intermediaries, and electronic, ECN-type markets, which offer speed, certainty of execution, control, and anonymity. The floor-based markets are known as *slow markets*, and the electronic venues are *fast markets*. Should regulation, in some way or other, consolidate the slow and fast markets? Not allowing trade-throughs implicitly does this. Unfortunately, the obligation to satisfy a quote posted in a slow market can slow down the swift operations of the fast markets.

Perhaps a customer is willing to sell shares at a few cents less (or buy shares at a few cents more) in an electronic market that offers speed, certainty of execution, control, and anonymity. Should this not be allowed? At this point, the resolution of this dilemma is pushing the Big Board to be both types of markets (a hybrid) in order to preserve trade-through protection for its marketplace. Whether or not this strategy will work, another issue is potentially being overlooked in the give-and-take of the SEC's comment period.

That is, as noted in various places in this book, price discovery is a major function of a market center. However, imposing strict price priorities across markets effectively prevents markets from competing with each other in terms of price discovery. There is irony in this. The flip side of U.S. public regulatory policy that has promoted competition is U.S. market fragmentation. The regulators have thought that intermarket linkages (e.g., the Intermarket Trading System, ITS) along with the trade-through rule counter the undesirable effects of fragmentation, but the trade-through rule itself undermines intermarket competition: How effective is price discovery competition between competitors who are required by rule to arrive at the same price?

What consequences would elimination of the trade-through rule have for the NYSE? As we explain subsequently, commission bundling and its companion, soft-dollar payments, have thus far helped the NYSE retain its order flow. Many, including the exchange, believe that the trade-through rule is also achieving something that the Big Board's former order-focusing rule (Rule 390) was designed to do—prevent internalization (the in-house execution of orders) and help keep order flow consolidated at the exchange. If the rule is eliminated, will the NYSE, as we know it, cease to be?

Other dire predictions of doom for the Big Board have not come to pass. The exchange's days were thought to be numbered following the elimination of fixed commissions in 1975 and after the removal of Rule 390 in 2000, but the NYSE is still receiving roughly 80 percent of the order flow. Nevertheless, as of this writing, the possible elimination of the trade-through rule is being taken very seriously, as it should be, by those concerned with the exchange's survival. Yet some believe that the exchange can fare perfectly well without the rule. Perhaps it will, just as long as the Big Board makes the right competitive decisions.

While fighting the removal of the trade-through rule in Washington, the exchange, as mentioned previously, has also been beefing up its own electronic trade execution system, Direct+. It is doing so expecting that the new regulations will allow fast markets to trade through slow markets but not other fast markets and that a beefed up Direct+ will qualify the Big Board as a fast market. Whether or not this tactic works to preserve the rule, it is not without risk even if it does succeed. If Direct+ attracts enough order flow away from the floor, the exchange could undermine its own slow market, the floor could collapse, and the NYSE could turn itself into an ECN.

The NYSE has kept its order flow in part because it has had so much of it to begin with. All else being equal, a larger market is more attractive to investors simply because it is large, and it is indeed difficult for a competing venue to attract orders from an established market center. But "order flow attracting order flow" is a two-edged sword. Once a major market center starts to lose it, it can enter a doom loop and the decline can accelerate into a rout as volume tips to its comptitors.

For some, maintaining the NYSE and its trading floor is a compelling reason for retaining the trade-through rule. For others, energizing competition is a compelling reason for eliminating the rule. Faced with this trade-off, we suggest the following. The underlying problem is not the trade-through rule itself—it is the fact that our markets are fragmented. The problem of fragmentation would best be resolved by the interplay of competitive forces in the marketplace, including a market's right to compete by the quality of price discovery that it offers. A freer, more competitive environment might induce the Big Board to further innovate and strengthen its market. Electronic call auctions, for instance, could help the exchange retain order flow in the face of competition from the fast markets. The electronic calls, because they would be held at specific points in time, would not risk tripping up the operations of the trading floor as might a continuous electronic transaction facility.

Any government-imposed trade-through rule will be complex—difficult issues to be addressed include operationalizing the distinction between fast markets and slow markets and assessing the advisability of having an order-by-order opt-out rule and/or a trade-through exemption with an appropriate de minimis provision. Any proposal will be hotly debated—the profitability of major sell side players depends on just how the legislation is crafted, and the major U.S. exchanges believe that the rule's elimination could result in their losing substantial order flow. On the plus side, rescinding the rule would tone down government involvement in the design of our markets, an unintended consequence that could possibly be quite desirable.

BEST EXECUTION

Best execution has been a holy grail in the United States since the enactment of the U.S. Congressional Securities Acts amendments in 1975. In mandating the development of a National Market System, the 1975 amendments stated, as a goal, that investors' orders be provided the opportunity to be executed, consistent with efficiency and *best execution*, without the participation of a dealer.

At the time the amendments were passed, institutional participation was far less than it is today, and the best-execution requirement was fashioned primarily with regard to retail order flow. Currently, however, attention has turned to institutional investors, a group for whom the requirement is appreciably more difficult to fulfill. As a consequence of the greater difficulty of specifying best-execution criteria for large orders, the concept of best execution, for institutional investors, is now being applied more to the efficiency of investment/trading *procedures*, than to the costs, per se, of specific transactions (as we discuss in further detail in Chapter 5, "Institutional Order Flow").

Increased attention is also being given to transaction cost analysis in the European arena, and best execution has gained attention on both sides of the Atlantic. In London, publication of the *Myners Report* in March 2001 lead to a protracted debate about (1) whether traditional fund management contracts give managers adequate incentives to minimize transaction costs, and (2), if not, what to do about it.[49]

What does the term *best execution* mean? The U.S. Congressional act did not say, and a widely accepted empirical definition has not since been developed. As discussed in Chapter 5, "Institutional Order Flow," the problem is multifaceted. First, market impact costs and opportunity costs are virtually impossible to measure with any kind of precision on a trade-by-trade basis.[50] Second, good benchmarks for assessing trading performance are difficult to define. Additionally, different kinds of orders require differential handling, depending on the needs of a trader, the size of an order, and the liquidity of the market for the shares being traded. In other words, the execution that is best depends on the particulars of the specific case at hand. Further, how does one measure best execution for orders that are broken into smaller pieces for execution over an extended period of time? And how does one specify a common set of best-execution procedures to apply to a broad, diverse population of participants?

The ambiguities involved in assessing trades with regard to best-execution criteria have not discouraged regulatory authorities from pursuing the objective in an attempt to ensure quality executions for public participants. Recently, the Financial Services Authority (FSA) in the United Kingdom released a discussion paper that reviews policy and invites public comments on the matter.[51] The document presents a broad array of questions concerning the implementation of a best-execution requirement.

Our own discussion of best-execution in Chapter 5 is focused largely on the impracticality of applying the criterion to institutional trades. Interestingly, the FSA (much as the Securities and Exchange Commission in the United States) is primarily focused on best execution as a "consumer protection tool," where the consumer is a retail customer. Accordingly, the assessment of best execution, for the most part, fits into the snapshot approach that we discussed in the earlier chapter. Namely, best execution is judged by matching a transaction price against other prices that exist at the time a trade is made.[52] Overlooked in the snapshot is the timing of order placement, including the submission of institutional orders in smaller tranches over extended periods of time.

Although a focus on the retail customer is understandable, best-execution criteria are applied to all trades. Indeed, it would present another level of complexity to stipulate just what trades are and what trades are not, subject to a best-execution requirement. Consequently, if best-execution criteria are not implementable for institutional orders, one might question the advisability of imposing the requirement for any orders. A reasonable alternative may simply be for firms to disclose to their customers the procedures they follow when placing their orders (this is suggested in the FSA's discussion paper) and to let competition take care of the rest. This thought is also echoed in the United States by a report on best execution by the Association for Investment Management and Research (AIMR).

The AIMR report was issued in November 2001. In the introduction, the report states, "Therefore, it is not feasible to define a single measurement basis for best execution on a trade-by-trade basis. Instead, the Guidelines focus on establishing processes, disclosures, and documentation, which together form a systematic, repeatable, and demonstrable approach to show that best execution compliance is consistent and effective."[53] The Investment Company Institute (ICI), in its comment on the AIMR report, puts this more strongly: "We recommend that the (AIMR) Guidelines clarify that best execution is not a quantifiable concept and that statistical measurements can be only one part of the overall assessment that firms may make in examining best execution."[54]

In assessing best execution, U.K. regulatory authorities give primary importance to the prices at which trades are made. Next in line is the time-liness of trades.[55] In Annex B of its discussion paper, the FSA presents brief summary statements about best execution from regulators in 13 different countries.[56] Of the 13 summaries, 5 include explicit reference to the time dimension.[57]

The regulators' focus on timeliness may be consistent with their focus on retail customers, but institutional participants commonly work their orders patiently in an attempt to get better prices.[58] In the United States, the AIMR report listed, in addition to the proper control of trading costs, that "firms need to (1) determine client trading requirements; (2) select appropriate trad-ing techniques, venues, and agents; (3) control the pace of liquidity search to avoid excessive market impact; (4) protect the interests of the clients and the proprietary information of decisions made by investment managers; and (5) monitor the results on a continuing and periodic review basis."[59]

As noted, the practice of patient order timing is not comprehended in a snapshot assessment of best execution.[60] The FSA, as reflected in the fol-lowing quote from its discussion paper, recognized this point in the context of its discussion of intraday liquidity variations:

> *At certain times of the day, dealing volumes may be low and wide spreads (the difference between buying and selling prices) may appear. At such times, it could be advantageous not to deal. However, the private customer may not be sufficiently well informed and in this case, the best execution rule (for example, the SETS price in the case of the UK equity market) does not provide any protection. Indeed, the SETS minimum could be a sanction for a poor price (even if that price were the best available at that time). This problem is most pronounced at the market open . . .*

We would amend the statement to refer more broadly to price discovery rather than to the bid-ask spread (which, of course, may also be viewed as a relevant factor).

Our final comment about a regulatory authority imposing a best-execution requirement is that the quality of executions achieved very much depends not just on the order placement decisions of individuals, but on the efficiency of the marketplace in which the individual participants are operating.[61] At the extreme, if a market becomes hypercontinuous under stressful conditions, best execution for an individual becomes a vacuous concept.[62] More generally, we suggest that the regulators focus, not on the handling of individual orders per se, but on the quality of prices discovered for the broad market as orders are aggregated and turned into trades.

COMMISSION BUNDLING

We next turn to *commission bundling*, a topic also discussed in Chapter 5, "Institutional Order Flow."[63] A major regulatory conundrum, the practice leads to buy side trading underperformance and has critical consequences for the quality of our markets. What should the regulatory authorities do about it? The matter is far from simple, and thus far no major action has been taken.

The heart of the buy side underperformance problem is the outsourcing by an asset manager of research, computer systems, and other support services to the sell side, with client assets used as payment. A fund management firm that provides such services internally or that makes explicit payments to third parties for them must bear the cost from its own capital and charge a management fee that makes the cost explicit to investors. Rather than doing this, a management firm has an incentive to outsource services in a manner that keeps the cost unobservable to investors.

The procedure works as follows. The fund manager pays hard-dollar commissions for trading serves and receives a soft-dollar rebate in return. The rebate is in the form of services and products that are not related to trading per se (e.g., research and computer systems). The procedure is opaque, and it necessarily involves broker-dealers in trading, not because they provide trading services that are desired in their own right, but because they are part of a system of invisibly transferring operating costs from the fund manager to the fund holder.

Obscuring the source of a fund's research through commission bundling is costly. The explicit dollar cost gap between traditional institutional brokerage and nonintermediated electronic trading is significant. Moreover, keeping intermediaries in the trading process can unnecessarily generate higher market-impact costs associated with a heightened demand for immediacy. The traditional explanation for immediacy demand (i.e., the opportunity cost of failing to trade ahead of an anticipated market move) is overstated. Rather, the buy side's demand for immediacy is in appreciable part endogenous to an intermediated environment that is characterized by front running.

Clients are unable to discipline commission bundling through performance monitoring because the damage to fund performance attributable to commission bundling is very difficult for fund holders to detect. Investors instead focus on ex ante information such as investment strategy and explicit costs. The common use of the volume weighted average price (VWAP) as a benchmark, because it can lead to trading inefficiencies and to trading costs being understated, also serves to support the practice of commission bundling.

Commission bundling works only in an environment where commissions are used to pay for trading services. Commissions are a standard means of payment in order-driven (agency) markets such as the New York Stock Exchange. In contrast, trades are made on a *net* basis in quote-driven (dealer) markets. That is, customers buy at the offer and sell at the bid, and the market maker's revenue is not commissions but the bid-ask spread. Interestingly, in the United States, an appreciable part of the order flow for Nasdaq stocks is now going to the ECNs, while, to date, these electronic markets have not made major inroads into the NYSE market. Neuberger, with a transatlantic perspective, stated, "Others have noted that low cost transaction systems have failed to get a large market share despite substantial apparent cost advantage (particularly true in Europe, but also to some extent in the United States). This suggests, they argue, that the investment managers may not have strong incentives to minimize trading costs."[64]

The drive of traders to reduce transaction costs is an important determinant of the quality of markets. Commission bundling weakens that drive. It does so for the obvious reason that trades are directed to brokers and to markets, not with sole reference to the most cost-effective way to handle a trade, but also because of the soft-dollar rebates obtained. Consequently, transaction costs are higher, but the higher costs are generally not observed by clients (market-impact costs in particular are very difficult to measure). Payments for the services that have been "softed" are also not visible to the client, and neither are the services that the agent has acquired. Consequently, many students of the market view soft-dollar payments with considerable discomfort.

Aronson of Aronson + Johnson + Ortiz had some words to say about soft-dollar practices at a Baruch College conference on April 29, 2003. While thinking back to the enactment of the 1975 Securities Acts amendments that precluded the return to fixed commission in the United States, he commented, "If you had told me at the time that twenty-eight years later we would have a soft-dollar industry that by various estimates is in the billions of dollars (those are hard dollars, not soft dollars) I would have bet you big money that you would be wrong. But, boy oh boy, was I wrong."[65] At the time the 1975 amendments were enacted, many observers attributed soft-dollar payments to commissions having been fixed at a level that was unrealistically high for large institutional trades. It was expected that the soft-dollar rebates would end under negotiated commissions. But the practice has remained in force. History has shown that more is involved.

What is going on? The difficulty a client faces in assessing the trading efficiency of a fund manager is a classical principal-agent problem. The ideal solution to the principal-agent problem is to design a contract between the fund manager and the client that gives the fund manager the proper incentive to minimize transaction costs for the client. Unfortunately, it is not clear how to accomplish this. As we have stressed, costs are very hard to measure, and the information required for performance monitoring is difficult if not impossible to get.

Brealey and Neuberger have analyzed the problem. One solution, they note, would be to relate the management fee to a fund's performance. But they further point out that the problem would then be that excessive risk would be shifted from the client to the manager. Another solution has been proposed by the Myners report—the management firm should charge a higher fee, but it, not the client, must pay the commissions. Brealey and Neuberger argue, however, that this can lead the manager to trade for the purpose of reducing commission costs but in a way that results in higher implicit execution costs.

As Neuberger has stated, "No contractual form is perfect. All contracts involve trade-offs."[66] We are left with the conclusion that the free market will not eliminate a practice (bundled commissions) that can undermine market efficiency. Recognizing this, some have recommended that government regulation disallow soft-dollar payments. But the regulatory intervention itself could have undesirable consequences. Ultimately, a more pleasing solution would be for plan sponsors (the clients) to understand more fully the negative impact that transaction costs have on fund performance and to demand better order handling. Not surprisingly, ignorance is at the heart of the principal-agent problem.

DEMUTUALIZATION

Exchanges have historically been organized as mutual organizations that are run on a nonprofit basis for the benefit of their members. Alternatively, an exchange can demutualize and be run on a for-profit basis for the benefit of shareholders. The members of a nonprofit organization can differ from the shareholders of a for-profit exchange, and the difference in organization structure has major implications for the efficiency of exchange operations and regulation.

A membership organization's objective is to increase the value of access privileges, which is reflected in the price of a seat. An equity-based, profit-maximizing firm's objective is to increase the price of its equity shares. With computer technology having made disintermediation possible, the difference between the two organizational objectives is critical. New technology that may increase the efficiency of a market center and its share value if the market center is equity-based can decrease the value of access privileges and the price of a seat if the market center is a membership organization. Consequently, some socially desirable innovations are more apt to be made by an equity-based organization that is more responsive to the needs of the ultimate customers (the natural buyers and sellers) than by a membership organization, which is responsive primarily to the needs of its broker-dealer members.

The first exchange to demutualize, the Stockholm Stock Exchange, incorporated as a for-profit company in January 1993. Steil had this to say about the change:[67]

> To give you an idea of how far Stockholm has come, that exchange was on its deathbed in 1991. But now it is a thriving international company and, having been absorbed by OM (the Swedish derivatives exchange operator and technology company) they have thousands of shareholders. It is itself listed on the Stockholm Stock Exchange. Foreigners own over a quarter of the shares. It has a market cap of about two billion dollars, and could easily be bought out tomorrow by a Reuters, or an IBM. If that isn't a strong incentive for producing efficient markets, I don't know what is.
>
> The share price of the Exchange went up over seven-fold within the first two years of operation. It is a remarkable success story. They knew that their future did not lie with the current members of the exchange, but with investors around the world. They were the first exchange in Europe to allow direct electronic access for institutional investors.

Following Stockholm's successful change of its governance structure, many other exchanges have followed suit. The Australia Stock Exchange, Euronext, the Toronto Stock Exchange, the London Stock Exchange, Deutsche Börse, and the International Securities Exchange, among others, are all equity-based. Nasdaq is equity-based, but, thus far, a commanding number of its shares are still being held by its parent company, the NASD. Exchanges moving toward the demutualized model include the Chicago Board Options Exchange, the Chicago Board of Trade, the Swiss Exchange, and the Tokyo Stock Exchange. The alternative electronic markets (ATSs and ECNs) are privately owned business firms, not membership organizations. In the summer of 1999, Richard Grasso, who at the time was CEO of the NYSE, stated that, by the next Thanksgiving, the Big Board would demutualize. But it never did. Was the exchange wise to have retained its membership structure?

The for-profit model has a clear advantage with regard to the problem of technological inertia. The members in a membership organization are the broker-dealer intermediaries who have traditionally been at the center of the market. As we have noted, this constituency understandably resists any technology innovation that would disintermediate them out of trading. The for-profit organizations are freed from this impediment. And they are better able to raise capital, to form alliances, and to make acquisitions without resistance from members.

On the other hand, a few questions can also be raised about the for-profit structure. Doubts have been expressed about the incentive of an equity-based, for-profit organization to perform as effectively the self-regulatory obligations that membership organizations have traditionally shouldered. One could further question the relative efficiencies of the for-profit and the demutualized organizations with regard to issues such as the development of network externalities and the provision of public goods–type services. Unfortunately, unambiguous answers are not readily obtained.

Ultimately, the selection of exchange governance structure should depend on the function that a market center wishes to perform. The operations of demutualized exchanges are centered on disintermediated, electronic trading platforms. Nasdaq, in moving toward a demutualized structure, has distanced itself somewhat from its dealer community and, in so doing, has focused attention on its own electronic platform, SuperMontage. Demutualization of the London Stock Exchange likewise went hand in glove with the introduction of London's electronic platform, SETS. With this in mind, let us return to the NYSE and consider the Big Board's business model.

The NYSE provides infrastructure. It has developed major electronic equipment for order handling and information dissemination, but does not base its operations on an electronic trade execution platform. Independent broker-dealer and specialist firms on the trading floor handle the orders and turn them into trades. The exchange is also heavily involved in self-regulatory activities. These two items—SRO operations and the trading floor—have given the NYSE its distinctive brand. Both are natural functions of a membership organization. Without a floor, the NYSE would not need members. Without members, its extensive surveillance operations would take on less importance and/or could be outsourced and/or could be turned over to a government regulator. Despite all the obvious positives, demutualization could have serious implications for the NYSE. It could cause the exchange to lose its brand and its dominance.

In the United States, the coexistence of demutualized organizations (e.g., the ATSs and ECNs) and membership organizations (e.g., the NYSE) has created another regulatory quandary. The registered exchanges and

Nasdaq (which has applied for exchange registration) are required to carry out and to pay for SRO operations while for-profit markets that are not registered as exchanges are not. The distribution of the financial burden across the different trading venues is strikingly uneven: In 2002, SRO operations cost the NYSE $120 million. That same year, Nasdaq paid the NASD $70 million for regulation.[68]

Some recompense may be found in the allocation of the tape revenue received from the sale of trade information. The revenue is distributed across markets according to the each market's proportionate shares of total trading activity. Thus, market centers that shoulder the bulk of the regulatory burden are the major recipients of the tape revenue. However, the amount to charge for market data is its own regulatory conundrum, and coupling tape revenue with the payment for SRO operations is of questionable merit.

CAVEATS FOR PUBLIC POLICY

The health of its equity markets is critically important to a nation. Economic growth depends on the ability of firms to obtain financial capital at reasonable cost, and the cost of equity capital depends on market quality. The collapse of a market under stress can have dire consequences for a national economy. For these reasons, issues concerning equity market operations and best execution have attracted considerable government attention in the U.S. and European arenas.

As long as there have been exchanges, participants have been concerned about market quality issues such as transparency, fragmentation, liquidity, price volatility, and trading costs. Also of major importance are principal-agent issues, technological inertia, price manipulation, and other abuses of power and position. However, our overriding focus in this chapter is not on the specific issues themselves, but on the role a government regulator should play with regard to them. Should markets, with all of their imperfections, be left free to evolve naturally, or should a government agency participate in designing market structure and in writing the rule book?

Regulation may be called for if an unregulated market would fail to achieve an optimal distribution of resources at appropriate prices. The rules of a market system must be set collectively by the body politic. The causes of market failure for the equity markets include the market power of some traders, dealers, and market centers; externalities; the public goods aspects of marketability services; principal-agent relationships and informational asymmetries; transaction price uncertainty; and technological inertia.

Following the enactment of the 1975 Security Act amendments, government has played an important role in the evolution of the markets. First and foremost, the regulatory authorities and the industry's own self-regulatory organizations (SROs) have sought to ensure an honest market. In addition, in the United States, starting in the 1970s, Congress and the SEC have been concerned with the competitive efficiency of the market for broker-dealer services. Some attention has also been given (primarily by the SROs) to the accuracy of the share prices being set in the market centers. Price discovery is a difficult goal to comprehend and to implement, however, and it has received insufficient attention in the debates concerning the design of trading systems.

Government involvement with market design has raised many questions. We share the concerns. Market architecture is highly complex. There is a lot involved that students of the market do not understand or agree about. The very measurements of market quality and best execution are subject to ambiguity. Market structure changes commonly have unintended consequences, especially in a rapidly evolving technological environment. And when a government-mandated structural change goes awry, government recognition, understanding, and appropriate corrective action, if ever taken, may not be forthcoming for years. It is far better to let alternative markets make their own decisions, reap their rewards, and accept the consequences of their mistakes as they battle for order flow in a competitive environment.

Is government intervention required to ensure sufficient competition in the industry, and how competitive is the current environment? On the one hand, we see technology innovation expanding the geographic reach of trading facilities, and increasingly, competition is taking place in a global environment. We also see the arrival of new firms and new trading modalities in the United States and Europe. On the other hand, major resistance to technological change persists, meaningful innovations are rare and far between, and the obstacles faced by a technology pioneer are daunting.

Because of network externalities, nothing is more important for the quality of a market than whether or not that market receives order flow. Consequently, it is extraordinarily difficult for a new entrant to put competitive pressure on an already established market, especially if the new entrant offers independent price discovery. Regardless of its inherent efficiency, a newcomer simply may not get the order flow required for its potential to be realized. This being the case, the established market has a weakened incentive to innovate and is more apt to follow the dictates of vested interests.

In conclusion, the vibrancy of competition and the ineffectiveness of competition combine to make good public policy extremely difficult to formulate. We advise minimal governmental intervention with regard to market architecture. For those who would like to see government play a more active role, we offer the following seven caveats.

1. Government agencies like to monitor that which they regulate. This leads to particular attention being given to performance characteristics that can easily be measured. Consequently, too much attention is given to readily observable aspects of market quality (such as bid-ask spreads), and insufficient attention is directed to more amorphous matters (such as the accuracy of price discovery).

2. Antitrust regulation has a well-established history in the United States with regard to markets in general and the securities industry in particular. From the unfixing of commissions and the elimination of off-board trading restrictions, to the implicit collusion lawsuit and decimalization, the U.S. regulatory authorities have been very concerned about the exercise of monopoly power. But there are counter-arguments that should also be paid attention to:
   - Security markets are natural monopolies because of strong network externalities in trading.
   - Countering the power of a network is the ability of a satellite market to free-ride on the prices established in a major market center.
   - Commissions and bid-ask spreads are only two components of transaction costs; market impact costs and errors in price discovery are likely of far greater importance. These factors should not be ignored simply because they are difficult to measure.

3. Eight exchanges in Europe have harmonized certain key features of their market structures. It is indeed desirable to synchronize various design features across different market centers. However, it is hazardous for a government agency to *mandate* structural change, especially across multiple markets. As noted, a mandated design feature is not easily withdrawn if it is found to be undesirable. A regulatory authority will commonly point elsewhere and try to fix the problem with further regulations. An unfortunate consequence is that, once government involvement in market design starts, the process tends to become self-perpetuating. Some U.S. observers believe that this has been happening in the United States. To date, the European governments have taken a less proactive role, and, thus far, there is no SEC of Europe.

4. With regard to fostering greater competition, considerable regulatory attention is commonly given to fairness. Under the rubric of fairness, it is argued that participants should have equal access to markets, that the playing field should be level, that markets should be transparent, and so forth. Unfortunately, all participants are not equal, and free mar-

kets are not necessarily fair.[69] Furthermore, all too often, a market that itself is being threatened by competitive pressure uses the fairness argument. Rather than strengthening its own efficiency, the beleaguered player seeks protection through regulatory intervention.

5. When the benefits of competition are extolled, the reference should be to competition in the marketplace. Unfortunately, competition also has a second forum. The market structure rules that are mandated, approved, or denied by a government body are a major determinant of who wins and who loses in the marketplace. Consequently, as regulatory involvement in rule making expands, competition grows fierce in the halls of government. In the United States, appreciable resources in the form of time and money have been devoted to swaying the decision makers in Washington in situations where clear answers do not exist. This, in the eyes of some, is unfortunate.

6. Vested interests and technological inertia exist. To these, we add a third: The regulatory process can also stymie innovation. In a competitive environment, innovations need to be made in a timely manner, but obtaining necessary regulatory approvals is typically a lengthy process. Furthermore, the power to deny change conveys the power to dictate change.

7. Our final caveat is that it is important not to loose faith in the efficacy of free market competition. As equity markets on both sides of the Atlantic continue to evolve, it is the force of competition, not the intervention of government, that should be depended on to induce markets to provide an environment that will make best execution more readily achievable for all.

NOTES

1. Paul Schreiber and Robert A. Schwartz, "Price Discovery in Securities Markets," *Journal of Portfolio Management*, summer 1986, pp. 43–48.

2. A broker who is an exchange member must serve as intermediary.

3. We discuss these developments in further detail in Chapter 8, "The Evolving Scene in the United States."

4. Gregory Bresiger, "SEC at Market Structure Crossroad," *Traders Magazine*, June 2003.

5. The typewriter analogy was suggested by Seymour Smidt. My thanks to Gautam Vora for calling my attention to the Dvorak keyboard.

6. People just learning to type are also younger (on average) than those already acquainted with the existing system and hence have more years to benefit from their knowledge (which increases their return on the investment).

7. See E. Bloch and R. Schwartz, eds., *Impending Changes for Securities Markets: What Role for the Exchange?* Greenwich, CT: JAI Press, 1979, p. 107.

8. A. Allen and L. Zarembo, "The Displaybook: The NYSE Specialist's Electronic Workstation," in H. Lucas and R. Schwartz, eds., *The Challenge of Information Technology for the Securities Markets: Liquidity, Volatility and Global Trading*, Homewood, IL: Dow Jones-Irwin, 1989.

9. E. Clemons and B. Weber, "London's Big Bang: A Case Study of Information Technology, Competitive Impact, and Organizational Change," *Journal of Management Information Systems*, spring 1990.

10. The use of electronic equipment for order routing and information display, on the other hand, is partial, not comprehensive change, and market professionals have had far less difficulty in accepting and adapting to this change.

11. See G. Stigler, "The Theory of Economic Regulation," *Bell Journal of Economics and Management Science*, spring 1971, for further discussion.

12. See D. Scarff, "The Securities and Commodities Markets: A Case Study in Product Convergence and Regulatory Disparity," in Amihud, Ho, and Schwartz, eds., *Market Making and the Changing Structure of the Securities Industry*, Lexington, MA: Lexington Books, 1985.

13. See E. Bloch, "Multiple Regulators: Their Constituencies and Policies," in Amihud, Ho, and Schwartz, 1985, op. cit.

14. Case material contained in this section draws on T. Dunfee, F. Gibson, J. Blackburn, D. Whitman, F. McCarty, and B. Brennan, *Modern Business Law*, New York: Random House, 1984; and D. Whitman and J. Gergacz, *The Legal and Social Environment of Business*, New York: Random House, 1985.

15. For instance, J. Jaffe, "The Effect of Regulation Changes on Insider Trading," *Bell Journal of Economics and Management Science*, spring 1974a; J. Jaffe, "Special Information and Insider Trading," *Journal of Business*, July 1, 1974b; J. Finnerty, "Insiders and Market Efficiency," *Journal of Finance*, September 1976; and D. Givoly and D. Palmon, "Insider Trading and the Exploitation of Inside Information: Some Empirical Evidence," *Journal of Business*, January 1985.

16. *Wall Street Journal*, November 17, 1986, p. 28.

17. 401 F.2d 833 (2d Circuit, 1968).

18. Interestingly, the standard of business behavior imposed on the securities transactions differed from that imposed on the purchase of land surrounding the site of the ore discovery. Texas Gulf Sulphur was free to purchase the land without any obligation to release information about the discovery.

19. Cady Roberts & Co., 40 S.E.C. 907 (1961).

20. *Chiarella v. U.S.*, 45 U.S. 222 (1980).

21. Statements by Justice Powell; see T. Dunfee, F. Gibson, J. Blackburn, D. Whitman, F. McCarty, and B. Brennan, op. cit.

22. *Dirks v. Securities and Exchange Commission*, U.S. Supreme Court 103 S. Ct. 3255 (1983).

23. A tip given to a relative or friend may also constitute an unjustified exploitation of nonpublic information. The court would view an insider who makes a gift of confidential information to a family member or friend as equivalent to the insider's trading personally on the information and then making a gift of the profits to the family member or friend.

24. Sterngold, "Wall Street's Army of Insiders," *New York Times*, May 18, 1986, section 3, p. 1.

25. Sterngold continued (p. 8), "At each company involved, the chief executive and his most trusted advisers usually know of the impending deals, and the board of directors, often numbering a dozen or more, must be allowed to debate and vote on the issue. The company's outside law firm is alerted, and at times the board of directors will have its own set of lawyers." And the list grows longer, for it also includes specialists and lawyers at the investment banking houses and at the commercial banks.

26. E. Berg, *New York Times*, May 16, 1986, p. D2.

27. Columbia Business School *Annual Report*, 1986, p. 18.

28. *Washington Post*, June 5, 2003, p. A01.

29. Controls to prevent egregious abuses of position are without question needed. There is scant disagreement, for instance, that short selling by insiders, price-volume manipulation, and the release of false information must be prohibited.

30. H. Manne, *Insider Trading and the Stock Market*, New York: Free Press, 1966.

31. E. Bloch, *Inside Investment Banking*, Homewood, IL: Dow Jones-Irwin, 1986.

32. In September 1982, the SEC established with Switzerland a system for handling SEC requests for information on insider trading. Prior to this understanding, bank secrecy laws in Switzerland would have prevented the disclosure of information concerning trades in U.S. stocks that were made on the basis of nonpublic information. Other countries with bank secrecy laws include the Bahamas, Panama, Bermuda, and the Cayman Islands.

33. *NYSE Fact Book*, 1974, 1976.

34. On April 24, 1972, commissions on trades in excess of $300,000 became subject to negotiation between customers and brokers.

35. U.S. Department of Justice, Inquiry into Proposal to Modify the Commission Rate Structure of the NYSE, SEC Release No. 8239, Washington, 1968.

36. See A. A. Sommer, Jr., "Comments on Professors Block, Lorie, and the Future," in Ernest Block and Robert A. Schwartz, eds., *Impending Changes for Securities Markets: What Role for the Exchanges?* Greenwich, CT: JAI Press, 1979, pp. 40–49.

37. The arguments presented by the exchange, along with an assessment of their validity, have been set forth in R. West and S. Tinic, "Minimum Commission Rates on New York Stock Exchange Transactions," *Bell Journal of Economics and Management Science*, autumn 1971, and S. Tinic and R. West, "The Securities Industry Under Negotiated Brokerage Commissions: Changes in the Structure and Performance of New York Stock Exchange Member Firms," *Bell Journal of Economics and Management Science*, spring 1980, pp. 39–40. This subsection draws heavily on both of these papers.

38. For analysis and further references, see West and Tinic (1971, op.cit.).

39. Economies of scale in order handling cause costs per share to be lower for bigger orders, but do not necessarily imply that average costs for a brokerage firm decrease as its trading volume expands, ceteris paribus.

40. Tinic and West (1980, op.cit.).

41. An equivalent elimination of fixed commissions was instituted in England in October 1986. The British deregulation is referred to as the "Big Bang."

42. Fixed commissions and off-board trading restrictions were both established by the Buttonwood Tree Agreement signed by 24 securities brokers on May 17, 1792. The buttonwood tree was located at what is now 68 Wall Street.

43. Securities Acts Amendments of 1975, *Conference Report*. House of Representatives Report No. 94-229, May 19, 1975, p. 94.

44. For further discussion, see S. Williams, "The Evolving National Market System," in Amihud, Ho and Schwartz, op. cit.

45. In the Securities Acts amendments, Congress had established the National Market Advisory Board (NMAB) to carry out the design function for the SEC. The board failed to achieve its objective within the two years it had been given. On December 12, 1977, after much wheel spinning and in the face of increasing impatience in Congress, the NMAB had its last meeting.

46. See *NYSE 2001 Fact Book*. The percentages refer to the percentage of volume and of trades reported on the Consolidated Tape in NYSE-listed issues. The participating market centers in addition to the NYSE were the Pacific, Chicago, Philadelphia, Boston, and Cincinnati Stock Exchanges, Instinet, and the National Association of Securities Dealers.

47. See the Nasdaq web site, "Market Data."

48. See Paula Dwyer and Amy Borrus, "The Crisis at Nasdaq," *Business Week*, August 11, 2003, p. 67.

49. See P. Myner, "Review of Institutional Investment: Final Report," HM Treasury, London, March 6, 2001. For further discussion, see R. Brealey and A. Neuberger, "Treatment of Investment Management Fees and Commission Payments: An Examination of the Recommendations Contained in the Myner's Report," Fund Managers Association, October 2001; and Neuberger's discussion in Schwartz, Byrne, and Colaninno, eds., *Call Auction Trading: New Answers to Old Questions*, Kluwer Academic Publishers, 2003.

50. More meaningful measures can be obtained by averaging measurements over a substantial number of trades.

51. Financial Services Authority (FSA), "Best Execution," discussion paper, London, April 2001.

52. In reviewing current policy on best execution, the FSA's discussion paper (FSA 2001) states, ". . . when dealing in securities traded on the Stock Exchange Electronic Trading System ('SETS'), to meet the best execution requirement, firms should achieve a price (whether on SETS or an alternative execution venue) which at least matches the best price available on SETS)" (p. 13). The document continues, "However, in markets where there is no single or central exchange such as an over-the-counter ('OTC') market, the practice that is followed to substantiate the achievement of best execution is to obtain three quotes from different market makers (and then to select the most favourable price)" (p. 13).

53. See AIMR (2001, op. cit.), p. 2.

54. Letter to the AIMR. See A. Lancellotta, *Letter to the Association for Investment Management and Research, Re: Proposed AIMR Trade Management Guidelines*, Investment Company Institute, Washington, DC, February 12, 2002.

55. Other considerations noted in the FSA's discussion paper include counterparty risk (see the discussion starting on p. 26).

56. The statements were extracted from the Forum of European Securities Commissions (2001).

57. Phrases contained in the quoted references were "within a reasonable period of time," "as rapidly as possible," "without undue delay," "within a reasonable time period," and "as fast as possible."

58. For further discussion, see N. Economides and R. Schwartz, "Electronic Call Market Trading," *Journal of Portfolio Management*, 1995, pp. 10–18.

59. See AIMR (2001), p. 3.

60. The FSA discussion paper (FSA 2001) p. 18. The paper also notes that "Timely execution is put forward as an important objective of customers, which it is argued, obviates the need for extensive researching of price. The argument is that the customer's requirement for immediate execution takes precedence over price: in this case, the customer is seeking speed of execution at the expense of foregoing the exercise of researching alternative prices" (p. 34). The FSA also notes, in an explicit reference to institutional customers, that ". . . execution may not be possible in a single transaction but a series of transactions might be necessary. With a large order, the choices for execution may be between (a) immediate execution and possibly incurring a significant price impact; or (b) patient execution . . . where the risk is that the price moves against the investor (who suffers an opportunity cost)" (p. 35).

61. In its discussion of best execution obligations, AIMR (2001), also noted that markets and exchanges should ". . . continually . . . seek to develop faster,

more efficient, and more reliable systems and structures to ensure that their market place maintains fair, transparent, and equitable trading practices."

62. By *hypercontinuous*, we mean that trades are occurring with such high frequency that transaction-to-transaction price volatility is so accentuated that price discovery breaks down.

63. Material in this section is adapted from R. Schwartz and B. Steil, "Controlling Institutional Trading Costs: We Have Met the Enemy, and It Is Us," *Journal of Portfolio Management*, vol. 28, no. 3, spring 2002, pp. 39–49.

64. See Anthony Neuberger, in R. Schwartz, J. Byrne, and A. Colaninno, eds., *A Trading Desk's View of Market Quality*, Kluwer Academic Publishers, 2004 forthcoming.

65. R. Schwartz, J. Byrne, and A. Colaninno, eds., *Coping with Institutional Order Flow*, Kluwer Academic Publishers, forthcoming 2004.

66. See A. Neuberger in R. Schwartz, J. Byrne, and A. Colaninno, eds., *A Trading Desk's View of Market Quality*, Kluwer Academic Publishers, 2004 forthcoming.

67. Remarks by Benn Steil made at a Baruch College conference, and printed in the conference volume, *Regulation of U.S. Equity Markets*, Robert A. Schwartz, ed., Kluwer Academic Publishers, 2001, pp. 16, 17.

68. Hilary Kramer, "Free the Nasdaq," *Wall Street Journal*, August 12, 2003.

69. In the United States, the SEC has sought, in the name of fairness, to protect retail customers and in the process has created a more difficult environment for instutional participants. However, the point has been widely made that an institutional investor, be it a mutual fund, pension fund, or other, is itself little more than an amalgam of many small individuals.

CHAPTER 12

Simulated
Trading

I n this chapter, we move closer to the markets themselves, to the real world where the rubber meets the road. We do so through the tool of computer simulation. Our trading simulation model, TraderEx, is on the CD that is packaged with this book. TraderEx will enable you to gain hands-on experience with trading from the vantage point of a day trader who will wish to end the day with a zero position.

OVERVIEW OF TRADEREX

TraderEx should help you to understand more fully how prices are set and how trades are made in an equity market. Price determination in the market is complex. Even though we intuitively recognize liquidity (or its converse, illiquidity), the concept is difficult to define, and the problem of

Robert A. Schwartz and Bruce W. Weber developed the simulation model for TraderEx discussed in this chapter. Oliver Rockwell wrote the software for the TraderEx version that is packaged with this book. TraderEx is owned by I-Smarts Partnership, which includes Schwartz, Weber, and William Abrams. Bruce Weber has participated as a coauthor of this chapter. Parts of this chapter have been adapted with permission from Robert A. Schwartz and Bruce W. Weber, "Economics of Market Making," Nasdaq's HeadTrader web site www.academic.nasdaq.com/ headtrader, © 2004, The Nasdaq Stock Market, Inc. Produced for the Nasdaq Educational Foundation. Adapted with permission insufficient liquidity is best understood by trying to buy or sell shares at reasonable cost, in a timely fashion, in a relatively thin market. By varying certain parameters in TraderEx, you can control the liquidity of the market you will be trading in and can see the effect that liquidity has on your trading performance.

The TraderEx Software

TraderEx reflects a real-world, order-driven market structure and, to an appreciable extent, captures the dynamic properties of price formation. Nevertheless, the version of TraderEx that you have is simplified in a number of ways vis-à-vis the real world. Most notably, the simulation is completely electronic, accepts only two basic types of orders (market and limit), does not allow for negotiation between large participants, incorporates just two assets (one risky security and cash), and is not linked to an external information feed on which you might base your own expectations of future share value.[1]

A trading simulation can be based on either (1) canned data or (2) computer-generated data. With canned data, quotes, orders, prices, and trades are taken from a historic transaction record, and the live participant trades against the historic prices. With computer-generated data, the simulation itself creates the market environment, the quotes, and the transaction record. TraderEx is based on computer-generated data, not canned data.

The canned data approach is limited in two respects. First, a live player's own orders cannot affect the record of past prices—they are what they are. In the real world and with TraderEx, the live trader's orders can affect the evolution of prices in the marketplace. Second, with canned data, it is not possible to rerun a simulation using different parameter settings and/or trading strategies, because a transaction record is the product of the specific market that produced it. In the computer-generated environment of TraderEx, a live player is able to rerun the simulation. This enables you to assess the impact of a parameter or strategy change on price formation while holding all else constant.

To be exciting, and to truly engage the live player, a simulation requires the following:

- Prices can be affected by the live player's actions. If you rush a large buy order to market, price will be pushed up. Similarly, if you rush a large sell order to market, price will be pushed down.
- You must have some basis for anticipating future price movements. As we have discussed in Chapter 2, "From Information to Prices," this would not be possible if prices followed random walks. Importantly, TraderEx is not just a random exercise—patterns of runs and reversals

exist. That is, the environment is structured so that both trending and mean reversion coexist. Consequently, trading in our simulated environment does not simply involve throwing darts. Your trades should be priced and sized in relation to your anticipation of future price changes.

- You must be able to replay a simulation run with the setting changed in some way. We suggested the desirability of doing this in our previous discussion. Because the simulation can be replayed, you can repeat a run and see what would have happened if you had followed a different strategy or had operated under a different market environment.

The TraderEx Model

The computer plays four major roles in TraderEx. First, it establishes a market background. That is, it generates a flow of public orders, establishes and updates the limit order book, and sets transaction prices. Second, the computer can give participants orders to execute. Third, it maintains a screen that displays an order book, the transaction record, and the live participant's trade blotter. Fourth, it captures performance data for online graphical display and for subsequent analysis. Postgame analysis is important for assessing a live participant's trading decisions and the quality of the market.

A simulation run is a sequence of discrete events over simulated time, which will pass more quickly than real time. It may take 30 minutes to run a one-day trading simulation. TraderEx offers two alternatives for advancing from event to event. First, with the *discrete events mode*, the live player advances the simulation from event to event by first clicking on the "GO" button, and then clicking on the advance arrow button ">" to trigger the next event. This mode should be used while first gaining familiarity with the simulation. In the *continuous time mode*, a time clock in the software advances the simulation automatically. In either mode, simulated time will progress more rapidly than actual time, so that a full trading day in TraderEx can ordinarily be completed in 30 to 60 minutes.

The time clock can be set at one of three speeds: slow, medium, or fast (S, M, or F). To initiate the continuous running mode, click on the "LIVE" button, which toggles off the GO and > buttons and begins to advance the clock automatically. As you gain familiarity with TraderEx, accelerating the clock is a good way to intensify the game's challenge. After the close of trading, the results are displayed and available for further analysis.

- The live trader places orders whenever he or she chooses. The machine orders are, on average, generated every x minutes (e.g., 5.5 minutes), where x is an exponentially distributed random variable.

- The size of a machine-generated order is determined by a random draw from a unimodal distribution that is skewed to the right (specifically, a gamma distribution). A given stream of orders is converted into a sequence of trades.

CONCEPTUAL FOUNDATIONS

TraderEx's machine-generated orders are all statistical events (i.e., each order is the result of a draw from one or more distributions). The statistical processes have been designed so that the output (orders and trades) is consistent with the conceptual foundations that we have established in the preceding chapters of this book. We start with the motives for trading. Following the classical distinction in the academic literature, informed traders and liquidity traders are our first two sources of machine-generated orders. To these we add a third: technical traders.

The Information Motive for Trading

Awareness of information that has not yet been reflected in market prices motivates the placement of an informed order. We handle the informed orders as follows. Let the variable P^* represent the price that would be set at any moment in time in an environment where all participants fully reveal their desires to buy and to sell shares. In this frictionless environment, orders would be instantly entered, sorted, aggregated, and matched to establish P^* as the clearing price. P^* could be considered a consensus value or, in economic lingo, an equilibrium value. Informed participants are informed, but not per se because they have privileged information about the fundamental determinants of share value that others do not possess. Rather, it is simply and directly because they know the value of P^* and act upon it in the market.

The informed trader will send a buy order to market if P^* is above the value at which shares can be bought (i.e., if it is above the market offer). Similarly, he or she will send a sell order to market if P^* is below the value at which shares can be sold (i.e., if it is below the market bid).

In TraderEx, P^* periodically updates from one value to another. The time span from one jump to the next is determined by random draw. Specifically, we model the arrival of a new P^* value as a Poisson process. The Poisson arrival process has the interesting property of being "memoryless." That is, the probability of a new value arriving in the next moment of time is constant, regardless of the length of time that has passed since the last arrival. The Poisson is a simple process to work with. The order arrival rate, λ, its one parameter, describes both its mean and variance. The rate at which information events occur can be changed by changing λ.

The size of each jump in P^* is also determined by a random draw. Each change in P^* is a return. We take the P^* returns to be lognormally distributed with a zero mean.[2] Therefore, each new value of P^* is obtained by multiplying its previous value by 1 plus the antilog of a draw from a lognormal distribution. The magnitude of the information events, and thus market volatility, can be changed by changing the variance parameter of the lognormal returns distribution.

By construction, successive changes in P^* are not serially correlated. In other words, P^* follows a random walk. But the informed participants are not the only source of orders that the machine generates, and P^* is only one input into the dynamic price formation in TraderEx. When P^* is between the bid and the offer, no informed orders are generated, and market orders to buy and to sell arrive with equal probability. When P^* is above the offer, the arrival rate of orders to buy is increased from 50 percent to 75 percent. When P^* is below the bid, the arrival rate of orders to sell is similarly increased from 50 percent to 75 percent.

The imbalance between buy and sell market orders that occurs when P^* is outside of the quotes pulls the market in the direction of P^*. This is a key dynamic for the live participant to be sensitive to. As you play TraderEx, keep asking yourself the question, "Where is P^*?" Typically it is not between the bid and the offer. But, like the children's book character, Waldo, it is very hard to find.

The Liquidity Motive for Trading

Informed orders are perfectly directionally correlated with each other. If one arrives on the market to buy, another will also arrive to buy until the market ask is raised above P^*. Similarly, if an informationally motivated order arrives on the market to sell, another will also arrive until the market bid is pushed below P^*. In contrast, orders from liquidity traders are completely uncorrelated with each other.

Each liquidity trader comes to the market because of his or her own idiosyncratic desire to trade. The idiosyncratic motive can be attributed to cash inflows or to expenditures that are unique to an individual (e.g., an inheritance that has been realized or a tuition bill that has to be paid). Further, because investors have divergent expectations, an individual is free to change an opinion for a reason that only he or she knows.[3] Thus liquidity (idiosyncratic) trades can also be attributed to individual reassessments of share value.

The computer-generated liquidity orders are produced by much the same process as the information-driven orders. For each order, the size, time of arrival, and price are all determined by random draws from the relevant distributions. The major difference is that the price attached to each liquidity order is not determined by P^*. Rather, the prices of these orders are set with the use of a double triangular distribution (the distribution has two modes) that is located with reference to the current market bid and ask quotations. One double triangular distribution is used for the liquidity-driven buy orders, and another, a mirror image of the first, is used for the liquidity-driven sell orders. The double triangular distribution for liquidity-motivated sell orders is shown in Exhibit 12.1.

In Exhibit 12.1, price is on the vertical axis, and the probability of a price being selected is on the horizontal axis. The top triangle has a maximum probability at the market offer of $26.15, and the lower triangle has a maximum probability at the market bid of $26.00. If the price that is picked by random draw is above the $26.00 bid, the order is placed on the book as a limit order to sell. If the price that is picked is at the $26.00 bid or below, the order is executable (at least partially). If the sell order is for more shares than are available at the bid, it will execute as much as possible at the bid and at each lower price down to and including its own limit price. At this point, any unexecuted remainder of the order is entered as a limit sell (an offer) at the selected price.

Because the market bid and offer are the location parameters for the double triangular distribution, the distribution shifts with the bid and the

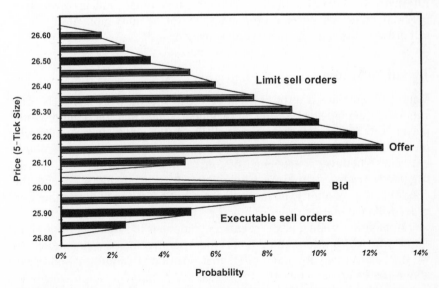

EXHIBIT 12.1 Double triangular distribution used for generation of liquidity-motivated sell orders.

offer. The distribution itself has a neutral effect on prices. If informed orders pull the quotes up (or down), the double triangular rises (or falls). If liquidity-motivated market orders eliminate limit orders from the book and thereby cause the offer to rise (or the bid to fall), the double triangular rises (or falls). No matter the price level, the liquidity-motivated orders will not cause it to revert back to a previous level. Neither will they reinforce a trend to a new level.

If liquidity orders were the only source of order flow and if, solely by chance, more buy orders are generated than sell orders, price would drift up over the course of a simulation run. Or if, solely by chance, more sells are generated than buys, price would drift down. If price were determined solely by liquidity orders, it would follow a random walk (aside from the bid-ask bounce). Any drift in prices could be explained by the cumulative impact of individuals (with divergent expectations) randomly and independently changing their assessments of share value. But liquidity orders are not the sole source of order flow in TraderEx.

In TraderEx, any drift that is caused by liquidity trading is constrained by the information-motivated order flow. That is, if a buy-sell imbalance from liquidity orders (without any P^* change) causes the quotes to drift up, informed orders to sell kick in once the bid quote rises above P^*. Similarly, informed buy orders kick in whenever an order imbalance causes the offer to fall below P^*. Thus the informed orders keep the quotes loosely aligned with P^*, the reflection of the fundamental determinants of share value. Alternatively stated, the informed orders cause price to mean-revert to a previous value whenever a preponderance of liquidity-motivated buy or sell orders causes the quotes to move away from P^*.

Technical Trading

Market technicians are the third source of order flow in TraderEx. The simulation includes one simple technical rule—that of a momentum player: Buy if price starts to rise, sell if price starts to fall. Specifically, the machine-resident momentum player operates according to the following rule: Whenever a sequence of four or more buy-triggered (or sell-triggered) trades or upticks (downticks) in the midquote occurs, the conditional probability is increased that the next machine-generated order will be a market order to buy (or a market order to sell).

Momentum trading is an essential component of TraderEx because of the way in which informed trading is incorporated into the simulation. As we have discussed, any jump in P^* that positions this information driver above the offer or below the bid triggers a preponderance of machine-generated buys or sells. These orders in turn cause prices to run up or to run down toward the new value of P^*. If this pattern were not muted in some way, it would be a bit too easy for a live participant to profit by buying or selling whenever price appears to be trending up or down. To make it more difficult for you to be a successful momentum player, we have incorporated the machine-resident momentum players.

The machine-resident momentum players do not make your life more complicated simply by jumping onto a run before you do. More critically, you will face uncertainty because the machine-resident momentum player can cause a false momentum move by kicking in when several same-side liquidity-motivated orders (either to buy or to sell) happen to arrive simply by chance. Further, following a change in P^*, the machine-resident momentum player will typically cause an otherwise justified price run to overshoot the new value of P^*. Both false runs and overshooting end up with price mean reverting back to a previous level.

Consequently, by including the machine-resident momentum players in TraderEx, we have built in reversal patterns as well as runs. This makes exploiting any price move far more difficult because you can never be sure if a run is real or how it will end. The coexistence of positive and negative serial correlation in TraderEx (as well as in real-world markets) masks the existence of each and keeps each from being arbitraged away.[4]

Bid-Ask Spread

In the real world and in TraderEx, the bid-ask spread does not exist because of chance. In Chapter 6, "Order-Driven Markets," we attribute the existence of the spread to the gravitational pull that a limit order on the book exerts on the placement of a contra-side order. Because of the desirability of executing with certainty at a posted bid or offer, a trader will submit a market order to buy rather than post a limit buy order in the close neighborhood of the market ask. Similarly, he or she will submit a market order to sell rather than post a limit order to sell in the close neighborhood of the market bid.

In TraderEx, only liquidity order flow puts limit orders on the book (informed participants and momentum players submit only market orders). The gravitational pull effect is achieved in TraderEx by use of the double triangular distribution that we have discussed with respect to the arrival of liquidity-motivated orders. Look closely at Exhibit 12.1 and notice that there are two price points between the bid and the offer. The probability of a limit order to sell being placed at 26.10 is only about 5 percent. If an order is placed at 26.10, the spread will narrow. The probability of a limit order to sell being placed at 26.05 is zero in Exhibit 12.1. The low (5 percent) probability and the 0 percent probability ensure the existence of a meaningful spread.

The location parameters of the double triangular distribution shift with the arrival of buy and sell limit orders, and hence with the relative thinness of the book. At times there is a nonzero probability that a sell limit will be placed within one tick (5 cents in Exhibit 12.1) of a posted bid or that a buy limit will be placed within one tick of a posted offer. Thus, from time to time, the market spread does equal the minimum tick size. This is not inconsistent with a gravitational pull effect. The important point is that the spread remains nontrivial in TraderEx because the probability of a spread reducing limit order being placed gets progressively smaller whenever the spread itself becomes increasingly tight.

As the spread narrows in the simulation, the probability of a spread-reducing limit order being placed decreases and the spread becomes more likely to widen; as the spread widens, the probability increases that a spread-reducing limit order will be placed and the spread becomes more likely to tighten. For some intermediate size, the spread is equally likely to widen or to tighten when it next changes. This size of spread may be considered an equilibrium value.

Ecology of the Order-Driven Market

In Chapter 6, "Order-Driven Markets," we state that a market can be thought of as an ecological system, because a balance between different types of participants is required for it to work. Most important, some participants must wish to buy when others wish to sell, and some must place market orders while others place limit orders.

The key to both balances existing in TraderEx is the liquidity-motivated order flow. When trading for their own idiosyncratic reasons (be it cash flow needs or an individual reassessment of share value), liquidity buy and sell orders are naturally interspersed. Further, because of our use of the double triangular distribution, market and limit orders are also interspersed. As we discuss in Chapter 6, share prices must mean-revert for the placement of limit orders to be justified. This is necessary for the machine-generated orders for the same reason that it is important for you.

As we have already discussed, price does mean-revert because of the overshooting caused by the momentum moves generated by technical participants. The compensation is there for limit order traders because price can be pushed up too high or down too low. When price has trended up too far, your limit order to sell might execute. If it does, you profit if and when price mean-reverts back down to a lower level. Similarly, when price has trended down too far, your limit order to buy might execute. If it does, you profit if and when price mean-reverts back up to a higher level. Play the role of a day trader and try this. Also try being a momentum player. You might discover that each strategy can earn a positive return if you are fortunate enough to detect and exploit a pattern.

OPERATING THE TRADEREX SIMULATION

This section introduces the TraderEx software and provides several examples of it in action, along with a few exercises that require running the TraderEx simulation. The TraderEx application requires about 1.5 megabytes of disk storage space. Once installed, it will have the following icon in the program folder where it is installed:

Traderex.exe

Click on the icon to launch the TraderEx simulation.

Getting Started

When you first bring up the TraderEx screen, you will see a text box with the software name, credits, and a disclaimer (See Exhibit 12.2). Click on Continue.

In the order-driven market structure and Day Trader role option, which we will use for illustration, you are able to enter buy and sell orders and to trade with the objective of earning a profit rather than seeking to accumulate a position. You should try to return your position to zero at the

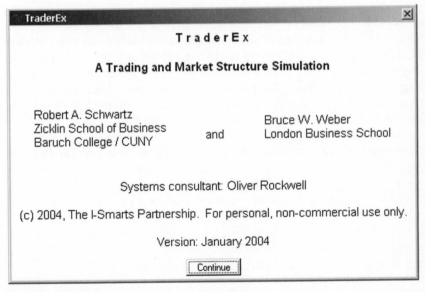

EXHIBIT 12.2 Opening text box for simulation.

```
┌─────────────────────────────────────────────────────────────────┐
│  ▓ ORDER-DRIVEN MARKET:  CENTRAL LIMIT ORDER BOOK (CLOB) SIMUL... │ ✕ │
│                                                                   │
│  Orders Arrive Every │5.5   │ Minutes                             │
│                                    Limit Order Percentage │90  │ % │
│  Daily Returns Volatility = │3   │ %                              │
│                                    Trading Day: 9:30 a.m-4:00 p.m. │
│  Order Size is 1 to 99 Units Maximum                              │
│                                                                   │
│                        │    Continue    │                         │
└───────────────────────────────────────────────────────────────────┘
```

EXHIBIT 12.3   Settings box with default values for simulation run.

end of the one-day simulation run. You may take long positions (owning shares in anticipation of price increases) or short positions (selling borrowed shares). Your objective in taking a short position is to profit from price decreases by repurchasing the borrowed shares (also known as *covering* the short position) at a lower price.[5]

Operations of the Market

Click on Continue. A parameter settings box will appear with the default values for the simulation run. Three settings can be adjusted: the order arrival rate, the daily returns volatility (of the $P*$ variable, discussed earlier in this chapter under "The Information Motive for Trading"), and the percentage of limit orders. (See Exhibit 12.3.)

The central limit order book (CLOB) is a consolidated set of the limit orders to buy and to sell. We assume that all trading takes place through the limit order book and that the limit orders in the book entirely determine the trade prices. Pricing follows a *walk-the-book* convention. In the walk-the-book algorithm, a market order that exceeds the size displayed at the best quote trades at multiple prices as it executes against an array of orders on the book. This contrasts with *block* pricing, in which the last slice of the limit order to trade sets the price for the entire trade.

To illustrate the difference, consider a market order to buy 25 that executes against the book shown in Exhibit 12.4. In a market that uses walk-

Bids	Price	Offers
	$23.40	20
	23.30	5
	23.20	10
15	23.10	

EXHIBIT 12.4   Order book before market order to buy 25 arrives.

Bids	Price	Offers
	$23.40	10
	23.30	
	23.20	
15	23.10	

EXHIBIT 12.5 Order book after the market order to buy 25 has arrived.

the-book pricing, the first 10 shares are bought at 23.20, the next 5 at 23.30, and the final 10 at 23.40. The purchase of 25 executes against several sell limit orders at the specific prices of those orders, giving the buyer in this case an average purchase price per share of $(10 \times 23.20) + (5 \times 23.30) + (10 \times 20.40)/25 = \$23.30$.

The seller of the initial 10 at 23.20 may feel regret about selling at this low price after seeing other sellers receiving 23.40 for their shares. In a market with a block pricing convention, the entire 25 are bought at 23.40, the price at which the last slice of the limit order executes. The limit order sellers at 23.20 and 23.30 receive higher prices than their limit orders indicated that they would accept. Notice that the order book at the completion of the order is the same regardless of the pricing algorithm used. (See Exhibit 12.5.)

The last entry to make before you can start playing TraderEx is to enter a random number seed from 1 to 10. This number determines the sample path that each of the simulation's distributions will draw from. Rerunning the simulation with the same seed value will re-create the same background conditions in the model. (See Exhibit 12.6.)

Playing the Simulation

After the random number seed has been selected, the market opens. The market's limit order book shows all orders to buy and to sell from 16.90 to 18.80. Notice that the highest bid is set by buy limit orders priced at 17.90

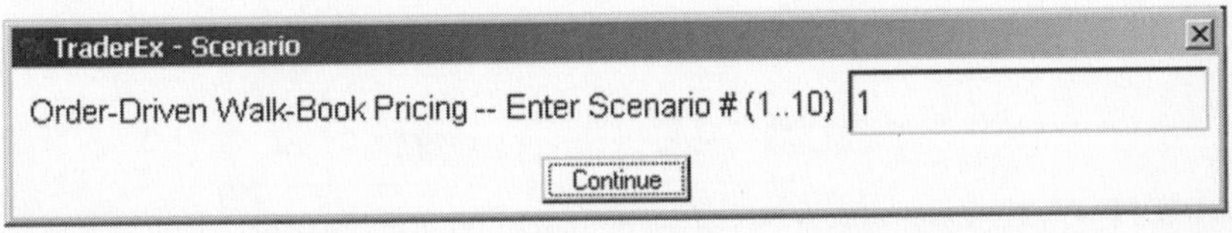

EXHIBIT 12.6 Selection of scenario number (random number seed).

for 18 units. The lowest-priced offer is from sell orders offering 25 units at 18.00. Except for the order book, the screen is empty—there are as yet no trades to report on the ticker. On the top of the screen is information about the time of day, number of trades, market index, share volume, the high and low prices of the day, the most recent trade price (last), and the volume weighted average price (VWAP). Right below the information strip is the ticker, which shows the price, size, and time of the recent trades. The ticker advances from left to right, with the most recent trade on the left.

Our position is recorded in the blotter in the center of the screen. The window below the blotter reports the most recent events (up to eight). Your relevant summary statistics are in the lower right of the screen.

In the first screen in Exhibit 12.7, the opening order arrives at 9:32 A.M. It is a market order to buy 25 units (i.e., 25,000 shares in our simulation's units). The current market offer quote is from the limit order(s) to sell 25 that is in the order book at 18.00. Hence, the market order will be filled in a single transaction.

After the user clicks the advance button "+>" at the bottom of the screen, the next display (Exhibit 12.8) shows the effect of the 25-unit buy order: a trade at 18.00 on the ticker and a revised low offer quote that is now at 18.40. A limit order to buy four has joined the book at 18.00. The

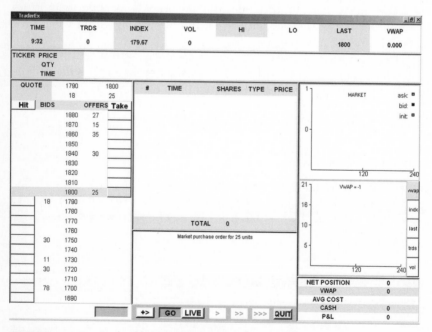

EXHIBIT 12.7   Computer screen after the opening order arrives.

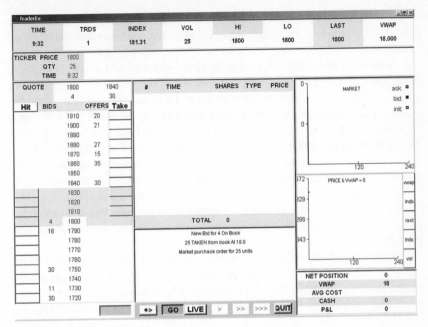

EXHIBIT 12.8   Computer screen after opening order executes and a new bid has been entered.

effect of the market order purchase is to increase the midquote from 17.95 to 18.15. Your new limit order to buy, which raises the bid to 18.00, further increases the midquote to 18.20. These count as two "momentum events" for the model's technical traders. Two more similarly bullish events in a row (trades on the offer side of the market or increases in the midquote) will trigger the momentum traders to begin submitting buy orders into the market.

The User's Trade Blotter and Performance

To illustrate the operations of the software, assume you have entered two orders as the live user: a market order to buy 25 and a limit order to buy 25 at 18.20. The market order was entered by clicking on the "Take" button at the top of the order book and entering the desired order quantity in the box that appears below the order book. If it had been a sell market order, you would have clicked on "Hit." To enter a limit order, you click on the box next to the price at which you wish to place your order. For a buy limit order, the box is on the left of the order book, and for a sell limit order it is on the right. Notice that boxes do not appear at prices where a limit order will not be accepted (i.e., buy limits cannot be entered at the offer price or greater, and, equivalently, sell limits cannot be entered at the bid or below).

After your two orders for 50 in total are entered and several machine-generated orders have arrived, the market screen appears as shown in Exhibit 12.9. Notice that your limit order at 18.20 has partially executed for 9 units; the remaining 16 units of your order are in the book at 18.20. Your two trades appear in the user's blotter, with your total position shown as 34. Your purchase price averages 18.347 per share. For a day trader, the goal would be to return the position to zero profitably by selling at 18.40 or greater. At this point, your profit and loss (P&L) is +1.79. That is the mark-to-market value of the 34 units (34×18.40) less the cash outflow (-34×18.347) to purchase the position. In general, shares are marked-to-market using the bid price for a long position and the offer price for a short position.

After these four trades, the volume weighted average price (VWAP) for the day is 18.216. VWAP is the average price at which the shares have traded so far in the day. VWAP is computed by summing the value of each trade and dividing by the total volume already traded. In this case, VWAP =

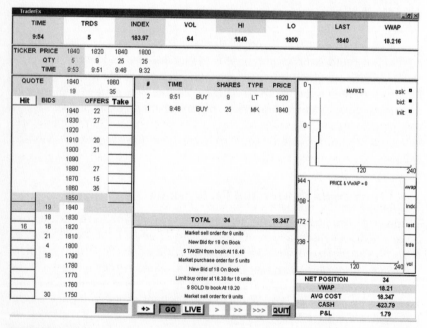

EXHIBIT 12.9 Computer screen after arrival of two live player orders and several machine-generated orders.

$[(5 \times 18.40) + (9 \times 18.20) + (25 \times 18.40) + (25 \times 18.00)]/64 = 18.216$. VWAP is a widely used benchmark in trading. Completing an instruction to buy shares near or below the VWAP price is often considered a sign of good performance. Selling near or above the VWAP price is similarly encouraged. Our discussion of VWAP in Chapter 5, "Institutional Order Flow," does point out major problems with using VWAP as a benchmark for performance measurement. Nevertheless, it is not an inappropriate statistic within the simplified context of our simulation.

Other Software Features

In the discrete events mode, you advance the simulation from event to event by first clicking on the "GO" button, then clicking on the advance arrow button "+>" to trigger the next event. This mode should be used while first gaining familiarity with the simulation. To go into the continuous time mode, the "Live" button must be clicked. Once in continuous mode, the ">", ">>", and ">>>" buttons set the speed to slow, medium, or fast. The initial setting is slow.

The TraderEx software has color coding for the graphs on the right side of the screen. In the upper right, the graph displays the ask, bid, and the initial price (init). In the graph at the lower right, you can click on the name to see a display of VWAP, index, last trade price (last), number of trades (trds), and trading volume (vol). The graph fills in over the trading day.

A text output file is created by TraderEx during each run. The data file will be located in whichever file folder the executable TraderEx program is in (TraderEx.exe). The file will have a name such as "TraderEx_040209_1534.out," which reflects the year (04), month (02), day (09), hour (15), and minute (34) of the end of the run. This ensures that each run has a unique output file. The file contains pertinent information about the trades and prices observed during the run. Each row, or record, in the file contains a snapshot of the market and information on any orders entered by you or trades generated by your orders.

The "comma delimited" file can be imported into Excel for analysis and graphing. Use the File Open command in Excel. After clicking on the file name (e.g., TraderEx_040209_1534.out), Excel's Text Import Wizard will open. Click on the "Delimited" button, then check off "Comma" as the delimiter, and select "General" as the data format.

The output file numbers will be placed into 17 columns in the spreadsheet in the following order: Order_Number, Day, Time, Trade_Number, Bid, Ask, Quantity_at_Bid, Quantity_at_Ask, High_Price_of_Day, Low_Price_of_Day, Last_Price, VWAP, Volume_for_Day, EQ_P (P*), Your_Order_Size, Your_Position, Your_Cash. Once the output file data is in Excel it can be analyzed and graphed.

Trading Exercises

1. Run the simulation for one day as a day trader, and return to a zero position by the end of the day. Note moments during the day when the spread is particularly narrow or wide.
   - What could explain the phenomenon of the spread narrowing and widening?
   - How does the size of the spread affect your trading decisions?
   - Were you able to return to a flat position and make a profit? What were the main factors that affected your profits?

2. Run the simulation and try to accumulate a net position of +500 units by the end of the day. As a goal, try to keep the average purchase cost below VWAP. Try to use both limit orders and market orders.
   - Did you buy all 500 units? Were you able to beat VWAP?
   - What influenced your performance relative to VWAP? Would you trade differently in a rerunning of the simulation?
   - What are the advantages and disadvantages of the two order types, limit and market?
   - Rerun the simulation with the same random number seed and accumulate a net position of −500 by the end of the day. Try to keep your average selling price above VWAP. How does selling a large quantity compare to buying for this particular market setting?

3. Consider the descriptions of the walk-the-book and block pricing algorithms in this chapter.
   - Which do you feel is a fairer approach to setting trade prices in an order book system?
   - What types of traders benefit from the block pricing approach? Who is disadvantaged?
   - Would you operate differently in a block pricing market?

4. The software has the ability to capture data in a file for postsimulation trade analysis. After completing the trading day specified in exercise 2, follow the instructions in the software to open the file in Excel or another spreadsheet package.
   - Graph the evolution of prices in a trading day. Show the bid, ask, and last trade price.
   - Add the P^* value to the graph and discuss how the market prices interacted with the P^* value and its changes.
   - In another graph, show how VWAP evolved over the course of the trading day and plot the points in time when your orders executed. Which of your trades were most profitable? Which were least profitable? How would your performance have changed if you had

traded your order to buy 500 units evenly over the trading day? Or all at or near the open? Or all at or near the close?

5. Here are some questions for postsimulation analysis.
   - Run the simulation and assess whether or not prices follow a random walk using the output file created during the run. What assessment technique did you use? What did you find?
   - In the context of the efficient markets hypothesis, do you think that the dynamic behavior of prices in TraderEx is weak-form efficient?

NOTES

1. We are developing more complex versions of the simulation, as well as a networked product that enables multiple live players to interact with each other and with the machine-generated orders. Information about these enhancements can be found on our web site www.baruch.cuny.edu/bctc/teachtech/traderex.htm.

2. With the mean equal to zero, the value of $P*$ does not systematically drift up or down over a simulation run.

3. We discuss divergent expectations in Chapter 2, "From Information to Prices."

4. See the discussion in Chapter 2, "From Information to Prices."

5. In TraderEx, borrowing costs and trading commissions are both taken to be zero.

Prices and Returns

E ach transaction price reflects the interaction of at least two orders—
a buy order and a sell order. Each return that is established reflects
two separate transaction prices—the price at the beginning of the
period over which the return is measured and the price at the end of the
period. All told, prices and returns are complex results of informational
change, liquidity change, and the mechanics of the market. In this appendix, we present technical details regarding the measurement of returns. We
also explain the effect of measurement interval length on the mean and
variance of returns and on the market model beta parameter, the variance
of residual returns, and the market model R^2.

THE MEASUREMENT OF RETURNS

A price exists at a specific moment in time. A return reflects a change in
price over a given period of time. We start our discussion of the measurement of returns by considering the time dimensions involved in the measurement of returns.

The Time Dimension

The time dimension enters the measurement of returns in a number of
ways: $T + 1$ points in time establish T time intervals; t identifies the tth

interval, $t = 1, \ldots, T$. The return for an interval is given an index that corresponds to the index for the interval. Thus r_t is the return over the interval $t - 1$ to t. If the length of the interval is changed, then the index on the return corresponds to the point in time that demarcates the end of the longer period. That is, R_T denotes the return from 0 to T if the full span is referred to, and r_T denotes the return from $T - 1$ to T if the Tth (last) short interval is referred to. Using this notation, the relevant time dimensions are as follows:

- *Points in time.* $T + 1$ points in time extend from the first (0) to the last (T).
- *Time intervals.* T time interval are indexed $t = 1, \ldots, T$, with the index on each interval corresponding to the count on the price observation at the end of that interval.
- *Time span.* The overall time span is of length T, and it comprises T short intervals.
- *Interval length.* The length of each interval is point in time t minus point in time $t - 1$ (e.g., one day or one week).
- *Unit period.* Both the overall time span and the shorter time intervals are measured as multiples of a *unit period of time.* For instance, if the unit period is one day, then both the time interval $t - 1$ to t and the overall time span, T, are measured in days.
- *Common period.* A return measured for one interval of time (such as a week) can be expressed as a rate per some other interval (e.g., per year). Converting all time rates into a common period sometimes facilitates analysis and evaluation.
- *Compounding frequency.* Interest can be compounded once per time interval, more frequently, or, in the limit, continuously.
- *Calendar time.* For theoretical analysis, time can be treated as an abstract concept. For empirical analysis, actual price observations are located in calendar time. With seasonal variability, secular trends, and/or nonstationary returns distributions, the exact location of the span $t = 0, \ldots, T$ in calendar time will affect the observed price behavior. Location in calendar time may be shifted on a large scale by, for example, using 2004 prices instead of 2003 prices, or on a small scale by using daily opening prices instead of daily closing prices.

PRICES

The term *price* can refer either to a transaction price or to a bid-ask quotation. *Transaction prices* are prices that have been established for trades already made. *Quotation prices* are ex ante expressions of the willingness of buyers and sellers to trade. We generally restrict the use of the term *price* to transaction prices and refer to bid-ask prices as *quotes*. The behavior of prices and quotes is studied by analyzing their change from one point in time to another.

Price changes are *returns*. Price changes computed by using points of time that are separated by an interval of specified length (such as one day) are identified as pertaining to that period (e.g., *daily returns*). Price changes computed for a sequence of prices recorded at the points of time that trades occur are *transaction-to-transaction returns*. For the most part, we deal with returns measured for specified time intervals.

In empirical work, prices are adjusted for stock and cash dividends paid during an interval so that the return measured for the interval is the total return—capital gains plus dividends. Therefore, if the closing price of a stock at time $t - 1$ is 50, the recorded closing price at t is 49, a dividend of \$.25 a share is paid, and t is the ex-dividend date, the adjusted price at t is 49¼, and the price change from $t - 1$ to t is 49¼ − 50 = −¾. Similar adjustments are made for stock splits. For instance, immediately following a 2 for 1 split, the price of a share is adjusted by multiple 2.

RETURNS

Price changes (returns) can be measured as price relatives, as dollar amounts, or as percentages. Arithmetic percentages can be converted into logarithmic values or into growth rates.

Assume a time span from 0 to T divided into equal intervals indexed $t = 1, \ldots, T$. The *price relatives* are

$$\frac{P_T}{P_0} = \left(\frac{P_1}{P_0}\right)\left(\frac{P_2}{P_1}\right) \cdots \left(\frac{P_T}{P_{T-1}}\right) \tag{A.1}$$

For the time interval 0, 1 we can write

$$P_1 = P_0 + \Delta P_1 \tag{A.2a}$$

$$P_1 = P_0(1 + r_1) \tag{A.2b}$$

$$P_1 = P_0 e^{\,g_1} \tag{A.2c}$$

Accordingly,

ΔP is the *dollar return*,

$$\Delta P_1 = P_1 - P_0 \tag{A.3}$$

r_1 is the *percentage return,*

$$r_1 = \frac{\Delta P_1}{P_0} = \frac{P_0 + \Delta P_1}{P_0} - 1 = \frac{P_1}{P_0} - 1 \qquad (A.4)$$

r_1^* is the *logarithmic return,*

$$r_1^* = \ln(1 + r_1) \qquad (A.5)$$

and g_1 is the *growth rate,*

$$g_1 = \ln\left(\frac{P_1}{P_0}\right) \qquad (A.6)$$

where ln indicates the natural logarithm (to the base e, $e = 2.7182\ldots$).

Generalizing for a succession of periods, $t = 1, \ldots, T.$

$$P_T = P_0 + \Delta P_1 + \ldots + \Delta P_T = P_0 + \sum_{t=1}^{T} \Delta P_t \qquad (A.7a)$$

$$P_T = P_0(1 + r_1) \ldots (1 + r_T) = P_0 \prod_{t=1}^{T} (1 + r_t) \qquad (A.7b)$$

$$P_T = P_0 e^{g_1} \ldots e^{g_T} = P_0 \prod_{t=1}^{T} e^{g_t} \qquad (A.7c)$$

For the overall time span we can also write

$$P_T = P_0 + \Delta P_T \qquad (A.8a)$$

$$P_T = P_0(1 + R_T) \qquad (A.8b)$$

$$P_T = P_0 e^{g_T} \qquad (A.8c)$$

where R_T is the percentage return over the whole time span. Equations A.7 and A.8 give

$$\Delta P_T = \sum_{t=1}^{T} \Delta P_t \qquad (A.9a)$$

$$1 + R_T = \prod_{t=1}^{T} (1 + r_t) \qquad (A.9b)$$

$$e^{g_T} = \prod_{t=1}^{T} e^{g_t} \qquad (A.9c)$$

Taking logarithms of (A.9c) gives

$$g_T = \sum_{t=1}^{T} g_t \qquad (A.9d)$$

It follows from Equations A.9a to A.9d that

- The average price change over the time span of length T is the arithmetic average of the price changes over the T short intervals that comprise it.
- $(1 + R_T)^{1/T}$ is the geometric mean of the $(1 + r_t)$. (The geometric mean of n observations is the nth root of the product of the n observations.)
- g_T is T times the arithmetic mean of the g_t.

Let $R_T{}^* = \ln(1 + R_T)$ and $r_t{}^* = \ln(1 + r_t)$. Then, from (A.7b) and (A.8b), we have

$$\ln\left(\frac{P_T}{P_0}\right) = R_T^* = \sum_{t=1}^{T} r_t^* \qquad \text{(A.10)}$$

From (A.8b) and (A.8c) we have

$$(1 + R_T) = e^{\,g_T} \qquad \text{(A.11)}$$

Taking logarithms of (A.11) gives

$$R_T^* = g_T \qquad \text{(A.12)}$$

The growth rate g_T is, therefore, a logarithmic return.

As seen in Equation A.7b, the $(1 + r_t)$ values are multiplicative returns: It follows from Equation A.9b that $(1 + R_T)^{1/T}$ is a geometric mean return. Multiplicative returns, geometric means, and especially the variance of multiplicative returns are cumbersome to deal with; additive returns, arithmetic means, and the variance of additive returns are not. For this reason, microstructure analysis frequently uses logarithmic returns (r^*) instead of arithmetic returns (r); the r_t^* are additive, and we can treat their arithmetic mean and variance.

THE INTERVALLING EFFECT

The *intervalling effect* is the way in which measures of returns behavior change as the measurement interval is varied. The relevant return measures include the following:

- Mean return (stock and index).
- The variance of returns (stock and index).
- Market model beta.

- The variance of residual returns.
- Market model R^2.

Following the previous discussion, taking logarithms of

$$\frac{P_T}{P_0} = \left(\frac{P_1}{P_0}\right) \cdots \left(\frac{P_T}{P_{T-1}}\right)$$

gives

$$R_T^* = \sum_{t=1}^{T} r_t^* \qquad (A.13)$$

Let the short time span $(t-1$ to $t)$ be the unit period. The intervalling effect is the effect on each of the five measures of increasing the interval T over which the long period return, R_T^* in Equation A.13 is measured.

Mean Return (Stock and Index)

Taking means of Equation A.13 and assuming the returns distribution is stationary, gives

$$E[R_T^*] = \sum_{t=1}^{T} E[r_t^*] = TE[r^*] \qquad (A.14)$$

It is clear from Equation A.14 that the mean logarithmic return increases linearly with T. For instance, the average weekly logarithmic return expressed as a rate per week is five times the average daily logarithmic return expressed as a rate per day.

The Variance of Returns (Stock and Index)

Taking the variance of Equation A.13 gives

$$\text{Var}(R_T^*) = \sum_{t=1}^{T} \sum_{u=1}^{T} \sigma_t \sigma_u \rho_{t,u} \qquad (A.15)$$

where σ_t (σ_u) is the standard deviation of returns in the tth (uth) short period and $\rho_{t,u}$ is the correlation between the tth short period return and the uth short period return, $t, u = 1, \ldots, T$.

The correlation between returns affects the relationship between the variance of the long-period return and the variances of the short-period returns. Because of this, the intervalling effect on variance depends on the correlation pattern in security returns. This correlation is *serial correlation:* the correlation between the returns in the time series $r_1, \ldots, r_T$.

To simplify the discussion, make the following two assumptions:

1. The returns distribution is stationary ($\sigma_t = \sigma_u$ for all short periods t, $u = 1, \ldots, T$).
2. $\rho_{t,u}$ is the same for all $|t - u|$. That is, if $t = 8$, $u = 5$, and thus the returns are three short periods apart, the correlation between these two returns is identical to the correlation between any other pair of returns that are three short periods apart (the ninth return and the twelfth return, the seventh and the fourth, and so on).

From assumption 1 we have

$$\sigma_t \sigma_u = \mathrm{Var}(r^*) \quad \text{for all } t, u = 1, \ldots, T \tag{A.16}$$

From assumption 2 we can write

$$\rho_{t,u} = \rho_{1,1+s} \quad \text{for } s = |t - u|, s = 1, \ldots, T - 1 \tag{A.17}$$

To illustrate, consider the following. Let the correlation between the return for $t = 4$ and the return for $u = 6$ be $\rho_{4,6}$. Because $|4 - 6| = 2$, the correlation is, by assumption 2, the same as the correlation between return 1 and return 3. Using the notation in Equation A.17, the correlation between return 1 and return 3 is $\rho_{1,1+2}$ ($s = 2$ in this case). Equation A.17 shows that $\rho_{4,6} = \rho_{1,3}$, an equality that follows from assumption 2.

How many $\rho_{t,u}$ are there in the series t, $u = 1, \ldots, T$ that are equal to $\rho_{1,1+s}$, for any $s = 1, \ldots, T - 1$? Consider the case where $T = 8$ and $s = 3$. The pairs of returns that are three periods apart in the set of eight returns are

1, 4
2, 5
3, 6
4, 7
5, 8

There are $8 - 3 = T - s$ pairings. Generalizing for all T and s, and substituting Equations A.16 and A.17 into Equation A.15 gives

$$\mathrm{Var}(R_T^*) = T\,\mathrm{Var}(r^*) + 2\,\mathrm{Var}(r^*) \sum_{s=1}^{T-1} (T - s)\rho_{1,1+s} \tag{A.18}$$

Equation A.18 shows that the variance of logarithmic returns increases linearly with T if there is no intertemporal correlation in the returns (if $\rho_{t,u} = 0$ for all $t \neq u$). It also follows that, for any value of $\text{Var}(r^*)$, the long-period variance $\text{Var}(R_T^*)$ will be larger if the intertemporal correlations are predominantly positive and will be smaller if the intertemporal correlations are predominantly negative.

Market Model Beta

The market model beta for a stock can be written as

$$\beta_i = \frac{\text{Cov}(R_i^*, R_m^*)}{\text{Var}(R_m^*)} \tag{A.19}$$

From the intervalling relations defined previously for the variance term, and given that

$$\text{Cov}(R_i^*, R_m^*) = \sigma_i \sigma_m \rho_{i,m}$$

it is clear that a stock's beta will be independent of the differencing interval if there is no intertemporal correlation in security returns [i.e., if $\text{Var}(R_{iT}^*)$ and $\text{Var}(R_{mT}^*)$ increase linearly with T and if the cross-correlation $\rho_{i,m}$ is the same for all T]. On the other hand, intertemporal correlation in returns will introduce an intervalling effect on the beta coefficient. With serial cross-correlation, the use of short-period returns causes beta estimates to be lower for relatively thin issues and higher for the largest issues. For a rigorous derivation of the intervalling effect bias in beta, see Cohen, Hawawini, Maier, Schwartz, and Whitcomb (1983a and 1983b).

The Variance of Residual Returns

The *variance of residual returns* behaves in the same way as the variance of returns—it increases linearly with T in the absence of serial correlation, at a faster rate in the presence of positive serial correlation, and at a slower rate if the serial correlations are predominantly negative. Residual variance is further affected if beta itself is dependent on T, with the effect depending on the impact that the intervalling effect on beta has on the average absolute size of the residual term.

The Market Model R^2

The squared coefficient of correlation for a regression equation shows the percentage of the variation in the dependent variable that is explained by change in the independent variable. For the market model regression,

$$R^2 = \frac{b_i^2 \, \mathrm{Var}(R_m^*)}{\mathrm{Var}(R_i^*)} \tag{A.20}$$

There will be no intervalling effect on R^2 if there are no intertemporal correlation patterns in security returns. This is because, in the absence of such correlation, beta is independent of T, and $\mathrm{Var}(R_m^*)$ and $\mathrm{Var}(R_i^*)$ both change linearly with T. On the other hand, intertemporal correlations cause an intervalling effect on R^2; the effect depends on the intervalling effect on beta and on the intervalling effect on the variance of R_m^* in relation to the intervalling effect on the variance of R_i^*. R^2 generally falls considerably as the differencing interval is shortened from, for example, monthly measurements to daily measurements or less.

From Portfolio Decisions to Trading in a Frictionless Environment

A frictionless world is elegant in its simplicity. Transaction costs are zero, there are no taxes or constraints (such as a short-selling restriction), the markets for all financial instruments are perfectly liquid, all investors are fully informed and, being fully informed, have the same (homogeneous) expectations concerning the distributions of future returns.

We consider the frictionless world in this appendix. Doing so highlights the major underlying determinants of share price and establishes a foundation for assessing the real world of investing and trading. We first show how equity shares are evaluated according to their risk and return characteristics in a frictionless environment. We start by considering an investor's optimal portfolio selection.

PORTFOLIO SELECTION

The first step in analyzing portfolio selection is to specify the objective of the representative investor. We then consider how the objective can be met in a frictionless world.

The Objective

Let three points in time $T = 0, 1, 2$ identify two time periods: (1) the period from 0 to 1 is a brief trading interval (e.g., one day), and (2) the period from 1 to 2 is an individual's holding period (e.g., one year). The individual seeks to maximize the expected utility of wealth that will be realized at the end of

370

the holding period $T = 2$. That person's utility function for wealth can be written as

$$U = U(W_2)$$

where the subscript 2 denotes wealth at $T = 2$.

The decision maker's portfolio at the start of the investment period $T = 1$ is described by the share holdings N_{i1}, $i = 1, \ldots, M$ assets. Assume a single holding period analysis. Thus for each ith asset, $N_{i1} = N_{i2}$. Therefore, we can suppress the time identification on share holdings and write

$$W_2 = \sum_{i=1}^{M} P_{i2} N_i$$

where P_{i2} is the price of the ith asset at time $T = 2$.

The investor controls the value of W_2 by his or her selection of the N_i. However, because the change of share value for each security is subject to variation, the investor does not have total control over the future value of the portfolio, but rather is faced with a set of uncertain outcomes. For this reason, the investor is not able simply to maximize utility. Rather, he or she makes decisions with reference to *expected* utility.

Following the standard approach, we take the investor's objective to be the maximization of the expected utility of wealth. Specifically, the investor seeks to

$$\underset{N_i}{\text{Max }} E[U(W_2)] = \underset{N_i}{\max} \int U(W)f(W)dW \qquad \text{(B.1)}$$

where E is the *expectations operator* and $f(W)$ is a *probability density function*. The maximization is with respect to the specification of the N_i.[1] That is, by optimally combining assets according to their risk and return characteristics, the investor obtains the N_i, $i = 1, \ldots, M$ that maximize the expected utility of W_2. Accordingly, we will consider how the risk-return characteristics of individual stocks are related to the risk-return characteristics of a portfolio.

It is straightforward to show that, given W_0, r is a linear transformation of W_2. Thus, given W_0, we can rewrite $U(W_2)$ as $v(r_p)$. The advantage of dealing with r_p rather than with W_2 is that the parameters of the returns distribution relate to a portfolio's composition and are independent of an individual decision maker's own wealth position.

We assume r_p, the return on the portfolio, to be normally distributed. This enables two parameters alone, mean and variance, to describe the returns distribution.[2] Therefore, for normally distributed returns, we rewrite $v(r_p)$ as

$$U(W_2) = f[E(r_p), \text{Var}(r_p)] \tag{B.2}$$

where $E(r_p)$ is the mean return and $\text{Var}(r_p)$ is the variance of returns over the investment period.[3]

From Equation B.2, it can be shown (and it is easy to accept intuitively) that risk-averse investors realize higher expected utility with a greater expected return (variance constant) or with a lower variance of returns (expected return constant). This is shown in Exhibit B.1, where we display a family of mean-variance indifference curves.

The investor maximizes expected utility by attaining the highest possible indifference curve in mean-variance (of returns) space. The arrow pointing to the northwest in Exhibit B.1 shows the direction of increasing utility.

The Mean and Variance of Portfolio Returns

Optimal portfolio selection is a maximization problem subject to the constraint given by the set of risk-return combinations available in the marketplace. To derive this constraint, it is necessary to compute portfolio mean and variance from the means, variances, and covariances of individual assets. This is done as follows.

Assume that any dividend declared during the period is paid at time $T = 2$, and let P_{i2} be the actual price plus the dividend per share. The return on the ith asset in the portfolio is

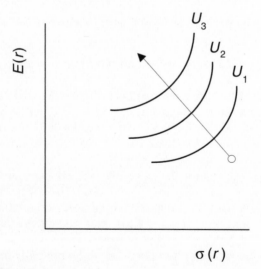

EXHIBIT B.1   Risk-averse investors realize higher expected utility with a greater expected return (variance constant) or with a lower variance of returns (expected return constant).

$$R_i = \frac{P_{i2}}{P_{i1}} = \frac{P_{i1} + \Delta P_i}{P_{i1}} = 1 + r_i \qquad \text{(B.3)}$$

where R_i is a *price relative*; $\Delta P_i = P_{i2} - P_{i1}$; and r_i has the standard returns dimension with which most people are more accustomed. R is used in some places in the text and r in others, depending on which is simpler in context to treat mathematically. The change in the value of a portfolio over the investment period is

$$\Delta W = \sum_{i=1}^{M} \Delta P_i N_i \qquad \text{(B.4)}$$

The return on the portfolio is

$$r_p = \frac{\Delta W}{W_1} = \frac{\sum_{i=1}^{M} \Delta P_i N_i}{W_1} \qquad \text{(B.5)}$$

Equation B.5 can be rewritten as

$$r_p = \sum_{i=1}^{M} \left(\frac{P_{i1} N_i}{W_1} \right)\left(\frac{\Delta P_i}{P_{i1}} \right) \qquad \text{(B.6)}$$

The dollar weight of the ith stock in the portfolio is

$$w_i = \frac{P_{i1} N_i}{W_1} \qquad \text{(B.7)}$$

Substituting Equation B.7 into B.6 and using the definition of r_i gives

$$r_p = \sum_{i=1}^{M} w_i r_i \qquad \text{(B.8)}$$

Taking expectations of Equation B.8 gives the expected mean return,

$$E[r_p] = \sum_{i=1}^{M} w_i E[r_i] \qquad \text{(B.9)}$$

Taking variances gives

$$\text{Var}(r_p) = \sum_{i=1}^{M} \sum_{j=1}^{M} w_i w_j \sigma_i \sigma_j \rho_{ij} \qquad \text{(B.10)}$$

where σ_i is the standard deviation of returns on the ith asset, and ρ_{ij} is the correlation between the return on the ith and the jth assets. Equations B.9 and B.10 show how the means, variances, and covariances for a set of stocks combined in a specific way (i.e., a specific set of portfolio weights) result in specific values for the mean and variance of returns for the portfolio.

The $\text{Var}(r_p)$ in Equation B.10 follows the rule that the variance of a sum is equal to the sum of the variances plus twice the sum of the covariances. To see this, consider the case where there are only two assets (asset 1 and asset 2):

$$\sigma_1\sigma_1\rho_{11} = \sigma_1^2 \qquad \text{for } i, j = 1, \text{ since } \rho_{11} = 1$$
$$\sigma_2\sigma_2\rho_{22} = \sigma_2^2 \qquad \text{for } i, j = 2, \text{ since } \rho_{22} = 1$$
$$\sigma_1\sigma_2\rho_{12} = \sigma_2\sigma_1\rho_{21} \qquad \text{for } i = 1, j = 2 \text{ and } i = 2, j = 1$$

Substituting into the variance equation gives

$$\sigma_p^2 = w_1^2\sigma_1^2 + w_2^2\sigma_2^2 + 2w_1w_2\sigma_1\sigma_2\rho_{12}$$

where $\sigma_1\sigma_2\rho_{12} = \text{Cov}_{12}$

The Constraint

Because different assets can be combined in a portfolio in many different ways, a feasible set of alternative portfolios is available to the decision maker. The decision maker adjusts the portfolio weights to obtain the one portfolio in the feasible set that maximizes his or her expected utility.

Equation B.9 shows that the portfolio's expected return is an average of the individual stock returns, with each return weighted by the stock's dollar importance in the portfolio. Equation B.10 shows that the relationship between the returns variance for the portfolio and the returns variances for the stocks is more complicated. To analyze the stock/portfolio variance relationship, write Equation B.10 for two stocks (A and B):

$$\text{Var}(r_p) = w_A^2\,\text{Var}(r_A) + w_B^2\,\text{Var}(r_B) + 2w_Aw_B\sigma_A\sigma_B\rho_{AB} \qquad \text{(B.11)}$$

If the returns on the two stocks are perfectly correlated ($\rho_{AB} = 1$), Equation B.11 is a perfect square. Thus we have

$$\text{Var}(r_p) = (w_A\sigma_A + w_B\sigma_B)^2 \quad \text{for } \rho_{AB} = 1 \qquad \text{(B.12a)}$$

and

$$\text{Var}(r_p) < (w_A\sigma_A + w_B\sigma_B)^2 \quad \text{for } \rho_{AB} < 1 \qquad \text{(B.12b)}$$

Taking square roots of Equation B.12 gives

$$\sigma_p = w_A\sigma_A + w_B\sigma_B \quad \text{for } \rho_{AB} = 1 \qquad \text{(B.13a)}$$
$$\sigma_p < w_A\sigma_A + w_B\sigma_B \quad \text{for } \rho_{AB} < 1 \qquad \text{(B.13b)}$$

We see that the portfolio return's *standard deviation* is the weighted average of the *standard deviations* of the individual stock returns if the stock returns are perfectly correlated with each other. Thus, we generally deal with means and standard deviations, even though the term *mean-variance analysis* is commonly used. Notice that the horizontal axis of Exhibit B.1 is labeled $\sigma(r)$. Mean-standard deviation indifference curves are also simpler to deal with on the utility side, although here, too, the term *mean variance* is commonly used.

For the moment assume a universe of two stocks (A and B) whose returns are perfectly (positively) correlated. The mean and standard deviation parameters for these stocks are shown in Exhibit B.2 by the coordinates of the points labeled A and B. In addition, the mean and standard deviation parameters for a portfolio combination of the two stocks are given by the coordinates of a point that lies on the straight line between A and B (this follows from Equations B.9 and B.13a). We have illustrated such a point by the one labeled P in Exhibit B.2. For simplicity, we have taken $w_A = w_B$. Accordingly, P is halfway between A and B, $E(r_p)$ is halfway between $E(r_A)$ and $E(r_B)$, and σ_p is halfway between σ_A and σ_B.

Next consider the standard deviation of portfolio returns for the more typical case of $\rho_{AB} < 1$. It is clear from Equation B.11 that a reduction in ρ (all else being constant) reduces $\text{Var}(r_p)$. Therefore, since Equation B.13a holds for $\rho = 1$, for $\rho < 1$ we must have

$$\sigma_p < w_A\sigma_A + w_B\sigma_B \tag{B.14}$$

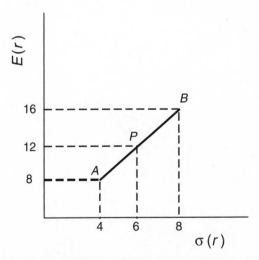

EXHIBIT B.2 Mean and standard deviation parameters for a two-stock (A and B) portfolio, $\rho_{AB} = 1$.

the result shown by Equation B.13b. For a given set of weights (w_A, w_B), the difference between σ_p and the weighted average of the standard deviations of the individual stocks depends on how far the correlation coefficient, ρ, is below unity. At the lower limit ($\rho = -1$), $\mathrm{Var}(r_p) = (w_A\sigma_A - w_B\sigma_B)^2$, from which it follows that $\mathrm{Var}(r_p)$ will be zero if $w_A/w_B = \sigma_B/\sigma_A$.

Note the direction of the inequality in Equation B.14. The effect of this inequality is shown graphically in Exhibit B.3. For the particular case where $w_A = 0.5$, $w_B = 0.5$, we have $E(r_p) = 12$ and $\sigma_p = 4.5 < 6$. More generally, the locus of all $E(r_p)$, σ_p points (for differing values of w_A and w_B) is a concave arc from A to B. The concavity of the arc reflects the fact that, for $\rho < 1$, portfolio diversification reduces the variance of portfolio returns.

Let a third stock (C) be introduced. As shown in Exhibit B.4, we now have a positively inclined concave arc between A and B and a second such arc between B and C. The point labeled AB on the first arc shows the mean-variance parameters of a two-stock portfolio defined by $w_A = 0.5$, $w_B = 0.5$.

The point labeled BC on the second arc shows the mean-variance parameters of a two-stock portfolio defined by $w_B = 0.5$, $w_C = 0.5$. What if the decision maker's wealth were divided between an AB-type portfolio and a BC-type portfolio?

Replication of the preceding discussion would show that the mean-variance parameters of this three-stock portfolio are given by the coordinates of a point on the concave arc from AB to BC. For instance, the weights $w_{AB} = 0.5$, $w_{BC} = 0.5$ (which are equivalent to $w_A = 0.25$, $w_B = 0.5$, $w_C = 0.25$) would identify a point such as the one labeled P in Exhibit B.4.

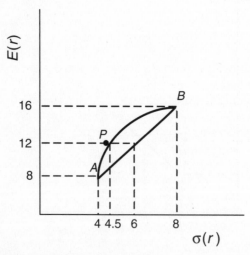

EXHIBIT B.3 Mean and standard deviation parameters for a two-stock (A and B) portfolio, $\rho_{AB} < 1$.

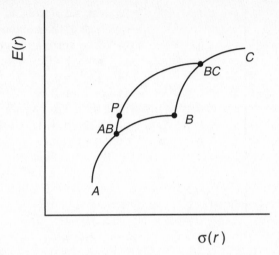

EXHIBIT B.4 Mean and standard deviation parameters for a three-stock (*A, B,* and *C*) portfolio.

The positively inclined mean-variance indifference curves in Exhibit B.1 reflect the fact that risk averters value expected returns but dislike returns variance. Therefore, given the existence of point *P* in Exhibit B.4, the risk-averse decision maker would not place all of his or her wealth in asset B. The reason is that the point labeled *B* lies below and to the right of the arc between *AB* and *BC* and thus is dominated by a multistock portfolio such as *P* that has a higher expected return and/or a lower returns variance. (Stock *B*, of course, is not dominated out; it enters the multistock portfolios. Stock *B* is only dominated out as a single-stock portfolio.) Less than perfect returns correlation explains the variance reduction associated with portfolio diversification, and this in turn explains why risk averters generally hold diversified portfolios.

The feasible set and the constraint can now be identified. These are illustrated in Exhibit B.5. Each little bullet in Exhibit B.5 shows the mean-standard deviation parameters for each asset the decision maker considers for inclusion in his or her portfolio. The dashed and solid lines on the outer border delimit the set of all feasible mean and standard deviation combinations, given the means, variances, and covariances for the individual stocks. For the most part, multiple-stock portfolios lie along the left-hand segment that passes through points *G*, *E*, and *F*, for reasons discussed in relation to Exhibit B.4. The constraint itself is the positively inclined, solid line segment between *E* and *F.* This is because, when the investor has achieved a portfolio along the *EF* arc, greater expected returns can be obtained only at the cost of higher variance, and lower variance can be

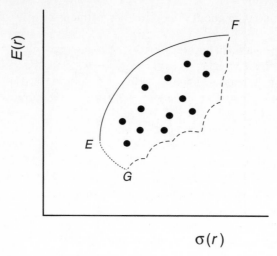

EXHIBIT B.5   Feasible set and constraint.

realized only at the expense of lower expected returns. Accordingly, this arc is called the *efficient frontier.*

The efficient frontier is the constraint. Note that the investor has made an efficient decision only if he or she has achieved a position where a trade-off is necessary to get more of a "good" or less of a "bad." Alternatively stated, the ability to improve one's position at no cost indicates a subopti-mal solution, and hence inefficiency.

The Optimal Portfolio Decision

The optimal portfolio is given by the point of tangency between the effi-cient frontier and the highest indifference curve the investor can reach. The tangency solution identifies the optimal mean-variance combination given the alternatives that are available and the investor's utility function. The solution is illustrated in Exhibit B.6 by the point labeled P^*. When port-folio P^* is selected, the decision maker achieves an expected return of $E(r)^*$, a standard deviation of σ^*, and an indifference curve labeled U^*. In Exhibit B.6, the optimal portfolio lies on the arc between point A and point B. Assume that point A is associated with a single stock. Point B may rep-resent either a single stock or a multistock portfolio; if the latter, assume that stock A does not enter portfolio B. We can consider the specific equa-tion that shows how A and B are combined to get portfolio P^*, and we may thereby determine stock A's weight (w_A^*) in P^*. In a similar fashion, we can obtain the weight (w_i^*) for any other ith stock in the portfolio. The weights express the investment decision.

Note the following about the optimal investment decision:

- Because for each ith asset $w_i = (P_i N_i)/W_1$, and since W_1 is given, determining optimal weights is equivalent to determining optimal dollar holdings in each asset. Therefore, for given market prices (the P_i), the individual's investment decision reduces to determining how many shares to hold of each stock (the N_i).
- The investment decision is implemented by buying or selling the appropriate number of shares of each asset given the solution for the optimal weights, initial portfolio holdings, and share prices.
- If the decision maker wants to hold N_i^* shares of the ith asset and currently holds N_0 shares, then he or she will seek to trade $N_i^* - N_0$ shares.
- There is no fundamental distinction between buyers and sellers in the securities market. Any trader is either a buyer or a seller, depending on his or her desired portfolio adjustment. $N_i^* - N_0 > 0$ indicates a buy decision, and $N_i^* - N_0 < 0$ indicates a sell decision.

For two reasons, the desired share holding for an asset depends on the price at which shares of the asset can be bought or sold. First, expected returns, variances, and covariances all depend on the relationship between initial prices (the P_{i1}) and end of period prices (the P_{i2}); hence, the optimal investment decision also depends on the initial prices. Second, the decision concerning the total dollar investment in a security is translated into the number of shares to hold (N_i^*) given the price per share (P_i).

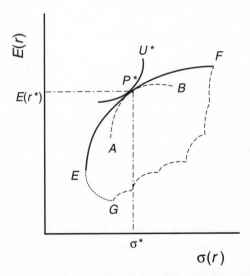

EXHIBIT B.6 Tangency solution identifying optimal mean-variance combination.

THE CAPITAL ASSET PRICING MODEL

This section shows how the portfolio selection model may be extended to obtain an equilibrium pricing model for risky assets. The formulation is the *capital asset pricing model* (CAPM). The CAPM was first developed by Sharpe, Lintner, and Mossin.[4] An alternative to explaining asset prices is *arbitrage pricing theory* (APT). See Ross and Elton, and Gruber for further discussion.[5]

Assume the following:

- Each investor has a single investment period, from T_1 to T_2.
- Each investor makes his or her portfolio decision with regard to the mean and variance of portfolio returns.
- Investors agree on the mean, variance, and covariance characteristics of individual securities; that is, investors have homogeneous expectations.
- Each investor can borrow or lend unlimited amounts of a risk-free asset at a risk-free rate of interest r_f.
- There are no taxes, transaction costs, short-selling restrictions, or other frictions in the market.
- Price and quantity (of share holdings) are continuous variables.
- No individual has the economic power to affect any price by his or her trading (i.e., the market is perfectly competitive).

The Capital Market Line

Introduction of a risk-free asset changes the efficient frontier (the arc from *E* to *F* in Exhibits B.5 and B.6). To see how, select a point on the *EF* arc, such as the point labeled *X* in Exhibit B.7. The risk-return parameters for combinations of the risky portfolio *X* and the risk-free asset are given by the dashed line from r_f through X.[6] The dashed line is above the *EF* arc in the region to the left of *X*. Hence, over this region, higher mean returns and/or lower returns variance can be obtained by combining the risky portfolio *X* and the risk-free asset.

Next consider the point labeled *M* along the *EF* arc. The risk-return parameters for combinations of the risky portfolio *M* and the risk-free asset are given by the solid line from r_f through *M*. Because the solid line is above the dashed line, the portfolio combinations it describes dominate the portfolio combinations described by the dashed line. That is, higher expected returns and/or lower returns variance can be obtained from portfolios on the solid line than from those on the dashed line. Because the solid line through *M* is tangent to the *EF* arc, no other line from r_f to any other point

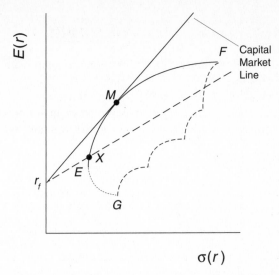

EXHIBIT B.7   Introduction of a risk-free asset changes the efficient frontier.

along the EF arc lies above the solid line through point M. Therefore, the efficient frontier with unlimited borrowing and lending at the riskless rate is the straight line that passes from r_f through M. This line is called the *capital market line*. Because investors have homogeneous expectations, they all make decisions with respect to this capital market line.

Each investor selects the specific risk-return combination given by the point of tangency between the capital market line and the highest indifference curve that he or she can attain, as illustrated in Exhibit B.8.

For each investor, the specific combination of the risky portfolio (M) and the riskless asset depends on the tastes of the individual. If (with reference to Exhibit B.7) the point of tangency is to the right of M, the investor borrows the risk-free asset and pays the rate r_f; if the point of tangency is to the left of M, the investor lends the risk-free asset and receives the rate r_f (as shown by the tangency solution depicted in Exhibit B.8). The combination of risky stocks, however, is the same for all investors—it is the portfolio M.

When the market is in equilibrium, all shares of all issues must be held by investors. Accordingly, M must be the market portfolio of all stocks. The capital asset pricing model shows how equilibrium share prices are determined for each security in the market portfolio. To obtain the equilibrium pricing relationships, first write the equation for the capital market line. From Exhibit B.8, it is clear that the intercept parameter is r_f and that the slope parameter is $[E(r_m) - r_f]/\sigma_m$. Accordingly, the equation for the capital market line is

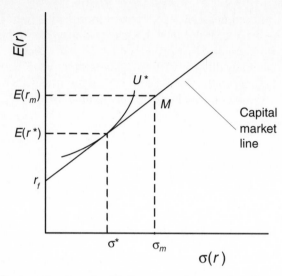

EXHIBIT B.8 Introduction of a risk-free asset changes the efficient frontier, the capital market line, and an investor's indifference curve.

$$E(r) = r_f + \left[\frac{E(r_m) - r_f}{\sigma_m} \right] \sigma \qquad (B.15)$$

Equation B.15 shows that the return on an equilibrium portfolio can be decomposed into two parts: (1) r_f compensates the investor for postponing the receipt of income (waiting), and (2) $\{[E(r_m) - r_f]/\sigma_m\}\sigma$ compensates the investor for risk. $[E(r_m) - r_f]$ may be viewed as the price of risk (i.e., what the market will pay the investor for accepting risk). In Equation B.15, the total compensation for risk taking is, therefore, the price per standard deviation of the market portfolio, which is $[E(r_m) - r_f]/\sigma_m$, times the amount of risk accepted, which is σ.

The Security Market Line

The capital market line shows the risk-return relationship to which an equilibrium portfolio must conform given the assumptions of CAPM. Individual securities, however, are not equilibrium portfolios, and thus they do not generally lie on the capital market line. An equation equivalent to Equation B.15, to which the risky securities must conform, is obtained by identifying the relevant measure of risk for each asset in the market portfolio.

The relevant measure of risk for the ith asset is the change in the risk of the market portfolio caused by a small change in the ith asset's weight in the market portfolio. That is, in keeping with the standard microeconomic pricing model, the compensation for risk bearing with regard to the ith asset equals the price of risk times the marginal increase in portfolio risk attributable to an increased investment in the ith asset. The change in portfolio risk is obtained by differentiating the standard deviation of the market portfolio with respect to the portfolio weight of the ith asset.

The derivative, which equals σ_{im}/σ_m, is obtained as follows. Since

$$\sigma_m = [\text{Var}(r_m)]^{1/2}$$

where

$$\text{Var}(r_m) = \sum_{i=1}^{M} w_i^2 \sigma_i^2 + \sum_{i=1}^{M}\sum_{j=1}^{M} w_{ij}\sigma_{ij}$$

the derivative of σ_m with respect to w_i is

$$\frac{d\sigma_m}{dw_i} = \frac{1}{2}[\text{Var}(r_m)]^{-1/2}\left[\frac{d[\text{Var}(r_m)]}{dw_i}\right] \tag{B.16}$$

with

$$\frac{d[\text{Var}(r_m)]}{dw_i} = 2w_i\sigma_i^2 + 2\sum_{j=1}^{M} w_j\sigma_{ij} \tag{B.17}$$

Therefore

$$\frac{d\sigma_m}{dw_i} = \frac{w_i\sigma_i^2 + \sum_{j=1}^{M} w_j\sigma_{ij}}{\sigma_m} \tag{B.18}$$

Since

$$r_m = \sum_{j=1}^{M} w_j r_j$$

and because[7]

$$\text{Cov}(r_i, w_j r_j) = w_j\sigma_{ij}$$

and

$$\text{Cov}(r_i, \sum_{j=1}^{M} w_j r_j) = \sum_{j=1}^{M} w_j\sigma_{ij}$$

we have

$$\sigma_{im} = \text{Cov}\left(r_i, \sum_{j=1}^{M} w_j r_j\right) = \sum_{i=1}^{M} w_i\sigma_{ij} = w_i\sigma_i^2 + \sum_{j+1}^{M} w_j\sigma_{ij} \tag{B.19}$$

Hence the numerator of Equation B.18 is σ_{im}, and

$$\frac{d\sigma_m}{dw_i} = \frac{\sigma_{im}}{\sigma_m} \tag{B.20}$$

QED

Replacing σ, in Equation B.15 with σ_{im}/σ_m, the measure of the ith stock's contribution *on the margin* to overall market risk, gives

$$E(r_i) = r_f + \left[\frac{E(r_m) - r_f}{\sigma_m}\right]\left(\frac{\sigma_{im}}{\sigma_m}\right) \tag{B.21}$$

Equation B.21 can be rewritten as

$$E(r_i) = r_f + \beta_i[E(r_m) - r_f] \tag{B.22}$$

where

$$\beta_i = \frac{\sigma_{im}}{\sigma_m^2}$$

Equation B.22 is the equation for the *security market line,* shown graphically in Exhibit B.9. The expected return/beta (β) characteristics of all efficiently priced securities (and portfolio combinations of securities) lie on the security market line, given the CAPM assumptions. Consequently, the market portfolio also lies on the security market line, as shown in Exhibit B.9 by the point labeled M, with coordinates $E(r) = E(r_m)$ and $\beta = 1.0$.

The Characteristic Line

Rewriting Equation B.22 gives the equation for a security's *characteristic line,*

$$r_i = r_f(1 - \beta_i) + \beta_i(r_m) \tag{B.23}$$

This equation is shown graphically in Exhibit B.10. The line can be estimated by regressing the returns for the ith security on the returns for the market portfolio.[8] The regression line passes through the *point of means* [the point in Exhibit B.10 with coordinates $E(r_i)$ and $E(r_m)$], and the slope parameter of the regression equation equals the security's returns covariance with the market return divided by the variance of the market return.[9] Therefore, Equation B.23 assessed at the point of means can be rewritten as Equation B.22.

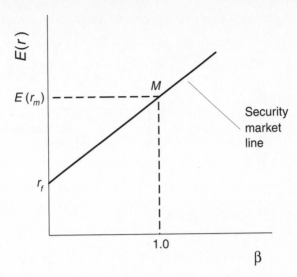

EXHIBIT B.9   The security market line.

Equilibrium Prices for Individual Assets

Equation B.22 can also be written as

$$\frac{E(r_i) - r_f}{E(r_m) - r_f} = \beta_i \qquad (B.24)$$

The numerator of the left-hand side of Equation B.24 is the excess expected return (over the risk-free rate) for the ith security, and the denominator is the excess expected return for the market portfolio. Equation B.24 shows that, in equilibrium, the excess return for the asset in relation to the excess return to the market is proportionate to the systematic risk of the stock.

The equilibrium price for the ith asset in the market portfolio is the value that equates the expected return for the asset with the expected return shown by the security market line, given the value of the asset's beta coefficient. As is next discussed, an arbitrage argument supports this equilibrium condition.

Exhibit B.11 restates the *security market line* as a relationship between the expected return on an asset (or portfolio) and the asset's covariance, $Cov(r_i, r_m)$. That is, the horizontal axis in Exhibit B.11 is beta (β), the horizontal axis in Exhibit B.9, times $Var(r_m)$. Exhibit B.11 also shows the expected return, covariance relationship for two different assets (A and B) and for two different portfolios, the market portfolio (M) and a portfolio C. Portfolio C is selected so that $Cov(r_c, r_m)$ equals $Cov(r_A, r_m)$.

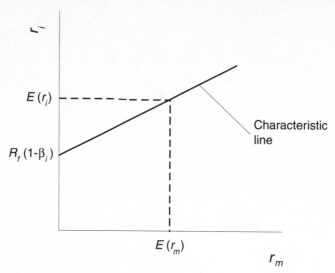

EXHIBIT B.10 The characteristic line.

Given asset B and the market portfolio, a portfolio such as C must exist. The reason is that portfolio C can be formed by combining asset B and the market portfolio in proportions w_B and w_m that satisfy

$$\text{Cov}(r_C, r_m) = w_B\text{Cov}(r_B, r_m) + w_m\text{var}(r_m) = \text{Cov}(r_A, r_m) \qquad \text{(B.25)}$$

with

$$E(r_C) = w_B E(r_B) + w_m E(r_m) \qquad \text{(B.26)}$$

The simultaneous existence of asset A and portfolio C presents an attractive investment opportunity. By simultaneously obtaining a long position in asset A and an offsetting short position in portfolio C, an investor can receive an expected return of $E(r_A) - E(r_C) > 0$. This is because, for any return on the market, the return for the long position (using Equation B.23 and adjusting the intercept parameter to reflect the additional expected return) is

$$r_{+A} = [r_f(1 - \beta) + E(r_A) - E(r_C)] + \beta(r_m) \qquad \text{(B.27)}$$

The return on the short position is

$$r_{-C} = -r_f(1 - \beta) - \beta(r_m) \qquad \text{(B.28)}$$

Hence, adding Equations B.27 and B.28 we have that, whatever the return on the market, the expected return to the hedged position is $E(r_A) - E(r_C)$,

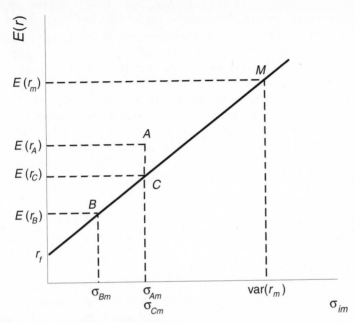

EXHIBIT B.11   The relationship between the expected return on an asset or portfolio and its covariance with the market.

and the beta for the hedged position is equal to zero. Because unrestricted short selling and zero transactions costs have been assumed, the investor can attain the hedged position by using the proceeds from selling C short to finance the long position in A. Hence, the return r_f is not required to compensate for the delayed receipt of income and, given the market price of risk, the hedged position would be taken by the investor.

If, alternatively, asset A were to map directly below point C in Exhibit B.11, a long position in portfolio C and an offsetting short position in asset A would yield a positive expected return of $E(r_C) - E(r_A)$. Again beta for the position would be zero, the return r_f would not be required, and the hedged position would be taken by the investor.

In general, if the expected return and beta characteristics of a risky asset do not describe a point on the security market line, a profitable arbitrage opportunity exists. This is because any point off the line implies the simultaneous existence of two investments with identical risk (beta), but different expected returns. Arbitrage trading will lead investors to acquire a long position in the underpriced asset and a short position in the overpriced asset.

Arbitrage is the process by which the prices of otherwise identical resources are brought into alignment with each other. The increased demand for a security with an expected return that is too high (given its beta) increases the asset's share price and lowers its expected return. Short selling a security with an expected return that is too low (given its beta) decreases the asset's share price and raises its expected return. The price changes brought about by the arbitrage trading continue until the expected return for each asset, given its beta coefficient, is brought into harmony with the relationship described by the security market line.

The capital asset pricing model implies that the market demand to hold shares of each risky asset is infinitely elastic at the equilibrium price. The reason is that the different assets and/or portfolios are perfect substitutes for one another and, being perfect substitutes, they must trade at the same price. Thus the price of each asset is determined, given its market risk (beta), the risk-free rate of interest, and the market price of risk.

THE MARKET MODEL

One of the major insights of the capital asset pricing model is that the return on a risky asset is related to the return on the market portfolio and that, through this relationship, the systematic (nondiversifiable) risk of the asset is established. The relationship between an asset's return and the market return can be expressed more generally by the market model equation.

The Market Model Equation

The return on a risky asset is a linear function of the return on the market under the frictionless world assumptions of the capital asset pricing model. The intercept parameter of the linear equation equals the risk-free rate of interest times one minus the asset's beta coefficient (see Equation B.23 for the asset's characteristic line).

The market model also relates the return on a risky asset to the return on the market portfolio. The equation for the market model is

$$r_{it} = a_i + b_i r_{mt} + e_{it} \qquad\qquad (B.29)$$

where b_i is the stock's beta coefficient as in Equation B.23, and e_{it} is the market model residual. The residual is that part of the price change for the stock that is not related to the return on the market. In the CAPM environment, a_i in Equation B.29 is $r_f (1 - b_i)$.

Systematic (Undiversifiable) versus Unsystematic (Diversifiable) Risk

We can use the market model to distinguish two types of risk: *systematic risk* and *unsystematic risk*. To see this, take variances of Equation B.29:

$$\text{Var}(r_{it}) = b_i^2 \, \text{Var}(r_{mt}) + \text{Var}(e_{it}) \qquad \text{(B.30)}$$

Because the return on the stock is partially explained by the return on the market index, part of the riskiness of the stock is explained by the underlying riskiness of all stocks. The first term on the right-hand side of Equation B.30 is the stock's systematic risk. Because the market-related component of a stock's return is perfectly correlated with the market, the systematic variance cannot be reduced by portfolio diversification. For this reason, systematic variance is often called *undiversifiable risk*. It is clear from Equation B.30 that if a stock's beta coefficient is greater than unity, the systematic variability of the stock's return is greater than that of the market. On the other hand, the systematic component of the stock's return is more stable than the return on the market portfolio if the stock's beta coefficient is positive but less than unity.

The second term on the right-hand side of Equation B.30 is the stock's unsystematic risk. Because the price movements for the stock are in part independent of general market movements, part of the riskiness of the stock is independent of the riskiness of the market. Because the residual return for one stock is uncorrelated with (1) the residual return on other stocks and (2) the return on the market index, unsystematic risk can be reduced by portfolio diversification. For this reason, it is often called *diversifiable risk*. In a frictionless environment, the risk-averse decision maker will hold a well-diversified portfolio to eliminate diversifiable risk.

VALUATION OF THE MARKET PORTFOLIO

We next show how the value of the market portfolio is determined in the frictionless environment. We start by obtaining the representative investor's demand curve to hold shares of the market portfolio.

The Investor's Demand Curve

We next show how the value of the market portfolio is determined in the frictionless environment. Assuming the market portfolio is traded as if it were a single risky asset, we first derive an individual investor's demand curve to hold shares of the market portfolio. To do so, we restate the utility (of wealth) function to make explicit the price at which shares of the market portfolio may currently be traded, and the mean and variance of future share prices.[10]

The demand curve to hold shares of the market portfolio may be obtained directly from the utility function. The derivation follows Ho, Schwartz, and Whitcomb.[11]

Assume the following:

- The investor's portfolio comprises a risk-free asset and one risky asset (shares of the market portfolio).
- Share price and share holdings are continuous variables.
- Short selling is unrestricted.
- The existence of a brief trading period, T_0 to T_1, followed by a single investment period, T_1 to T_2.
- All transactions made during the trading period are settled at point in time T_1.
- The investor seeks a portfolio at the beginning of the investment period (at time T_1) that will maximize the expected utility of wealth to be realized at the end of the investment period (at time T_2).
- Investor expectations with respect to the share price at the end of the investment period (at time T_2) are exogenously determined (expectations are independent of the current price of shares).
- Investors are risk averse.

The following variables are used:

$C_0 =$ holdings of the risk-free asset at the beginning of the trading period (T_0).

$C_1 =$ holdings of the risk-free asset at the beginning of the investment period (T_1).

$N_0 =$ number of shares of the market portfolio held at the beginning of the trading period (T_0).

$N_1 =$ number of shares of the market portfolio held at the beginning of the investment period (T_1).

$R_0 - 1 =$ risk-free rate of interest over the trading period.

$R_1 - 1 =$ risk-free rate of interest over the investment period.

$P_1 =$ price at which shares of the market portfolio are purchased or sold during the trading period.

$P_2 =$ price at which shares of the market portfolio can be sold at the end of the investment period (T_2).

$Q =$ number of shares traded by the investor at the beginning of the investment period (T_1); $Q > 0$ indicates a purchase; $Q < 0$ indicates a sale.

The Model   The decision maker starts the *investment period* with C_1 dollars of the risk-free asset and N_1 shares of the market portfolio (the risky asset). Therefore, wealth at T_2 is given by $C_1R_1 + N_1P_2$. As of T_1, this wealth is uncertain because P_2 is uncertain. As of T_1, the expected utility of end of period wealth can be written as

$$EU(C_1R_1 + N_1P_2) \tag{B.31}$$

The decision maker starts the *trading period* with C_0 dollars of the risk-free asset and N_0 shares of the risky asset. If during the trading period the decision maker were to exchange holdings of the risk-free asset for Q shares of the risky asset at a price of P_1, the *expected utility of end of period wealth*, written as a function of P_1 and Q, given N_0 and C_0, would be

$$h(P_1,Q|N_0,C_0) = EU[(C_0R_0 - QP_1)R_1 + (N_0 + Q)P_2] \tag{B.32}$$

where $C_0R_0 - QP_1 = C_1$ and $N_0 + Q = N_1$. Equation B.32 can be rewritten as

$$h(P_1,Q|N_0,C_0) = c + gQ(a - bQ - P_1) \tag{B.33}$$

where $c = U(W) - \pi N_0^2 U'(W)/R_1$
$g = U'(W)R_1$
$a = [E(P_2) - 2\pi N_0]/R_1$
$b = \pi/R_1$
$\pi = -\dfrac{1}{2}[U''(W)/U'(W)]\,\text{Var}(P)$

The step from Equation B.32 to Equation B.33 involves expanding (Taylor expansion) the investor's utility around the expected value of wealth if the investor does not trade. The procedure is a convenient way of introducing the variance term into the utility function. Two further assumptions are required to obtain Equation B.33: (1) The third derivative of utility with respect to wealth is small enough to ignore; and (2) the squared deviation of the expected rate of return on the risky asset from the risk-free rate is small enough to ignore.

Before analyzing Equation B.33, we first identify two measures of an investor's risk aversion and define an investor's risk premium.

Risk Aversion   The two measures of risk aversion are: (1) $R_A = -U''(W)/U'(W)$ is a measure of absolute risk aversion; and (2) $R_R = WR_A$ is a measure of relative risk aversion. Because we have $U'' < 0$ for a risk-averse decision maker, we have $R_A, R_R > 0$ for risk aversion. Larger values of R_A and R_R indicate higher degrees of risk aversion. R_A is a measure of absolute risk aversion because it reflects the decision maker's reaction to uncertainty in relation to the *absolute* (dollar) gains and losses in an uncertain situation. R_R is a measure of relative risk aversion because it reflects the decision maker's reaction to uncertainty in relation to the *percentage* gains and losses in an uncertain situation.[12]

Risk Premiums   A *risk premium* is the minimum dollar compensation a decision maker requires to hold a risky asset in place of an alternative that involves no risk. Specifically, a decision maker would be indifferent between a riskless investment with a certain return of D dollars and a risky investment with an expected dollar return of $E(Z)$ equal to D plus the investor's risk premium. In general, the investor's risk premium depends on his or her utility function and initial wealth and on the distribution of Z.

Pi (π) in Equation B.33 is a risk premium: π equals one-half of R_A (the measure of the investor's absolute risk aversion) times $\text{Var}(P_2)$, which measures the absolute (dollar) risk attributable to holding one share of the market portfolio. The uncertainty associated with holding N shares of the risky asset is $\text{Var}(NP_2) = N^2 \, \text{Var}(P_2)$; thus the total risk premium for holding N shares is

$$\pi_T = \pi N_1^2 \tag{B.34}$$

Dividing Equation B.34 by N_1 $(= N_0 + Q)$ gives the risk premium per share (the average risk premium):

$$\pi_A = \pi N_1 \tag{B.35}$$

Differentiating Equation B.34 with respect to N_1 gives the risk premium for a marginal share (the marginal risk premium):

$$\pi_m = 2\pi N_1 \tag{B.36}$$

Dividing Equation B.36 by P_1 expresses the marginal risk premium as a percentage of current price:

$$\pi_{M\%} = \frac{\pi_M}{P_1} = \frac{2\pi N_1}{P_1} \tag{B.37}$$

The return on the combined portfolio of N_1 shares of the market portfolio and C_1 dollars of the risk-free asset is

$$r_P = \left(\frac{P_2}{P_1} - 1\right)\left(\frac{P_1 N_1}{W}\right) + \left(1 - \frac{P_1 N_1}{W}\right)r_f \tag{B.38}$$

and the variance of the return on the combined portfolio is

$$\text{Var}\left[\left(\frac{P_2}{P_1}\right)\left(\frac{P_1 N_1}{W}\right)\right] = \left(\frac{N_1}{W}\right)^2 \text{Var}(P_2) \tag{B.39}$$

Thus the investor's risk premium associated with the uncertain return realized from the combined portfolio is

$$\pi_{rp} = \left(\frac{N_1}{W}\right)^2 \pi \qquad (B.40)$$

The various risk premiums identified here are used in the subsection "Interpretation" that we get to shortly.

The Reservation Demand Curve   Equation B.33 can be used to obtain both a *reservation price demand curve* and an *ordinary demand curve*. We consider the reservation demand curve first.[13]

The reservation price for a purchase or a sale is the maximum price the decision maker would be willing to pay to buy a given number of shares ($Q > 0$) or the minimum price the decision maker would be willing to receive to sell a given number of shares ($Q < 0$) when the only alternative is not to trade at all. Equation B.33 shows that, if no trade is made (i.e., if $Q = 0$), the decision maker's expected utility is equal to c. The reservation price for any value of Q is the price that equates the expected utility [$h(P_1, Q|N_0, C_0)$] if the trade were made, with the expected utility (c) if no trade were made. Thus the reservation price for any value of Q is given by

$$h(P^R, Q|N_0, C_0) = c \qquad (B.41)$$

where P^R is the reservation price associated with the trade of Q shares. Given Equation B.33, for Equation B.41 to be satisfied, we must have $a - bQ - P_1 = 0$. Hence the reservation price demand curve is

$$P^R = a - bQ \qquad (B.42)$$

The Ordinary Demand Curve   Using Equation B.33, we can also obtain the ordinary demand curve. At any value of P_1, the decision maker selects the value of Q that maximizes expected utility. Hence, the ordinary price demand curve is given by

$$\frac{\partial h}{\partial Q}(P^o, Q|N_0, C_0) = 0 \qquad (B.43)$$

where P^o is the "ordinary" price associated with the trade of Q shares. Therefore, differentiating h in Equation B.33 with respect to Q, setting the derivative equal to zero, and rearranging gives

$$P^0 = a - 2bQ \qquad (B.44)$$

D^R, the reservation curve given by Equation B.42, and D^0, the ordinary curve given by Equation B.44, are shown graphically in Exhibit B.12. Note the following about the two curves:

- For both curves, the parameter "a" shows the price at which Q is zero, and hence the price at which the initial number of shares (N_0) will be held.

The price intercept for the reservation and ordinary demand curves can be obtained by substituting $Q = -N_0$ into Equations B.42 and B.44, respectively. The intercept for the ordinary demand curve is $E(P_2)/R_1$, the present value (at the risk-free rate) of the price expected for point in time T_2. The intercept for the reservation demand curve is $[E(P_2) - N_0]/R_1$.

- The location of D^R depends on initial share holdings. The location of D^0 does not.
- Both curves are linear. Linearity is a consequence of an assumption made to simplify the derivation: The squared deviation of the expected rate of return on the risky asset from the risk-free rate is small enough to be ignored. The assumption is reasonable for the neighborhood of $E(P_2)/R_1$, but is not acceptable for prices sufficiently different from $E(P_2)/R_1$. Consequently, linearity is a reasonable approximation only as long as the price (P_1) of the risky asset does not deviate too far from the present value of the expected future price. One might expect the demand curve to hold shares of the market portfolio to be convex from below, such that it does not intersect the quantity axis. This is because, with zero storage cost, the investor would hold an unlimited number of shares at a sufficiently low price per share.
- The slope (dP/dQ) of the reservation demand curve given by Equation B.42 is half that of the ordinary demand curve given by Equation B.44.
- The slope of the demand curve would be zero (the price elasticity of demand would be infinite) if the risk premium were zero (i.e., if the investor were risk neutral), in which case the market portfolio and the risk-free asset would be perfect substitutes.

Interpretation

The previous subsection shows the demand curve to hold shares of the market portfolio for a representative investor given the risk-free rate of interest, expectations of P_2, and the investor's utility function. Exhibit B.13, which reproduces part of Exhibit B.12, shows that:

- If the price per share of the market portfolio is P_1, the investor will hold N_1 shares.
- The reservation price for the N_1 shares equals $E(P_2)/R_1$ minus the present value of the risk premium per share, π_A/R_1. The equation for D^R

Price per share

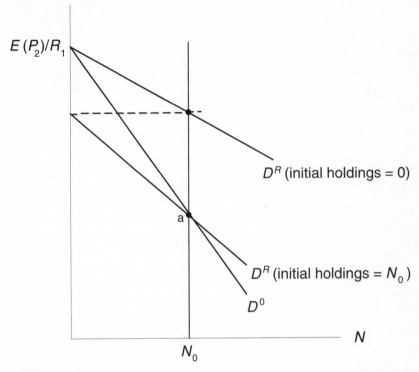

EXHIBIT B.12 D^R the reservation curve in Equation B.42, and D^0, the ordinary curve in Equation B.44.

when $N_0 = 0$ is $[E(P_2)/R_1] - bn_1$, and $bn_1 = \pi_A/R_1$ (from the definition of b and Equation B.35).

- Because the slope (DP/DN) of the ordinary demand curve is twice that of the reservation curve, $[E(P_2)/R_1] - P_1 = 2\pi_A/R_1$.
- The present value of the total risk premium π_T/R_1 equals the area of the rectangle $[E(P_2)/R_1]ABP^R$, which, consistent with Equation B.34, equals $\pi(N_1)^2/R_1$.
- *Consumer surplus*[14] equals the area of the rectangle P^RBCP_1, which equals the area of the triangle $[E(P_2)/R_1]CP_1$.

The Risk Premium and the Market Price of Risk   When the investor has traded the optimal number of shares of the market portfolio at the market-determined price per share, his or her risk premium can be

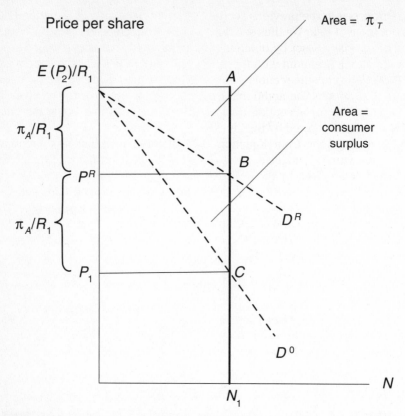

EXHIBIT B.13 The relationship between the reservation curve, ordinary curve, total and average risk premium, and consumer surplus.

related to the market price of risk. To see how, assess the ordinary demand curve at $P^0 = P_1$:

$$P_1 = \frac{E(P_2)}{R_1} - \frac{2\pi N_1}{R_1} \tag{B.45}$$

Multiplying by R_1/P_1, rearranging, and recognizing that $[E(P_2)/P_1] - 1 = E(r_m)$ and $R_1 - 1 = r_f$, we get

$$\frac{2\pi N_1}{P_1} = E(r_m) - r_f \tag{B.46}$$

Therefore, from Equation B.37 we have

$$\pi_{M\%} = E(r_m) - r_f \tag{B.47}$$

As discussed in the previous section, the right-hand side of Equation B.47 is the price of risk. We thus see that the investor achieves an optimal holding of the risky asset by obtaining the number of shares that equates the marginal risk premium with the market price of risk. This result is consistent with the consumer choice model: Price is equated with marginal value. Here, the price is the additional expected return the investor receives as compensation for accepting risk, and the marginal value is the marginal risk premium required by the investor.

It is apparent from Equation B.36 that the marginal risk premium increases with N. For a given price of risk, if the investor holds fewer shares than the value given by the ordinary demand curve, the marginal risk premium will be less than $E(r_m) - r_f$; consequently, the investor will increase his or her share holdings until his or her marginal risk premium has risen to equality with the market-determined price of risk. Alternatively, if the investor holds more shares than the value given by the ordinary demand curve, the marginal risk premium will be greater than $E(r_m) - r_f$; consequently, the investor will reduce his or her share holdings until the marginal risk premium has fallen to equality with the market-determined price of risk.

The Investor's Optimal Point on the Capital Market Line   The demand model can be used to assess the investor's optimal point on the capital market line (Equation B.15). From Equation B.40 we have

$$\pi = \pi_{rp}\left(\frac{W}{N_1}\right)^2$$

which, using $R_A = -U''(W)/U'(W)$, the measure of absolute risk aversion, can be written as

$$\pi = \frac{1}{2}R_A \text{Var}(r_p)\left(\frac{W}{N_1}\right)^2 \tag{B.48}$$

Because $\sigma_p = (NP/W)\sigma_m$, we have $\text{Var}(r_p) = \sigma_p(NP/W)\sigma_m$ and can write Equation B.48 as

$$\pi = \frac{1}{2}R_A\sigma_p\left(\frac{PW}{N_1}\right)\sigma_m \tag{B.49}$$

Substituting Equation B.49 into Equation B.46 and simplifying gives

$$R_R\sigma_P = \frac{E(r_m) - r_f}{\sigma_m} \tag{B.50}$$

where $R_R (= WR_A)$ is the measure of relative risk aversion.

Equation B.50 shows that for the investor to hold an optimal portfolio, the market price of risk per standard deviation of the market portfolio must be equal to the investor's coefficient of relative risk aversion times the standard deviation of the combined portfolio's return.

Letting $w = N_1P_1/W$, substituting $w\sigma_m = \sigma_p$ into Equation B.50 and rearranging gives

$$w = \frac{E(r_m) - r_f}{\text{Var}(r_m)R_R} \tag{B.51}$$

Equation B.51 shows that the percentage of wealth that the risk-averse investor invests in the market portfolio is positively related to the expected return $E(r_m)$, and negatively related to r_f, $\text{Var}(r_m)$, and R_R. Investors all face the same values of $E(r_m)$, $\text{Var}(r_m)$, and r_f, but differ according to their degree of risk aversion. More risk-averse investors (larger R_R) have smaller optimal values of w and hence are more apt to lend at the risk-free rate (which implies $w < 1$); less risk averse investors (smaller R_R) have larger optimal values of w and hence are more likely to borrow at the risk-free rate (which implies $w > 1$).

The right-hand side of Equation B.50 is the market price of risk per standard deviation of the market portfolio. As discussed in the section on the capital asset pricing model, the total compensation for risk taking is the price of risk times the number of standard deviations the investor accepts (here, the standard deviation of the combined portfolio). Multiplying both sides of Equation B.50 by σ_p, we obtain

$$R_R\text{Var}(r_p) = \left[\frac{E(r_m) - r_f}{\sigma_m}\right]\sigma_p \tag{B.52}$$

Adding r_f to both sides of Equation B.52 gives the investor's total compensation for waiting and for risk taking:

$$E(r_p) = r_f + R_R\text{Var}(r_p) = r_f + \left[\frac{E(r_m) - r_f}{\sigma_m}\right]\sigma_p \tag{B.53}$$

Equation B.53 shows that the location of the investor's optimal point on the capital market line (Equation B.15) depends on his or her measure of relative risk aversion (R_R).

The ith Risky Asset's Point on the Security Market Line   The demand model can also be assessed to show the location of a risky asset on the security market line (Equation B.22). Equation B.47 shows that the marginal risk premium for each investor, as a percentage of P_1, will equal $E(r_m) - r_f$. Therefore, for each investor,

$$\frac{R_A \text{Var}(P_2) N_1}{P_1} = E(r_m) - r_f \qquad \text{(B.54)}$$

It follows from the equation for the ordinary demand curve (Equation B.44) that investors with lower values of R_A hold a larger number of shares, such that the product $R_A N_1$ is the same for all investors. Because $r_m = (P_2/P_1) - 1$, $\text{Var}(r_m) = \text{Var}(P_2)/P_1^2$. Substituting $\text{Var}(r_m)P_1^2 = \text{Var}(P_2)$ into Equation B.54 and simplifying gives

$$R_A \text{Var}(r_m) P_1 N_1 = E(r_m) - r_f \qquad \text{(B.55)}$$

Using $P_1 N_1 = wW$ we obtain

$$wR_R \text{Var}(\text{r}_\text{m}) = E(r_m) - r_f \qquad \text{(B.56)}$$

Equation B.56 can be interpreted as an equilibrium condition for each investor. Because $wR_R = R_A N_1 P_1$, and because the product $R_A N_1$ is constant across investors, wR_R is constant across all investors. [It is also clear from Equation B.51 that the product wR_R must be constant across all investors, because $E(r_m)$, r_f, and $\text{Var}(r_m)$ are the same for all.]

The equilibrium condition for each investor with respect to the market portfolio implies an equilibrium condition for each investor with respect to any ith risky asset in the market portfolio. The CAPM shows that the relevant measure of risk for the ith risky asset is $\beta_i = \sigma_{im}/\text{Var}(r_m)$. Therefore, writing $\text{Var}(r_m) = \sigma_{im}/\beta_i$, substituting into Equation B.56 and multiplying both sides by β_i we get

$$wR_R \sigma_m = \beta_i [E(r_m) - r_f] \qquad \text{(B.57)}$$

Adding r_f to both sides of Equation B.57 gives

$$E(r_i) = r_f + wR_R \sigma_{im} = r_f + \beta_i [E(r_m) - r_f] \qquad \text{(B.58)}$$

Equation B.58, assessed at $w = 1$, shows that the expected return for the ith risky asset depends on its covariance with the market return, and on the measure of relative risk aversion for an investor whose optimal combined portfolio contains the market portfolio only. The equation also shows that the ith risky asset's specific location on the security market line (Equation B.22) depends on the covariance of the asset's return with the return on the market portfolio, as discussed in the section about the CAPM.

Market Equilibrium

Determination of the equilibrium market price of risk can be visualized as follows. Arbitrarily select a value of $E(r_m) - r_f$ and consider the number of shares of the market portfolio that investors in aggregate will seek to hold, as each attempts to obtain the specific number of shares given by his or her ordinary demand curve at the particular value of $E(r_m) - r_f$. If the total number of shares demanded exceeds the total number of shares available, excessive buying pressure will increase the price of a share of the market portfolio, and $E(r_m) - r_f$ will decrease. Alternatively, if the total number of shares demanded is less than the total number of shares available, excessive selling pressure will decrease the price of a share of the market portfolio, and $E(r_m) - r_f$ will increase. The equilibrium value of the price of risk, $[E(r_m) - r_f]^*$ is the price that equates the aggregate desire to hold shares of the market portfolio with the total number of shares available to be held.

For the capital markets to achieve equilibrium, an equilibrium value for the risk-free rate, r_f, must also be attained. If r_f is below its equilibrium value, investors in aggregate will seek to borrow more of the risk-free asset than they are willing to lend, thus putting upward pressure on r_f. Alternatively, if r_f is above its equilibrium value, investors in aggregate will seek to lend more of the risk-free asset than they are willing to borrow, putting downward pressure on r_f. The equilibrium value of the risk-free rate, r_f^*, is the rate that equates the aggregate desire to borrow the risk-free asset and the aggregate desire to lend the risk-free asset.

Therefore, when the capital markets are in equilibrium, (1) the number of shares investors in aggregate wish to hold of the market portfolio equals the number of shares available, and (2) the amount of the risk-free asset they wish in aggregate to lend equals the amount they wish in aggregate to borrow. When the market has achieved this equilibrium, each investor will hold the specific number of shares that equates his or her own marginal risk premium with the equilibrium market price of risk, $E(r_m)^* - r_f^*$.

The capital market equilibrium is described graphically by Exhibit B.14. The expected return on the market portfolio is shown on the vertical axis, and the *number of shares outstanding* (NSO) of the market portfolio is shown on the horizontal axis. Each of the upward-sloping r_f curves show the relationship between the expected return on the market portfolio and NSO for the associated value of r_f. $E(r_m)$ is determined given NSO and r_f because (1) the marginal risk premium is established by the aggregate demand curve evaluated at NSO, and (2) the marginal risk premium equals $E(r_m) - r_f$. For a given value of r_f, $E(r_m)$ is an increasing function of NSO because the marginal risk premium is an increasing function of NSO.

Let r_{f2} be greater than r_{f1}. The upward-sloping line labeled r_{f2} is above the line labeled r_{f1} because (1) the equilibrium value of the risk premium is determined for a given value of NSO, and (2) the higher the risk-free rate, the higher must be the expected return on the market portfolio for the risk premium to equal its equilibrium value.

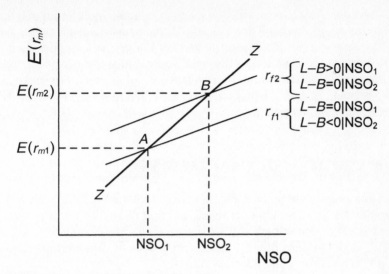

EXHIBIT B.14   Capital market equilibrium.

Let $L - B$ (aggregate lending minus aggregate borrowing) stand for investors' net aggregate desire to lend at the risk-free rate. For a given value of NSO, the higher the risk-free rate, the larger $L - B$ is. Information concerning the net desire to lend is given in Exhibit B.14 by the labels shown for the two r_f curves. The upper curve shows, for the rate r_{f2}, that $L - B > 0$ when the number of shares outstanding is NSO_1, and that $L - B = 0$ when the number of shares outstanding is NSO_2. The lower curve shows, for the rate r_{f1}, that $L - B = 0$ for $NSO = NSO_1$, and $L - B < 0$ for $NSO = NSO_2$.

Given a value for NSO, the capital market is in equilibrium if $L - B = 0$ and if the market price of risk equals each investor's marginal risk premium. Such an equilibrium is shown in Exhibit B.14 by point A for $NSO = NSO_1$ and by point B for $NSO = NSO_2$.

At point A, $L - B = 0$ with $r_f = r_{f1}$, given that $r_f = r_{f1}$, the marginal risk premium for NSO_1 equals the price of risk with $E(r_m) = E(r_{m1})$.

At point B, $L - B = 0$ with $r_f = r_{f2}$, given that $r_f = r_{f2}$, the marginal risk premium for NSO_2 equals the price of risk with $E(r_m) = E(r_{m2})$.

Notice that the equilibrium value for the risk-free rate is shown to be higher if the number of shares of the market portfolio is $NSO_2 > NSO_1$. This is because (1) as NSO increases, the risk premium increases; (2) r_f constant, the risk premium increases by $E(r_m)$ increasing; but (3) if $E(r_m)$ were to increase r_f constant, $L - B$ would become negative; and hence (4) r_f must also increase to maintain $L - B = 0$.

Because r_f increases with NSO, capital market equilibrium will lie on the more steeply inclined line labeled *ZZ* that passes through points *A* and *B*. The intersection of *ZZ* and the vertical line at the exogenously determined value of NSO identifies the equilibrium values of the expected return to the market portfolio and the risk-free rate of interest. For example, if NSO = NSO_1, $E(r_m)^* = E(r_{m1})$, and $r_f^* = r_{f1}$. Alternatively, if NSO = NSO_2, $E(r_m)^* = E(r_{m2})$ and $r_f^* = r_{f2}$.

INDIVIDUAL STOCK VALUATIONS

We have established that the riskiness of a stock (or portfolio) can be measured by the stock's beta coefficient and that the expected return for the stock is a function of beta (β). We now use a simple discounted cash flow (DCF) model to show how the stock's price is set by discounting future dividends at an appropriate discount rate (k).

The Discounted Cash Flow Model

Assume a company's earnings are expected to grow at a steady rate of g per year for the unlimited future and that, at the end of each year, a constant percentage of earnings is paid out as dividends to investors (the remainder is retained so that the firm's assets can grow at the rate g). The investor who buys a share of the firm's stock can be thought of as purchasing an infinite stream of annual dividend payments that also grows at the rate g. The price of a share can be determined by assessing the dividend stream using a risk-appropriate discount rate to obtain a present value.

Evaluating a stock that has just gone ex-dividend, we can write[15]

$$P_0 = D_0(1 + g)/(1 + k) + \ldots + D_0[(1 + g)/(1 + k)]^\infty \qquad \text{(B.59)}$$

which, being the sum of an infinite geometric progression, can be rewritten as

$$P_0 = D_1/(k - g) \qquad \text{(B.60)}$$

Similarly, we expect share price one year hence to be

$$P_1 = D_2/(k - g) \qquad \text{(B.61)}$$

Substituting $D_1(1 + g)$ for D_2 in Equation B.61 and dividing by Equation B.60 gives

$$P_1/P_0 = (1 + g) \qquad \text{(B.62)}$$

Thus g is also the rate at which the stock's price appreciates.

Solving Equation B.60 for k we have

$$k = D_1/P_0 + g \tag{B.63}$$

Equation B.63 shows that k is an expected return that comprises a dividend yield and a capital appreciation component. P_0 is set in the marketplace so that the dividend yield, D_1/P_0, is sufficient to give shareholders their required return, given the growth rate, g. That is, if returns are too low, P_0 falls and the dividend yield increases; if returns are too high, P_0 increases and the dividend yield falls.

Determination of the Risk-Appropriate Return

$E(r)$ is an expected return for the stock; k is an expected return that an investor requires as compensation for holding the stock. In equilibrium, $E(r)$ must equal k. If $E(r) < k$, P_0 will fall and $E(r)$ will increase; if $E(r) > k$, P_0 will rise and $E(r)$ will decrease. In the frictionless world, the capital asset pricing model gives the equilibrium expected return. Using Equation B.58 and the condition $E(r) = k$, write

$$k = r_f + \beta[E(r_m) - r_f] \tag{B.64}$$

From Equation B.47, $[E(r_m) - r_f]$ can be interpreted as the marginal risk premium for the market portfolio expressed as a percentage of price. Multiplying this term by the stock's beta coefficient gives us the marginal percentage risk premium for the stock. Thus the expected return equals the risk-free rate plus the marginal percentage risk premium.

The Relationship between k and Market Capitalization

The relationship between k and market capitalization (the value of shares outstanding) is most simply shown for the market portfolio for which β is unity. Let r_f and the expectation of the future share price of the market portfolio be constant, and consider the consequence of a decrease in the market portfolio's current price from P_H to P_L: The expected return for the market portfolio is higher and the risk premium paid by the market is raised in equilibrium. Thus, to maintain $E(r_M) = k_M$, the marginal risk premium required by the investor must also be higher. This is consistent with our demonstration in the section "The Market Portfolio" that, in a CAPM environment, the investor's demand curve to hold shares of the market portfolio is downward-sloping. Hence the aggregate market's demand to hold shares of the market portfolio is also downward-sloping. It follows that, ceteris paribus, k is larger for greater market capitalization, with the specific functional relationship depending on the utility functions of investors.

The discussion suggests that k is not exogenously determined, but rather depends on the size of the market portfolio. This implies that the price of the market portfolio is not an intrinsic value that can be found by security analysis, but rather is determined in the marketplace by the forces of demand and supply.

ORDER PLACEMENT AND THE DETERMINATION OF MARKET PRICES

In keeping with the rest of the chapter, the analysis in this section assumes costless trading. In the frictionless environment, the agent simply transmits buy and sell order functions to the market and trades the appropriate amount at whatever price is established on the market. We start with the investor's demand to hold shares of the market portfolio.

The Investor's Demand Curve

A representative investor's demand to hold shares of the market portfolio (Equation B.44) is shown in Exhibit B.15. The investor's current holdings are identified by the dashed vertical line at N_0. The subscript 0 here refers to an initial share holding; alternative share holdings will be denoted by subscripts 1 and 2. Similar subscripts will be used for the price variable. P_0 is the price at which the investor would be willing to hold N_0 shares of the market portfolio. At any price greater than P_0, the decision maker would like to hold fewer shares; at any price lower than P_0, he or she would like to hold more shares. The geometry is shown in Exhibit B.15.

If the price in the frictionless market is P_1, the investor will want to hold N_1 shares, and he or she will achieve this by buying Q_1 shares. If, instead, the price is P_2, the investor will want to hold N_2 shares, and he or she will achieve this by selling Q_2 shares, and so forth.

Note the following about the demand curve to hold shares and the associated buy-sell order curves:

- We have suppressed the i subscript that denotes the ith asset, because the discussion in this chapter relates to the demand to hold shares of one particular asset, the market portfolio. Because we now consider the full set of participants in the market for a stock, the subscript j has been introduced to identify the jth investor-trader, $j = 1, \ldots, \zeta$.

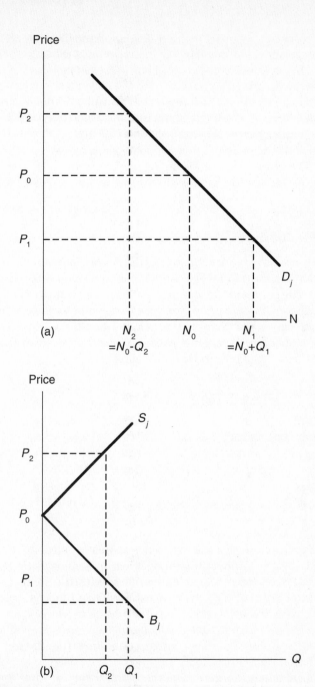

EXHIBIT B.15 Investor's demand curve and buy and sell curves: (a) the demand curve (b) the buy and sell curves.

- The buy-sell functions for the individual trader branch off the price axis at a value determined by the intersection of the investor's demand curve (D_j) and the dashed vertical line at N_0 that denotes the number of shares the jth investor holds.
- N_0 constant, the point of intersection depends on the location of the demand curve. Accordingly, shifts in D_j are associated with shifts in the buy-sell order curves shown in Exhibit B.15(b).
- D_j constant, the point of intersection depends on the size of share holdings. Therefore, each trade is accompanied by a shift of the buy-sell order curves (the curves shift down with a purchase and up with a sale).

Market Equilibrium

Given each investor's order functions (the S_j and B_j trade curves) and an environment where trading is costless, each investor submits his or her complete trade curves to the market. The reason is twofold. First, the order size associated with each price along the trade curves will have been accurately written given that that price is in fact set on the market. Second, the environment guarantees that the investor realizes only one execution.

For the individual buy and sell functions,

$$B_j = f_j(P) \qquad \text{(B.65)}$$
$$S_j = g_j(P) \qquad \text{(B.66)}$$

the aggregate buy and sell functions are

$$B = \sum_{j=1}^{\zeta} f_j(P) \qquad \text{(B.67)}$$

$$S = \sum_{j=1}^{\zeta} g_j(P) \qquad \text{(B.68)}$$

The aggregate functions are shown graphically in Exhibit B.16. Unlike the B_j and S_j curves for an investor shown in Exhibit B.15, the market curves B and S can intersect each other because the locations of D_j and of the vertical line at N_0 vary across investors. When the aggregate buy and sell trade curves intersect, prices exist at or below which some investors are willing to sell and at or above which other investors are willing to buy. Hence, trades occur. For the configuration shown in Exhibit B.16, Q^M shares will trade at a price of P^M.

Trading eliminates orders from the B and S curves. After the subtraction of Q^M shares from both the B and S curves, the trade curves will have

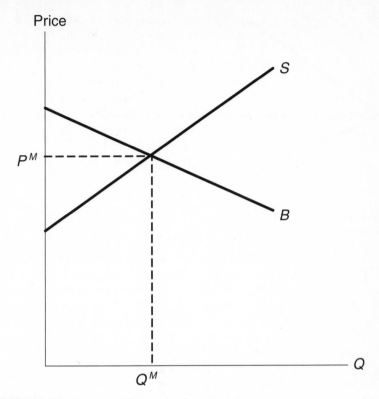

Price

P^M

Q^M

Q

S

B

EXHIBIT B.16   Aggregate buy and sell curves.

shifted to the left until the intersection point shown in Exhibit B.16 is at the price axis, as shown in Exhibit B.17(a).

The process of trading harmonizes the jth decision maker's investment desires with the market. As shown in Exhibit B.17(b), the trade curves the jth investor submitted to the market will have resulted in the purchase of Q_1 shares at the price P^M. Exhibit B.17(c) shows that, after the trade, the vertical line that denotes that investor's holdings has shifted from N_0 to $N_0 + Q_1$. Consequently, the vertical line now intersects D_j at the market price, P^M. Thus, after the trade, the jth investor is holding exactly the number of shares that he or she would like to hold at the current market price.

If the investor were to submit a new set of trade curves to the market after the trade, the curves would appear as shown in Exhibit B.17(d). Note that the new trade curves necessarily branch off the price axis at P^M. Because this is true for each trader, mutually profitable trading

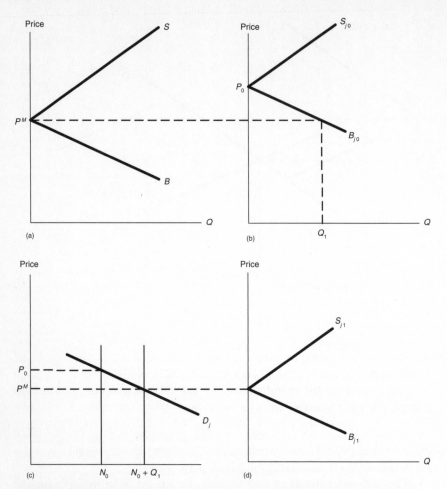

EXHIBIT B.17   Adjustment of an investor's holdings (Q) in relation to a market determined price (P^M): (a) aggregate buy and sell curves after trades have eliminated all crossing orders; (b) the jth investor's initial trade curves result in the purchase of Q_1 shares, at the price P^M; (c) after the purchase of Q_1 shares, the vertical line intersects the jth investor's demand curve at $N_0 + Q_1$ shares; (d) the jth investor's buy and sell curves immediately after the purchase of Q_1 shares.

opportunities do not exist immediately after a trading session for any pairing of market participants. Therefore, one round of trading in the frictionless environment harmonizes the trading propensities of all investors and leaves no desire to recontract.

The market's aggregate demand curve to hold shares of the risky asset can now be identified: It is the curve labeled D in Exhibit B.18(b).

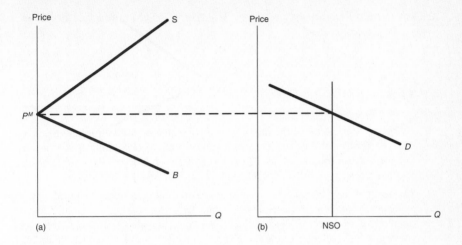

EXHIBIT B.18 Market buy and sell curves and demand curve: (a) the buy and sell curves; (b) the demand curve.

The relationship between the market's trade curves, B and S [as shown in Exhibit B.18(a)], and the market's demand curve, D, is the same as that which relates B_j and S_j to D_j (as shown in Exhibit B.15).

Unlike the case for an individual, the market in aggregate must hold a *given* number of shares—the aggregate *number of shares outstanding* (NSO). Thus, we take the vertical line at NSO as fixed and locate the aggregate demand curve, D, in relation to it. In equilibrium, D crosses the vertical line at P^M, the price that has been established on the market. Alternatively stated, the equilibrium price for the market can be obtained by assessing $D = D(P)$ (the market demand equation) at $D = $ NSO. Because the market in aggregate must hold the number of shares outstanding, and because this number is given, a separate supply equation is not needed to obtain a solution. (There are two equations, $D = D(P)$ and $D = $ NSO, and two unknowns, D and P.)

The vertical line at NSO is not a supply curve in the following sense. If total corporate earnings, dividends, growth, and so on, are unaffected by the number of shares outstanding, then any change in NSO due, for example, to a stock split or stock dividend, would be associated with an equal but opposite percentage change in share price (for instance, a 2 for 1 stock split would result in the share price being halved). This being the case, with demand propensities constant, shifts of the vertical line at NSO would trace out a locus of equilibrium prices that is a negatively inclined, convex curve of unitary elasticity. It would be misleading to consider this curve the market demand curve for an asset. Therefore, NSO should not be interpreted as a supply curve.

NOTES

1. There are alternatives to the maximization of expected utility: for instance, the maximization of the geometric mean return and various safety first criteria. For further discussion, see E. Elton and G. Gruber, *Modern Portfolio Theory and Investment Analysis*, 6th ed. New York: John Wiley & Sons, 2002.

2. The assumption that arithmetic returns are normally distributed simplifies the analysis. Empirically, returns distributions are more nearly lognormal. A third moment of the returns distribution, *skewness*, has also been considered in some portfolio selection models. For further discussion, see E. Elton and G. Gruber, op. cit.

3. There are two other conditions under which utility can be written as a function of mean and variance: (1) quadratic utility and (2) lognormally distributed returns. Economists differ in their willingness to assume quadratic utility. The empirical evidence suggests that returns distributions are approximately lognormal, however, and the assumption of lognormality is widely accepted. To simplify the discussion here, we assume that returns are distributed normally.

4. W. Sharpe, "Capital Asset Prices: A Theory of Market Equilibrium Under Conditions of Risk," *Journal of Finance*, September 1964; J. Lintner, "Security Prices and Maximal Gains from Diversification," *Journal of Finance*, December 1965, pp. 587–615, and "The Valuation of Risk Assets and the Selection of Risky Investments in Stock Portfolios and Capital Budgets," *Review of Economics and Statistics*, February 1965; and J. Mossin, "Equilibrium in a Capital Asset Market," *Econometrica*, October 1966.

5. S. Ross, "The Arbitrage Theory of Capital Asset Pricing," *Journal of Economic Theory*, December 1976; E. Elton and G. Gruber, *Modern Portfolio Theory and Investment Analysis*, 4th ed. New York: John Wiley & Sons, 1991.

6. Return variance for the risk-free asset is zero, and there is no covariance of return between the risk-free and the risky assets. Therefore, the locus of mean, standard deviation values for the combined portfolio is a straight line, with the standard deviation for the combined portfolio being equal to $w_x\sigma_x$, where w_x is the weight of the risky portfolio in the combined portfolio.

7. The covariance of a variable (x) with the weighted sum of two other variables ($w_y y + w_z z$), is equal to the weighted sum of the covariance between x and y, and the covariance between x and z. The proof is

$$\begin{aligned}
\text{Cov}(x, w_y y + w_z z) &= E[(x - \overline{x})(w_y y + w_z z - w_y \overline{y} - w_z \overline{z})] \\
&= w_y E[(x - \overline{x})(y - \overline{y})] + w_z E[(x - \overline{x})(z - \overline{z})] \\
&= w_y \text{Cov}(x, y) + w_z \text{Cov}(x, z)
\end{aligned}$$

8. Tests for the CAPM typically regress excess returns for the stock on excess returns for the market, using an equation of the form

$$r_i - r_f = a + b[E(r_m) - r_f]$$

where the parameter a is expected to be zero, and the parameter b is the estimate of beta.

9. The slope parameter, b, of any regression equation $y = a + bx$ is equal to $\text{Cov}(y,x)/\text{Var}(x)$.

10. The manipulation of the utility function involves a procedure called Taylor expansion. For a discussion of the Taylor procedure, see, for example, R. G. D. Allen, *Mathematical Analysis of Economists*. London, England: Macmillan, 1960.

11. T. Ho, R. Schwartz, and D. Whitcomb, "The Trading Decision and Market Clearing Under Transaction Price Uncertainty," *Journal of Finance*, March 1985.

12. For further discussion, see J. Pratt, "Risk Aversion in the Small and the Large," *Econometrica*, January 1964.

13. This subsection and the one that follows are based on Ho, Schwartz, and Whitcomb (1985, op. cit.).

14. The term *consumer surplus* is a monetary measure of the benefits of trade. Specifically, it is the maximum amount that a consumer would be willing to pay for a given number of units traded minus the amount that he or she actually pays. Analogously, *producer surplus* is the monetary receipt from selling a given number of units minus the minimum amount the producer would be willing to receive for the total number of units traded.

15. Equation B.59 is meaningful only for $g < k$. When it is clear in context, we have, for simplicity, suppressed the subscript i on k and $E(r)$ that would identify a specific security.

Dimensions of Informational Efficiency

In this appendix, we present further detail on five dimensions of informational efficiency that were set forth in Chapter 2, "From Information to Prices": (1) efficiency with regard to existing information, (2) efficiency with regard to information-gathering activities, (3) the informational accuracy of equilibrium prices, (4) the informational accuracy of market-clearing prices, and (5) the dynamic efficiency of information dissemination.

EFFICIENCY WITH REGARD TO THE EXISTING INFORMATION SET

Investors make decisions in relation to information in two ways. First, they search for situations in which they think the market has mispriced an asset given the asset's risk-return characteristics. When such a situation is found, an investor takes a position that enables him or her to profit if and when prices are appropriately adjusted in the market. Second, even if all assets are appropriately priced, a selection of alternative mean-variance-efficient portfolios exists, and the investor uses information concerning the risk-return characteristics of securities to select an optimal portfolio (given his or her unique tastes for risk and return). The discussion that follows focuses on the first use to which information may be put.

The decision maker formulates returns expectations by assessing publicly available information, his or her own private information, and current market prices. If, on the basis of the assessment, the risk-adjusted expected return for an asset appears abnormally high, the decision maker seeks to buy additional shares. Alternatively, if the expected return seems abnormally low, the decision maker seeks to sell shares (if he or she is long in the asset), to short the stock, or simply to ignore the stock (if short selling is restricted). A negative return on the stock is a positive return to the investor with a short position. Therefore, by shorting a stock, a trader who is bearish in relation to the market may also anticipate positive returns.

Abnormal returns on an investment are, by definition, returns that are either higher than an investor would require or lower than the investor must receive to make the investment. Therefore, abnormally high returns are "bought" (by buying the shares or shorting the stock), and abnormally low returns are "sold" (by selling shares or covering a short position). Buying pressure increases current prices and thus decreases expected returns. Selling pressure decreases prices and thus increases expected returns to a long position (and reduces expected returns to a short position). Because of the effect of purchases and sales on current prices, transactions that exploit the abnormal returns also eliminate them. It follows that abnormal expected returns are eliminated when investors achieve portfolios that are optimal, given the information set.

The first condition for informational efficiency is that abnormally high returns cannot be realized by exploiting the existing information set. The condition is equivalent to requiring that investors have maximized their expected utilities by obtaining efficient portfolios, given the information that they possess.

EFFICIENCY WITH REGARD TO INFORMATION GATHERING ACTIVITIES

Efficiency with regard to information-gathering activities involves (1) recognizing the trade-off between producing private information and inferring information from market prices, (2) individual participants achieving optimality with regard to the trade-off, and (3) the market in aggregate achieving equilibrium. We start with the trade-off.

The Trade-Off

Assume an investor anticipates a particular mean and variance of returns, given the level of price at which the stock is currently trading. Also assume that, on the basis of logic and past experience, that investor has some understanding of how a new bit of information would alter the stock's price. At a cost, he or she can attempt to obtain that information before its impact is fully reflected in market prices. If successful, the investor benefits from the price adjustment the news will trigger.

With divergent expectations, an individual may also profit from information that has already been widely distributed. For instance, let there be some information bit that an individual might interpret differently than the market in the short term. If that individual were indeed more astute in his or her assessment of the information, then in the longer term he or she would realize a return from it even if the news has already been assessed by others and has had its impact on market prices. By pursuing a further investigation, the individual is producing private information.

As time goes by, truth reveals itself. As it does, some investors find that their anticipations were correct, and others find that they were wrong. Therefore, the return to information includes the profits one can achieve by being more correct than the market. This is a difficult game to play, and few believe that they can consistently play it with success. Nevertheless, security analysis is potentially valuable, even to decision makers who cannot beat the market by being among the first to receive news.

One need not, however, attempt to obtain information directly along the lines discussed previously. An investor can also *infer* informational change from market prices. That is, on the basis of past experience, the investor can interpret price changes as signals (albeit noisy signals) that some new information bit has been released. Therefore, rather than directly looking for the information, the investor may decide to let the price change signal the information.

We define four categories of investors with regard to expectations:

1. *The rugged individualists.* Such people conduct their own security analysis, develop their own assessment of how a stock might perform in the future, and are totally unaffected by what others might think. For these people, future expected price levels are independent of a stock's current price.

2. *The sheep.* These investors exercise no independent judgment. Rather, they simply assume that the price set on the market is the correct price. This being the case, any price change is interpreted as signaling new information on the future value share price will attain, but does not change expected returns. For these people the change in future expected price levels is proportionate to change in a stock's current price.

3. *The exaggerators.* These people assume that current price changes understate the impact of informational change. Thus they believe that any percentage increase or decrease in current price is associated

with a greater percentage increase or decrease in future expected price levels.

4. *The rest of us.* Decision makers in this category think for themselves and come to their own conclusions, but also respect the market's collective judgment as reflected in security prices. These people revise their expectations of future price levels as current prices change, but do so less than proportionately.

What value might price signaling have to a member of the sheep category? From time to time, new funds are invested in the market and old funds are withdrawn. Knowledge (or the belief) that the risk-return characteristics of a security have not changed is relevant for portfolio decisions made in relation to the injection or withdrawal of funds. In addition, the realization (or belief) that the risk-return characteristics of a security regain their previous values after the stock has adjusted to news may prevent the investor from mistakenly buying or selling after an opportunity has passed. In this regard, it may be advisable to act as a sheep if one does not have a preferential position vis-à-vis the information flow or special insight into information's meaning. Furthermore, the investor may in fact benefit from signals inferred from price changes. For instance, if prices do not adjust instantly and accurately to new equilibrium values, the investor may profit by quickly entering orders. Tests using filter rules have shown that trading strategies based on past price changes do in fact generate excess gross returns (although transaction costs make them, on net, unprofitable).[1]

Technical analysts (chartists) in particular believe that profitable trading rules can be formulated on the basis of patterns exhibited by past price movements. Although charting is not accepted by many, the belief that the ebb and flow of investor reactions, psychology, and so on, introduce predictable, repetitive patterns is not, per se, erroneous. The reason for questioning the premise of the chartists is that in an informationally efficient environment, the exploitation of such price patterns would eliminate them, as we have discussed in Chapter 2, "From Information to Prices."

In conclusion, information is valuable whether received directly or inferred from prices and whether received before or after the market has had a chance to adjust to it. However, when it is received sooner and directly (rather than later and inferred), it is (1) more valuable and (2) more costly to obtain. This is why a trade-off exists in information gathering. The second condition for informational efficiency is that this trade-off is optimally resolved. We next explain what this means.

Individual Optimality

Consider one individual's decision of whether or not to purchase a single bit of information concerning a corporation. As discussed previously, the alternative for an investor who does not purchase the information is to make a portfolio decision regarding the corporation's stock on the basis of the stock's market price and other readily available information.

The value of the information bit to any specific decision maker depends on the quality of the anticipations he or she can formulate, given that information, in relation to the quality of the market's anticipations (which are reflected in the current price of the asset). The faster (relative to other market participants) the specific individual can obtain the information bit and the better he or she is as an information processor (relative to other market participants), the greater is the value of the information. The investor should look for information not yet gathered by others and for new information that is not highly correlated with existing information.

Suppose a specific investor is moderately efficient at obtaining and assessing information. The larger the number of other investors who are informed and the more efficient others are as information gatherers and processors, the less likely it is that that investor would realize a competitive advantage by obtaining the information bit. If the decision maker's abilities were low enough in relation to the market, then he or she might do better to let others obtain and process the information, and simply turn to price as an unbiased signal of the information.

The second condition for informational efficiency—that additional information-gathering and -processing activities do not generate abnormal profits—is equivalent to the requirement that an investor obtain information directly if its incremental value is greater than its incremental cost, or infer it from market prices if its incremental value is less than its incremental cost (including the opportunity cost of time).

Market Equilibrium

We have established that the value of additional information to each individual depends, not just on the information itself, but also on that individual's efficiency vis-à-vis others at information gathering and processing. The market is in equilibrium with respect to a piece of information if all individuals for whom that information's value exceeds its cost obtain it, and if all individuals for whom that information's value is less than its cost infer it from the market price of the asset.[2] In such an equilibrium, the information-gathering activities that are undertaken are on net profitable, but additional information gathering does not yield positive net returns.

To establish the existence of an equilibrium amount of information gathering for the market, first consider a situation where no one actively seeks additional information directly, but all participants base their expectations entirely on current market prices and on whatever information was publicly available in the past. The informational content of security prices declines, and prices soon convey very noisy signals. In such a market, an investor with even a small amount of additional effort is able to spot some extraordinary situations—a stock paying a $15 dividend, offering much promise of dividend growth, and trading at $20 a share; some other stock trading at $75 a share even though the company has slashed its dividend and is about to collapse. In such an environment, additional information-gathering activities clearly are profitable.

What would the situation be if many investors were informed? The informational content of security prices would then be high, and prices would convey a far less noisy signal. In this case, all but the most efficient information processors might find that the quality of prices set in the market is too good to beat. Accordingly, most people might simply follow the crowd rather than attempt to outguess the market. In the limit, if all share prices were to reflect all information fully and were not noisy signals, there would be no return to additional information gathering.

This may seem to imply a paradox: On the one hand, if stock prices were to reflect all information fully, no one would undertake security analysis. On the other hand, if no one were to undertake security analysis, stocks could not be appropriately priced.

There is no paradox. An equilibrium amount of information gathering exists. At one extreme, if virtually no one looks for information, the net returns to information gathering are likely to be positive for at least the most efficient information gatherers and processors. At the other extreme, if nearly everyone looks for information, the net returns to information gathering are likely to be negative for at least the most inefficient information gatherers and processors. In equilibrium, an equilibrium number of investors are informed:

- The informed are those who are the most efficient at the process and/or those for whom information has the greatest value.
- For the marginal information gatherer, the value of the information just equals the cost of obtaining it.
- Those for whom the value of information is less than the cost of obtaining it infer the information from prices.

A market that has achieved such an equilibrium is informationally efficient with regard to the intensity with which information-gathering activities are pursued.

THE INFORMATIONAL ACCURACY OF EQUILIBRIUM PRICES

Prices act as constraints that lead individuals to use resources optimally, given supply and demand conditions.[3] In traditional, deterministic economics, *nonstochastic prices* convey no information about the resources themselves—market participants are assumed to have complete information to begin with. On the other hand, when outcomes are uncertain and information is incomplete, prices play an important informational role. Prices are a mechanism for information transfer (from the informed to the uninformed) and for the aggregation of diverse information bits (for both informed and uninformed traders). This section considers the efficiency with which prices perform these two functions.

With divergent expectations, a security's price reflects a weighted average opinion of all investors in the market. The more weight the market gives to the opinions of those who are better informed, the greater is the informational accuracy of the equilibrium prices. The third condition for informational efficiency is that informationally meaningful equilibrium prices are achieved.

Whose expectations might the equilibrium prices reflect? People who believe themselves to be the most efficient at information gathering and processing are most likely to become informed traders (as noted, others will simply let price be their signal). With regard to the distribution of the informed, two factors affect the dollar strength of each person's opinion and hence the weight of his or her conviction in the market.[4] The first factor is the accuracy of the decision maker's opinion, and the second factor is the decision maker's wealth.

The dollar strength of an anticipation is correlated with the accuracy of that anticipation to the extent that truth carries its own conviction. Unfortunately, the presence of some bull- (or bear-) headed fools in the market makes the association between truth and conviction somewhat less than perfect.

The wealth an individual has realized in the financial markets is his or her reward for having invested successfully in the past, and, to an extent, the quality of a decision maker's earlier anticipations is correlated with his or her current abilities as a forecaster. Therefore, current wealth should be positively related to the accuracy of current opinion. However, this association is also less than perfect. Few are able to predict consistently well over time. Furthermore, some inefficient information processors may be richly rewarded by chance, and some efficient information processors may not do well—also by chance.

With regard to the informational efficiency of equilibrium prices, we conclude that even in a market that is informationally efficient in other respects, prices are noisy signals. We may never be sure who the most efficient information processors are by spotting the winners. Consequently, expectations remain divergent and the market does not completely achieve informationally accurate prices.

THE INFORMATIONAL ACCURACY OF MARKET CLEARING PRICES

The preceding section considered the informational accuracy of equilibrium prices. Equilibrium prices are values determined by the intersection of the aggregate buy and sell order functions of all traders. We now consider the informational accuracy of market-clearing prices.[5] Market-clearing prices are values that clear all crossing buy and sell orders that have been written in relation to the underlying order functions. The difference between an equilibrium price and a clearing price is shown in Exhibit C.1. The fourth condition for informational efficiency is that market-clearing prices do not diverge from equilibrium values.

The downward-sloping line labeled B_j in Exhibit C.1(a) is the buy order function of the jth trader. The trader's anticipations of the clearing price are shown by the bell-shaped curve drawn on the vertical axis. $E(P)$ is the expected clearing price. Let the trader submit just one order point (a single price and a single quantity) to the market. Assume a call market-trading environment.[6] Then, given the buy order function (B_j), expectations of the clearing price (as described by the bell-shaped curve) and the call market arrangement, the optimal order for the jth trader to submit is a point such as P_j, Q_j, (labeled a) on the curve RB_j.[7]

The equilibrium price for the asset and for the trading session is shown in Exhibit C.1(b) by the intersection of the aggregate buy and sell order functions. P^* is the equilibrium price, and Q^* is the equilibrium number of shares traded. In the case depicted in Exhibit C.1(b), we have set P^* equal to $E(P)$. In other words, the representative investor has been assumed to have an unbiased, rational expectation of the clearing price. This accuracy of expectations need not be satisfied in any given trading session, however.

The asset's *clearing price* for the trading session is shown in Exhibit C.1(c) by the intersection of the curves labeled B' and S'. B' and S' are not aggregates of the individual order functions, but of the individual order points [such as the single point a, in Exhibit C.1(a)]. In the case depicted in Exhibit C.1(c), the market clearing price is P', and the number of shares

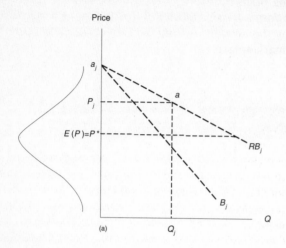

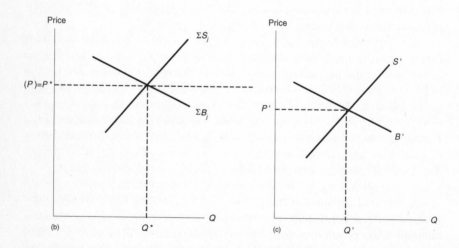

EXHIBIT C.1   A market-clearing price (p') can differ from an equilibrium price (p^*): (a) determination of the optimal buy order point of the jth trader; (b) determination of the equilibrium market price P^* by aggregating investor buy and sell order functions; (c) determination of the market-clearing price P' by aggregating investor buy and sell order points.

traded is Q'. Under transaction price uncertainty, P', in general, differs from $P*$, as shown in the exhibit. Likewise, Q', in general, differs from $Q*$.[8]

Because the clearing price can (and in general does) differ from the equilibrium price, the informational accuracy of the market-clearing price is impaired. That is why the accuracy of price discovery is an important operational issue for a marketplace.

THE DYNAMIC EFFICIENCY OF INFORMATION DISSEMINATION

The four efficiency criteria thus far considered concern static efficiency. We now turn to the fifth requirement, the dynamic efficiency with which information is disseminated in the investment community.

The efficiency of information dissemination has two dimensions: (1) the time needed for new information to be fully reflected in market prices and (2) the sequential order in which the information is disseminated among investors. After change has occurred in a company's fortunes, investors should learn of it quickly, and the change should be quickly reflected in market prices. This is true for both equity and efficiency: Market prices provide better signals to decision makers if they reflect current, rather than outdated, information. But because information dissemination is not instantaneous, some investors are bound to receive news before others.

On June 18, 1815, Napoleon was defeated at Waterloo. A carrier pigeon took news of the British victory to Nathan Rothschild in London. In a single day, Rothschild reaped a fortune by buying shares from uninformed, and quite frightened, traders (he was also credited with having saved the London Stock Exchange). Rothschild's profit was not due to the news. It was due to his having received the news first.

A tremendous amount of information is disseminated in today's markets, and only seconds may separate many investors in the receipt of news. Nonetheless, certain investors still receive information before others, and some may do so consistently. Thus we should continue to question the informational dynamic efficiency of the markets.

Investors receive information at different times for two reasons: (1) They are not equally efficient and aggressive as information gatherers, and (2) some people have a preferential position vis-à-vis the information flow. The efficiency and aggressiveness of investors should be rewarded, and they are. The returns to these people are the profits they receive from the price adjustments that occur when others lag behind them in the receipt and analysis of news. In part, it is the scramble to benefit from the price adjustments that accounts for the informational static efficiency of a market. Nevertheless, the process of information dissemination should be fair.

On August 15, 2000, the U.S. Securities and Exchange Commission took a major step to promote full and fair disclosure of new information by adopting a new rule, Regulation FD. Reg FD addressed the problem of selective disclosure of information by requiring that a listed company must publicly disclose any information that it has provided to some stock analysts and/or to any other securities market professionals who may themselves seek to trade on the basis of that information.

For some people, information is a by-product of a service they provide that has no relation to information gathering. The proofreader in a securities firm or a lawyer in a merger case, for instance, may receive information that has not yet been released to the public. When these people profit from their prior receipt of information, we may observe certain proofreaders and lawyers being grossly overpaid for their services. No economic function is served by this overpayment. On the contrary, the feelings of inequity that it can engender can have harmful repercussions.

Insiders are deemed to have a preferential and unfair advantage vis-à-vis the information flow. Accordingly, these people are restricted in their freedom to trade shares of their corporation's stock. Insiders must file with the SEC after trading, and they are not allowed to trade on news that has not yet been made public. We discuss insider-trading restrictions further in the Chapter 11, "Regulation."

A trade-off exists between the dynamic efficiency and the static efficiency of a market. The greater the flow of information in the market, the more accurate are the prices that are set and the more static efficient is the market. But the flow of information is positively related to the return to information, and the return to information is in large part the price adjustments an informed trader profits from when he or she receives the news first. Therefore, *dynamic inefficiency* motivates the information-gathering activities that make a market static efficient.

That such a trade-off exists is not surprising. Information gathering, like trading, is a manifestation of disequilibrium behavior. Also, as with trading, information gathering helps to repair imbalance in the market and to bring prices back to equilibrium values. It is too much to expect that the dynamic process by which equilibrium is regained will generate no undesired side effects. If we want prices that are the best possible signals of information, we must let those who have the best information (insiders included) trade with a minimum of restrictions. Alternatively, if we do not want insiders consistently to exploit the uninformed public, we must settle for prices that are noisier reflections of the information set. This is indeed a difficult trade-off.

NOTES

1. A *filter rule* is a decision to buy if price goes up x percent and to sell if price goes down x percent, where the value of x sets the strength of the filter. See S. Alexander, "Price Movements in Speculative Markets: Trends or Random Walks," *Industrial Management Review*, May 1961, and S. Alexander, "Price Movements in Speculative Markets: Trends or Random Walks No. 2," *Industrial Management Review*, spring 1964.

2. The discussion concerning market equilibrium draws heavily on S. Grossman and J. Stiglitz, "Information and Competitive Price Systems," *American Economic Review*, May 1976. Used with permission.

3. The discussion in this section draws on S. Figlewski, "Market 'Efficiency' in a Market with Heterogeneous Information," *Journal of Political Economy*, August 1978. Used with permission.

4. The *dollar strength* of an investor's opinion is the funds he or she commits to a position in light of the strength of his or her conviction.

5. The discussion in this section draws on T. Ho, R. Schwartz, and D. Whitcomb, "The Trading Decision and Market Clearing Under Transaction Price Uncertainty," *Journal of Finance*, March 1985. Used with permission.

6. In call auction trading, buy and sell orders that could be matched and executed are batched together for a multilateral trade, at a single price, at a predetermined point in time when the market "called." We discuss this trading environment further in Chapter 6.

7. The curve labeled RB_j reflects reservation prices. At a quantity, a *reservation price to buy* is the highest price a participant would be willing to pay for that entire quantity when the alternative is not to buy at all. A *reservation price to sell* is similarly defined as the lowest price the participant would be willing to receive for the entire quantity when the alternative is not to sell at all.

8. The simplest way to show that P' and $P*$ generally differ is to show the special conditions under which they will be the same. There are two necessary conditions: (1) Buyers and sellers must all expect a clearing price of $P*$ (the equilibrium price), and (2) the distribution of buyers and the distribution of sellers must be symmetric. These two conditions can both hold in any given trading session only by chance.

The Concept of Self-Regulation

Every market needs basic rules and common practices for there to be trading, and every market needs regulation to enhance market quality by bringing fairness, orderliness, and consistency. To achieve a highly efficient market, trading procedures require a great deal of regulatory attention, and both the traded instruments (the securities) and the listed companies must be focal points of regulation. In particular, a high degree of standardized disclosure and transparency about listed companies is a prerequisite for public confidence.

Stock exchanges are typically among the most regulated markets, with the most standardized procedures designed to deliver extremely high efficiency and speed. Nevertheless, regulation also reduces the freedom of market participants. Therefore, there should be "as much regulation as necessary, but still as little as ever possible." In the future, as competition among market infrastructures increases, an optimum regulatory structure and an optimum combination of government regulation and self-regulation will be crucial to ensuring an exchange's competitiveness. Regulation must also be appropriate to the needs of the investor. Government regulation can provide a strong foundation in key areas by defining overarching principles (e.g., the responsibilities of professional traders vis-à-vis their customers). This provides a first-line guarantee of confidence in a market.

Regardless of whether it is a for-profit organization or a mutual

---

The discussion in this appendix is presented, as much as possible, in generic form so that it might be maximally applicable to a broad array of markets on both sides of the Atlantic. Some differences from market to market are, of course, inevitable.

organization, an exchange runs a *regulated business*. Regulation, organization, technology, systems, and logistics are key functions of an exchange. In so far as it sets, supervises, and enforces its own rules, an exchange is typically called a *self-regulatory organization* (SRO). Self-regulation sets the detailed rules for every aspect of the marketplace. To a large extent, an exchange is defined by its rule book. From a broad perspective, the following may be said of an exchange (and its rule book):

- It is generally regarded as a "public utility" that has the task of establishing good liquidity and low transactions costs.
- It is a place to build market size and efficiency for public companies and members.
- It has a neutral position within the market.
- It creates value by establishing and applying rules and regulations that ensure fair and transparent price discovery.[1] Good price discovery is one of the main assets of an exchange.
- It is vital to a market economy.

The *overall objectives* of exchange rules and regulations are:

- Investor protection.
- System protection.
- The achievement of a fair and orderly market.

To meet these goals, an exchange must have independence and the freedom to operate within its own particular regulatory environment. As with any form of marketplace, there will always be some risk whenever buyers and sellers come together. Investors will never be able to operate in a zero-risk environment. The goal of an exchange is to reduce risk to a minimum without imposing undue administrative burdens on market participants.

The expanding globalization of securities markets is leading to *competition in regulation* between national and/or supranational capital markets. What happens if the rules and regulations in one particular marketplace are too burdensome, inefficient, or inconsistent, and therefore not competitive in one marketplace? Under these conditions, investors (especially institutional investors with the necessary clout and sophistication) will route their orders to another marketplace where the regulatory structure is more advantageous. This is easily done with the use of modern technology that enables an investor, with a simple mouse click, to move his or her order from one market to another.

Orders can be redirected in today's markets almost totally unrestricted by either volume or place. The process is called *regulatory arbitrage*. With regulatory arbitrage, the advantages of a marketplace can be rapidly devalued. Regulatory arbitrage by participants makes it of utmost importance that an exchange's legal framework be sufficiently competitive. If it is not, the consequences can be huge. And if an exchange is not successful in the international competition for liquidity, the cost of shareholder equity can rise significantly.

The regulatory functions necessary for an exchange to function effectively comprise the following.[2]

The Primary Market

- Vetting of prospectuses.
- Admissions to listing and trading.

The Secondary Market

- Supervision of trading.
- Market surveillance:
  In real time (for instance, monitoring for price manipulation).
  Posttrade (e.g., looking for insider trading by members, intermediaries, and/or customers.
- General rules of business (including relevant aspects of clearing and settlement).
- Overseeing member positions and market risk (including clearing risk when a central counterparty is used).
- Ongoing obligations concerning financial reporting and disclosure and the dissemination of price and other sensitive information.
- Monitoring compliance with corporate governance regulations.

Membership (Admission and Vetting)

- Member firms and other market participants.
- Traders.

The rules and regulations of an exchange contribute to market efficiency on both a national and an international level, and self-regulation is an effective way to establish the rules and regs.[3] Delegating to an exchange the competence and power to set its own rules and regs is usually stated in a national or federal law, typically in the form of some type of "securities exchange act."[4] The law sets the legal framework and general objectives, but delegates the establishment of rules to the exchange.

Based on the framework established by law, the exchange establishes its own rules, although these, in turn, usually must be approved by a national or federal "securities commission."[5] This form of self-regulation means that authoritative orders are not established by the government authorities, but by the private organizations. The principle is widely accepted and practiced in other industries.[6] Self-regulation relies on an appropriate interplay between a government's authority to approve and supervise and an exchange's right as a private organization to define its rules. The exchange acts as a *regulatory agent* with the delegation and assignment of competency, but the independent authority and autonomy in rule setting is carried out within a clearly specified and prescribed legal framework:

- No extensive interpretation or delegation of competence is allowed outside the legal framework.
- Legislation may be at several levels, with the regulatory authority defining detailed regulations.[7]

Government regulation and self-regulation should not be thought of as conflicting with each other, but as complementing each other. Optimum regulation represents a cooperative effort by the government regulator and the SRO, with the greater power of the former and the superior flexibility of the latter being combined to create the right environment. Finding the appropriate mix of government regulation and self-regulation is more of an art than a science. It is a customized, tailor-made mix of (1) principles that remain unchanged over a long period of time and (2) the many facets of the market that are in permanent development. Ideally, the mix is defined in a cooperative effort to produce the proper checks and balances without incurring unnecessary limitations on the operation of competitive market forces. We provide an example of the regulatory competencies in Exhibit D.1.

A blueprint of rule making must include various items that we show in Exhibit D.2. The items are organized in three phases: the delegation of power, specification of rules and regulations, and government regulatory authority.

Phase I: The Delegation of Power
- The delegation of power to a regulated exchange by means of national or federal legislation (a securities or stock exchange law) allows the exchange to set its own rules and regulations. The law in question must explicitly delegate this power to establish rules.
- The competencies must be clearly specified and covered by the delegating legislation.

Phase II: Specification of Rules and Regulations
- The rules and regulations are specified by the exchange organization in consultation with market participants (the general assembly, board of

	Development/ Maintenance of Regulation	Implementation/ Application/ Supervision	Supervision	Enforcement/ Surveillance 1, Minor Sanctions	Enforcement/ Surveillance 2, Major Sanctions
Listing	Exchange	Exchange	Exchange	Exchange	Exchange
Ongoing disclosure	Exchange	Exchange	Exchange	Exchange	Exchange
Trading procedures (traders and firms)	Exchange	Exchange	Exchange	Exchange	GR
Trading firms					
▪ Management	GR	GR	GR	GR	GR
▪ Financials	Exchange/GR	Exchange	Exchange	Exchange/GR	GR
▪ Infrastructures	Exchange/GR	Exchange	Exchange	Exchange	Exchange
Investors	GR/exchange	Exchange/GR	GR	GR	GR
Insider trading violations	Exchange	Exchange	Exchange/GR	GR/DA	GR/DA
Market manipulation	Exchange	Exchange	Exchange/GR	GR/DA	GR/DA

Note: GR = government regulator; DA = district attorney.

EXHIBIT D.1 Regulatory competencies (an example).

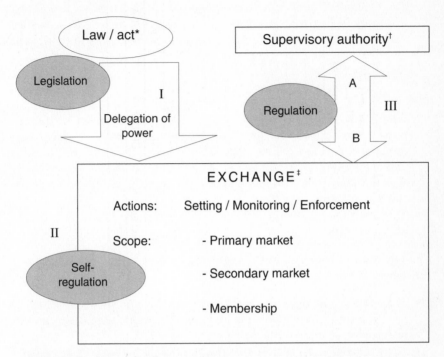

EXHIBIT D.2 A blueprint of rule making: (1) stating the power to set rules and the power to delegate rule-setting competence; (2) see, for example, the *SEC mission:* "Whenever pursuant to this title the commission is engaged in rulemaking, or the review of a rule of a self-regulatory organization, and is required to consider or determine whether an action is necessary or appropriate in the public interest, . . ." (Securities Exchange Act of 1934, Section 3f; also, nearly identical, the Securities Act of 1933, Section 2b, and the Investment Company Act of 1940, Section 2c); The three acts build the *legislative foundation for exchange and securities regulation in the United States;* (3) An exchange in this chart is a *self-regulating organization* (SRO).

---

*States the power to set rules and the power to delegate rule-setting competence.

†See, for example, the SEC mission: "Whenever pursuant to this title the commission is engaged in rule making, or the review of a rule of a self-regulatory organization, and is required to consider or determine whether an action is necessary or appropriate in the public interest,. . . ." The Securities Exchange Act of 1934, Section 3f. See also the Securities Act of 1933, Section 2b, and the Investment Company Act of 1940, Section 2c. The three acts build the legislative foundation for exchange and securities regulation in the United States.

‡An exchange in this chart is an SRO (self-regulating organization).

directors, user groups, traders, back-office and IT staff, external experts, lawyers, market architects, etc.).

- The exchange's draft rules may be subject to approval by its general assembly or board of directors and the national or federal securities exchange commission, or other appropriate supervisory authority (or authorities in the case where supranational bodies are involved).

Phase III: The Government Regulatory Authority

- Where government supervisory authorities are involved in the approval, they check the proposal in legal, market, and technology terms and decide to either approve or reject.[8] If approved, the rules and regulations are implemented within a determined period of time. If rejected, they must be amended to include, change, or remove provisions as required.
- The government supervisory authorities themselves have the right to call in experts.

The checks and balances in the regulatory process[9] can include the following:

- The government supervisory authorities act as approval authorities in terms of form and content, and they have the right to approve, change, or reject all or parts of the proposal.
- The exchange must require that the corresponding party contractually commits itself to fulfill the regulatory requirements, which also concerns fair treatment of all involved parties (e.g., the members).
- Strict rules exist on how to determine the composition of exchange corporate bodies. For instance, the board of directors must include issuers, investors, and independents among its members.
- The self-regulatory activities of an exchange are systematically examined and monitored by the national supervisory authority.
- The decisions of an exchange, based on its rules and regulations, are subject to appeal to, and remedy by, independent bodies.
- Ongoing supervisory and reporting obligations exist with respect to the government authority.

The following principles of self-regulation apply to the setting of rules. A rule must be:

- Set only when necessary (as we have previously noted, the rule for this is, "as much as necessary and as little as possible").[10]
- Set only within the limitations of the legislation.

- In line with market needs.
- Implementable, enforceable, and therefore effective.

Self-regulation is a specific, controlled, and supervised procedure. Rules are set with a very high degree of direct or self-responsibility. The procedure makes the actions of the exchange predictable, and the process builds up the trustworthiness of the exchange (thereby ensuring legal clarity). As a result, the actions of the regulatory authorities must be consistent, comprehensible, and credible.

The advantages of self-regulation are self-evident. In the current environment, where technology is quickly evolving, where product differentiation is a key issue, and where clarity for market participants is of utmost importance, it is of great advantage that the people who are defining and ultimately setting the rules be as close as possible to the important issues. Self-regulation of the marketplace means faster, more flexible, and more effective adaptation to a fast-changing environment. Self-regulation, being faster than the alternative (legal) procedure, reduces the potential for crippling regulatory lag. One cannot emphasize enough that the ability to respond quickly to market developments is of major strategic importance. Being able to capitalize on and to integrate the know-how of the market participants are key. Wrong developments should be avoided and balanced through subsequent government control and monitoring.

On the other side of the coin, often-mentioned disadvantages of self-regulation include the possibility that unfettered competition could become impaired by cartelized practices, that weaker players in the market could be placed at an unfair disadvantage, and that interest groups or stronger players may sway the regulatory process (an act that is referred to as *regulatory capture*). And so the debate continues. We conclude that there is no ideal regulatory model, that the proper balance between government regulation and self-regulation must be placed in the context of the particular market at issue. But we also bear in mind what Montesquieu (1689–1755) wrote in his treatise, "De l'Esprit des Lois" (1748): "Useless laws weaken necessary laws." Accordingly, the law that defines the foundation upon which the rules of a market are set should include three items:

1. Restricted regulatory breadth.
2. Clearly specified and limited regulatory depth.
3. Wide delegation of competencies.[11]

These preconditions for successful self-regulation are absolutely necessary to enhance market quality.

NOTES

1. A *rule* is typically established by the exchange itself, in consultation with its members. A rule may or may not need to be formally approved by a regulator. A *regulation* is typically established by *external* regulators, or by internal "self-regulators."

2. This can be achieved either by the exchange setting its own rules and/or monitoring compliance, or by the exchange receiving responsibility for enforcement of regulations defined by external (typically government) regulators.

3. The national or federal law-setting body has—besides self-regulation—two other regulatory alternatives:
   1. A *very comprehensive law* with wide scope and very specific level of detail. This is the case in Germany. Disadvantage: Adaptation is time-consuming and difficult; every time the law needs to be changed, the whole heavyweight procedure has to be followed.
   2. A *central supervisory authority* explicitly (e.g., the Securities and Exchange Commission in the United States—Securities Act 1933 and Securities Exchange Act 1934) or implicitly (e.g., the Securities and Exchange Surveillance Commission in Japan—Securities and Exchange Law 1948) receives far-reaching competence to regulate the securities and exchange business. This approach can be very flexible, as rules and regulations can be established at a lower, more informal level than primary or secondary legislation. Disadvantage: There's a lack of legal certainty.

   It is important, even if such authorities are set up, that there still remain important areas requiring self-regulation because of the need for rule making close to the marketplace itself.

4. In the United Kingdom, this is the Financial Services and Markets Act (FSMA), 2000; in Switzerland, it is the Swiss Stock Exchange Act, March 23, 1995.

5. For instance, the Securities and Exchange Commission (SEC) in the United States, Financial Services Authority (FSA) in the United Kingdom, and the Federal Banking Commission in Switzerland.

6. For instance, in the field of accounting:
   - The International Accounting Standards Board (IASB) has established the International Financial Reporting Standards (IFRS).
   - The U.S. Financial Accounting Standards Board (FASB) has established the standard U.S. generally accepted accounting principles (GAAP).
   - There are domestic auditing standards.
   - There are international auditing standards (e.g., International Standards on Auditing, established by the International Federation of Accountants, IFAC).
   - There are analyst regulations, established by the industry itself.
   - There are corporate governance standards and codes.

7. This is the case, for instance, in the United Kingdom. In the regulatory structure in the United Kingdom, the FSA:

- Is an independent nongovernmental body that has statutory powers under the Financial Services and Markets Act 2000 (FSMA). The government is responsible for the overall scope of the FSA's regulatory activities and powers.
- Exercises its powers over recognized investment exchanges (RIEs) through rules and guidance on how the FSA interprets the recognition requirements prescribed by the Treasury. RIEs must satisfy the recognition requirements on a continuing basis.
- Expects an RIE to take its own steps to ensure that it continues to satisfy the recognition requirements and other obligations in or under FSMA when considering any changes to its business or operations. The FSA does not generally approve the detailed wording of an RIE's rules, but considers whether rule changes proposed by an exchange enable it to continue to satisfy the recognition requirements.

8. The SEC, for example, describes its mission at its web site (www.sec.gov) thus: "to administer and enforce the federal securities laws in order to protect investors, and to maintain fair, honest and efficient markets."

9. For further reading in achieving market integration, see Scott McCleskey, *Achieving Market Integration*, Butterworth-Heinemann, 2004, p. 153.

10. *Indications of necessity* (which can be described and regulated only in concrete cases) include:
    - Comparisons based on a quantifiable scale and compared with the overall law setting the procedures and the specific issue that has to be regulated.
    - Consequences of the rules for the sanctioned persons and companies.
    - Scope of regulated persons and companies.
    - Political importance.
    - Organizational and administrative impact in realizing the rules (implementation and enforcement).

    Regulation must be kept to the minimum. New regulation must be triggered by a clear and comprehensive objective, a significant "return on investment," a timely and target-oriented implementation, and an effective application. Careful attention must be given not just to creating and maintaining rules and regulations, but also to abolishing them.

11. Competencies to regulate as closely as possible to the corresponding market know-how of practitioners (e.g., trading rules and matching algorithms) should therefore be taken into account by the exchange.

Selected Readings

MICROSTRUCTURE BOOKS

Amihud, Y., T. Ho, and R. Schwartz, eds. *Market Making and the Changing Structure of the Securities Industry*. Lexington, MA: Lexington Books, 1985.

Avgerinos, Y. V. *Regulating and Supervising Investment Services in the European Union*, Palgrave MacMillan, 2003.

Bloch, E., and R. Schwartz, eds. *Impending Changes for Securities Markets: What Role for the Exchange?* Greenwich, CT: JAI Press, 1979.

Buck, J., ed. *The New York Stock Exchange: The First 200 Years*, New York 1992.

Cohen, K. S., R. Maier, R. Schwartz, and D. Whitcomb. *The Microstructure of Securities Markets*. Englewood Cliffs, NJ: Prentice Hall, 1986.

Garbade, K. *Securities Markets*. New York: McGraw-Hill series in finance, 1982.

Harris, L. *Trading & Exchanges: Market Microstructure for Practitioners*. London: Oxford University Press, 2003.

Lucas, H., and R. Schwartz, eds. *The Challenge of Information Technology for the Securities Markets: Liquidity, Volatility, and Global Trading*. Dow Jones-Irwin, 1989.

O'Hara, M. *Market Microstructure Theory*. Cambridge, MA: Basil Blackwell, 1995.

Schwartz, R. *Equity Markets: Structure, Trading, and Performance*. Harper & Row, 1988.

Schwartz, R. *Reshaping the Equity Markets: A Guide For the 1990s*. HarperBusiness, 1991. Reissued by Business One Irwin, 1993.

Schwartz, R., ed. *Global Equity Markets: Technological, Competitive and Regulatory Challenges*, Irwin Professional, 1995.

Schwartz, R., ed. *The Electronic Call Auction: Market Mechanism and Trading*. Kluwer Academic Publishers, 2001.

Schwartz, R., and A. Colaninno, eds. *Regulation of U.S. Equity Markets*. Kluwer Academic Publishers, 2001.

Schwartz, R., J. Byrne, and A. Colaninno, eds. *Call Auction Trading: New Answers to Old Questions.* Kluwer Academic Publishers, 2003.

Schwartz, R., J. Byrne, and A. Colaninno, eds. *A Trading Desk's View of Market Quality,* Kluwer Academic Publishers, forthcoming 2004.

Schwartz, R., J. Byrne, and A. Colaninno, eds. *Coping with Institutional Order Flow,* Kluwer Academic Publishers, forthcoming 2004.

Steil, B. *The European Equity Markets: The State of the Union and an Agenda for the Millennium,* London: European Capital Markets Institute and the Royal Institute of International Affairs, 1996.

OTHER PUBLICATIONS

Adams, G., G. McQueen, and R. Wood. "The Effects of Inflation News on High Frequency Stocks Returns," *Journal of Business,* forthcoming 2003.

Admati, A., and P. Pfleiderer. "A Theory of Intraday Patterns: Volume and Price Variability," *Review of Financial Studies* 1, 1988, pp. 3–40.

Alexander, S. "Price Movements in Speculative Markets: Trends or Random Walks," *Industrial Management Review,* May 1961.

Allen, A., and L. Zarembo. "The Displaybook: The NYSE Specialist's Electronic Workstation," in H. Lucas and R. Schwartz, eds., *The Challenge of Information Technology for the Securities Markets: Liquidity, Volatility and Global Trading.* Homewood, IL: Dow Jones-Irwin, 1989.

Allen, R. G. D. *Mathematical Analysis for Economists.* London: Macmillan, 1960.

Amihud, Y., and H. Mendelson. "Asset Pricing and the Bid-Ask Spread," *Journal of Financial Economics* 17, 1986, pp. 223–249.

Amihud, Y., and H. Mendelson. "Dealership Market: Market Making with Inventory," *Journal of Financial Economics* 8, pp. 31–53, 1980.

Amihud, Y., and H. Mendelson. "Trading Mechanisms and Stock Returns: an Empirical Investigation," *Journal of Finance* 42, 1987, pp. 533–555.

Amihud, Y., H. Mendelson, and B. Lauterbach. "Market Microstructure and Securities Values: Evidence from the Tel Aviv Stock Exchange," *Journal of Financial Economics* 45, 1997, pp. 365–390.

Andersen, T., T. Bollerslev, A. Das. "Variance-Ratio Statistics and High-Frequency Data: Testing for Changes in Intraday Volatility Patterns," *Journal of Finance* 56, 2001, pp. 305–327.

Association for Investment Management and Research (AIMR), "Trade Management Guidelines," Charlottesville, VA, November 12, 2001.

Bagehot, W. (pseudonym). "The Only Game in Town," *Financial Analysts Journal* 8, 1971, pp. 31–53.

Barclay, M. "Bid-Ask Spreads and the Avoidance of Odd-Eighth Quotes on Nasdaq: An Examination of Exchange Listings," *Journal of Financial Economics* 45, 1997, pp. 35–60.

Barclay, M., W. Christie, J. Harris, E. Kandel, and P. Schultz. "The Effects of Market Reform on the Trading Costs and Depths of Nasdaq Stocks," *Journal of Finance* 54, 1999, pp. 1–34.

Baumol, W. *Economic Theory and Operations Analysis*, 4th ed. Englewood Cliffs, NJ: Prentice Hall, 1977.

Beiner, N., and R. Schwartz. "The Option Properties of Limit Orders in Call and Continuous Environments," in Robert A. Schwartz, ed., *The Electronic Call Auction: Market Mechanism and Trading, Building a Better Stock Market*, Kluwer Academic Publishers, 2001.

Berkowitz, S., D. Logue, and E. Noser. "The Total Cost of Transactions on the NYSE," *Journal of Finance*, 1988, pp. 97–112.

Bessembinder, H., and H. Kaufman. "A Cross-Exchange Comparison of Execution Costs and Information Flow for NYSE-Listed Stocks," *Journal of Financial Economics* 46, 1997, pp. 293–319.

Bessembinder, H., and R. Subhrendu. "Trading Costs and Return Volatility: Evidence From Exchange Listings," working paper, University of Utah, 2002.

Bessembinder, H. "Trading Costs and Return Volatility: Evidence from Exchange Listings," unpublished working paper, Emory University, 1998.

Biais, B., P. Hillion, and C. Spatt. "An Empirical Analysis of the Limit Order Book and the Order Flow in the Paris Bourse," *Journal of Finance* 50, 1995, pp. 1655–1689.

Bikhchandani, S., D. Hirshleifer, and I. Welch. "A Theory of Fads, Fashion, Custom, and Cultural Change as Informational Cascades," *Journal of Political Economy* 100, 1992, pp. 992–1026.

Bloch, E. "Multiple Regulators: Their Constituencies and Policies," in Amihud, Ho, and Schwartz (1985).

Blume, L., D. Easley, and M. O'Hara. "Market Statistics and Technical Analysis: The Role of Volume," *Journal of Finance* 49, no. 1, 1994, pp. 153–181.

Bradford, D., A. Shleifer, L. Summers, and R. Waldman. "Positive Feedback Investment Strategies and Destabilizing Rational Speculation," *Journal of Finance* 45, 1990, pp. 379–395.

Bradley, H. "Views of an 'Informed' Trader," reprinted by AIMR 2002 from the AIMR proceedings, *Organizational Challenges for Investment Firms*. Charlottesville, VA: AIMR, May 2002.

Brealey, R., and A. Neuberger. "Treatment of Investment Management Fees and Commission Payments: An Examination of the Recommendations Contained in the Myners Report," *Fund Managers Association*, October 2001.

Brennan, M., and A. Subrahmanyam. "Market Microstructure and Asset Pricing: On the Compensation for Illiquidity in Stock Returns," *Journal of Financial Economics* 41, 1996, pp. 441–464,

Bresiger, G. "SEC at Market Structure Crossroad," *Traders Magazine*, June 2003.

Campbell, J., A. Lo, and A. C. MacKinlay. *The Econometrics of Financial Markets.* Princeton, NJ: Princeton University Press, 1997, pp. 48–80.

Chakraborty, S., M. Pagano, and R. Schwartz. "Bookbuilding,," Baruch College working paper, 2004.

Chakravarty, S., and C. Holden. "An Integrated Model of Market and Limit Orders," *Journal of Financial Intermediation* 4, 1995, pp. 213–241.

Chakravarty, S., R. Wood, and R. Van Ness. "Decimal Trading and Market Impact," working paper, University of Memphis, May 2002.

Chan, L., and J. Lakonishok. "Institutional Trades and Intraday Stock Price Behavior," *Journal of Financial Economics*, 1993, pp. 173–199.

Chordia, T., and B. Swaminathan. "Trading Volume and Cross-Autocorrelations in Stock Returns," *Journal of Finance* 55, 2000, pp. 913–935.

Christie, W., and P. Schultz. "Why Do Nasdaq Market Makers Avoid Odd-eighth Quotes?" *Journal of Finance* 49, 1994, pp. 1813–1840.

Christie, W. "A Minimum Increment Solution," *Traders Magazine*, November 2003, p. 40.

Clary, I. "Why Hasn't the SEC Turned Down Nasdaq?" *Securities Industry News*, August 18, 2003, p. 4.

Clemons, E., and B. Weber. "London's Big Bang: A Case Study of Information Technology, Competitive Impact, and Organizational Change," *Journal of Management Information Systems*, spring 1990.

Cohen, K., and R. Schwartz. "An Electronic Call Market: Its Design and Desirability," in Lucas and Schwartz (1989).

Cohen, K., G. Hawawini, S. Maier, R. Schwartz, and D. Whitcomb. "Friction in the Trading Process and the Estimation of Systematic Risk," *Journal of Financial Economics* 12, 1983a, pp. 264–278.

Cohen, K., G. Hawawini, S. Maier, R. Schwartz, and D. Whitcomb. "Estimating and Adjusting for the Intervalling-Effect Bias in Beta," *Management Science* 29, 1983b, pp. 135–148.

Cohen, K., S. Maier, R. Schwartz, and D. Whitcomb. "Transaction Costs, Order Placement Strategy, and Existence of the Bid-Ask Spread," *Journal of Political Economy*, April 1981, pp. 287–305. Reprinted in Hans Stoll, ed., *Microstructure: The*

Organization of Trading and Short Term Price Behavior, Edward Elgar Publishing Limited, 1999, pp. 76–94.

Conrad, J., K. Johnson, and S. Wahal. "Institutional Trading and Soft Dollars," *Journal of Finance* 56, 2001, pp. 397–422.

Cooper, K., J. Groth, and W. Avera. "Liquidity, Exchange Listing, and Common Stock Performance," *Journal of Economics and Business*, February 1985.

Copeland, T. E. "A Model of Asset Trading Under the Assumption of Sequential Information Arrival," *Journal of Finance* 31, no. 4, 1976, pp. 1149–1168.

Copeland, T. E., and D. Galai. "Information Effects on the Bid-Ask Spreads," *Journal of Finance* 38, 1983, pp. 1457–1469.

Coughenour, J., and K. Shastri. "Symposium on Market Microstructure: A Review of Empirical Research," *Financial Review* 34, no. 4, pp. 1–28.

Cox, C., and B. Kohn. "Regulatory Implications of Computerized Communications in Securities Markets," in Saunders and White (1986).

Cushing, D., and A. Madhavan. "Stock Returns and Institutional Trading at the Close," *Journal of Financial Markets* 3, 2000, pp. 45–67.

Daniel, K., D. Hirshleifer, and A. Subrahmanyam. "Investor Psychology and Security Market Under- and Overreactions," *Journal of Finance* 53, 1988, pp. 1839–1885.

Dann, L., and W. Mikkelson. "Convertible Debt Issuance, Capital Structure Change and Financing-Related Information," *Journal of Financial Economics*, June 1984.

Dann, L., D. Mayers, and R. Raab. "Trading Rules, Large Blocks and the Speed of Price Adjustments," *Journal of Financial Economics*, January 1977.

DeLong, Bradford J., A. Shleifer, L. H. Summers, and R. J. Waldman. "Positive Feedback Investment Strategies and Destabilizing Rational Speculation," *Journal of Finance* 45, 1990, pp. 379–395.

Demarchi, M., and S. Thomas. "Call Market Mechanism on the Paris Stock Exchange, in Schwartz (2001).

Dimson, E. "Risk Measurement When Shares Are Subject to Infrequent Trading," *Journal of Financial Economics* 7, 1979, pp. 197–226.

Domowitz, I., and B. Steil. "Automation, Trading Costs, and the Structure of the Securities Trading Industry," *Brookings-Wharton Papers on Financial Services*, 1999, pp. 33–92.

Domowitz, I., and B. Steil. "Innovation in Equity Trading Systems: The Impact on Transactions Costs and the Cost of Capital," *Technological Innovation and Economic Performance*, Princeton University Press, 2001.

Dunfee, T., F. Gibson, J. Blackburn, D. Whitman, F. McCarty, and B. Brennan. *Modern Business Law*. New York: Random House, 1984.

Dwyer, P., and A. Borrus. "The Crisis at Nasdaq," *Business Week*, August 11, 2003.

Easley, D., and O. Maureen. "Price, Trade Size, and Information in Securities Markets," *Journal of Financial Economics* 19, 1987, pp. 69–90.

Easley, D., H. Soeren, and O. Maureen. "Is Information Risk a Determinant of Asset Returns?" *Journal of Finance*, 2002.

Economides, N., and R. Schwartz. "Electronic Call Market Trading," *Journal of Portfolio Management*, 1995, pp. 10–18.

Economides, N., and R. Schwartz. "Equity Trading Practices and Market Structure: Assessing Asset Managers' Demand for Immediacy." *Financial Markets, Institutions and Instruments* 4, no. 4, 1995, pp. 1–46.

Elton, E., and M. Gruber. *Modern Portfolio Theory and Investment Analysis*, 4th ed. New York: John Wiley & Sons, 1991.

Elyasiani, E., S. Hauser, and B. Lauterbach. "Market response to Liquidity Improvements: Evidence from Exchange Listings," *Financial Review* 35, 2000, p. 1.

Fama, E. "Efficient Capital Markets: A Review of Theory and Empirical Work," *Journal of Finance*, May 1970.

Fama, E. "The Behavior of Stock-Market Prices," *Journal of Business*, January 1965.

Fama, E., L. Fisher, M. Jensen, and R. Roll. "The Adjustment of Stock Prices to New Information," *International Economic Review*, February 1969.

Fang, C., K. Gautam, and Z. Lu. "The Patterns of Returns, Raw Returns and Excess Returns, Before and After Institutional Trading Are Striking," *Institutional Trading and Stock Returns*, 2000, pp. 2–3, 6.

Fant, L., and E. O'Neal. "Temporal Changes in the Determinants of Mutual Fund Flows," *Journal of Financial Research* 23, no. 3, 2000, pp. 353–371.

Figlewski, S. "Market Efficiency in a Market with Heterogeneous Information," *Journal of Political Economy*, August 1978.

Financial Services Authority (FSA), "Best Execution," discussion paper, London, April 2001.

Finnerty, J. "Insiders and Market Efficiency," *Journal of Finance*, September 1976.

Fisher, L. "Some New Stock-Market Indexes," *Journal of Business* 16, 1966, pp. 191–225.

Fleming, M., and E. Remolina. "Price Formation and Liquidity in the U.S. Treasury Market: The Response to Public Information," *Journal of Finance* 54, 1999, pp. 1901–1915.

Forum of European Securities Commissions, "Standards and Rules for Harmonizing Core Conduct of Business Rules For Investor Protection," consultative paper, Paris, February 2001 (ref. Fesco/00-124b).

Foster, F. "An Empirical Investigation of the Agreement Among Underwriters and the Selling Contract: The Effects of SEC Rule 415," working paper, Duke University Fuqua School of Business, 1987.

Foucault, T. "Order Flow Composition and Trading Costs in a Dynamic Order Driven Market," *Journal of Financial Markets* 2, 1999, pp. 99–134.

Francioni, R. "Marktformen zum Handel von Unternehmensanteilen," in *Wertorientiertes Start-Up-Management*, edited by Ulrich Hommel and Thomas C. Knecht, Verlag Franz Vahlen, München, 2002, pp. 541–562.

Francioni, R. "Der Börsengang von Mittelstands- und Familienunternehmen," in *Planung, Finanzierung und Kontrolle im Familienunternehmen*, edited by Jeschke/Kirchdörfer/Lorz, Verlag C.H. Beck, 2000.

Francioni, R. "Der Neue Markt im Kontext europäischer Wachstumssegmente," in *Handbuch Europäischer Kapitalmarkt*, edited by Prof. Dr. Hummel, 2000.

Francioni, R. "Doppelnotierung Neuer Markt/Nasdaq (Co-Autor: Dr. Barbara Böhnlein)," *in Zugang zum US-Kapitalmarkt für deutsche Akeintengesellschaften*, edited by Prof. Rüdiger von Rosen and Dr. Werner G. Seifert, 1998.

Francioni, R. "German Equity Market Development as a Response to Investor Needs," in *Institutional Investor Needs, Trading Costs and Equity Market Structure (Symposium)*, edited by Deutsche Börse, 1995.

Francioni, R., *La supériorité en terme de liquidité du système de transactions électronique IBIS sur le parquet*, in Bruno Biais, Didier Davydoff, et Bertrand Jacquillat, eds., *Finance Organisation et qualité des marchés financiers*, December 1997.

Fung, W., R. Schwartz, and D. Whitcomb. "Adjusting For the Intervalling Effect Bias in Beta: A Test Using Paris Bourse Data," *Journal of Banking and Finance* 9, 1985, pp. 443–460.

Gaastra, F. *The Dutch East India Company, Expansion and Decline*, Leiden, 2003.

Garman, M. "Market Microstructure," *Journal of Financial Economics*, June 1976.

George, T., and C. Hwang. "Information Flow and Pricing Errors: A Unified Approach to Estimation and Testing," *Review of Financial Studies* 14, 2001, pp. 979–1020.

Gerety, M., and H. Mulherin. "Price Formation on Stock Exchanges: The Evolution of Trading within the Day," *Review of Financial Studies* 7, 1994, pp. 609–629.

Givoly, D., and D. Palmon. "Insider Trading and the Exploitation of Inside Information: Some Empirical Evidence," *Journal of Business*, January 1985.

Glass, S., and W. Wagner. "The Dynamics of Trading and Directed Brokerage," *Journal of Pension Plan Investing*, 1998, pp. 53–72.

Glosten, L., and L. Harris. "Estimating the Components of the Bid/Ask Spread," *Journal of Financial Economics* 21, 1988, pp. 123–142.

Glosten, L., and P. Milgrom. "Bid, Ask and Transaction Prices in a Specialist Market with Heterogeneously Informed Traders," *Journal of Financial Economics* 14, 1985, pp. 71–100.

Glosten, L., "Is the Electronic Open Limit Order Book Inevitable?" *Journal of Finance* 49, 1994, pp. 1127–1161.

Glosten, L., and P. Milgrom. "Bid, Ask, and Transaction Prices in a Specialist Market with Heterogeneously Informed Traders," *Journal of Financial Economics* 13, 1985, pp. 71–100.

Goetzman, W., and N. Peles. "Cognitive Dissonance and Mutual Fund Investing," *Journal of Financial Research* 20, 1997, pp. 145–158.

Goldman, M., and A. Beja. "Market Prices vs. Equilibrium Prices: Returns Variance, Serial Correlation, and the Role of the Specialist," *Journal of Finance*, June 1979.

Goodhart, C. *Monetary Theory and Practice: The UK Experience.* London: Macmillan, 1984.

Granger, C. "Spectral Analysis of New York Stock Market Prices," *Kyklos*, January 1963.

Greenwich Associates. "Advances and Anomalies in 'Nontraditional' Trading," A Report to Institutional Investors in the United States, 1999.

Grossman, S., and J. Stiglitz. "Information and Competitive Price System," *American Economic Review*, May 1976.

Handa, P., and R. Schwartz. "Limit Order Trading," *Journal of Finance*, 1996, pp. 1835–1861.

Handa, P., R. Schwartz, and A. Tiwari. "Price Improvement and Price Discovery on a Primary Market: Evidence from the American Stock Exchange," *Journal of Portfolio Management*, fall 1998.

Handa, P., R. Schwartz, and A. Tiwari. "Quote Setting and Price Formation in an Order Driven Market," *Journal of Financial Markets* 6, pp. 461–489.

Handa, P., R. Schwartz, and A. Tiwari. "The Economic Value of a Trading Floor: Evidence from the American Stock Exchange," *Journal of Business*, April 2004, pp. 331–355.

Hansen, Lars P. "Large Sample Properties of Generalized Method of Moments Estimators," *Econometrica* 50, 1982, pp. 1029–1054.

Harris, L. "A Transaction Data Study of Weekly and Intradaily Patterns in Stock Returns," *Journal of Financial Economics* 16, 1986, pp. 99–118.

Harris, L. "Does a Large Minimum Price Variation Encourage Order Display?" working paper, University of Southern California, 1996.

Harris, L. "Optimal Dynamic Order Submission Trading Strategies in Some Stylized Trading Problems," working paper, University of Southern California, 1994.

Harris, L. "Stock Price Clustering and Discreteness," *Review of Financial Studies* 4, 1991, pp. 389–415.

Harris, M., and A. Raviv. "Differences of Opinion Make a Horse Race," *Review of Financial Studies* 6, 1993, pp. 473–506.

Hasbrouck, J., and R. Schwartz. "Liquidity and Execution Costs in Equity Markets," *Journal of Portfolio Management*, spring 1988, pp. 10–16.

Hasbrouck, J., and G. Sofianos. "The Trades of Market Makers: An Empirical Analysis of NYSE Specialists, *Journal of Finance* 48, no. 5, 1993, pp. 1565–1594.

Hasbrouck, J. "Assessing the Quality of a Securities Market: A New Approach to Transaction-Cost Measurement," *Review of Financial Studies* 6, 1993, pp. 191–212.

Hasbrouck, J. "One Security, Many Markets: Determining the Contributions to Price Discovery," *Journal of Finance* 50, no. 4, pp. 1175–1199.

Hau, H. "Location Matters: An Examination of Trading Profits," *Journal of Finance* 56, no. 5, 2001, pp. 1959–1983.

Heiner, R. "On the Origins of Predictable Behavior," *American Economic Review* 73, 1983, pp. 560–595.

Hess, A., and P. Frost. "Tests for Price Effects of New Issues of Seasoned Securities," *Journal of Finance*, March 1982.

Ho, T., and H. Stoll. "Optimal Dealer Pricing Under Transactions and Return Uncertainty," *Journal of Financial Economics* 9, 1981, pp. 47–73.

Ho, T., R. Schwartz, and D. Whitcomb. "The Trading Decision and Market Clearing Under Transaction Price Uncertainty," *Journal of Finance*, March 1985, pp. 21–41.

Hong, H., and J. Wang. "Trading and Returns Under Periodic Market Closures," *Journal of Finance* 55, 2000, pp. 297–354.

Hong, H., and J. Stein. "A Unified Theory of Under-Reaction, Momentum Trading and Overreaction in Asset Markets," *Journal of Finance* 54, 1999, pp. 2143–2184.

Huang, R., and H. Stoll. "Dealer Versus Auction Markets: A Paired Comparison of Execution Costs on Nasdaq and the NYSE," *Journal of Financial Economics* 41, 1996, pp. 313–357.

Huang, R., and H. Stoll. "Market Microstructure and Stock Return Predictions. A Paired Comparison of Execution Costs on Nasdaq and the NYSE," *Review of Financial Studies* 7, 1994, pp. 179–213.

Huang, R., and H. Stoll. "The Components of the Bid-Ask Spread: A General Approach," *Review of Financial Studies* 10, 1997, pp. 995–1034.

Hui, B., and B. Heubel. "Comparative Liquidity Advantages Among Major U.S. Stock Markets," *DRI Financial Information Group Study*, Series no. 84081, 1984.

Jaffe, J. "The Effect of Regulation Changes on Insider Trading," *Bell Journal of Economics and Management Science*, spring 1974a.

Jaffe, J. "Special Information and Insider Trading," *Journal of Business*, July 1, 1974b.

Jain, P., and J. Gun-Ho. "The Dependence Between Hourly Prices and Trading Volume," *Journal of Financial and Quantitative Analysis* 23, 1988, pp. 269–284.

Jones, C. M. "A Century of Stock Market Liquidity and Trading Costs," working paper, Columbia University, 2002.

Kalay, A., L. Wei, and A. Wohl. "Continuous Trading or Call Auctions: Revealed Preference of Investors at the Tel Aviv Stock Exchange," *Journal of Finance* 57, 2002, pp. 523–542.

Kavajecz, K. "A Specialist's Quoted Depth and the Limit Order Book," *Journal of Finance* 54, 1999, pp. 747–771.

Keim, D., and A. Madhavan. "The Anatomy of the Trading Process," *Journal of Financial Economics*, 37, 1995, pp. 391–398.

Keim, D., and A. Madhavan. "The Cost of Institutional Equity Trades," *Financial Analysts Journal*, 1998, pp. 50–69.

Keim, D., and A. Madhavan. "The Upstairs Market for Large-Block Transactions: Analysis and Measurement of Price Effects," *Review of Financial Studies* 9, 1996, pp. 1–36.

Keim, D., and A. Madhavan. "Transactions Costs and Investment Style: An Inter-Exchange Analysis of Institutional Equity Trades," *Journal of Financial Economics* 46, December 1997, pp. 265–292.

Kendel, M. "The Analysis of Economic Time Series," *Journal of the Royal Statistical Society*, Series A, 1953.

Keynes, J. M. *General Theory of Employment, Interest and Money*, New York, 1936.

Ko, K., S. Lee, and J. Chung. "Volatility, Efficiency and Trading: Further Evidence," *Journal of International Financial Management and Accounting* 6, 1995, pp. 26–42.

Kramer, H. "Free the Nasdaq!" WSJ.com, The Wall Street Journal Online, August 14, 2003.

Kraus, A., and H. Stoll. "Price Impacts of Block Trading on the New York Stock Exchange," *Journal of Finance* 27, 1972, pp. 569–588.

Kraus, A., and R. Stoll. "Parallel Trading by Institutional Investors," *Journal of Financial and Quantitative Analysis* 7, 1972, pp. 2107–2138.

Kyle, A. "Continuous Auctions and Insider Trading," *Econometrica* 53, 1985, pp. 1315–1335.

Lancellotta, A. *Letter to the Association for Investment Management and Research, Re: Proposed AIMR Trade Management Guidelines*, Investment Company Institute, Washington, DC, February 12, 2002.

Lee, C., and M. Ready. "Inferring Trade Direction from Intraday Data," *Journal of Finance* 46, 1991, pp. 733–746.

Lesmond, D., J. Ogden, and C. Trzcinka. "A New Estimate of Transaction Costs," *Review of Financial Studies* 12, 1999, pp. 1113–1141.

Levhari, D., and H. Levy. "The Capital Asset Pricing Model and the Investment Horizon," *Review of Economics and Statistics* 59, 1977, pp. 92–104.

Lintner, J. "Security Prices, Risk and Maximal Gains from Diversification," *Journal of Finance*, December 1965.

Lintner, J. "The Aggregation of Investor's Diverse Judgments and Preferences in Purely Competitive Security Markets," *Journal of Financial and Quantitative Analysis*, December 1969.

Lintner, J. "The Valuation of Risk Assets and the Selection of Risky Investments in Stock Portfolios and Capital Budgets," *Review of Economics and Statistics*, February 1965.

Lo, A., and A. C. MacKinlay. "Stock Market Prices Do Not Follow Random Walks: Evidence from a Simple Specification Test," *Review of Financial Studies* 1, 1988, pp. 41–66.

Lo, A., H. Mamaysky, and J. Wang. "Foundations of Technical Analysis: Computational Algorithms, Statistical Inference, and Empirical Implementation," *Journal of Finance* 55, 2000, pp. 1705–1770.

Lockwood, L., and S. Linn. "An Examination of Stock Market Return Volatility During Overnight and Intraday Periods 1964–1989," *Journal of Finance* 45, 1990, pp. 591–601.

Loss, L. *Securities Regulation*, Boston: Little, Brown, 1961 (supplemented 1969).

Madhavan, A., and M. Cheng. "In Search of Liquidity: Block Trades in the Upstairs and Downstairs Markets," *Review of Financial Studies* 10, 1997, pp. 175–204.

Madhavan, A., and V. Panchapagesan. "Price Discovery in Auction Markets: A Look Inside the Black Box," *Review of Financial Studies* 13, 2000, pp. 627–658.

Madhavan, A., M. Richardson, and M. Roomans. "Why Do Security Prices Change? A Transaction-Level Analysis of NYSE Stocks," *Review of Financial Studies* 10, 1997, pp. 1035–1064.

Madhavan, A. "Market Microstructure: A Survey," *Journal of Finance* 3, no. 3, 2000, pp. 205–258.

Mandelbrot, B. "Forecasts of Future Prices, Unbiased Markets, and 'Martingale' Models," *Journal of Business*, January 1966.

Manne, H. *Insider Trading and the Stock Market.* New York: Free Press, 1966.

Marsh, P. "Equity Rights Issues and the Efficiency of the UK Stock Market," *Journal of Finance*, September 1979.

McCleskey, S. *Achieving Market Integration: Best Execution, Fragmentation and the Free Flow of Capital.* Butterworth-Heinemann, December 2003.

McIninsh, T., and R. Wood. "An Analysis of Intraday Patterns in Bid/Ask Spreads for NYSE Stocks," *Journal of Finance* 47, 1992, pp. 753–764.

Mikkelson, W., and M. Partch. "Stock Price Effects and Costs of Secondary Distributions," *Journal of Financial Economics*, June 1985.

Miller, M. "Volatility, Episodic Volatility and Coordinated Circuit-Breakers," in *Pacific-Basin Capital Market Research*, vol. 2, S. G. Rhee and R. Chang, eds. New York: North Holland, March 1991.

Mossin, J. "Equilibrium in a Capital Asset Market," *Econometrica*, October 1966.

Muscarella, C., and M. S. Piwowar. "Market Microstructure and Securities Values: Evidence from the Paris Bourse," *Journal of Financial Markets* 4, 2001, pp. 209–229.

Myners, P. "Institutional Investment in the United Kingdom: A Review," *The Myner Report*, March 2001.

Myners, P. "Review of Institutional Investment: Final Report." London: HM Treasury, March 6, 2001.

Neuberger, A. Chapter 1, "Recent Evidence on Market Quality," in Schwartz, Byrne, and Colaninno (2004).

New York Clearing House, *Historical Perspective*, published by the New York Clearing House, 2003.

New York Stock Exchange, Inc. "The Rule 80A Index Arbitrage Tick Test," Interim Report to the U.S. Securities and Exchange Commission, January 1991.

Nofsinger, J., and R. Sias. "Herding and Feedback Trading by Institutional and Individual Investors," *Journal of Finance* 54, 1999, 2263–2295.

Odean, T. "Volume, Volatility, Price and Profit When All Traders Are Above Average," *Journal of Finance* 53, 1998, pp. 1887–1934.

Osborne, M. "Brownian Motion in the Stock Market," *Operations Research*, March/April 1959.

Ozenbas, D., R. Schwartz, and R. Wood. "Volatility in U.S. and European Equity Markets: An Assessment of Market Quality," *International Finance* 5, no. 3, winter 2002, pp. 437–461.

Pagano, M., and A. Röell. "Auction and Dealership Markets: What Is the Difference?" *European Economic Review* 36, 1992, pp. 613–623.

Pagano, M., and A. Roell. "Transparency and Liquidity: A Comparison of Auction and Dealer Markets with Informed Trading," *Journal of Finance* 51, 1996, pp. 579–611.

Pagano, M., and R. Schwartz. "A Closing Call's Impact on Market Quality at Euronext Paris," *Journal of Financial Economics* 68, 2003, pp. 439–484.

Parlour, C. "Price Dynamics in Limit Order Markets, *Review of Financial Studies* 11, pp. 789–816 and studies 10, 1998, pp. 103–150.

Pastor, L., and R. F. Stambaugh. "Liquidity Risk and Expected Stock Returns," working paper, University of Chicago, 2001.

Perold, A., and E. Sirri. "The Cost of International Equity Trading," working paper, Harvard University, 1993.

Plexus Group, "The Official Icebergs of Transaction Costs," Commentary #54, The Plexus Group, 1998.

Pratt, J. "Risk Aversion in the Small and the Large," *Econometrica*, January 1964.

Rawls, J. "*A Theory of Justice*," The Belknap Press of Harvard University Press, 1975.

Roberts, H. "Stock Market 'Patterns' and Financial Analysis: Methodological Suggestions," *Journal of Finance*, March 1959.

Roll, R. "A Simple Implicit Measure of the Effective Bid-Ask Spread in an Efficient Market," *Journal of Finance* 39, 1984, pp. 1127–1139.

Ross, S. "The Arbitrage Theory of Capital Asset Pricing," *Journal of Economic Theory*, December 1976.

Samuelson, P. "Proof That Properly Anticipated Prices Fluctuate Randomly," *Industrial Management Review*, spring 1965.

Sanger, G., and J. McConnell. "Stock Exchange Listings, Firm Value, and Security Market Efficiency: The Impact of Nasdaq." *Journal of Financial and Quantitative Analysis*, March 1986.

Scarff, D. "The Securities and Commodities Markets: A Case Study in Product Convergence and Regulatory Disparity," in Amihud, Ho, and Schwartz (1985).

Scholes, M., and J. Williams. "Estimating Betas From Nonsynchronous Data," *Journal of Financial Economics* 5, 1977, pp. 309–328.

Schreiber, P., and R. Schwartz. "Efficient Price Discovery in a Securities Market: The Objectives of a Trading System," in Amihud, Ho, and Schwartz (1985).

Schultz, P. "Regulatory and Legal Pressures and the Costs of Nasdaq Trading," *Review of Financial Studies* 13, 2000, pp. 917–957.

Schwartz, R., and B. Steil. "Controlling Institutional Trading Costs: We Have Met the Enemy, and It Is Us," *Journal of Portfolio Management* 28, no. 3, spring 2002, pp. 39–49.

Schwartz, R., and B. Steil. "Equity Trading III: Institutional Investor Trading Practices and Preferences," in *The European Equity Markets: The State of the Union and an Agenda for the Millennium*, Benn Steil, ed. Great Britain: The Royal Institute of International Affairs, 1996, pp. 81–106.

Schwartz, R., and B. Weber. "Economics of Market Making," Nasdaq's HeadTrader web site.

Schwartz, R., and D. Whitcomb. "The Time-Variance Relationship: Evidence on Autocorrelation in Common Stock Returns," *Journal of Finance*, 1977, pp. 41–55.

Schwartz, R., and R. Wood. "Best Execution: A Candid Analysis," *Journal of Portfolio Management* 29, no. 4, summer 2003, pp. 37–48.

Schwartz, R., and J. Shapiro. "The Challenge of Institutionalization for the Equity Markets," in *Institutional Investors: Challenges and Responsibilities*, Arnold W. Sametz, ed. Homewood, IL: Dow Jones-Irwin, 1991.

SEC Market Data Concept Release, Release No. 34-42208, December 9, 1999.

SEC Release No. 34-42208; File No. S7-28-99, Regulation of Market Information Fees and Revenues, December 10, 1999.

SEC Release No. 34-42450; File No. SR-NYSE-99-48, NYSE Rulemaking: Notice of Filing of Proposed Rule Change to Rescind Exchange Rule 390, February 23, 2000.

SEC, Institutional Investor Study Report, H.R. Doc. No. 92-64, 92d Cong. 1st Sess. 1971.

Securities Acts Amendments of 1975, Conference Report. House of Representatives Report No. 94-229, p. 94, May 19, 1975.

Sharpe, W. "Capital Asset Prices: A Theory of Market Equilibrium Under Conditions of Risk," *Journal of Finance*, September 1964.

Sharpe, W. *Investments*, 3d ed. Englewood Cliffs, NJ: Prentice Hall, 1985.

Sias, R., and L. Starks. "Return autocorrelation and institutional investors," *Journal of Financial Economics* 46, 1997, pp. 103–131.

Siegfried, Bley, *Börsen der Welt*, Frankfurt, 1977.

Silber, W. "Innovation, Competition, and New Contract Design in Futures Markets," *Journal of Futures Markets*, summer 1981.

Sirri, E., and P. Tufano. "Costly Search and Mutual Fund Flows," *Journal of Finance* 53, 1998, pp. 1589–1622.

Smidt, S. "Can We Get There from Here?" in Amihud, Ho, and Schwartz (1985).

Sofianos, G., and I. Werner. "The Trades of NYSE Floor Brokers," working paper, New York Stock Exchange, 1997.

Sofianos, G. "Trading and Market Structure Research," Goldman Sachs, May 2001.

Steil, B., D. Victor, and R. Nelson. *Technological Innovation and Economic Performance*. Princeton, NJ: Princeton University Press.

Stemgold, J. "Wall Street's Army of Insiders," *New York Times*, May 18, 1986, section 3, p. 1.

Stigler, G. "The Theory of Economic Regulation," *Bell Journal of Economics and Management Science*, spring 1971.

Stoll, H. "Friction," *Journal of Finance* 4, 2000, pp. 1479–1515.

Stoll, H. "Principles of Trading Market Structure," *Journal of Financial Services Research*, 1992.

Stoll, H. "The Stock Exchange Specialist System: An Economic Analysis," *New York University Salomon Center Monograph Series in Finance and Economics* 2, 1985.

Stoll, H. "The Supply of Dealer Services in Securities Markets," *Journal of Finance* 33, 1978, pp. 1133–1151.

Stone, D. "Future Shock Is Here," in E. Bloch and R. Schwartz (1979).

Summer, A. "Comments on Professors Bloch, Lorie and The Future," in Bloch and Schwartz (1979).

SWX Swiss Exchange, "The SWX Platform and Associated Systems," November 2002, p. 4.

Tinic, S., and R. West. "The Securities Industry Under Negotiated Brokerage Commissions: Changes in the Structure and Performance of New York Stock Exchange Member Firms," *Bell Journal of Economics and Management Science*, spring 1980.

U.S. Department of Justice, "Inquiry into Proposal to Modify the Commission Rate Structure of the NYSE," SEC Release No. 8239, Washington, DC, 1968.

Venkataraman, K. "Automated Versus Floor Trading: An Analysis of Execution Costs on the Paris and New York Exchanges," *Journal of Finance* 56, 2001, pp. 1445–1485.

Wagner, W., and M. Edwards. "Best Execution," *Financial Analysts Journal* 49, no. 1, 1993, pp. 65–71.

Wagner, W. "The Essential Role of Market Makers," *Traders Magazine*, Thomson Media, May 2002.

Wagner, W. Testimony before the *House Committee on Financial Services*, March 12, 2003.

Wall, J. "The Competitive Environment of the Securities Market," in Y. Amihud, T. Ho, and R. Schwartz (1985).

Watkins, S. "Is the Specialist System Doomed?" *Traders Magazine*, November 2003, p. 35.

Werner, I., and A. Kleidon. "UK and US Trading of British Cross-Listed Stocks: An Intra-Day Analysis of Market Integration," *Review of Financial Studies* 9, 1996, pp. 619–664.

West, R., and S. Tinic. "Minimum Commission Rates on New York Stock Exchange Transactions," *Bell Journal of Economics and Management Science*, autumn 1971.

Whitman, D., and J. Gergacz. *The Legal and Social Environment of Business.* New York: Random House, 1985.

Williams, S. "The Evolving National Market System," in Y. Amihud, T. Ho, and R. Schwartz (1985).

Wood, R., T. McInish, and K. Ord. "An Investigation of Transactions Data for NYSE Stocks," *Journal of Finance* 40, 1985, pp. 723–741.

Wunsch, R. S. "What's Driving Market Structure? Technology or Regulation?" in Schwartz (2001).

About the Authors

Robert A. Schwartz is Marvin M. Speiser Professor of Finance and University Distinguished Professor in the Zicklin School of Business, Baruch College, City University of New York. Before joining the Baruch faculty in 1997, he was Professor of Finance and Economics and Yamaichi Faculty Fellow at New York University's Leonard N. Stern School of Business, where he had been a member of the faculty since 1965. Professor Schwartz received his Ph.D. in Economics from Columbia University. His research is in the area of financial economics, with a primary focus on the structure of securities markets. He has published numerous journal articles and 11 books, including *Reshaping the Equity Markets: A Guide for the 1990s*, Harper Business, 1991 (reissued by Business One Irwin, 1993). He has served as a consultant to various market centers including the New York Stock Exchange, the American Stock Exchange, Nasdaq, the London Stock Exchange, Instinet, the Arizona Stock Exchange, Deutsche Börse, and the Bolsa Mexicana. From April 1983 to April 1988, he was an associate editor of *The Journal of Finance*, and he is currently an associate editor of the *Review of Quantitative Finance and Accounting*, the *Review of Pacific Basin Financial Markets and Policies*, and *The Journal of Entrepreneurial Finance & Business Ventures*, and is a member of the advisory board of *International Finance*. In December 1995, Professor Schwartz was named the first chairman of Nasdaq's Economic Advisory Board, and he served on the EAB until spring 1999.

Reto Francioni has been Chairman and President of the SWX GROUP since May 2002. The Swiss Exchange Group comprises virt-x (a stock exchange in London), SWX Ltd. (a securities exchange in Zurich), a partnership in Eurex (the world's leading derivative exchange) and in STOXX (the index company).

Prior to assuming his current position, Reto Francioni was the Co-CEO of Consors Discount Broker AG, Nuremberg, from April 2000. Earlier in his career, in 1993, he was appointed to the Executive Board of Deutsche Börse AG (which includes Eurex, Xetra, and Clearstream) in Frankfurt, where he was responsible for its entire cash market. In 1999, he became Deputy Chief Executive Officer. He was an initiator of the group's thrust toward internationalization. Earlier in his career, he held management positions in the securities exchange and banking industry, and was a director in the finance division at Hoffmann LaRoche Ltd., Basel.

Reto Francioni has a master's degree and Ph.D. in law from Zurich University. He is an adjunct professor of Economics and Finance at the Zicklin School of Business, Baruch College, City University of New York.

About the CD-ROM

INTRODUCTION

TraderEx, as discussed in greater detail in Chapter 12, is an interactive computer simulation designed to provide hands-on experience in making tactical trading decisions. You enter your orders into a computer-driven market that generates its own order flow and that can respond directly to your orders. You see your results in real time and can analyze them after each simulation run. You are free to experiment with your order placement.

Robert A. Schwartz and Bruce W. Weber developed the simulation model for TraderEx discussed in Chapter 12. Oliver Rockwell wrote the software for the TraderEx version that is packaged with this book. TraderEx, copyright 2004, I-Smarts Partnerships, all rights reserved, is owned by I-Smarts Partnership, which includes Schwartz, Weber, and William Abrams. Bruce Weber has participated as a coauthor of Chapter 12, which discusses the TraderEx software at length. Further information about enhancements to the simulation model can be found on our web site, www.baruch.cuny.edu/BCTC/teachtech/traderex.htm.

Please see the ReadMe file on the CD-ROM for additional information.

MINIMUM SYSTEM REQUIREMENTS

Make sure that your computer meets the minimum system requirements listed in this section. If your computer doesn't match up to most of these requirements, you may have a problem using the contents of the CD.

For Windows 95, 98, 9x, Windows 2000, Windows NT4 (with SP 4 or later), Windows Me, or Windows XP:

- PC with a Pentium processor running at 120 Mhz or faster.
- At least 32 MB of total RAM installed on your computer; for best performance, we recommend at least 64 MB.
- A CD-ROM drive.

USING THE CD WITH WINDOWS

To open and use the trade simulator, follow these steps:

1. Insert the CD into your computer's CD-ROM drive.
2. A window will appear with the following options: Install, Explore, and Exit.

    Install: Gives you the option to install the supplied software on the CD-ROM.

    Explore: Enables you to view the options in a directory structure. A menu should bring you directly to a list of contents—you can start the simulation or view a ReadMe file.

    Exit: Closes the autorun window.

If you do not have autorun enabled, or if the autorun window does not appear, follow these steps to access the CD:

1. Click Start, select Run.
2. In the dialog box that appears, type *d*:\setup.exe, where *d* is the letter of your CD-ROM drive. This brings up the autorun window described in the preceding set of steps.
3. Choose the Install, Explore, or Exit option from the menu. (See step 2 in the preceding list for a description of these options.)

TROUBLESHOOTING

If you have difficulty installing or using any of the materials on the companion CD, try the following solutions:

- *Turn off any antivirus software that you may have running.* Installers sometimes mimic virus activity and can make your computer incorrectly believe that it is being infected by a virus. (Be sure to turn the antivirus software back on later.)
- *Close all running programs.* The more programs you're running, the less memory is available to other programs. Installers also typically update files and programs; if you keep other programs running, installation may not work properly.
- *Reference the ReadMe:* Please refer to the ReadMe file located at the root of the CD-ROM for the latest product information at the time of publication.

USING THE SOFTWARE

More detailed instructions for the TraderEx software can be found in Chapter 12 of *Equity Markets in Action*.

USER ASSISTANCE

If you have questions about the contents of the CD-ROM, contact Wiley Technical support and they can forward your question to the author.

If you need assistance, or have a damaged disk, please contact Wiley Technical Support at:

Phone: 800-762-2974

Outside the United States: 317-572-3994

Web site: www.wiley.com/techsupport

To place additional orders or to request information about Wiley products, please call 800-225-5945.

CUSTOMER NOTE

PLEASE READ THE FOLLOWING

By opening this package, you are agreeing to be bound by the following agreement:

This software product is protected by copyright and all rights are reserved by the author, John Wiley & Sons, Inc., or their licensors. You are licensed to use this software on a single computer. Copying the software to another medium or format for use on a single computer does not violate the U.S. Copyright Law. Copying the software for any other purpose is a violation of the U.S. Copyright Law.

This software product is sold as is without warranty of any kind, either express or implied, including but not limited to the implied warranty of merchantability and fitness for a particular purpose. Neither Wiley nor its dealers or distributors assumes any liability for any alleged or actual damages arising from the use of or the inability to use this software. (Some states do not allow the exclusion of implied warranties, so the exclusion may not apply to you.)

Index

DATE DUE
